Justifying Intellectual Property

JUSTIFYING INTELLECTUAL PROPERTY

ROBERT P. MERGES

HARVARD UNIVERSITY PRESS
Cambridge, Massachusetts
London, England
2011

Library of Congress Cataloging-in-Publication Data

Merges, Robert P.
Justifying intellectual property / Robert P. Merges.
p.   cm.
Includes index.
ISBN 978-0-674-04948-2 (alk. paper)
1. Intellectual property—Philosophy.   I. Title.
K1401.M475 2011
346.04'8—dc22   2010047516

This book is much like me:
A bit long, a bit wordy,
And totally dedicated to my family:
Jo, Robbie, and James

Contents

Preface

Several years ago I told my esteemed and experienced Berkeley colleague Jesse Choper that I was beginning work on this book. After he heard a bit about my plans, his response was this: "Oh, I get it. Taking a Big Swing, are you?" Now as I look back on the whole project—prefaces having the invariably paradoxical quality of being written at the end, but appearing at the beginning—I can see that he was right. I had reached a point where I needed to disrupt the scholarly rhythm I had fallen into: a staccato series of law review articles, punctuated by casebook revisions, with the occasional "think piece" woven into the mix. I wanted to take on something bigger, more sustained; to go back to the dugout, pick up a bigger bat, and swing from the heels. This book is the result of that fateful, and very foolish, decision.

So up I strode, ready to take a big hack at some tough issues in my primary field of study, intellectual property (IP). I wanted to defend IP rights against a host of charges leveled in recent years: that IP was no longer necessary in the digital age; that the field is an incoherent tangle of made-up rationales and half-baked theories; that IP, whatever it is, is not really property at all. But I wanted to do more than simply defend the IP edifice as it stands. I wanted to suggest some ways that this area of law could be trimmed and tailored to better serve its main purpose, which for me has always been protecting creative works as a way of honoring and rewarding creative people. And so the title of this book has a double meaning. I want to justify IP rights, in the sense of defending them from various critiques;

but I also want to justify it in the sense of justifying a margin, or a line of type—to straighten it out, neaten it up, make it a bit more orderly.

Here is how I plan to go about it. I will talk mainly about three things: (1) ideas on property held by important philosophers, both old (Locke and Kant), and not-so-old (John Rawls, Robert Nozick, Jeremy Waldron); (2) close examination of these ideas with the specifics of IP chiefly in mind; and (3) ways these ideas might help in understanding the future of property rights in our increasingly digitized and networked world.

Carrying this out has taken longer than I planned and been harder than I thought. But it has also been something I can only describe as very close to fun. It is an odd idea of fun to get up several hours before the rest of the family, pour a cup of coffee, and anguish over just exactly what some complex text is trying to say to me, or what I really think about some gnarly tangle of a conundrum, or—worst of all!—how to set those thoughts into a series of words and a string of sentences that hang together in a semblance of sense and order. The challenge is something like crossing a wide, raging river that howls along at spring flood, with only a vague notion that there may be a few submerged stepping stones to hold you upright. If that sounds like an outing most sane people would gladly avoid, I am sure you are right. As for my own part, I found it irresistible.

On my rambles in IP law, I met with all sorts of notions and theories. As I grappled with them, three in particular stood out to me: (1) a Kantian conception of property, which lends itself to an even-handed theoretical approach to IP rights, balancing freedom of action for owners with the interests of others in the community (and which fits with the ideal of distributional justice expounded by John Rawls); (2) the importance of "midlevel principles" of IP theory, intermediate between deeply held foundational commitments and doctrinal and factual details; and (3) the idea of rewards proportioned to effort or value, which operates as a deep mainspring driving the wheels and mechanisms of many IP doctrines. I call this third idea the proportionality principle, which is itself exemplary of the midlevel principles just mentioned.

A word about these principles is in order. If we have learned anything in this world of ours it is that one person's heartfelt conviction does not entitle him to inflict it on others just because it is intensely and sincerely felt. As explained in the Introduction and shown in Part I, I found the solid normative grounding for IP law that I had been looking for in philosophical writings on property. (The Introduction also explains why this grounding is perfectly consistent with most analytical work on IP, particularly in the law and economics tradition.) But although I see in these writings a firm footing for the field, you may not agree. This normative grounding may leave you cold, or bored, or put you off entirely. What to do? How could I set out my best case for the philosophical foundations of the field as I had pieced them together, while leaving room for others to find or make foundations more conducive to their own closely held feelings and ideas? Once I put the issue this way, the answer was clear. I just needed to borrow from the deep literature on political pluralism, especially the work of John Rawls and, among contemporary legal philosophers, Jules Coleman. What is needed is a set of ideas, a vocabulary, that transcends and ties together multiple foundational conceptions. Discourse at this midlevel permits generalization from specific cases and discrete fact patterns, while avoiding head-on clashes over ultimate convictions. Midlevel principles cannot and should not prevent or displace all disagreement, but they do create a forum for disagreement that is more amenable to effective interchange and, ultimately I believe, resolution.

The reason it is important to preserve a safe space for argument and discourse in the IP field is that so much is at stake. For whatever foundation the field ultimately rests on, it is quite clear to me that it has a crucial role to play in contemporary economic life. IP rights allow people to make a living with their creative talents. This "propertization of labor" allows composers, musicians, novelists, and inventors to leverage their creative work, turning their effort into saleable assets. This not only enhances their income, it buys freedom. A creative person can work when and where she wants, with whom she wants, making money by selling copies of what she produces. And ownership of the work product gives her control over how it reads or sounds or works, how it is packaged and marketed. These advantages of IP rights are the practical, workaday manifestation of the abstract-sounding value of "autonomy" that philosophers (especially Kant and Hegel) have long associated with property rights. The case study of Harry Potter author J. K. Rowling late in the book puts these benefits on display.

Stated simply, IP rights make creative work a more viable job for more people, and this basic fact explains why IP is still worth studying. Even though ownership is often mediated by large companies, IP allows more creative people to own what they make. The language surrounding IP rights rings with the message that ownership confers control and dignity. Workers receive wages, but IP owners are paid in *royalties*. This linguistic signal carries an important social message about the status of creative effort. It shows well the value that is attached to this type of work—value that is realized in concrete form only because of IP rights.

Writing can be a solitary business but, fortunately for me, scholars are a sociable lot. We have to be; without people to talk with, people to challenge our pet ideas and push back against our opinions, we would seldom get very far in our thinking. I owe a huge debt to the many, many colleagues with whom I have discussed and developed my ideas over the years. I include here only a partial list, with the admonition that it is surely very far from comprehensive. (If I have left you out, I apologize for my hubris and/ or incomplete memory.)

For help with orientation in the philosophical literature, my Berkeley colleague Chris Kutz was invaluable. I also want to thank Stephen Munzer of UCLA Law School and Justin Hughes of Cardozo Law School, who both oriented me in different ways to the philosophical literature I draw on. Finally, kudos to my former colleague Jeremy Waldron, whose contributions have left a very significant mark on my thinking, as this book will attest. And a nod as well to Kent Greenawalt of Columbia, Robert Ellickson of Yale, and Richard Epstein of Chicago, three experienced scholars whose guidance and support at different times and in different ways proved crucial to my thinking. I also want to thank Henry Smith of Harvard and Carol Rose of Yale / Arizona for being such close and supportive readers of my work over the years. Thanks also to Samuel Fleischaker for helpful information on philosophical issues related to Adam Smith.

I thank workshop organizers and faculty participants at the following schools, all places where I first tried out some of the ideas developed in this book:

Cardozo School of Law, Case Western Law School, Columbia Law School, the University of Houston School of Law, and the University of Virginia Law School. Finally, I thank my Berkeley colleagues who listened to a number of presentations on various chapters of the book. Special thanks to Robert Barr (fellow IP devotee and, more importantly, devoted Red Sox fan), Amy Kapczinski, Peter Menell, Pam Samuelson, Tala Sayed, Suzanne Scotchmer, and Molly Van Houweling, my friends and colleagues at the Berkeley Center for Law and Technology—who together make up the finest scholarly home any academic could ever wish for. Other Berkeley colleagues who helped me one way or another include Bob Berring, Jesse Choper, Jan Vetter, Eric Talley, and the late Phil Frickey, from the law school; and Rich Gilbert, David Mowery, and Carl Shapiro from the economics/business faculty at Berkeley. Dean Chris Edley deserves special mention for allowing me the time and space to work on this book, along with his predecessor Herma Hill Kay. And, for the record, regular summer research funding did not hurt a bit, either. Among non-Berkeley people, Dan Burk, Rebecca Eisenberg, Mark Lemley, John Duffy, Rochelle Dreyfuss, Stu Graham, Ashish Arora, Richard Nelson, Hal Edgar, Jane Ginsburg, Adam Mossoff, Joe Miller, Mark Janis, Doug Lichtman, Dietmar Harhoff, Maureen

O'Rourke, Andrea Ottollini, Giuseppe Mazziotti, Hsung-Mei Hsiung, and Graeme Dinwoodie (Oxford don and Patriots fan extraordinaire) deserve special mention. Many thanks also to the quartet extraordinaire of treatise authors in the IP field, Don Chisum, Paul Goldstein, Tom McCarthy, and David Nimmer, whose expertise and friendship over the years has been invaluable. I do not want to forget the many judges and government officials who have informed my views over the years, chief among them (pun intended) Judge Randall Rader of the Federal Circuit, and also including Judge Richard Posner, the late Judge Giles Rich, Judge Richard Linn and Judge Ronald Whyte, together with the many judges who have passed through Berkeley as part of our Federal Judicial Center IP "bootcamps" over the years (masterminded by my high-energy colleague and fellow Berkeley Center for Law and Technology (BCLT) cofounder Peter Menell).

Thanks also to my loyal research assistants over the past few years, without whom I could not have amassed and sifted all the secondary literature that grows so profusely in the IP field: Susan De Galan, Amit Agarwal, Ranganash Sudarshan, and Ana Penteado. Ultimately my debt extends back to many former RAs, including Jeff Kuhn, Ines Gonzalez, and Celeste Yang; and even to some of my earliest RAs at Boston University, Rob Cobert, Joe Kirk, Rob Rieders, Brett Sokol, and so many others. I also owe a huge debt to the invaluable daily assistance of Chris Swain, David Grady, and Louise Lee. And, for talented and professional assistance translating my rough drawings into polished illustrations, Brittany Elise Salmon.

Two who assisted me deserve special mention: Ben Petersen, Berkeley Law class of 2009, whose help on every chapter was invaluable (and whose delayed start at work was a boon to me beyond measure); and Elizabeth Knoll of Harvard University Press. Little did she know when she popped into my office over three years ago and innocently asked, "Working on anything interesting?" what she was getting into.

For general moral support, not to mention support of a more material nature, a shout-out to my cofounders, colleagues, and friends at the IP business and investment firm Ovidian Group, LLC., whose clients bring home the real-world value of IP rights every day: Alex Cohen; Steven Horowitz; Lisa McFall; Joe ("the CEO") Siino; the newest Ovidian, Satya Patel; plus Sheri Siino and Emily Leavitt.

Everyone, especially scholars, needs to spend some time outside their heads once in a while. For help in this department, I thank all my friends at Davis Community Church, including the Rev. Marylynn Tobin; fellow DCC Worship Band musicians (especially our music director, David Deffner); plus John Hannan, the Saturday morning Starbucks crowd (Tom Newcombe and Tim Masterson, ringleaders), and Tim Mooney; and of course all the kids I have coached and managed over the years, especially the Davis Little League Cubs of 2007–2009 and the (champion!) flag football Patriots of 2009, plus my coaching buddies Tom "Hitch Pass" Hall and Kevin Bunfill.

And finally, my family: Jo, Robbie, James; Mom and Dad; and brothers Bruce, Paul, and Matt. "Acknowledgment" is a thin reed on which to hang what I owe them; it is like a pilot acknowledging the help of the air in doing what he does. Better to say they are the medium I move in, the reason I do what I do, the sustenance and support that make it possible to be who I am. I am profoundly grateful to them, in a way that no simple acknowledgment could capture. Especially my wife, Jo. Imagine being married to a guy who would write a book like this, full of abstruse terminology and obscure digressions. Well, she has to do more than imagine it, she has to live it. And for that I remain grateful and in no small part amazed.

Justifying Intellectual Property

CHAPTER ONE

Introduction

Main Themes

INTELLECTUAL PROPERTY (IP) law today is like one of those sprawling, chaotic megacities of the developing world—Mexico City, maybe, or Shanghai. Construction cranes are everywhere. The old city center—the ancient core of the field—is today surrounded by new buildings, new neighborhoods, knots of urban growth, budding in every direction, far off into the distance. As a longtime resident, an old-timer who for a good number of years now has walked the streets and taken in the scenes, I find myself with decidedly mixed feelings about all this. I marvel at the bold, new energy unleashed in the old burgh, and I am not a little pleased at the prosperity it has brought. But I also feel a distinct sense of unease. The helter-skelter of new growth, proliferating at times with no regard for the classic lines and feel of the old city, brings a slight case of vertigo—a feeling of being lost amid the familiar. It's an exciting time, to be sure; but a confusing time too.

This book is a reconnaissance and renewal mission, undertaken in the precincts of my strangely familiar town. It is part archaeological dig, going back to the roots of the place to regain a sense of why it was founded, where it was centered, and what the city's original outline looked like. It is also part mapping expedition, an effort to put in place a high-altitude conceptual map of the cityscape—one of those marvels of modern graphic design, with stylized lines for the main roads, and a color key for main features—something akin to the New York City subway map. The idea is to cut through the noise and new construction, to locate the trunk roads and main boulevards that give this place its distinctive form and shape. And this book is, finally, an exercise in city planning: it lays out principles and guidelines drawn from the deep well of history, to structure and channel all the new growth. My goal is not to stop the growth, or to dictate all its features at a fine level. It is instead to make sure that with each new extension of the old city, basic themes and motifs from the historical core are picked up, replicated, and carried forward. As the city grows, I want it to retain its essential character.

The archaeological part of my mission is a search for foundations. Although all legal institutions emerge out of social practices and become formalized over time, an inquiry into historical origins forms only a small part of this book. The major archaeology I undertake is *conceptual:* in extending property to intangible items, what are the best justifications, and how do they shape the contours and limits of the field? In other words, what are the conceptual patterns, the basic formative ideas, that have inspired and animated the "cityscape" I am surveying? It is these questions, and not the fascinating (but for my purposes tangential) linear march of historical events (first this act, then this case, and so on), that motivate Part I of this book.

Current convention has it that IP law seeks to maximize the net social benefit of the practices it regulates. The traditional utilitarian formulation— the greatest good for the greatest number—is expressed here in terms of rewards. Society offers above-market rewards to creators of certain works that would not be created, or not created as soon or as well, in the absence of reward. The gains from this scheme, in the form of new works created, are weighed against social losses, typically in the form of the consumer welfare lost when embodiments of these works are sold at prices above the marginal cost of their production. IP policy, according to this model, is a matter of weighing these things out, of striking the right balance. At the conceptual level at least, the process involved is not particularly complex. It is easy to picture the toting up of costs and benefits, and to think of a good policy as one that equilibrates the scale at just the right point—the point that maximizes the number and quality of new creative works without costing society an arm and a leg.

The process is simple but, practically speaking, not at all easy. Impossibly complex, in fact. Estimating costs and benefits, modeling them over time, projecting what would happen under counterfactuals (such as how many novels or pop songs really would be written in the absence of copyright protection, and who would benefit from such a situation)—these are all overwhelmingly complicated tasks. And this complexity poses a major problem for utilitarian theory. The sheer practical difficulty of measuring or approximating all the variables involved means that the utilitarian program will always be at best aspirational. Like designing a perfect socialist economy, the computational complexities of this philosophical project cast grave doubt on its fitness as a workable foundation for the field.

In my research, I have become convinced that with our current tools we will never identify the "optimal number" of patented, copyrighted, and trademarked works. Every time I play the archaeologist and go looking for the utilitarian footings of the field, I come up empty. Try as I might, I simply cannot justify our current IP system on the basis of verifiable data showing that people are better off with IP law than they would be without it.[1] Maximizing utility, I have come to see, is not a serviceable first-order principle of the IP system. It is just not what IP is really all about at the deepest level.

This is a truth I avoided over the years, sometimes more subtly (for example, heavily weighing the inconclusive positive data, showing IP law is necessary and efficient, discounting inconclusive data on the other side), and sometimes less so (ignoring the data altogether, or pretending that more solid data were just around the corner). But try as I might, there was a truth I could never quite get around: the data are maddeningly inconclusive. In my opinion, they support a fairly solid case in favor of IP protection—but not a *lock*-solid, airtight case, a case we can confidently take to an unbiased jury of hardheaded social scientists.

And yet, through all the doubts over empirical proof, my faith in the necessity and importance of IP law has only grown. I seem to have a lot of company. Countless judges begin their IP decisions with one or another familiar "stage setter" about how IP protection exists to serve the public interest, often intoning one of a few stock passages penned in a spare moment by Thomas Jefferson. But these utilitarian platitudes quickly give way to doctrinal details, which often show the unmistakable imprint of something more fundamental, something beyond utility—revealing, at the end of the exercise, its real purpose and justification. That is, courts often wind up talking about IP rights *as* rights. Being courts, they are understandably too busy getting through their important work to notice the significance of this move. But in this book I make it my purpose to notice. And make no mistake, the shift from social utility to fundamental rights talk *is* an important one. For as we have learned from John Rawls, Jeremy Waldron, and others before them (particularly Immanuel Kant), the hallmark of a right is that social utility alone is not reason enough to override it. Waldron speaks to this when he distinguishes handily between "mere interests" and true *rights*. Despite the frequency of utilitarian rhetoric in the IP field, I have come to see that courts often understand IP rights (at least implicitly) as rights in the full and true sense. Perhaps more surprisingly, at least to me, I have come to agree with them.

Preliminaries: Is IP "Really" Property?

I will argue in this book that there is a basic logic to the law of property, and that it applies to intangibles as well as physical things. Because there is a lot of resistance to this from various quarters, I had better state my best case here at the outset.

To begin, I must concede that on one narrow view of what "property" is, I cannot succeed. There are those who claim that property the *concept* is and always will be a prisoner of its origins, that it is rooted in and can never grow out of its formative association with physical, tangible things, most notably (in the Anglo-American tradition) land. Anyone who sees things this way will always see intellectual property as an awkward transplant. For them, the idea of property contains certain historical-essentialist traits that cannot be altered to better adapt it to intangible things. As applied to intangibles, property will always have the feel of a northern fir in the tropics, or a damp fern in the high desert. It just does not fit. And any conceptual adaptation, any strenuous breeding program that produces a concept that *does* fit would result not simply in a small variant. It would create something fundamentally new and different, a new species entirely; and whatever it was called, it could not be called property. (One lexical clue to this argument is that only property in land is called "real" property.) For those who subscribe to this theory, intellectual property can best be described as a sort of protracted analogy, a standing metaphor. It borrows some of the basic outline of property but cannot be considered seriously as an actual and true branch of this fundamental legal category.

I disagree. I do not see property in this historical-essentialist way. For me, property is a broad and roomy concept. It has a distinct (and fascinating) history, to be sure. But its origins do not imply constraints or limits. The very wide range of things that property concepts have been applied to suggests to me an expansive and highly adaptable legal category. Land, tools, trees, minerals, water, fractional ownership claims, legal obligations to pay money—these and many, many other things are subject to property's wide embrace. Over its long career, property has shown a restless capacity to jump from one arena into another, morphing and adapting as it goes. While some of its distinctive features were shaped by its early history, I believe this history supplied property not with a set of burdensome constraints, but largely with a highly adaptable and flexible conceptual vocabulary that renders it wonderfully adaptive to all sorts of new things and situations. This vocabulary is singularly effective in structuring relations between legal actors and unique things of value to them. Property has proven robust because, like a spoken language that grows and spreads, it has shown itself quite capable of absorbing new dimensions and changing in significant ways, while retaining fidelity to certain core principles that provide its basic structure.

The most important core principle of the institution of private property is this: it assigns to individual people control over individual assets. It creates a one-to-one mapping between owners and assets.[2] I argue in this book that this one-to-one mapping is the best way to handle intangible assets, just as it is with most other assets. For me, it is this powerful logic of individual control that makes property appropriate and appealing; it has little to do with the nature of the assets in question. That is why I see IP as a perfectly plausible, and even desirable, system for administering intangible assets. The logic of decentralized control and coordination—that is, individual ownership—makes just as much sense to me for intangible assets as it does for physical assets and the other objects of traditional property law.

Another major objection to the property model in IP law centers on the high transaction costs of property rights. Critics with this orientation do not dwell on essentialist arguments. Their point is more about the consequences of assigning property rights to intangibles, and in particular, the transactional bottlenecks and costly nightmares that this entails. There are many variations on this basic objection, but most share this thought: while IP rights may make sense for some things, or may have at one time, in the context of a rapidly evolving, high-throughput information economy, IP represents a major frictional "drag."

I address this objection—with which I have a limited degree of sympathy—at several places in this book. My basic point throughout is that high transaction costs point to *reforms* in IP law, rather than the need to scrap it altogether. Compared to critics who emphasize this point, I am both more confident in the ability of economic players to "work around" transactional chokepoints and more convinced that, notwithstanding these transactional challenges, the best starting point remains a commitment to individual ownership of assets. Ultimately, I seek to learn from "transactional pessimists" but not join their movement.

Efficiency as One Midlevel Principle of IP Law

My earlier talk of IP as a "right" might sound like I am adopting a "natural law" perspective on IP, one that avoids completely any discussion of economic efficiency. Not so. Let me make clear right here that I am not proposing that we banish questions of efficiency from IP law. Such a proposal would relegate a huge amount of helpful scholarship—some of it my own!—to the deleted file repository of history. The trick is to understand that efficiency is a second-order goal—a "midlevel principle." Though I discuss foundational principles later in this introduction, I will take a moment now to explain the difference between a midlevel principle such as efficiency and a truly foundational concept.

Efficiency is an important goal of any area of law, and IP is no exception. The imprint of this important principle is all over IP law; indeed, many aspects of the social practice known as IP law cannot be effectively explained without reference to the principle of efficiency. As I mentioned earlier, however, despite its pervasive impact on the practices that make up IP law, efficiency is not an adequate foundational or normative principle. It cannot explain large features of the IP landscape (moral rights being one of many examples). And, try as we might, law and economics scholars have never established an efficiency-based (or utilitarian) justification for the field. There is no lock-solid proof that overall social welfare would decline if IP protection were suddenly removed. True, there are plenty of *indications,* plenty of data to support the notion that IP rights are overall a good thing for the economy. But there is no proof in the form that a scientist, or even a rigorous social scientist, would accept as unequivocal. The famous conclusion of the eminent economist Fritz Machlup in a study for the U.S. Senate was that it is not clear we would establish IP rights if starting from scratch today, but it would be unwise to get rid of them given that we already have them. The vast empirical literature in the field generated since then has done much to illuminate the wisdom of discrete practices and doctrines; but no one has produced evidence sufficient to dislodge Machlup's basic conclusion. At a personal level, my interest (and belief) in efficiency led me to try to ground or justify the entire field on this idea. My failure to do so, and the path opened up by this failure, led me to write this book.

I also reject another principle that many have proposed (usually implicitly) as a possible foundation of the IP field: preserving and maximizing the public domain. Scholars have promoted this agenda under a number of rubrics. One centers on the idea that IP law serves the same function in the world of information that environmental law serves in the natural world: to guard as many things as possible from the rapacious grasp of privatization. In environmental law, this is the stewardship principle, the idea that our job is to protect nature's wondrous but limited bounty from those who would appropriate it for personal gain. This concept lies behind environmental law's preservationist agenda. In IP law, this concept is what I call "the nonremoval principle," which says that information and ideas in the public domain must not be taken away or privatized. This is the second midlevel principle that unites and helps organize the field.

Although I believe nonremoval is an important goal of the IP system, it is simply not robust enough to form a first-order principle. In this, it suffers from the same defect as utilitarianism. If you look carefully at various rules, doctrines, and institutional practices of the IP system, you will see much evidence of the nonremoval principle at work. And certainly for many practical purposes, promoting the agenda of nonremoval is a worthy aim. But just as with efficiency, nonremoval does not work as a normative foundation for the field. The reason is simple: it does not account for important practices and values evident throughout the field. For example, public domain concepts have nothing to tell us about the rules governing claims to priority (who was first, and deserves a right); the outcome of a priority contest in trademark and patent law is usually that one of the rival claimants will come away with a property right, so a policy favoring a maximal public domain has little place in such a contest. Likewise for the rules governing remedies and compensation when an IP right has been infringed. The core issue here is measuring harm to the rightholder, and nonremoval does not enter in. Even where nonremoval figures into a rule, it is often not the only principle at work. This is true with respect to rules about how much originality or creative spark is needed for a work to be worthy of copyright or patent protection. Nonremoval surely forms part of the rationale for these requirements. But another part comes from the idea that an IP right ought to be proportional to the contribution of a creative work. This idea, which I call "the proportionality principle," is in my view central to IP law; it is perhaps *the* major midlevel principle and is covered in depth in Part II, Chapter 6, of this book. The fact that we need supplementary concepts such as proportionality is a dead giveaway that nonremoval is not by itself sufficiently robust to support the entire conceptual weight of the field.

It is plain to me now that although I thought I was starting at the bottom when I began exploring efficiency and nonremoval as foundations of the IP field, I was actually starting in the middle. In this I am not alone. The very accomplished legal philosopher Jules Coleman traces the same path in the introduction to his book *The Practice of Principle.*[3] I use Coleman's terminology (in Part II) when I describe the four midlevel concepts at the heart of IP law. Like Coleman, I believe that these midlevel principles serve a vital function. They tie together a whole range of disparate rules, doctrines, and institutional practices in the IP system. It is not surprising in retrospect that I would commence my review of IP law by looking into these principles. They form an integral part of the connective tissue of the field. And in fact, as for Coleman, it was only by thoroughly grasping these principles and coming to terms with their limitations that I could begin to see the need for a foundational layer underneath them.

Before I introduce these foundations, however, I need first to complete my overview of the midlevel principles. In addition to (1) efficiency and (2) nonremoval, both discussed earlier, I have identified two more: (3) proportionality (mentioned briefly above), and (4) dignity.

Throughout IP law there is an impulse to tailor a creator's property right in a way that reflects his contribution. This is the proportionality principle. There is a distinctly Lockean flavor to this principle (though it makes sense on utilitarian grounds as well), especially as Locke has been adapted to IP by legal scholar Justin Hughes. At its heart it is about basic fairness: the scope of a property right ought to be commensurate with the magnitude of the contribution underlying the right. Proportionality shows up in all sorts of IP rules, from infringement and remedies issues in copyright, to the requirements of patentability, to various trademark doctrines. It shows itself most clearly when a creator claims a right whose value is grossly disproportionate to the actual contribution at issue. In this situation, IP law finds a way to prevent the awarding of a disproportionate right. In copyright law, a very small piece of copyrighted material may hold the key to a large and lucrative market. "Lockout codes" on video game consoles serve as a good example. Ownership of a copyright in such a code can in effect translate into ownership of the right to control the market for games that are compatible with the console. Under some conditions, this exclusive control might make sense. But, according to several important cases, mere ownership of the copyrighted codes should not confer such control.[4] The same principle is at work in patent rules denying effective control over large markets to creators who did not significantly contribute to the founding and growth of those markets. Opportunistic patentees often try to sail into a thriving market on clever strategies designed to capitalize on the pioneering work of others. But they usually run headlong into stiff countering winds. Sooner or later, judges and legislators push back against the unfairness of these strategies, on the premise that they are not consonant with the deeper purpose of the patent system. In Chapter 6 I use a simple parable and diagram—the Parable of the Bridge—to describe how the proportionality principle manifests in these cases.

The fourth midlevel principle in IP law is the dignity principle. It captures the idea that in many cases works covered by IP rights reflect and embody personal attributes of individual creators, therefore justifying special protection for some aspects of creative works. The dignity principle is most evident in so-called moral rights, which protect the creator of a work even after other rights to the work are sold or transferred. The dignity interest can be thought of as an invisible string that connects individual creators with their works, and that survives even a formal act of legal alienation. For historical reasons, this principle is more fully developed in continental European IP systems. Even so, it finds expression (muted as it may be at times) in the IP law of the United States, where many (including me) feel it ought to have a more prominent place.

On Foundational Pluralism, or "Room at the Bottom"

Now that I have set out an overview of the midlevel concepts, I am eager to dig deeper and talk about what lies underneath, at the conceptual foundations of the field. But before I do, I need to digress for a moment. I want to say a few words about the relationship between foundations and midlevel principles.

Although I have arrived at my understanding of foundations over many years of study, I do not believe my ideas have any claim to exclusivity. The deontological foundations I describe in Part II are not the only plausible grounding for the field. As I said earlier, the current data (in my opinion anyway) are close to forming a lock-solid utilitarian case for IP. More data might tip the balance, leading me and perhaps others to believe that the field is basically all about net social utility, or perhaps that it can be justified by either set of core values, utilitarian or deontological rights. But this leads to a question: What would it do to our thinking about the field if the deep substratum could be changed under our feet—if in the face of new learning we suddenly substituted one "foundation" for another?

The answer at the operational level is: not much. That's because the operational principles of the IP system are the midlevel principles I identified earlier. Efficiency, Nonremoval, Proportionality and Dignity—these basic principles, which form the conceptual backbone of the field, are largely independent of the deep conceptual justifications of IP protection. Except in a few boundary cases, they rarely do much direct work, or make a large practical difference, to the IP system in its day-to-day operation.

What about at the theoretical level? What would it do to our understanding of the field if we shifted from one foundation to another? I answer that by way of an analogy. In John Rawls's book *Political Liberalism*,[5] he does a masterful job of carefully pulling apart and then reconstructing the idea of pluralism. Rawls said that in a liberal democracy, there is need for a sort of "public space" based on an "overlapping consensus" drawn from multiple, sometimes divergent foundational commitments. Through the proper construction of a liberal set of institutions, citizens can simultaneously hold to their deepest commitments (for exanple, fundamental values, religious faiths, and the like) and join together in a common understanding with others who hold equally strong but not necessarily congruent commitments.[6] Liberal democracy, in other words, permits each individual to hold resolute personal beliefs while participating in civil society with others who may hold just as strongly to a contrary set of beliefs.[7] And a really workable consensus, according to Rawls, includes not just a working agreement at the operational level but also a set of shared moral commitments, part of what Rawls terms "public reason."[8] These commitments constitute a level of "public moral discourse" separate from each individual's deepest foundational commitments. According to Rawls, an overlapping consensus must include this level of moral agreement if it is to be robust—if it is to be flexible enough to adapt to new problems and situations.[9]

My theory of IP includes this foundational pluralism. I am open to more or better evidence on the net social effects of IP protection. For me, a lock-solid utilitarian case might someday unseat deontological rights as the field's foundation. In the meantime, the great virtue of pluralism is that I can engage in a meaningful way with those who are already convinced of the utilitarian account, those who hold firmly to deontological rights, and those who place their faith in other foundations altogether. Midlevel principles provide our common space, our place of engagement. They are like a musical score, allowing us all to play together, even if we disagree about the deep wellsprings or ultimate significance of our shared performance, our common musical practice. The midlevel principles allow us to be tolerant about questions of ultimate importance. In my theory, the conceptual hierarchy includes a ground floor that is airy and capacious. There is room at the bottom.

What about those who disavow the appropriateness of and need for any foundational theory whatsoever—those who would claim that the midlevel principles I discuss in this book represent the deepest theoretical level that IP law can and should aspire to? They might consider why the four midlevel principles I discuss (or any alternative set they might come up with) emerged as the appropriate organizing principles of the field. Isn't it possible that a deeper metaprinciple informed the emergence and relative weighting of these principles? Understanding why a midlevel principle emerges in a field, and recognizing its limits and its relationship to other midlevel principles, can indicate the presence of a deeper organizing influence at work below the midlevel principles.

But a stout nonfoundationalist may of course reject this suggestion as well. Because many of my friends and fellow travelers in the law and economics community may feel this way, I want to direct a few words their way.

Here is an analogy: Say you and I are scientists, old pals from way back who have worked long and hard in the lab in our chosen field. Suddenly I am plagued by doubts about where nature came from, why it is the way it is. I read widely and decide there is some sort of unseen intelligence, some higher power behind the whole thing, that set the universe in motion. My doubts go away and I rejoin you in the lab. My day-to-day work does not change, but I am somehow more serene about the whole enterprise, I have found a grounding for it that makes sense to me.

That's what the normative grounding in Part I of this book is like—it helps me push on through foundational doubts. I am not saying that Kant and Locke are in any sense theological figures; just that they serve the same purpose for me as the spiritual-theological reading does for the scientist in my analogy. They provide a grounding outside the contours of my field as conventionally practiced, one that helps me resolve foundational doubts and get back to work confidently "inside" my field.

The important point is that I do not want you to think that this book, especially Part I, undermines my prior work or my commitment to analyzing detailed doctrines and rules, and the institutions that surround them, from the perspective of efficiency. In the vast majority of cases, the new normative grounding does not affect my view of correct policy in any way. It may help me resolve borderline cases, and perhaps might lead me to favor an owner or rightholder in a close case or at the margin. But mostly, it simply helps me frame the field. It gives me a stronger foundation for the conventional kinds of work you and I have always done. You may have no need for foundations. The system we have may need no deeper motivation or justification than that it has always had. My simple point is that this perspective was no longer sufficient for me. So I went on a deep exploration, the results of which are in Part I. Whether you see the need to join me or not, do not doubt that for the most part my views on right policy and the best way to look at our field operationally have not changed much at all.

Let us return now to the issue of foundations. I have already said that neither efficiency nor nonremoval is a foundational idea in IP law. But if not these, then what *are* the most fundamental ideas? First, IP is property. This may seem fairly obvious (it's right there in the name of the field, right?), but given the current state of IP scholarship, it is not. IP scholarship is in the midst of a vast upheaval, caused in equal parts by the revolution in digital (and other) technologies and the rapid extension of IP law into these new technological domains: ownership of genes, Internet domain names, digital music "sampling," open source software, and many others. Anyone who follows the popular press has seen the stories about the revolutionary challenges to IP law. This process of upheaval and extension has jarred many a scholar out of the view that IP is really property, or at least that property concepts are really still at the heart of the field. Many fine scholars (Larry Lessig, Mark Lemley, Tim Wu, and my colleague Peter Menell) question aspects of IP's status as property; in so doing, they helped push me to think hard about the issue. They led me back to the field's roots, while keeping me from a too-facile set of answers, the attractive (to me) but ultimately simplistic classical libertarian view of property associated with Richard Epstein (and Robert Nozick before him). While I would like to believe that a "night watchman state" is the ideal for IP, I see now that it is not. Lessig, Lemley, and the others have taught me well that optimal policy in the IP field involves more than simply providing a clear set of property rights and then getting the government out of the way. This is a good starting point, as far as I am concerned, but it is not the end of the story. Government must monitor more than the initial conditions of appropriation; it must keep track of how these property rights are assembled and deployed, and what consequences—economic and social—follow from their use in specific settings. Because property (like all rights) permits private individuals to bring the power of the state to bear against other citizens, the conditions surrounding the use of this power are always relevant, always of interest to the legal system. So the government's interest in IP rights does not end when the rights are awarded. It extends to the long period during which property owners use rights to control and exclude other people. Acquisition and appropriation are only the first movement in the concerto of government concern with IP rights; they are not the finale. It is my position that treating IP as property is not in any way inconsistent with a concern for the environment and conditions in which property rights are deployed—the "postgrant" situation—and that this necessarily requires attention to distributional issues. Nothing in the label *property* limits me to a consideration only of the initial act of appropriation or grant, as some would have it. It is equally within the office of property as an institution to care about how much property is held by various individual people and legal entities, and how that property is used. None of this is in any way at odds with the simple idea that IP really is property.[10]

The second major realization that led to this book was that, if IP is really property, I should look for guidance in the literature on philosophical treatments of property. Books such as Jeremy Waldron's *The Right to Private Property*,[11] Stephen Munzer's *A Theory of Property*,[12] together with the books these works draw on—books by Locke, Kant, and Rawls—were all fair game. Although none of these works covered IP in any detail (most cover it very lightly, if at all), they all provided excellent grounding in the first principles of property. Collectively, they led me back to the principles on which this vital social institution is founded. More importantly, they led me away from a simplistic "just clearly define the rights and let the market sort things out" sort of view—the libertarian option I mentioned earlier. Instead, all these authors argue for a much richer, more complex, at times more confounding understanding of what property is all about. I came to see that they laid as much stress on the *limits* and *exceptions* to property claims (based most often on the needs of others, or "third-party claims") as they did on the justifications for appropriating property in the first place. They led me back, then, to two connected ideas, which together form a truly liberal conception of property: first that property is essential to a fair society, and second that it is imbued with important limits and constraints.[13] In writing this book I hope to translate these foundational writings into the IP context—to write a liberal theory of intellectual property law, with all that this means. This theory's foundational components, as described by Locke, Kant, and others, are a commitment to individual ownership as a primary right, respect for third-party interests that conflict with this right, and, from the philosophy of John Rawls, an acceptance of redistributive policies intended to remedy the structural hardships caused by individual property rights. A liberal theory of IP rights will always remember that property is a *grant* from the government. It embodies an individual right, backed by social institutions—a right that is *personal* yet not *selfish*.

So my aim is to bring together social practices and institutions; midlevel principles, such as efficiency and proportionality; and the foundational concepts of Locke, Kant, and Rawls, in a single coherent theory of the IP field. Figure 1.1 summarizes the conceptual approach to the IP field that I describe throughout this book and serves as a high-altitude map of the terrain ahead.

So what are the first-order principles I am referring to? Stating them as succinctly as possible, they are (1) Lockean appropriation, (2) Kantian (liberal) individualism, and (3) Rawlsian attention to the distributive effects of property. I explain these principles in Part I, Chapters 2 and 3. For present purposes, I want to flag a few points from the later discussion that may help put these concepts into context.

John Locke's appropriation theory is one of the traditional "first principles" of the field, unlike Kant's autonomy theory. (The IP casebook, or

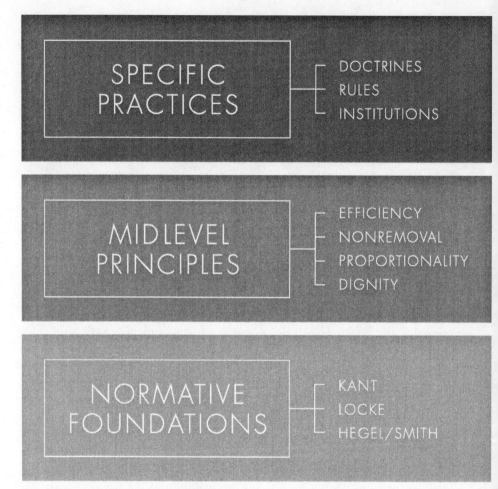

Figure 1.1. A conceptual approach to IP

textbook, I coauthored begins, predictably enough, with an excerpt from Locke's *Two Treatises of Government*.) But I try to go a bit deeper with Locke than the main run of IP literature. In this introduction I can give only a brief sample of what I mean by this; the full account must be left to Chapter 2.

Starting with Locke's famous "labor theory" of appropriation, I question the convention that he relies primarily on a metaphor of "mixing" one's labor with materials found in nature. Applying labor *to* things, rather than mixing labor *with* things, seems a more apt description of what Locke was trying to say. This emphasis on applying labor achieves two important goals, one theoretical and the other more practical. At the level of theory, it relieves some of the difficulties, noted by critics, that are caused by the emphasis on mixing. These difficulties are evident in Robert Nozick's famous example of the person who claims ownership of the ocean after pouring a can of tomato juice into it. Talk of mixing shifts our attention away from the labor involved in mixing to the thing that is mixed; in Nozick's example, from the effort of pouring the juice to the juice itself.[14] The *reductio ad absurdum* flavor of Nozick's example is the implicit comparison between the tiny volume of the juice and the immense volume of the ocean. How could adding the former justify a property claim to the latter? The absurdity disappears when we return to Locke's intended subject, the expenditure of effort as a ground for property rights. He was *not* interested in trying to justify expansive property claims with scholastic treatments of tiny bits of new matter infecting massive amounts of old matter. He paid no attention to the relative weights or volumes of the "thing added" and the preexisting thing. He did not talk about what was added *as* a thing at all. He was concerned with *labor*—with how expending effort leads to justified claims of property. By making *effort* the subject of his inquiry, he naturally limited the scope of the resulting property claims. We need not get lost in the Nozickian metaphysics of admixtures, so long as our focus never strays from Locke's primary topic: the labor itself. How much labor was involved? And how was the preexisting thing changed or affected by that labor? If we stick to these questions, we avoid absurd hypotheticals and keep to the spirit of Locke.

More practically, an emphasis on applying labor works much better for IP rights. The creator of a new work claims property not by virtue of contributing some new *thing* to a preexisting thing, but to the transformation of the preexisting thing by the expenditure of labor. Inventors, authors, composers, and the like do not add physical items like juice to the prior art or to culture; they add effort and, on that basis, claim property rights. A renewed emphasis on labor or effort therefore pays off handsomely when it comes to understanding the right to appropriate and its relationship to IP law.

After restoring Locke's account of appropriation, I explore some other dimensions in Locke scholarship beginning with his treatment of third-party effects from appropriation—how Locke handles the interests of those impacted by appropriation. Contrary to the conventional view among IP scholars, I (following others, especially Jeremy Waldron) find Locke's theory of appropriation to have crucial social and egalitarian strands. I believe this more egalitarian Locke to have important lessons to teach us about the proper reach of IP law, so I devote a good bit of space to these aspects of Locke's thought in Chapter 2.

The basic foundations of IP law are individual autonomy and freedom. These are formative ideas from Immanuel Kant, so it might just as well be said that Kantian philosophy belongs, along with Locke, at the bottom of the foundation. I must hasten to say that Kant was not much in my mind when I started this book. For me, reading Kant with an eye toward IP theory has been a revelation. I was aware of his foundational writings on epistemology, and—like everyone—I knew something about his seminal ethical theory (the categorical imperative, and all that). But reading Kant on property rights opened my eyes to a host of interesting ideas that I had only been aware of at the vaguest level. The relationship of property to individual will, individual choice, and individual freedom; the importance of possession as a concept, rather than an empirical fact; the idea that the formation of government (or "civil society") precedes, rather than follows, the establishment of property rights (as in Locke); and above all, the marvelous vistas opened up by Kant's characteristically *conceptual* approach to philosophy—these ideas washed over me as I was writing this book, slowly at first, and then insistently and rapidly. The real revelation for me was in discovering the excellent fit between Kant's famous a priori concepts and the problems and contours of IP law. Having been schooled largely in the law and economics tradition of U.S. IP law, I was accustomed to thinking about IP law in the familiar terms of Anglo-American empiricism and utilitarianism. I was delighted and surprised to find a rich alternative. Kant's conceptual approach—an approach based on carefully worked out deontological truths, rather than empirical facts and social practices—provided wonderful clues and insights to many of the questions that had long bothered and perplexed me about my field. Paradoxically, I also found that this conceptual approach is enormously helpful in understanding actual institutions and social practices—that the conceptual is a great aid to understanding the practical.[15] I slowly realized why the conventional utilitarian account of IP law had been so dissatisfying to me. What I *thought* was the foundation of my chosen field of study, at least in its current state, could not bear the weight I had been asking of it. Something more fundamental was needed to support the structure of the field. Kant, with his emphasis on individual autonomy and the value of each person, provided just that foundation. And Kant's *style of thought* is equally important. Looking back, it should have been apparent that there would be a good match between this most conceptual of philosophers and IP law, this most conceptual of legal fields (which Joseph Story, in the early eighteenth century, famously described as "the metaphysics of the law"). But it was not apparent, at least not to me. I hope as you read Chapter 3, on Kant and IP law, you will come to agree about the "goodness of fit" between Kant's approach to philosophy and the foundational issues at the heart of the IP field. For now, a quick glimpse at some Kantian ideas will give the general idea.

Kant has complex ideas about creativity, ideas that track well with the structure of IP law. He begins with some primitive notions—the individual, his or her will, and the extension or application of that will onto objects. For Kant, the desire to shape and control things external to the self (that is, objects) is a powerful impulse for human beings. A project involving an external object may require that a person shape or control that object over a period of time. Therefore, human freedom depends, to some degree, on the ability to relate to an object in this way, to control and shape it over time. For some objects, this might be achieved by a persistent physical grasping, but this is obviously a limited strategy. Some objects are too big, hard to grasp, and so forth; generally, a more robust type of possession beyond physical grasping would be more effective in promoting the freedom to work on an object over time. Kant believes that this broader concept of *possession* is crucial to human freedom—so crucial, in fact, that it provides the impetus behind the creation of formal legal institutions, and hence civil society itself. For Kant, legal ownership is central to human freedom. Freedom, ownership, formal law, and then civil society: this is the key conceptual progression in Kant's legal and political philosophy.

Contemporary theorizing about IP rights begins a long, long way from Kant's system of thought, which is exactly why exposure to Kant can be so useful. Scholars today do not see individual freedom and the individual ownership it demands as the chief purpose of IP law. For most of them, IP law is strictly instrumental, a means to the ultimate end of net social welfare or the like. Kant cuts through this instrumental view as if wielding a knife blade. His thought upends amorphous concepts of collective interest and utilitarian balancing, replacing them with the bright, sharp idea of personal autonomy. The result is a more clear-headed focus on IP as a right, and on third-party interests as aspects or dimensions that are reached when we move outward from the starting point of the individual. Kant's thought very effectively separates third-party *interests* from individual *rights*, a distinction I believe is essential to a proper understanding of IP law, especially at this point in the development of the field. An infusion of Kant promises to help correct the recent and intense emphasis on the rights of users and consumers of IP—a point I press in Part III.

Recasting IP in terms of Kantian rights does more than rebalance the field at the conceptual level, however. It leads to some immediate policy payoffs. Concern for autonomy, to take perhaps the most important example, goes beyond placing the rights of creators at the top of the legal hierarchy. It also means a thoroughly practical concern with the working conditions and economic prospects of creative professionals. Though this topic must await Chapter 7 for full development, the groundwork is laid in the discussion of Kantian property in Chapter 3. Autonomy is about something more than properly locating a set of legal rights at the apex of a conceptual pyramid. To be meaningful, it must have some cash value, so to speak; it must translate into putting a few dollars in one's pockets. Creative people are rarely free to create, and cannot effectively shape their destiny, if they cannot control and have little prospect of being paid for their creative work. Autonomy, it must be recalled, means "self-rule," the ability to steer oneself according to one's own plan and design. There is little chance of doing this in a sustained way without ownership over the products of one's creativity. Ownership confers both control and the prospect of compensation—the two practical dimensions of the abstract Kantian notion of autonomy.

So autonomy, in the Kantian sense, follows from conceiving of property as a right. But to speak of IP, or property more generally, in these terms (as a right) may sound like the beginning of a libertarian harangue. You may be familiar with the genre: an author makes a case for property as a right coequal with other fundamental rights; the sad plight of property, relative to other rights, is described (often with a disquisition on how modern governments have lost the way so painstakingly laid down by the early disciples of the "classical liberal" scripture); and the culprit (modern, redistributive government—the demon "welfare state") is identified, censured, and sentenced to a radical near-starvation diet, the better to return to its originally intended form, a sort of bantamweight overseer of robustly defined but minimally supervised entitlements.

Whatever else this kind of program is, it is not in my view consistent with Kantian foundations. For while Kant saw property as a right, and while all rights that deserved the title were fundamental, governments were absolutely *not* limited in purpose to defining or recognizing initial entitlements and then getting out of the way. Kant's Universal Principle of Justice pushed in quite the opposite direction. This principle, which serves as the baseline definition for justice in Kant's legal philosophy, says that actions (including claims to property) are fair or just only when "the freedom of the will of each . . . coexist[s] together with the freedom of everyone in accordance with a universal law."[16] And there is no easy way to dodge concern for "the freedom of everyone" by arguing for the sufficiency of some sort of theoretical equal freedom to claim property, as against actual prospects for property acquisition and actual distributions of property holdings. Kant clearly rejects the easy libertarian path, calling instead for deep and true engagement with the interests of third parties. There is no getting around the difficulty of what Kant asks of civil society: to both respect individual property claims at a deep level and to simultaneously care about the practical impact of individual property claims on the lives and fortunes of others. Kant's thoroughgoing egalitarianism requires that legal rules relating to property maximize the freedom of all members of civil society.

This is a stringent pair of demands. Taken together, they seem to state something close to a paradox. It would take some real work to sort out, in a detailed way, how to reconcile these competing demands to arrive at a coherent set of principles for a property regime. Unfortunately, Kant did not see fit to do so. Outside of a few scattered examples of specific property issues (including an intriguing but brief passage on literary property rights),[17] Kant's work is silent on the details of how to balance the rights of appropriators and the interests of third parties.

Fortunately, just such a body of thought is ready to hand. It is the property theory of John Locke, and in particular the Lockean provisos and other limitations on appropriation. Kant's more schematic ideas on meliorating the third-party effects of individual property rights lead straight back to the Lockean principles first discussed in Chapter 2. So in this way Kant's work fits nicely with Locke's, and Chapters 2 and 3 blend together to form a consistent description of the normative foundations of IP law.

That description is far from comprehensive, however. In particular, justifying individual acts of appropriation, and explaining principled limits on those acts, falls short of a comprehensive consideration of the overall societal impact of the institution of IP rights. For this comprehensive, systemwide view I needed the twentieth-century philosophical literature on property and distributive justice, and hence, of course, the work of John Rawls. In Chapter 4 I apply Rawlsian conceptions of the fair society to the problem of IP protection. The major question is whether individual awards of IP can be justified in light of their effect on the overall distribution of resources in society. A key question is whether it is fair to privilege creative works, which result from individual talent and effort, given that (according to Rawls) no one can be said to deserve their native talent, and also that societal resources are usually required to develop and apply that talent.

In addressing these issues I draw on the work of scholars who argue persuasively that dedicated development and application of talent gives rise to a legitimate desert claim, and hence, in my view, a justified claim to IP rights. Yet I also acknowledge Rawls's original point, that much individual action is the result of pervasive social influence, so that society too has a legitimate interest—but not a coequal right—in the results of individual initiative. The societal interest is made manifest at three different points in the life of an IP right. First, and most conventionally, third-party interests are "baked into" the right; they form part of the structure of the right from the moment it is granted. Time limits and affirmative user rights are examples. Second, the state rightfully monitors each IP right after its grant. Courts in particular intercede when postgrant conditions coalesce in a way that confers disproportionate leverage on a rightholder. User defenses and limits on legal remedies give primary expression to this impulse, which is described in depth in Chapter 6, The Proportionality Principle.

The third moment when societal interests enter into the IP picture occurs after a creative work has been exploited and money has been earned. In keeping with Rawlsian theory, society retains the right to claim some of the money that flows from individual creative works. Practically speaking, this means that it is fully legitimate for the state to tax the proceeds of individual works covered by IP rights. In addition to the Kantian core, reflecting the unique contribution of each creative person and the state's recognition of individual autonomy, there is a Rawlsian dimension as well. I illustrate this balanced conception with a diagram showing the "deserving core" that belongs by right to all creators, and the "social periphery" representing society's interest in each creative work.

This conception of individual property coupled with state-backed limitations and taxation is hardly novel. In fact, it combines two of the most conventional building blocks of Western socioeconomic systems. I emphasize this approach only because I think IP theorists often overlook it. Most choose to channel all their discussion of the proper balance between individual and society into the arena of IP law itself, as though each doctrine and each controversy must be engineered so as to get the balance right. It ought to come as a relief to be reminded that the conventional instrument of taxation is available to redress distributive imbalances, and that therefore we do not need to design every doctrine of IP law as a precision instrument designed to optimize overall distributive justice. The more systemic view supplied by Rawls's way of thinking can get us out of the unproductive and often divisive trap of thinking that each individual rule of IP must balance out perfectly. Rawls's approach frees us from this excessively internalist perspective and ought to be embraced for that reason alone.

I BEGAN by tracing the skeletal components of the contemporary IP cityscape, the midlevel principles. Next, I dug up the submerged foundations of IP law: the field's formative concepts, derived from Kant and Locke, plus Rawls (with the caveat that other foundations are conceivable as well). Now I proceed to the material covered in Part III, a survey of some of the detailed institutions and rules that make up the surface and texture of IP law. I have two aims. First I describe some broad structural concerns that arise when discrete property rights, granted to individuals for the foundational reasons I explain in Part I, and enforced and applied by courts according to principles laid out in Part II, come to be amalgamated and centralized in the hands of large corporate owners. Next I look at two important flashpoints in the contemporary discourse over IP law: digital works and pharmaceutical patents.

After this assessment of the way things are, I also look ahead in Part III. In Chapter 10, I draw on important critiques of IP—some substantive, relating to new technologies, others purely conceptual—that have appeared in the past fifteen years or so. Against some aspects of these critiques, I defend the field, arguing that IP rights continue to make sense even in the context of new technologies and conceptual challenges. At the same time, some aspects of these critiques are helpful adjuncts to the property-based traditions of the field. These I promote as useful wrinkles, new additions that cohere with and supplement the basic logic of property rights that has served society long and well.

The substantive critiques that IP experts have leveled in recent years touch on all sorts of issues. Two of the most frequent targets are copyright protection for digital works and pharmaceutical patents. I tackle these topics in Part III, where I extend and apply the concepts from Part I and the principles from Part II. I aim to show that these concepts and principles are more than useless artifacts or sterile taxonomic labels; instead, they are capable of bearing fruit, of doing real work in contemporary policy debates.

However, before we can apply the foundational concepts of Parts I and II, we must address a vital preliminary issue: what might be called the problem of corporatization. The principles and concepts we address early in this book are almost always described in terms of a stylized scenario involving a lone creator figure and his audience. Critics of these principles have often pointed out that the real-world conditions in the industries that "produce" IP-protected creations are far different. Very large teams of people work together, each member contributing only a small part of the larger creation, which is owned in many cases by a large corporate entity, often in conjunction with a large portfolio of other, similar works. The paradigm cases might be the Walt Disney Company for copyrighted films, and a large pharmaceutical or semiconductor company for patented inventions.

The reality of corporate ownership—and its sharp contrast with the idealized world of a lone creator—has a central place in the literature critical of IP rights. Indeed, one prominent critique argues that the romanticized notion of the heroic, lone creator was a myth created in the latter days of the Enlightenment and is perpetuated today by large companies that use it cynically to advance their own self-interest. Whether the strong form of this argument is true, there is a fundamental disjuncture between the individual creator, who forms the stylized backdrop for foundational IP principles of the Lockean and Kantian variety, and the reality of large corporate "IP factories." And for some critics, this disjuncture is fatal; for them it means those foundational principles have little salience for IP policy.

In Chapter 7, Creative Professionals, Corporate Ownership, and Transaction Costs, I traverse and then reject these objections. My argument follows two main paths. I first point out that stories of the demise of the small creator are overblown; individual creators continue to make important contributions to culture and commerce. More importantly, if we widen the angle of vision just a bit, we can see that individual creators working in *small teams*—often in small start-up companies—play a very important part in contemporary IP-driven creativity. My initial thrust, in other words, amounts to a refutation of the basic premise of the critics' notion that creative activities are now highly concentrated in large corporate entities.

The second part of my answer concedes that large corporations account for the preponderance of IP ownership in some industries. The question then becomes whether the foundational principles behind IP protection are still persuasive when large companies hold IP rights. Can IP law, based on rewarding individual effort and encouraging individual autonomy, retain its justification when IP ownership flows to a large corporate entity? The answer I give is a qualified yes. I begin by recognizing that corporate employers are not simply faithful agents of individual creators, and therefore that large IP-owning companies are not ideal "creator collectives." There is, as a consequence, some dilution in the justification of IP rights. Put another way, it is important for the legal system to recognize that corporate IP owners mediate between the creative interests of the professional creators they employ and the business objectives of their managers. In some cases, this means that if IP law is to stay true to its foundational principles, legal rules must be tilted in favor of individual creators, at the expense of corporate owners. I give two examples. First, there are the rules that govern long-lasting copyright licenses, typically from small or independent creators to large corporate entities. A novelist who licenses "film rights," for example, may argue later that the license should not be interpreted to cover an interactive DVD version of the movie based on the novel. Courts have struggled with these cases, at times interpreting the original licenses broadly and thus favoring the original licensee, and at times ruling the other way, in favor of the novel's copyright owner. I come down in favor of proposals to systematically favor the individual creator in the interpretation of these licenses—the novelist in my example. A rule interpreting license grants narrowly—and therefore systemically favoring the small creator in this situation by giving him a chance to negotiate a new, separate license for a new, unforeseen technology—comports best with the foundational principles of IP law.

The second legal issue that bears on the relationship between small creators and large corporate owners relates to the "rules of exit." These are legal rules and doctrines that control how easy it is for an employee to leave a large company and start a new business. Because IP assets will often form the cornerstone of a new business start-up, ex-employers sometimes claim ownership of the ideas and technology upon which former employees found new start-up companies. Although I recognize the logic of large-scale corporate ownership,[18] I also see the importance of liberal rules of employee "exit." IP claims by large corporate entities should be carefully scrutinized to ensure they are not being used to prevent the formation of legitimate start-up companies. The misuse of IP along these lines cuts directly against the formative principles (effort, autonomy, and so forth) on which the IP system is based.

After acknowledging the problems of large corporate ownership, I consider and reject the stronger version of this argument: that creators are tiny peons in the larger corporate structure, and large corporate interests have so thoroughly co-opted the development of IP law that IP as it stands has become completely dissociated from the interests of individual creators. This is simply wrong. Though large corporate IP owners are not perfect agents of the creators they represent, the fact remains that large entities provide a professional home for many creative professionals today. Because of this, the interests of these large companies are often at least roughly aligned with those of the creative professionals they employ. This is why I advocate a more nuanced view than that of the full-time critic of large companies, one that recognizes there is sometimes a divergence between the interests of IP creators and the large companies that own much IP, but also that large organizations have an important role as employers and sometimes champions of creative professionals. I argue that corporate ownership is an important feature of the ecosystem that supports individual creative professionals; that incremental change in IP rules makes sense in some cases; but also that as long as new entry and a certain industry dynamism is possible there is no reason to suppose that industry structure is so anathema to the individual creator that the basic premise of IP law has become irrelevant.

THESE GENERAL THOUGHTS about the structure of IP-based industries give way, in Chapters 8 and 9, to a discussion of problems and conditions in two particularly IP-intensive industries, digital entertainment and media (Chapter 8) and pharmaceuticals (Chapter 9). The idea is straightforward:

to apply the basic principles developed in the early parts of the book to some difficult contemporary issues—to put the theory through its paces, so to speak. In the process, I suggest some ways in which the foundational principles of the field can be brought to bear on some major challenges in these important industries. The idea throughout is to address contemporary problems with the tools and principles that form the basic building blocks of IP law, to confront new issues by remaining true to the property right foundations of the field.

In the context of digital copyright, the concepts of Part I and the principles of Part II yield two important insights. The first is a corrective, bringing our attention back from the places it has wandered to in contemporary discourse, which are all about the revolutionary nature of the Internet and digitization in general. After the basic grounding in the logic of property as a right granted to meritorious creators, it is easier to see the Internet for what it is: a revolution primarily in the means by which creative works reach their audiences. And this makes it harder to fall into a common trap, which is to get so caught up in this revolutionary distribution technology that we make *it*—and not the creators of digital works, the traditional beneficiaries of IP rights—the focus of our interest, and our policies.

It is as if society had developed a revolutionary new technology for car engines that makes it possible for the average car owner to go 500 miles per hour. A group of scholars emerges to argue that the goal of the legal system ought to be to enable as many people as possible to drive as fast as possible. Anything that interferes with this goal is "antitechnology." Danger to pedestrians and bicyclists, concern for old neighborhoods and historic districts—these are irrelevant. The rhetoric of "regulation" and "control of technology" fills the pages of law reviews; the implicit premise is that any considerations that cut against the new technologies in any way are retrogressive, outdated, and reactionary. Arguing for rules that blunt the potential harm from this new high-speed capability brings immediate condemnation.

Just such a technocentric approach now dominates IP law, which is a shame. I argue that scholars should not get too caught up in the euphoria over the Internet. Instead, we need to keep faith with the basic ideas that have shaped the field, that give it structure. Scholars of the digital era have preached that "the Internet changes everything," and indeed there have been huge changes in the way creative works are delivered to people, and in the things people can do with them once they have them. But the new technologies of dissemination have not changed one important fact: creative works still require effort, and (in many cases) a projection of the individual will, or personality. Since effort and individuality are the essence of IP, property rights in creative works continue to make sense even in the Internet era.

Those who fail to see this essential continuity overlook the durable truths concerning creative works. A quick read of some books and articles in the technocentric vein proves the point. Lawrence Lessig's *Code Version 2.0*,[19] Jessica Litman's *Digital Copyright*,[20] and a host of similar writings repeatedly emphasize the radical discontinuity between the pre-Internet and Internet eras when it comes to technologies for distributing creative works. In this school of thought, the driving force of change is also the explanatory fulcrum on which the IP field hinges. The basic idea is simple: Because the technologies by which creative works are disseminated have changed drastically, our thinking about the field must change drastically as well. This is what I mean by technocentrism.

Technocentrism leads to two critiques of contemporary IP law. First is what might be called the unbalancing thesis. Scholars start with the idea that preexisting laws were formed on the basis of mostly unstated assumptions about what creators and consumers could do. Since those assumptions are now outdated—in particular, since creators now have much greater control over the uses of their works—the law has become unintentionally unbalanced. The idea (an old one in legal circles) is that the *practical* impact of a legal regime is a combination of "law on the books" together with real-world constraints and conditions, one of which is the state of technology surrounding application of the law. While the law on the books has not changed in many cases, these scholars argue that the practical impact or effective clout of the law has changed drastically. A common example concerns the distribution of written material—a magazine article, for instance. In the old, pre-Internet days, people could easily pick up a copy of a magazine at a bookstore or newsstand and read it for a while without paying for it. Libraries existed for the most part to facilitate shared access to individual printed works. Today, the owner of a digital version of the magazine can—and this is a crucial point—*in theory* monitor and charge for every use of the magazine, every user who glances at it or reads it over.[21] So the literal application of existing law preventing the making of copies means, many scholars say, that the owners of copyrights today have far more and far stronger property rights *in effect* than in the old days.

The premise behind the unbalancing thesis is correct: the real-world environment plays a crucial role in determining the actual impact of legal rules. But there is a problem as it is applied. Scholars promoting this idea have failed to push it all the way through. They overlook the fact that although the physical/technological environment has changed now that creative works are routinely digitized, the *business reality* has changed as well. So although the digital era has made possible much tighter technical restrictions on creative works, it has also made it much more important for copyright owners to permit all sorts of free sampling and reuse of creative works. This sort of liberality is dictated by the market: users want this sort of freedom, and owners must give it to them if they are to have any chance of seeding and developing the market for their works.

Chapter 9 considers the complex issue of patents on pharmaceuticals of use to suffering populations in the developing world. This is a classic conflict, pitting the rights of pharmaceutical companies against the ethical claims of a destitute group. The ideas developed in Parts I and II can be put to good use in sorting out the respective claims involved. Though Locke and Kant provide support for the basic notion that property makes an appropriate reward for the research effort of pharmaceutical companies, it is the limiting principles and constraints from their theories of property that really come to the fore. Locke's charity proviso, for example, is directly relevant. Under this proviso one whose survival depends on access to resources controlled by another has a legitimate property right to the resources. Locke's notion of charity thus extends to the point where destitute populations whose lives are truly at stake have a strong claim to life-saving pharmaceuticals. Likewise, Kant's Universal Principle leads to the same result. The effects of pharmaceutical patents on destitute populations represent an extreme limitation on their autonomy, and so the rights of the patent owners must give way.

There is however a significant boundary around the access rights of the destitute. Severe and persistent inroads on the patent rights of pharmaceutical companies may threaten the long-term viability of the drug industry's research program. Future generations may suffer the consequences. Under what Rawls called the "Principle of Fair Saving," more generally known as the problem of intergenerational equity, it would be wrong to redistribute resources today so as to threaten the welfare of future generations. In the case of pharmaceutical patents, this implies the need for limits to the right of access that follow from a straightforward application of the Lockean and Kantian principles to this case.

CHAPTER 10 SERVES as a précis of the main arguments in the book. Its primary point is that property still makes sense. The one-to-one mapping of individual owner to discrete assets remains a crucial and compelling social institution even in the modern era. There remains a strong argument for recognizing and rewarding creative work with true legal rights, thereby converting that work from hourly wage labor into a freestanding *economic asset* wherever possible. Nurturing professional creators means encouraging not only individual and small-team ownership, but also large corporate entities, which form an important part of the ecosystem that nurtures and supports individual creative professionals.

At the same time, I reiterate in Chapter 10 that just because IP rights should be real rights does not mean they must be *absolute* rights. In addition to the built-in limits on appropriation suggested by Locke, Kant, and the midlevel principles of Chapter 5 (chiefly nonremoval and proportionality), there is society's right to levy taxes on the proceeds from works covered by IP rights. As explained in Chapter 4, this is one of the most effective ways to maintain IP rights as an institution while recognizing society's contribution to and interest in each IP-protected work.

Limiting property rights and taxing IP-covered works are not the only ways to accommodate the needs of consumers and users. As I explain in Chapters 7 and 8, I favor cheap and easy IP permission and licensing mechanisms, together with simple waiver techniques that permit binding dedication of rights to the public. In the long-standing debate over incentives versus access, creators/owners versus consumers/users, I argue that this is the right combination. Rightholders can continue to receive rights, while consumers and users can gain access to the works they want to use, if resources are directed to creating efficient transactional mechanisms. These will allow IP rights to flow through commercial channels as smoothly, or almost as smoothly, as do the works covered by those rights. We need to recognize that, in a world with numerous IP rights, the market for creative works necessitates also a (separate, but related) market for the *rights covering those works,* and that IP policy ought to encourage market making in this secondary market.

I also call for a simple and binding mechanism for waiver—allowing a rightholder to make a binding dedication of his works to the public and thus implementing a "right to include" that is coextensive with the traditional right to exclude at the heart of IP, and property generally.

PART ONE

FOUNDATIONS

CHAPTER TWO

Locke

BECAUSE OF HIS ENORMOUS INFLUENCE, it makes sense in any serious discussion of property to start with the writings of John Locke. But because there are limits to how much can be usefully packed into a single chapter, I need to lay out up front what I choose to emphasize.

I will concentrate on only those aspects of Locke's thought that contribute directly to understanding the normative foundations of IP law. Even on these topics, I can only summarize, because so much has been written. There are a number of reliable guides capable of giving the full-out, languorous tour of Locke Country. My itinerary is much more limited. Even with respect to Locke's writings on property, to say nothing of his coverage of broader topics, much of what Locke writes about has little connection to the problems that concern me. So after the briefest overview of the big picture, we will linger only in those regions of Locke's thought that have special meaning for the topic at hand. Ours will be a limited trip for a particular purpose, always keeping in mind our ultimate destination, an understanding of normative property theory as it relates to IP today.

We begin with a brief introduction describing why Locke addressed issues of property acquisition in the first place. After gaining a sense of his motivation, we plunge right into the heart of his property theory, the famous passages where he talks about the original commons (or "state of nature"), and labor as a justification for property rights. The emphasis here is on the core Lockean concepts: why adding labor to "found things" can ground property claims; what types and amounts of labor are needed to secure rights; and the limits and qualifications on property—including, of course, the three Lockean "provisos." Though many scholars in and out of the IP field have acknowledged the provisos in their writings on Locke, many have limited their attention to one or at most two (typically, spoliation and sufficiency). The third, Locke's charity proviso, has important and largely overlooked ramifications for the IP field, as I explain. Full consideration of the provisos, added to a basic understanding of Locke's theory of appropriation, gives us a more three-dimensional Locke: more nuanced than the traditional cardboard cutout of Locke the libertarian.[1] We reclaim a philosophical figure capable of supporting a more egalitarian and truly liberal theory of property. This is just what we need in the IP field today, as I argue in Part III of this book.

The "Goodness of Fit" between Locke and IP Rights

Whether it is worthwhile to set out across the Lockean landscape depends on the "goodness of fit" between Locke's property theory and IP rights.[2] A fair number of scholars argue that the theory does not fit at all. Not me. I think Locke's theory applies equally well, if not better, to intellectual property. I will give three reasons. First, Locke's focus on appropriation from a "state of nature" fits much more accurately the usual "origin story" of our own time. Though unclaimed wilderness continues to be domesticated, and though it is perfectly accurate to speak of new property rights along various frontiers (most notably in the Amazon, described by property rights economists Lee Alston, Gary Libecap, and others),[3] a large fraction of the land surface of the earth has already been claimed, in most cases long ago. Fresh appropriation from a background of unowned or widely shared material is much more common today in the world of IP than in the world of tangible assets. Indeed, in the vast majority of cases, although there may be important antecedents to a particular work of authorship or inventorship, most intellectual property rights (IPRs) are newly claimed property rights, as opposed to what the law defines specifically as derivative works or "improvement inventions." At least in the developed world, Locke's canonical situation of a gatherer of apples or acorns at work in a commonly owned field of trees is in practice much more common in the IP world than in the world of physical property today. And, contrary to conventional accounts,[4] the intellectual commons is not shrinking—it is growing. The more intellectual creations we humans come up with, the more we make possible. To use a catchphrase from scientific research, this sphere of activity presents us with an "endless frontier."[5] The stock of public domain information, from which individual creators draw, fits closely with Locke's conception of a vast realm of common resources. The starting conditions for his theory, in other words, are met quite often with respect to intellectual creations, so his theory works especially well in this domain.[6]

But Locke is relevant for other reasons as well. At a deep level, the logic of his thinking applies to intellectual products at least as well as to the objects of physical property. This is so for two basic reasons. First, the "givenness" of the background materials out of which property is forged by labor is very apparent in the world of IP. What we call the public domain is an important, pervasive backdrop against which IP rights are defined. If some simple parallels are accepted (described in the section "Locke's Common and the Public Domain," below), then the symmetry between Locke's state of nature and the public domain becomes quite apparent. The claiming of IP rights out of the public domain follows the same logic as the emergence of property rights from the state of nature.

Second, it is well understood that for Locke, labor plays a crucial role in both justifying and bounding property rights. Again, there are strong parallels to the world of IP rights. Although some well-known doctrines in IP law provide that "mere" labor (or hard work) is not always enough to establish an IPR, nontrivial creations presumably requiring significant effort are often said to be at the heart of IP law. Although labor is relevant in establishing some real property rights, it is a much larger, and much more prominent, part of the IP landscape. So Locke is more pertinent to IP.

Finally, on a biographical note, Locke described his own work as labor: I am "employed," he wrote, "as an Under-Labourer in clearing Ground a little, and removing some of the Rubbish, that lies in the way to Knowledge."[7] The point is simple: Locke recognizes the work required in researching and writing, and so implicitly at any rate legitimizes a labor-based property claim for the end product of this type of work. Clearing ground and removing rubbish are exactly the kinds of manual labor that justify property claims in Locke's discussion of appropriation.[8] Gathering acorns and apples is not too different from this. Stooping and collecting are related, conceptually, to Locke's image of writing as clearing ground and removing rubbish. If writing is metaphorical grunt work, there is every reason that it should lead to the same result as actual grunt work: a valid claim to legitimate property.

Locke's Theory of Appropriation

The State of Nature and the Original Common

Locke begins his account of property by acknowledging what virtually all of his contemporaries understood, that God had given the earth to mankind. He adds that the gift was to people in common.[9] The origin of things was God, as everyone then knew; and He had given the earth to human beings collectively rather than piecemeal to individuals; "nobody has originally a private Dominion, exclusive of the rest of Mankind, in any [part of the earth or its products]."[10] This starting point shaped the basic task Locke set for himself: to explain how, out of a gift to all in common, individual property rights might arise.[11]

Individual appropriation makes sense only when we understand the purpose of the divine gift. The earth and all that it yields was "given to Men for the Support and Comfort of their being."[12] The divine directive was that mankind should survive and thrive, and the earth and all it contained was the means by which this purpose could be effectuated. To make use of the great gift of the world, humans must take hold of things, and consume them. In other words, they must *appropriate* them out of the original commons: "[T]here must of necessity be a means to appropriate them some way or other before they can be of any use, or at all beneficial, to any particular Man."[13] Individual appropriation is necessary, he says, because original acquisition through common consent is unworkable. The only way to fulfill the divine directive is to permit individuals to gain control over resources without first obtaining permission from everyone else. By a similar line of reasoning, Locke offers nontheological, or consequentialist, arguments in favor of individual appropriation.[14] Both arguments go to support the conclusion that individual appropriation is right and proper.[15] In this fashion Locke establishes the essential foundation of a system of private property rights—a one-to-one mapping between individual people and discrete economic resources.[16] But what is the connection between fulfilling the divine directive and the institution of property? Why should the act of appropriation give rise to the specific institution of ownership we call property? To answer these questions, Locke introduces the idea of work, or labor:

> Though the Earth, and all inferior Creatures be common to all Men, yet every Man has a Property in his own Person. This no Body has any Right to but himself. The Labour of his Body and the Work of his Hands, we may say, are properly his. Whatsoever, then, he removes out of the State that Nature hath provided and left it in, he hath mixed his Labour with it, and joyned to it something that is his own, and thereby makes it his Property. It being by him

removed from the common state Nature placed it in, it hath by this labour something annexed to it that excludes the common right of other Men.[17]

Notice two things. First, Locke speaks of Nature (as an expression of the divine will or presence) as having "left" or "placed" the earth in common for all people. When appropriation occurs, it is by a "taking out of" this common state. Second, the way one takes something out of the common is to labor or work on it—to expend effort. Common ownership, in other words, is the default state; individual appropriation comes about through effort, which is required to alter the default condition.

Why effort? The answer comes at the end of this section, when Locke writes: "For this 'labour' being the unquestionable property of the labourer, no man but he can have a right to what that is once joined to, at least where there is enough, and as good left in common for others." One owns one's labor "unquestionabl[y]". By extension, one owns whatever one's labor is "annexed to" or "mixed with." The axiomatic ownership of labor (which stems from ownership of one's body) thus provides the solid ground on which legitimate appropriation is built.

To summarize: Resources are common. One owns one's body, and the labor that is produced by it. Annexing or mixing one's labor with resources found in the common gives rise to property rights—a legitimate claim to ownership. Locke extends the chain of reasoning further in the *Second Treatise,* by arguing that on the basis of this prepolitical right to individual appropriation, people come together to form governments. The overall effect then is to overthrow the divine right theory of political sovereignty. The earth was not deeded by God to Adam and Eve, and hence by descent to the current monarch. It was instead given to all, and parts of it become the subject of individual ownership rights through the expenditure of labor.

Locke's Common and the Public Domain

Locke's notion of the original common fits well with the IP concept of the public domain. This is obvious at the intuitive level, but requires a more searching defense in light of certain technical objections. I will make the intuitive case first and then address the technical issues.

Property arises from two stark facts in Locke's setup. Natural resources in the state of nature are given to all in equal measure.[18] Each person has what property lawyers would call an undivided partial interest in the entirety of the state of nature. Yet to do anything useful with these resources, an individual has to somehow bring them into his or her control—to gather them or eat them, for example. If, to make use of a resource, each person had to get permission from its rightful owner (humanity as a whole), that person would starve.[19] In a state of nature, there is no mechanism for getting this permission.[20] The impossibility of group-level consent, coupled with the divine directive that humanity was not put here to waste away, points directly to individual appropriation.

I want to argue in this chapter that labor is capable of grounding claims over intellectual assets as well as tangible items such as land, crops, and the like. But what is the equivalent of the state of nature when it comes to IP? What takes the place of natural resources in their native, unclaimed state? What is it that someone in the IP world finds strewn about in a rough and unimproved condition, ready for appropriation through labor? The answer is the public domain.

It is a commonplace of IP theory today that virtually all new intellectual creations draw from the public domain—the vast trove of shared, unowned material that precedes and surrounds the individual creator. Indeed, modern IP theory often pays such strong tribute to the role of the public domain that it shortchanges the individual labor needed to transform items from this domain into something creative and new. However, Locke and Kant return always to personal effort and individual ownership as the root of property, and thereby offer a much-needed corrective to a single-minded emphasis on the public domain. I do not mean to imply that the public domain is unimportant, that individuals create their works in a vacuum, ex nihilo. (I can say without irony that I come to praise the public domain, and not to bury it.) But I do claim this: the addition of individual labor is what transforms public domain starting materials into a unique creative product. So for IP the public domain serves the same function as the state of nature in Locke's property theory. It supplies the raw material, the thick scattering of unowned resources, that surrounds the individual creator.

A little later I address some technical objections to a Locke-based rationale for IP. But two objections are so glaring I need to take them on immediately. The first is that Locke's state of nature is populated by tangible items, whereas the public domain consists of mostly intellectual things— stories, inventions, drawings, essays, and a host of other manifestations of human creativity. These intellectual objects are famously different from tangible items in that more than one person can use them simultaneously. Economists say they are "nonrivalrous": your use of a story idea does not make it impossible for me to use the same idea at the same time, in the way that your use of an apple or acorn does. Second, Locke says that God provides the state of nature for the use of all. Until the first claimant labors, it is not and never has been owned. The public domain is different. Some of it consists of material that was created by individual human labor and was previously subject to ownership claims that have lapsed or expired. A subsequent claimant, coming across something in the public domain, sometimes draws on things that were created (and owned) by others, rather than drawing on purely new and never-claimed resources. Is this an important difference?

Let me take the first objection first. It is tempting to argue that there is no need for property where goods are nonrivalrous. If I write a story, many people can read it at the same time without interfering with each others' access to it. This is how a story differs from an acorn or apple. Because it is so easy to share an item like this, it is natural to argue that society ought to prohibit individual claims and let everyone use it simultaneously.[21]

This thought lies behind certain statements by IP scholars that IP law creates "artificial scarcity," a term that suggests a state of affairs where information moves from one person to another in a free and frictionless way. In such a setting, the imposition of IP rights, which are after all designed to exclude others from the use of information, serves only to slow down the natural fluidity of information exchange.

There is much to say on this score. A thorough vetting of what nonrivalry means for IP law would take us far into the depths of Locke's provisos, a task I put aside for now.[22] But at this point, when we are just putting out from shore, it makes sense to limit the discussion to a simple, intuitive critique of those who take the nonrivalrous nature of information as the supreme guide to IP policy. The problem is that the pace and velocity of information exchange is not the only relevant issue in the world of IP. The generation of new information is equally important. Newness matters, originality matters. IP is about more than how quickly information changes hands. It is also about the nature of that information, in particular the stimulation of new and in some cases unique contributions to the great flow of information coursing through society.

How does this relate to the state of nature and the public domain? Go back to the idea that original creators work from starting materials they find in their environment. Few would bother laboring to recast, reshape, or improve them if that work had to be shared with all comers. For Locke, while it was true that anyone coming upon a field strewn with acorns or apples could take possession of them, it was also true that these items were not nearly as useful in their native state as they were after they were gathered. Implicit in his account was the idea that the produce of nature had to be sorted, organized, and collected to make it serviceable for human ends. To make found items useful, in the quest to survive and thrive, requires labor.

Here is where we encounter problems with the theory of "nonrivalry uber alles." Those obsessed with this motif in IP law see loaves of bread all around them, and think only of how to multiply it, slice it, and get it into the greatest possible number of hands. Locke's approach, echoed in the old children's story, asks "but who will bake the bread?" Sharing has become so effortless—a lifetime's work can be uploaded or e-mailed in an instant—that we lose sight of how much work was required to create things in the first place. As with Locke's acorns and apples, so in the world of creative work: it takes effort to pick and choose, gather and collect, rework and reshape, extend and create. The scattered, random plenty of the state of nature/public domain is only a starting point; it is the place where labor begins. Crowning this labor with property serves two ends: it honors the effort involved and calls forth more of it. So it was, Locke thought, for humans in the state of nature. And so it is, today, for humans faced with the vast, unorganized public domain. Information may be easy to share, but novel and useful information is still hard to create. Therefore property still makes sense.

Property and human flourishing—that is the key relationship. Locke's theory is less about the nature of the objects appropriated—whether they are tangible and rivalrous, or intangible and nonrivalrous—and more about human prospering through individual appropriation. As Richard Ashcraft puts it,

> [T]he first stage of the state of nature—the original condition in which God places mankind—is one in which property is defined in naturalistic and moral terms, where the key concepts are freedom of one's person, labor, use, the right to subsistence, and the Law of Nature of God's will. . . . It is a mistake [however] to believe that the moral features characteristic of the first stage simply disappear with the invention of money and the other historical developments that characterize the second stage of the state of nature. . . . For, as we have seen, Locke certainly believes that the natural right to subsistence is carried forward in time as an enforceable moral claim in the most advanced or civilized state of society.[23]

Because I believe IP rights do promote human flourishing, I believe they are completely consistent with Locke's theory, even though intellectual works draw on and consist of nonrivalrous goods.[24]

Now for the second objection. In Locke's set-up, things in the state of nature are given by God, while the public domain is for the most part made by humans. It is one thing to add labor to something God-given and found in a native state; perhaps it is another to justify individual rights by adding labor to something over which prior rights may have lapsed. Maybe this difference calls into question the entire parallel between the public domain and the state of nature.

Then again, maybe not. Material that was formerly covered by an IP right has much the same status as unowned resources in Locke's state of nature. Both constitute a commons. The public domain, like the state of nature, is available for all to draw on. No one has a superior claim to it, as compared with anyone else. Until an individual puts some work into the item drawn from the public domain, there can be no property claim. Because no one has a superior claim on it, and anyone may labor on it, the public domain is a completely egalitarian resource. In the end, it is not important who makes resources available for all to draw on, God (for natural resources) or people (for intellectual creations). It is only important that the resources are available to all in an unowned form, waiting for individual effort to transform them.

Removal from the Public Domain

So the state of nature/public domain analogy works fairly well. Yet it is possible to read Locke's "initial appropriation" theory as pertinent only to primitive states of development, where economic activity is based on removal of tangible goods from the common.[25] Before moving on, we need to counter this thought. We will have to show that the basic concepts Locke employs to justify appropriation in the state of nature carry over to creative work in a modern economy where information and IP rights form an important part of wealth and commerce. In terms of Locke's theory, we need to confront the idea of removal. In the state of nature, appropriation is effected by physical removal. There is no direct equivalent when it comes to creative work in the realm of ideas. The nonrivalrous nature of information makes it impossible to physically remove it in most cases.[26] What then does removal from the common mean in this setting?

It means roughly what it does for tangible items. Locke's ideas work perfectly well in the context of creative work, so long as we picture removal not as something literal and physical, but as something arising from a necessary convention or shared understanding—a social fact, instead of a natural fact. This will, it is true, require a bit of maneuvering through a few passages in Locke's writings. But without too much strain, we arrive at the conclusion that the public domain in the IP realm is equivalent to the tangible commons in the state of nature.[27]

In Locke's account things are taken out of general circulation by the exercise of labor, an act of appropriation. Locke relies on certain features of the natural world, especially that laboring on a specific tangible object transforms that object, to ground natural law property claims that precede (and in some sense necessitate) the founding of a formal government by agreement. Describing removal as less naturalistic and more a matter of social convention might seem to reverse the Lockean sequence; when social conventions about removal of information goods replace natural facts, this implies that some sort of government or prior agreement is already in place. But this is not as it seems. There is to begin with a conventional aspect to Locke's state of nature that is sometimes overlooked: the concept of natural law may be seen as a sort of transcendent prior agreement among prepolitical people. Even so, IP rights do require a more elaborate political structure; IP as we know it seems an unlikely institution to arise in the state of nature. Yet Locke's discussion of initial appropriation is still relevant. That is because the state of nature is only partly an anthropological-historical account. It is primarily a hypothetical setting used to derive certain fundamental truths, such as when individual property is justified, and when a shared government must recognize the resulting legal rights. These truths apply equally well to the assignment of IP rights, which necessarily occurs after civil society has been established. True, drawing from the public domain does not effect a physical removal of tangible items. But this does not bring intellectual creativity outside Locke's conceptual ambit. What matters is that there are basic principles about property rights, and that these principles transcend—conceptually precede—the specific rules of an actual government.[28] The shared understanding of these principles, and not the physicality of resources, is the key to Locke's hypothetical state of nature.[29]

Whether we are talking about gathering acorns in the state of nature, or adapting a well-known literary plot or piece of technology from the public domain, the basic logic is the same. That which is found in the state of nature must be transformed and adapted. Gathering and organizing acorns or apples in this setting necessarily means that those same acorns or apples will not be useable by others. The award of a property right, made to encourage human flourishing, dictates this result.

IP critics point out that information is different—that my use of a piece of information need not take away from your enjoyment of it. But if my use interferes with your ability to flourish, this runs afoul of the Lockean paradigm. If I copy a work you created, you may be harmed even though you may still use your copy. My use may not take the information out of your hands; but it may take some money out of your pocket. And this I must not do if it would interfere with your ability to flourish—with your right to exploit the things you have improved with your labor. *This* is the key point Locke makes. The relationship between labor, appropriation, and human flourishing lies at the heart of Locke's thinking. His property theory is not a theory about noninterference with tangible goods that have been labored over. It is a theory about why individual appropriation helps people to survive and thrive. Locke's theory does not concern itself with the difference between tangible and intangible assets; that is largely irrelevant. It is centrally concerned with the conditions under which an individual claim to property may be justified in light of the overarching goal of human flourishing. If I use something you have worked on, and that harms you, interferes with your ability to thrive, I may be in violation of your property. This is true whether or not you are left with anything after my use. The nature of the thing you created does not really matter. What matters is that you worked on it, and that my use of it interferes with your legitimate claim to it based on that work. Again, the important issue is not the nature of the asset involved, rivalrous versus nonrivalrous. It is whether my use interferes with your ability to flourish: to earn something, for example, for your labor. This applies to nonrivalrous things, those things covered by IP rights, equally as much as to rivalrous, tangible things.

The Centrality of Labor

The need to survive and thrive therefore justifies removal from nature. But what justifies an individual claim to a specific resource—a specific, discrete property right? Why must removal be accompanied by the exclusive rights of possession, use, and so on, that together compose the specific right we call property? Why does the promotion of human thriving, in other words, require the institution we call property, with all its attendant attributes? The answer for Locke is labor.

In Lockean theory, property is grounded in the combination of labor with found and unowned things. Because they are so important to Locke's account, I want to take the time to spell out with some precision Locke's ideas about labor, and the application of labor to unowned things. This lays the foundation for what comes later, when I apply Lockean concepts to the special problems of IP.

The conventional shorthand for Locke's theory of property acquisition is the "labor theory." His basic argument is that one may legitimately take property out of the state of nature by virtue of one's labor—by the act of gathering, in the case of apples and acorns, or the act of clearing and cultivating in the case of land. These examples raise all sorts of questions about Locke's theory; indeed, if one reads only the famous apple and acorn vignettes, one might well question whether Locke's account rises to the level of a theory at all. But there is much more in Locke's *Second Treatise* than these scattered examples. And it is largely the expositive text that answers the important questions. For our purposes, those questions include: Why does laboring on something legitimate a property claim to it? What kind of labor did Locke have in mind as being sufficient to ground a property right? And how much labor is required to justify securing property rights? When we have answered these, we will have the basis for a discussion of how (and how well) Locke's theory applies to the case of intellectual property.

THE "MIXING" METAPHOR

Lockean property requires that labor be combined with something found. Locke uses several different phrases to describe the nature of this combination. He begins his chapter on property by saying a person becomes an owner when "he hath mixed his labor with" something found in nature.[30] In other parts of the text, he says labor is "added to" or "joined with" things that are found. Despite varying terminology, Locke's basic framework is clear and consistent. Yet the mixing metaphor has caused some serious misunderstanding among Locke scholars. This has special salience in the case of IP, because the concept of mixing—and especially the critique of it—has often been employed as a vehicle for criticizing the Lockean theory of property as it applies to IP rights. Thus it is crucial for my purposes to address the mixing metaphor and deconstruct the critique it has engendered.

The critique I have in mind figures prominently in Robert Nozick's famous "tomato juice" hypothetical. In Nozick's little parable, a person standing on a beach empties a can of tomato juice into the ocean. The person then claims ownership of the entire ocean, on the premise that a thing that was unquestionably owned (the tomato juice) has been mixed with something found in the state of nature (the ocean). Jeremy Waldron varies the formula a bit, imagining instead a person who adds a diamond ring to a vat of drying cement. In both cases, the evident absurdity of the property claims that come from mixing illustrates the limitations of Locke's ideas and invites rejection of or adjustments to his theory.[31] The weakness in Locke's thinking is said to derive from the amorphous quality of property claims based on mixing. From this it is argued that labor itself is an insufficient or at least overly vague ground on which to base a property claim. Although I agree with Nozick and Waldron that Locke needs to be fleshed out in some ways, I disagree with their critique of the mixing metaphor, and so think that labor is capable of a crisper and sharper set of property entitlements than they indicate.

The Nozick-Waldron examples have a similar structure. Both posit a person who owns something free and clear—ownership of the tomato juice (Nozick) and ring (Waldron) is simply assumed. This already-owned thing is then mixed with something that is, at the beginning of the story, unowned: the ocean, or the vat of cement. Both authors then employ what they take to be Locke's general recipe for property rights—owned thing plus unowned resource gives rise to property claim—to cook up some absurd results which they then use as a platform to question the solidity of Locke's overall structure.

I think there are a host of problems with the Nozick-Waldron examples, which I try to explain in the paragraphs that follow. Briefly, my points are as follows: (1) Nozick and Waldron posit ordinary chattels (tomato juice, a ring) as already-owned things, in place of labor, while Locke believed that labor is a very special type of already-owned thing, one that is uniquely capable of grounding a theory of property when combined with unowned resources; (2) the Nozick-Waldron examples illustrate the difficulty of identifying limits to the appropriator's property claim, but this is less a function of inherent defects in Locke's theory, and more a function of redirecting attention away from labor (which, when joined to other resources, implies sharper ownership boundaries or at least limits to property claims as determined by the degree of effort involved); and (3) the mixtures envisioned in the Nozick-Waldron examples are fanciful thought experiments, far removed from the sorts of practical examples Locke used; examples closer to Locke's purpose—to show that property, growing out of labor, is essential for human beings to survive and thrive—do not typically produce the absurd results of Nozick and Waldron.[32]

The first thing to notice about the Nozick and Waldron examples is that neither of the already-owned things, the things being mixed with the unowned resource, is itself "labor." Nozick and Waldron want to explore the logic of Locke's theory, which they take to be quite general. Any already-owned thing will do, as long as it is mixed or added to an unowned resource. They assume, in other words, that if we posit unquestioned ownership over an external thing, it should behave the same way in Locke's theory as labor did in his examples. Initial ownership is what matters most; the precise thing that is owned initially is unimportant.[33]

This is where Nozick and Waldron go wrong. By avoiding reference to the specific thing whose initial ownership Locke had posited (labor), they have tried to generalize a formula that was meant to be very specific. It is not by chance that Locke starts with a particular already-owned thing—the body, and its labor—and builds his theory on that. For Locke, there is something very special about labor. This explains why scholars often call his theory of property acquisition the "labor theory," instead of the "owned plus unowned thing" theory, or "the general mixing theory." At the center of Locke's writing on property is not a general class of already-owned things, but one unique, unquestionably already-owned thing: labor.

There are two reasons why this matters, and they translate into two criticisms of the Nozick-Waldron examples. The first has to do with the

ethical status of the already-owned thing. In Locke's scheme, labor is literally a Godlike quality, best captured in the notion that man's labor mirrors
God's original workmanship in creating humans and the world.[34] Mixing
this special, ethically charged type of thing with unowned resources is obviously therefore quite different from mixing just any old already-owned
thing. Because labor is special, mixing or joining labor has special consequences. The Nozick-Waldron examples ignore this by abstracting away
from labor. In their effort to generalize, they lose the force of Locke's original emphasis on labor.

Labor has extra force because it is "of the body," it is an external manifestation of a person's self. Because we possess our persons, labor is the
most personal of "possessions." The notion of labor as deeply personal is
similar to Hegel's view that property is necessary to encourage the extension of one's personality into the external world outside the self.[35] (As we
will see in the next chapter, there are also strong overtones of this same
idea in Kant's property theory.) So one might say that my criticism of
Nozick and Waldron is that they have overlooked this Hegelian aspect of
Locke: that because of its special, personal status, labor is unique in its
capacity to ground property claims when mixed with unowned resources.
Their examples feature ordinary chattels—tomato juice, a ring—in place
of labor, and while their substitutions create interesting problems, they do
so by quietly smuggling out of the conversation the very subject that
Locke chose as the starting point for his discourse.

LABOR AND NATURAL OWNERSHIP BOUNDARIES

There is a second reason why Nozick and Waldron's examples prove to be
misleading. This has to do with one special quality of labor: when mixed
or joined, it more typically suggests clear-cut, natural limits on the scope
or extent of the resulting combination. It is easier to grasp a commonsense
dividing line between such a combination and the remaining unowned resources out of which it comes. Labor suggests a more natural boundary.[36]

To see why, consider Nozick's example. Its lesson is clear: Locke's idea
of mixing is flimsy, because there are no apparent limits to the scope of the
property claim that results when tomato juice is mixed with the ocean. But
compare this with Locke's examples. Is there any doubt that it is easier to
tell the limits of the ownership claim in the case of gathering acorns or
apples? Obviously, only the acorns or apples that are actually acted on by
the person's labor—those that are picked up—are subject to a claim of
ownership. The boundary between these, and the other apples and acorns
still lying on the ground, is quite clear. A more distinct boundary appears

if we turn Nozick's example in a more Lockean direction, by imagining that labor instead of tomato juice was joined or mixed with some ocean water—say, by taking some water out of the ocean with a bucket. Can there be any doubt that the property claim of the laborer would be limited to the water in the bucket? Does not the mixing of labor in this example avoid the absurd boundary problem of Nozick's tomato juice example?

The ability of labor to create a more natural boundary when mixed with other things is also apparent if we consider a variation on Waldron's example. Although there is a logical boundary around the entirety of the unowned resource in his example—all the cement in the vat—there is no way to separate out how much of this cement should now be owned by the person who threw the (already-owned) ring into the cement. But again, the conundrum is strictly a product of Waldron's choice of the ring as the already-owned thing. Focusing on labor instead yields less of a conundrum. As much cement as someone shovels out of the vat might be a reasonable estimate of the scope of the property right resulting from a labor-plus-cement combination. Or, if someone diligently stirs all the cement in the vat, for example to mix in a required ingredient, this might well justify a claim to all the resulting cement.

By the same token, stirring or mixing only part of the cement vat would yield a claim only over a portion of the cement. While the *precise* boundary might be difficult to define with absolute precision, at a general level it would be fair and rational to permit appropriation only of that portion of the cement touched or affected by the labor. Reasonable minds might differ on exactly where to draw this line, but most would agree that the "touched by labor" principle *does* define such a line—and that this is enough to defeat the reductio ad absurdum of the Nozick/Waldron hypotheticals.

The de-emphasis on labor is only part of what ails these hypotheticals, though. The other problem is overreliance on the image of mixing. This image makes it very difficult to draw clear lines between the labored-on resources and the remaining, unowned resources. To mix, as we understand it, is to thoroughly blend or intermingle. The complex or entity formed when labor is combined with a preexisting thing has this quality: the labor is evenly interspersed throughout it; the labor is thoroughly blended with it; the labor in some sense suffuses it. So the natural boundaries between the resources affected by the appropriator's labor and all other resources are blurred and indistinct.

But overemphasis on mixing makes Locke's theory more problematic than it really is. It is interesting in this connection that in Locke's time the word *mix* may have more closely denoted the conjoining of discrete items, as opposed to blending or suffusing.[37] Locke often uses synonyms for mix that strongly imply his intended meaning was closer to conjoin than to blend. It is true that Locke begins his chapter by saying a person becomes an owner when "he hath mixed his labor with" something found in nature; but he immediately adds that property results because the person had "joyned to it something that is his own." So from the start, the verb "joining" is used interchangeably with "mixing." Likewise, just after the famous acorn- and apple-gathering examples, Locke summarizes: "That labour [that is, the labor of the gatherer] put a distinction between them [the acorns and apples] and common. That *added something* to them more than Nature, the common Mother of all, had done; and so they became his private right."[38] He sounds the same theme at numerous other places in the chapter on property. When talking about labor, he speaks repeatedly in these terms: For example, "bestow[ing]" labor (*Second Treatise*, [hereafter 2T] at § 30, Laslett at 289), "inclos[ing]" (2T at § 32, Laslett at 291) land with labor, "labour[ing] on" (2T at § 34, Laslett at 291), and most often "annex[ing]" labor (see, for example, 2T at § 27, Laslett 288, and § 32, Laslett at 291). As these examples suggest, the metaphysics of mixing qua blending (as in Nozick's tomato juice story) were not of much interest to Locke. The point once again is simply that mixing or joining labor (rather than something else) to an unowned resource suggests a more tractable, more logical, property boundary.[39]

The defect that Nozick and Waldron have located, then, is really a function of their examples, rather than a flaw in Locke's theory. That theory, though imperfect, is far more useful when we keep our eye on the ball—on labor as a special category of thing. And this is true whether we are considering labor as applied to physical things, or (as in the case of IP) intangible resources.

KEEPING SIGHT OF THE *PURPOSE* OF LABOR

My final complaint about the Nozick-Waldron examples is that though they are clever, they are far removed from any practical appropriation situation one is likely to encounter. They take us away from the things Locke was centrally concerned with, human flourishing and the role of labor. When we hold fast to these concerns, we see that the purposive quality of labor provides an excellent justification for property over intellectual creations.

The Nozick-Waldron critique wanders far from the essence of Locke's thought. Locke's property rights grow out of the most basic, solid, practical realities of human existence. Appropriation has nothing to do with fanciful thought experiments. It originates in the primitive need to survive, and then thrive, in the world.

So Nozick's example has a distinctly un-Lockean flavor. A property claim over all the water in the entire ocean—to what end? What could you do with it, how would it help you survive? Even aside from the provisos, the expenditure of labor on such a project seems pointless and therefore strikes me as something that would hold no interest for Locke.[40] His concern was the application of labor to unowned resources for highly practical purposes—survival, or more generally, human flourishing. Arguing about purely metaphysical claims of ownership over a vast and not immediately usable resource seems a project scarcely worthy of Locke's attention.[41]

I can isolate the issue of purposiveness by posing a variant on Nozick's example. Instead of mixing tomato juice with the ocean, imagine mixing labor with it instead. For instance, someone wades into the ocean with a canoe paddle and stirs around some ocean water. This example highlights labor, in place of Nozick's tomato juice, as the already-owned thing in the appropriation equation. With that change, wouldn't this mixing of labor and ocean lead to a Lockean claim of property in the entire ocean? Again, I would say no, for the simple reason that here labor is applied for a pointless purpose. It is not connected to surviving or thriving; it has no other purpose, really, than to create a clever hypothetical example. And that is one reason why stories like this pose difficulties in identifying boundaries between what is legitimately appropriated and the remaining unowned resources. Labor is applied, for no obvious practical reason, to a vast complex of unowned resources. The limits of a labor-based property claim are therefore hard to identify. Compare this to a situation where labor is applied for an important practical end, such as physical survival or a desire to thrive. In this case, the purpose behind the effort suggests a natural limit to the resulting property claim. In this connection, it is no accident that all of Locke's examples of "primitive" appropriation involve removing resources from their native state.[42] They are removed in order to nourish the gatherer.[43] The scope of the property is proportional to the labor; limitations on the scope of the claim are suggested by the gatherer's purpose, which is to eat what is gathered, and thus to survive.[44] These examples contain the germ of a more general idea. Labor, directed to a useful end, justifies private appropriation. And the scope of the appropriation is determined by the extent of the labor.[45]

Summary: "Annexation" and Proportionality

Let me summarize what I have been saying. Talk of mixing brings with it a host of complications. And so I prefer to call Locke's approach the labor annexation theory. Labor is applied to, attached to, and directed at preexisting resources, in a way that makes something entirely new. This mental image of adding to, rather than mixing with, is more faithful to Locke and more useful for the task at hand. It also points the way to two related issues. Employing the concept of annexation, we can avoid some of the objections that Waldron and others have made to Locke's theory. More than this, we will find in the notion of annexation the raw material for an important principle that runs through all of IP law—the proportionality principle described in detail in Chapter 6. The upshot is this: Locke's theory, once we eliminate some of the objections that arise from the mixing metaphor, provides a compelling justification for IP, and a robust account of proportionality, one of its more important features.

In addition to the well-known provisos, which we take up soon, and which are so to speak "external" to his theory of appropriation by labor, there are limiting, cabining elements even *within* his theory of initial appropriation. The emphasis on labor as a special class of already-owned thing, and the requirement that property arise only insofar as labor is annexed to (not blended with) things, both operate to limit appropriation in significant ways under Locke's theory. And most importantly, labor grounds property for the purpose of surviving and thriving. All of which is to say: Locke's theory of appropriation is altogether more modest, and more tractable, than it has often been given credit for. It is essential to keep this in mind when we apply it to IP law, a sphere in which its supposed expansiveness has given rise to many a complaint.

Having now identified a limitation on the reach of property that emanates from Locke's treatment of appropriation, it makes sense to turn to other limits. And so, the provisos.

Locke's Provisos

When we come to the "provisos" in his theory of property, Locke's text admits of a number of different interpretations. Because of the resulting controversies, and because the provisos hold great promise for resolving some difficult issues in IP law, it is necessary to look at them in some depth.

Locke signals the importance of the provisos in his chapter on property by their location. They appear immediately after he introduces labor and original appropriation, starting with paragraph 27:

> For this Labour being the unquestionable Property of the Labourer, no Man but he can have a right to what that is once joyned to, at least where there is enough, and as good left in common for others.[46]

The stricture to leave "enough, and as good . . . for others" is referred to as the sufficiency proviso. In paragraph 31 Locke adds what is generally called the spoliation or waste proviso:

> It will perhaps be objected to this, That if gathering the Acorns, or other Fruits of the Earth, etc., makes a right to them, then anyone may ingross as much as he will. To which I answer, Not so. The same Law of Nature, that does by this means give us Property, does also bound that Property too. God has given us all things richly. . . . But how far has He given it to us? To enjoy. As much as anyone can make use of to any advantage of life before it spoils; so much he by his labour fix a property in. Whatever is beyond this, is more than his share, and belongs to others. Nothing was made by God for Man to spoil or destroy.[47]

Soon after this general statement, Locke moves to a more detailed description of the reason for this need to "bound" property—the potential for a person's appropriation to harm others. In paragraph 33, explaining why taking and improving land in the state of nature might be defended, he says:

> Nor was this *appropriation* of any parcel of *Land*, by improving it, any prejudice to any other Man, since there was still enough, and as good left; and more than the yet unprovided could use. So that in effect, there was never the less left for others because of his inclosure for himself. For he that leaves as much as another can make use of, does as good as take nothing at all.[48]

Then in the next paragraph we read:

> God gave the World to Men in Common; but since he gave it to them for their benefit, and the greatest Conveniences of Life they were capable of drawing from it, it cannot be supposed he meant it should always remain common and uncultivated. He gave it to the use of the Industrious and Rational, (and Labour was to be his Title to it;) not to the Fancy or Covetousness of the Quarrelsome and Contentious. He that had as good left for his improvement, as was already taken up, needed not complain, ought not to meddle with what was already improved by another's Labour: If he did, 'tis plain he desired the benefit of another's Pains, which he had not right to, and not the Ground which God had given him in common with others to labour on, and whereof there was as good left, as that already possessed, and more than he knew what to do with, or his Industry could reach to.[49]

There is a fair degree of debate among Locke commentators about how to read these passages. Because this debate bears on the application of Locke's theory to important issues in IP law, we will take some time to traverse it now.

One initial question is this: do these passages state two provisos, or only one? As we will see, this is important in the context of IP. Traditionally, when it comes to IP, it has been thought easy to satisfy the sufficiency condition, because IP rights attach only to original creations and only insofar as they are original. When the resulting rights are broad, they may appear to cover much material that will never in fact be exploited by the rightholder. It is helpful in this setting, therefore, to determine whether sufficiency and waste state separate, independent conditions for property, or whether in some cases only one condition need be satisfied. Much depends on how broadly one conceives of the spoliation limitation; under the more narrow view I espouse a bit later in this chapter, there is perhaps not so much at stake in considering whether sufficiency states the sole qualification for property. Even so, the two-versus one proviso argument has much to teach about the nature of the sufficiency proviso, which is in turn important to resolving some contentious debates in the Locke-IP literature. So in we plunge.

We start with Jeremy Waldron, who has provided a close, careful, and mostly persuasive reading of Locke's text. Waldron's version of Locke says that sufficiency is sufficient (in the logical sense) but not necessary: meeting the sufficiency proviso is not a *requirement* of legitimate appropriation, but where satisfied, it justifies a claim to property. [50] Put differently, a person can obtain a valid claim over an object even if he fails to leave others with "enough, and as good." Waldron's chief argument centers on situations where resources are scarce. In such a case, Waldron's view is that strict adherence to the sufficiency proviso would mean that no one could legitimately appropriate any resources. This, Waldron says, would be absurd given Locke's insistence that all resources have been given to mankind for the purpose of fostering human survival. [51]

As for spoliation, Waldron contends in effect that it is not a true proviso at all. If you can satisfy the sufficiency condition, you are home free; there is no further requirement that your appropriation avoid all spoilage. Appropriation that meets the sufficiency condition is necessarily modest, and hence, nonwasteful. So the prohibition on spoilage is automatically satisfied when appropriation leaves "as much and as good for others." Where spoliation does enter the picture is when the sufficiency condition cannot be satisfied. Under conditions of scarcity, appropriation is permitted even though one is unable to leave enough and good for others. But in such a state, appropriation is limited to that amount that the appropriator will not waste. Thus only when the sufficiency condition is inoperative does spoliation step in to limit what one can take.

Many scholars disagree with both parts of Waldron's formulation. They continue to insist that sufficiency should take its place beside spoliation as a full-blown Lockean proviso. For them, Locke's comments on leaving "enough, and as good" extend to all appropriations, and not just those made under conditions of relative abundance in the state of nature. By the same token, for these scholars an appropriator who satisfies the sufficiency requirement does not simply thereby demonstrate nonspoliation. On this view, it is possible for someone to take objects from the common, leaving "enough, and as good" for others, and yet allow those objects to spoil. In such a case, sufficiency will be satisfied, but spoliation will not be—and hence the appropriation will be illegitimate according to Locke's theory.

As with Waldron's position, there is some solid textual support for the two-proviso view. Locke says "nothing was made by God for man to spoil or destroy." It is easy to see in this language an absolute prohibition against spoilage, regardless of whether identifiable people are made worse off— regardless of the status of the sufficiency condition, that is. This interpretation meshes with biographical information about Locke's personal distaste for waste of any kind.[52] Even if the sufficiency requirement is met, no legitimate appropriation can occur where spoilage or waste will result.[53]

The prohibition on taking things only to let them spoil is often defended on the ground that it helps leave as many opportunities as were available to an initial appropriator. But this brings us back to sufficiency: what if, regardless of how much person A may take, there is an abundance left for persons B, C, D and so on? This line of thinking would again seem to render the spoliation proviso superfluous.[54] Although this is surely true, it ignores an important strain in Locke's thought.[55] Locke strongly implies that spoilage is not only potentially harmful to people who may come later. It is, utterly aside from its effect on other would-be appropriators, a sort of intrinsic affront to nature, an action that is in itself just wrong. From this perspective, spoilage has the ring of an absolute prohibition, one that applies regardless of whether the spoilage directly harms anyone else.

Thus for me, despite the rigor of Waldron's arguments, I tend to agree with the full-blown "two-proviso" view. Spoliation should be avoided even when the sufficiency proviso is complied with fully. I explain the appeal of this argument in the context of IP rights a bit later in this chapter. But for now, we must return to the first proviso, on sufficiency, as this must be considered prior to spoliation in Locke's schema.

Reliance and the Sufficiency Proviso

Before turning to the problem of waste, it is important to discuss one further aspect of the sufficiency proviso. Most traditional accounts—or at least, most accounts defending IP rights—stress that a properly run IP system will usually permit property claims only over things that people create from the common storehouse of material open to all. This means that if the system is running properly, rights will only be awarded to someone who has contributed something new, something that is distinct from the "public domain" that existed before the specific creation at issue. Because the public domain is necessarily conserved in such a system, it is widely assumed that the sufficiency proviso is routinely satisfied. Someone who merely appropriates what he himself added to the public domain must necessarily leave "as much and as good" for others. After the appropriation of what was added, those others have access to the same starting materials that the individual creator drew from. The prohibition on claiming these starting materials is assumed to necessarily satisfy Locke's sufficiency proviso.

In a highly insightful law review article in 1989, the legal scholar Wendy Gordon refuted this conventional argument.[56] She showed that it was logically possible for someone to create wholly original material, yet still deprive others of "as much and as good" as the creator had access to originally. The key to Gordon's argument is the notion of an expanding baseline. An original creator can add something that others come to depend on in an important way. Later, if that creator tries to remove what he or she has added, people may experience an important loss. She uses several examples to illustrate the idea:

> That an intellectual product is new, would not have otherwise existed, and may initially bring benefit to the public, does not guarantee that later exclusions from it will be harmless. . . . [O]nce a creator exposes her intellectual product to the public, and that product influences the stream of culture and events, excluding the public from access to it can harm. For example, assume that A takes substances from the common from which, with great ingenuity, she manufactures an enzyme that greatly improves one's health. Because of its salutary properties, a decision is made to include the enzyme in the drinking water. The benefits, however, come at the cost of a particular form of addiction: some people who drink the enzyme become unable to metabolize carbohydrates without continued intake of this elixir. To people so affected, ordinary food becomes valueless for nourishment—it is useless unless eaten along with the enzyme. In such a case, the fact that the common continues to have an ample supply of both food and the elements from which the enzyme can be made is not sufficient to protect the public from harm. The addicted public also needs A's knowledge of how the enzyme is manufactured, for without it, they will starve in the midst of plenty. If, after the enzyme is put into the water supply, the inventor is given a right to prohibit others from using her manufacturing technique, addicted members of the community are worse off in their ability to use the common than they were before.[57]

The notion that an IP owner can do no wrong, so long as the right covers only the creator's original contribution, has a long pedigree, extending back to John Stuart Mill and beyond.[58] It is closely related to the maxim "the greater includes the lesser," employed in innumerable IP cases over the years.[59] The (greater) power to withhold a new creation from the public entirely includes the (lesser) power to make it available and then withdraw it. Gordon's examples expose the limits of this idea and her contribution is to switch the focus from the rights of the creator to the effects on others when these rights are exercised. She compares the situation of these others with that of the creator prior to creation of the IP in question, and shows that they may differ in important ways.

Original creation, according to Gordon, can shift the baseline. The creator's contribution adds so significantly to what was there that it is wrong to permit the creator to pull back what he or she contributed, to remove it from circulation. To see this, imagine a Prodigious Waterbearer. Imagine that this hardworking person, through great effort, carries bucket after bucket from deep wells, and thereby raises by several feet the water level in a lake. Once others who live along the lake adjust, by building waterfront homes, docks, and beaches, it would be unfair for the Prodigious Waterbearer to say, "I am taking back all the water I contributed. And you, other people, have no right to complain; I will leave the lake as I originally found it." The others have come to rely on the extra water as a permanent part of the lake. Indeed, what they think of as "the lake" necessarily includes this extra water. They experience the diminishment of the lake as a real loss. To them, the situation is exactly as if the Prodigious Waterbearer had scouted the lake out before his exertions and then, the day he was to begin the long process of bringing new water to the lake, discovered that the lake had been lowered by several feet. The point of the story, and the key to Gordon's insight, is that the Prodigious Waterbearer fundamentally changes the lake, such that changing it back does not leave other people in the same position they were in. The lake, as they have come to know it, would no longer be the same if the contribution of the Prodigious Waterbearer were removed. These other people have come to count on the lake as they know it—to *rely* on it retaining the shape and depth they have known. This reliance interest gives them a voice in what happens to the lake, which in turn limits or constrains the right of the Prodigious Waterbearer to later remove what was originally contributed.

Gordon tells a number of stories that illustrate the force of this reliance interest. Probably the most persuasive is her account of cultural contributions that come in some sense to acquire "canonical" status. She uses as her example certain films by Walt Disney. But other examples come readily to mind, such as the Harry Potter books, Barbie dolls, and the *Lord of the Rings* trilogy. These canonical, iconic works are the equivalent of great increases in the water level of the lake of culture. Each in its own way has profoundly affected popular culture. They are widely shared reference points and have contributed widely shared tropes (magic and muggles; or dwarves and elves in Middle Earth). All are widely used as the common currency of cultural exchange. To allow their proprietors to completely remove them from the cultural stock would be to significantly deplete the pool of common references that people can draw from in writing new works, or even communicating with each other. It would be as if, Gordon argues, someone had removed some common reference points or shared cultural icons prior to creation of these famous works. We would find it wrong if J. K. Rowling, just as she was starting the first Harry Potter book, had been forbidden to read and build on myths and legends about magicians and their apprentices. Just so, Gordon argues, we would be wrong to permit Rowling to pull the Harry Potter books, and the great cultural tidewaters they carry, from general circulation today. Just as Rowling relied on very old, shared stories, a post-Rowling author (and audience) ought to be able to rely on the Harry Potter stories. Rowling has raised the level of the cultural lake, and she cannot now unmake her contribution. Once the Prodigious Waterbearer has done the work, it cannot be rolled back. The lake is forever changed.

I have borrowed a few measures from Gordon's reliance theme in my own work.[60] In so doing I add a twist of my own: explicit recognition of the labor or effort of those who use, adapt, and popularize a canonical work. Stated in terms of Lockean theory, I have tried to add the labor of users and consumers into the property rights analysis. By bringing attention to this offsetting source of labor, I have tried to expand the scope of the reliance argument. I see it as more than a limitation on the rights of the canonical work's creator; it is also, potentially, a source of affirmative rights for the group of people who have worked hard in reliance on the original, canonical work.[61]

Even in its standard form, however, the reliance argument is powerful. Let us return to Wendy Gordon to see why. Let me say first that I am strongly sympathetic to the goal of her original article on natural law and IP rights, which was to justify First Amendment limits on IP rights using the very same natural law principles often employed to defend an absolutist-libertarian vision of IP rights. But many who have followed Gordon do not stop at this point. Instead, they build on the logic of Gordon's approach to argue for a highly restrictive vision of IP rights. For these critics, Gordon's reliance argument becomes an all-purpose weapon, good for bludgeoning IP rights across the board.[62] The basic idea is that we are barraged by cultural images, which we neither choose to receive nor have the power to turn away from. The only way to salvage our dignity, and in some sense our identities, is to take these elements of culture and capture them, manipulate them, comment on them, and otherwise "make them our own." It is unfair, these critics say, to expose us to all this IP-protected culture, and then argue that we are no worse off if the owners of culture assert their IP rights to restrict our uses of it. We become enmeshed in it by virtue of being suffused with it. As a consequence, we must be allowed to copy and appropriate it. We are indeed far worse off, the argument goes, having been exposed to this tidal wave of culture which is then protected by expansive IP rights. Gordon's reliance argument, writ large.

I have two objections to this extension of Gordon's idea. First, I think it wildly overestimates the number of works that raise the cultural water level appreciably, and thus it exaggerates the magnitude of the public's reliance interest in access to these works.[63] And second, it ignores or dismisses the significant legal and practical limitations on IP owners who attempt to remove or pull back their works from the common stock.[64] It ignores the conventional tools available to prevent frustration of the public's reliance interest, leading to overly expansive claims about the failure of IP law to implement Locke's vision, and therefore the need for fundamental reform.

There are far fewer Prodigious Waterbearers than many IP critics think. Most contributions to culture are more like isolated drops in the lake. Removing them, by asserting IP rights over them, would barely cause a ripple. It is also extremely difficult, given the tools available, for a waterbearer to lower the water level. First Amendment principles, IP doctrine, self-interest, and enforcement costs all conspire to make it difficult and unprofitable to overenforce IP rights, thereby pulling a protected work back from public accessibility.[65] Removing a work covered by IP from the public stock is the equivalent of scooping water out of the lake one drop, or perhaps one bucket, at a time. Thus, although Gordon's account is fascinating from a theoretical perspective, she tells a story that applies to only a handful of works. And even for those, the conventional tools very often protect people's reliance interest. Her story simply does not support radical new tools to rein in IP rights based on Locke's sufficiency proviso.

I can restate my disagreement with Wendy Gordon's heirs this way: It is usually easy to meet the sufficiency proviso when ideas or intangibles are appropriated. The nature of IP law is such that most claimants can leave "enough, and as good" for others after they appropriate what they need. And in only a few cases will reliance by others on the continued availability of a work threaten to undermine the sufficiency condition.

The Importance of Spoilage in IP Law

As compared with sufficiency, Locke's other proviso, the one prohibiting "spoilage" due to excess appropriation, may at times present a more significant challenge. To see why, we must first review what Locke meant by spoilage and relate it to the very different context of information and IP rights. Although intangible assets do not literally rot or spoil, IP can at times promote wasteful overappropriation of the sort that Locke was concerned with. Indeed, when we cut through the superficial details of Locke's description of spoilage, we will see that the proviso against waste supplies a critical answer to the sometimes challenging problem of overclaiming in IP law.

We begin with the work of philosopher Gordon Hull, whose account of Lockean theory and IP rights features the provisos, especially spoliation. Hull first establishes that Locke's theory of appropriation applies equally to tangible and intangible assets. In fact, Hull argues that for Locke intellectual creations are the paradigmatic case of labor mixed with items from the commons.[66] He then moves on to the provisos. After defending spoliation as a separate and distinct requirement for Lockean property, and traversing some parts of Locke's text that seem to imply that the possibility of spoliation ends with the advent of civil society, Hull considers spoliation in the context of IP rights. For Hull, this proviso is especially important. He claims that it applies broadly to the IP field.[67]

However, I find Hull to be absolutely wrong in his central claim that the prohibition on waste dictates a highly constrained version of IP protection.[68] The central problem with his account comes right at the beginning. He rejects a superficial and literal interpretation of Locke's discussion of spoilage, with its strong whiff of primitive agricultural products left to rot in the sun and barren land left in its rough and uncultivated natural state. Hull turns away from Locke's examples and looks instead at the more general concepts informing and shaping them. At this more penetrating level Hull finds what he says is the essence of Locke's notion of waste: a prohibition on failing to improve people's lives when there is a feasible chance to do so. As Hull puts it, "Waste therefore happens when the product of labor that could improve somebody's life is allowed to irrevocably lose its value before it actually does so."[69] Although I approve of Hull's move from physical spoliation to something deeper and more abstract, I think he has gone about it all wrong. The deep principle he identifies, based on potential improvements to someone's life, which he restates as the idea of frustrated (or unmet) demand, completely distorts the logic of Locke's concern with waste. For spoilage to occur, it is necessary that someone else have a use for the item in question. But equally essential, and far more important in the IP context, is that the owner of the item must truly not use it at all, must let it go completely to waste.

Hull's fundamental problem is that he has identified the wrong guiding principle. For if frustrated or unmet demand constitutes spoilage, private market exchange necessarily causes massive amounts of "waste." Yet this runs precisely counter to a huge body of evidence pointing to the opposite conclusion: market exchange is well known to be the most efficient and therefore least wasteful mechanism for allocating goods in many situations. By Hull's logic, anyone who has ever been "priced out of the market" for anything—that is, anyone whose personal demand for an item led him to value it below the market price—has experienced an episode of Lockean waste. So every time I walk by a car dealership with unsold Maserati cars, I can argue that those cars are being "wasted." I want one, I am willing to pay for one, just not at the market price. What a waste!

This cannot work as a definition of waste. Just because my willingness to buy a Maserati drops away at the market price does not add up to an instance of waste. The real key, the guiding principle that Locke was driving at, is not unsatisfied demand, but a thing that has been appropriated and then put to no productive use at all. In Lockean terms, waste would apply if an absurdly wealthy person were to buy the entire output of the Maserati factory for a given year, and then let the cars sit unused in a warehouse for several hundred or so years until they are unusable. The cars in this example are never used by anyone; they sit in storage, rotting away, and no one ever gets to use them.

Rotting Maseratis do have their equivalents in the world of IP. Some patents claim embodiments that the patent owner never intends to use, and that no one else can make effective use of until the patent expires. And some patent owners have used their property rights to completely suppress an entire technology, though I think these instances are much less common than many conspiracy theorists would like to think. Even granting these occasional examples of Lockean waste, it is obvious that they are far different from cases of everyday "frustrated demand," where an owner's pricing decision leaves some potential buyers out in the cold, unwilling to pay the going price.

Some who would apply Lockean concepts to IP run into problems with spoliation because of the ready reproducibility of many assets covered by IP rights.[70] Scholars inclined this way make the following mistake. They first invoke the nonrivalrous nature of things covered by IP rights.[71] Next they say that, because of this, we can imagine a limitless (and often virtually costless) supply of such things.[72] Then comes the mistake: those who want one or more units of the thing in question, but who are unwilling to pay the market price, are being deprived of something that they could and should have. So imagine the owner of an asset covered by an IP right sets a price such that 100,000 units are sold. Imagine further that there are 10 million people who would have some use for the asset if it were given away. In this tale, all units from 100,001 to the 10 millionth unit are "wasted." It is an easy mistake to make, because it is so easy to hypothesize the existence of all these extra units. Once this large stock of hypothetical units is conjured in the imagination, it seems like a real loss to be told that they will not be allowed to come into existence. A legal rule, property, seems to get in the way of the "natural" multiplication of a useful thing for the many who might want it. All those copies, so easy to make, wasted; all those hands reaching for them, empty.[73]

On the contrary, though, the fact that these hypothetical copies never come into existence is not an instance of waste. For Lockean waste to occur, the concept, idea, or other original creation that is embodied in these copies would have to spoil completely. Its creator would have to elect to put it—the idea itself—on the shelf forever and make no use of it whatsoever. So long as he or she does not do that—so long as the creation is put to use to some extent, and for some purpose—it is no concern to Locke how many instances of the concept are put into circulation, or at what price. The Lockean asset is the concept or idea. This is what the creator labors to produce, mixing elements found in the prior art or public domain with some individual spark. It follows that only someone who never embodies it in any tangible medium at all, or who embodies a rough version of it in a single prototype and just lets it sit somewhere, unused, has engaged in Lockean spoliation. As long as someone gets some use out of the concept, it has not been wasted. The fact that some people, beyond the actual users, would have liked to use it (at a reduced price, or for free) has nothing to do with Lockean waste at all.[74]

SPOLIATION AND OVERCLAIMING

The small literature on Lockean waste in IP has generated one useful insight: legal rules, if poorly designed, can lead to wasted resources. The creator of an original work may receive a property right that covers an excessive range of works, stretching far beyond the scope of the original. Where such is the case, and where many variations of the original work are never developed or perfected, these unmade variants may be said to have been wasted. IP rules that systematically encourage creators to claim much more than they have in fact produced through their efforts may therefore bring about a fair amount of spoilage in the true Lockean sense.[75]

My point about spoilage here turns on a subtle distinction, so I want to take a moment to spell it out clearly. Start with a conception of some sort of creative work—an idea for a novel, play, movie; or an invention. At some point, if the work is to be made concrete and available to others, it will almost always have to be set down in some tangible form. Call this the original instance or original embodiment of the work. What I have called "the work" is a mental construct, an idea; the original embodiment of that idea is the first tangible instance of it. The way IP law operates, the creator of the work will almost always be able to obtain a property right that extends beyond the original embodiment of the work. The property right will almost always cover the original embodiment plus some number of variations on the original. In other words, IP law starts from the original and constructs a class or genus—a sort of virtual category—of potential embodiments that the property right will protect. It is this class or genus, this set of all variants on the original work, that is the real subject of IP law.

Now, when I speak about waste I am speaking about the parameters of this class or genus. If the class or genus is too large, many of the variants it embraces may never actually be made or used. Too many of the potential embodiments covered by the property right will never be built, made, or implemented. Potential embodiments such as these might be said to suffer spoilage in the Lockean sense. To return to the Maserati example I used earlier, consider some sort of IP right over a certain Maserati design. Now imagine that this right has been defined too broadly. It covers far more variants on the original design than is warranted—far more variants than are fairly encompassed by the actual original design. Maserati itself will never sell more than a few of these variants. And Maserati's broad IP right may keep others from building these variant designs as well. The many variants that are never built, the many variations on the original design that never see the light of day—these might be an example of waste.[76]

COMPLICATIONS: OF USEFUL FENCES AND
OPTION VALUES

The picture we have traced so far presents a stark dichotomy. Some claimed embodiments are put into use. Others, such as the unbuilt Maserati designs, are not, so they spoil. We need at this point to add some detail to this sketch of things. Doing so brings complexity, but also adds realism, to our view of spoliation.

The first complication we need to introduce is something of a paradox: in the world of IP, and elsewhere too, something does not have to be *in use* to be *useful*.[77] Put another way, under some circumstances a thing can sit on the shelf and yet still serve a useful purpose. Here is a straightforward example: someone gathers stones to defend himself against an enemy, in such numbers that the enemy dares not attack. These stones are surely of use, even though they in some sense are not being actively deployed. The essence of deterrence, in fact, is just this—to serve by not being used.

Sometimes IP rights serve a similar purpose. Imagine for example that an inventor conceives of a new chemical compound that serves a useful purpose, such as a more environmentally friendly chemical for dry-cleaning clothes. Although there is one preferred chemical structure that works best, there are three other workable variants of the compound that will do a serviceable job. The chemical structure of these variants might differ by having a slightly different "side group" that attaches to the main body of the compound. If the inventor of the dry cleaning compound receives a patent, that patent might well cover all four versions of the compound. But again, only one of them will actually be developed and commercialized. Are the other three variants an example of Lockean spoilage—are they wasted because they are never put into circulation?

I think not. The three unused variants serve an indirect purpose. By keeping out competition in the market for the compound, the patent on these variants makes it possible for the inventor to develop and commercialize the one workable compound. Thus, the property right on the uncommercialized variants is useful as a fence. The negative, exclusionary power of the rights over these variants prevents entry that would undermine the value of the property right over the version of the compound that is commercialized. In this way, a portion of an IP right may serve an indirect use by preventing an incursion into the other, more valuable part of the right.[78] An analogy to real property might help here. A buffer zone between grazing lands and crop lands may keep roaming animals from damaging the crops. In this way, property rights over undeveloped areas may be essential to getting value out of the developed areas. The entire parcel taken together, crop land plus buffer zone, may serve a useful purpose even though not every corner of it has been intensively developed.[79]

This example introduces a spatial dimension into our analysis of spoilage. To determine whether one part of a property right is spoiling, we look to the relationship between it and the scope of the right as a whole. Now I want to introduce yet another dimension, this one temporal. The portions of a right that are being used may change over time, requiring us to take the long view in deciding whether there is any waste going on. And once this is understood, we can push the insight one step further: yet unused portions of a right may have value solely because they preserve the possibility of future development. This is an important feature of IP rights: they provide their owners with future options.[80] Consider again the example of the dry cleaning chemical. Imagine that one of the four variants of the compound covered by the patent is the easiest to develop, given existing technology. Now imagine that a breakthrough in process technology several years after the compound is invented makes another of the variants much cheaper to produce. This second variant was not in use when the patent was granted, yet it was still covered by the patent and available for development several years later. Because the technologies surrounding a patented invention are constantly changing and developing, this is an important component of the value of many patents. On the date the patent is granted, these yet-to-be-developed variants are only potentially valuable. But one of them might end up being the most valuable embodiment of all. One way to put this is to say that when the patent is granted, it gives its owner an option to develop any of the as-yet unrealized variants. If the option value of a patent is high, that may well indicate that some of the yet undeveloped embodiments of the invention may in the future prove to be commercially important.[81]

This example counsels caution in applying the waste proviso.[82] Until it is certain that yet undeveloped variants will never in fact be put into use, we should refrain from declaring spoliation and invalidating a portion of the property right. Locke is concerned with abject waste. Until we are fairly certain that a variant will never be placed in service—that, in effect, the option on that embodiment is unlikely to be exercised—we should not presume it will be wasted in the Lockean sense.

The Charity Proviso

IP scholars have not had much to say about the charity proviso in Locke's second treatise. Writings on Locke and IP cover appropriation in depth, as well as the other provisos, spoliation and sufficiency. The omission of careful discussions of charity is a bit puzzling, given that the charity proviso is absolutely central to Locke's thinking. Whatever the reason, this leaves a serious hole in the IP-Locke literature. The paragraphs that follow are a brief treatment—a sketch, to be honest—of this topic. They are given with the strong caveat that a longer discussion is sorely needed.

WHAT DOES LOCKE MEAN BY "CHARITY"?

It is best, when trying to get a firm grip on these issues, to begin with careful attention to Locke's actual words. Here is the main passage on charity, from the *First Treatise*, paragraph 42:

> God the Lord and Father of all, has given no one of his Children such a Property, in his peculiar Portion of the things of this World, but that he has given his needy Brother a Right to the Surplusage of his Goods; so that it cannot be

justly denied him, when his pressing Wants call for it. And therefore no Man could ever have a just Power over the life of another, by right of property in Land or Possessions; since 'twould always be a Sin in any Man of Estate, to let his Brother perish for want of affording him Relief out of his Plenty. As Justice gives every Man a Title to the product of his honest Industry, and the fair Acquisitions of his Ancestors descended to him; so Charity gives every Man a Title to so much out of another's Plenty, as will keep him from extreme want, where he has no means to subsist otherwise. . . . [83]

To understand this passage, a little context is necessary. It appears in a long section of the *First Treatise* in which Locke is grappling with—and of course rejecting—various arguments in favor of the principle of absolute monarchy. The specific argument under discussion in the paragraphs preceding this passage concerns a biblical text from the book of Genesis, which absolutists had cited as authority for the notion that extant monarchs were merely the latest in a line that descended directly from Adam.[84] This argument Locke rejects out of hand. He maintains first that the biblical text really says that dominion was given to the human species as a whole and not Adam in particular. He goes on to say that, even if the absolutists were right about the bestowal of some sort of world ownership on Adam, this entitled him only to a conventional right of property and did not automatically form the basis of a claim to political authority. Ownership and political sovereignty are thus for Locke separate concepts.

But back to charity. The idea of charity has a dual purpose here. It first undermines the link between property ownership and absolute political power upon which Locke's opponents relied. If property ownership always comes with an implied limitation—a hidden, reserved set of claims by the destitute—then it is surely not capable of serving as the foundation for absolute political power. Because of the charity proviso, no property owner has the stark power over life and death that the absolutists were trying to defend.[85] In addition, charity plays a crucial part in Locke's conception of the prepolitical scheme of rights. Even in the state of nature, before civil society has been established, the charity proviso embodies the foundational idea that all property—all of nature, all of life—was given by God for the maintenance and development of the human race. For Locke, it was sheer folly to look to property as a source of absolute power; the only absolute dominion Locke recognizes is that of a beneficent Deity, who endowed humanity with a cornucopia of resources so that we might flourish and grow. This is the central (and to me, inspiring) point one comes away with after reading Jeremy Waldron's *God, Locke and Equality:* the roots of Locke's conception of property lie in a deeply religious sensibility. This is often missed in contemporary, secular readings of the *Two Treatises,* the most egregious being those that attempt to use Locke to justify thoroughly libertarian agendas in which property ownership is the highest set of rights society can bestow. Though these broader issues may seem quite remote from issues of IP policy, I think they help to understand Locke's basic outlook on property, to put it in context. It is useful to know where Locke's liberal theory of property came from, so we can better apply and adapt it to the case of IP.

To summarize, Locke says that people in desperate need have a claim on the assets held by legitimate owners. For Locke, the destitute have title to the goods they need to survive, even when those goods are otherwise legitimately held by others, either through valid original appropriation or a subsequent transfer from an original acquisition.

HOW SHOULD THE CHARITY PROVISO
BE ENFORCED?

Locke is a bit unclear on how the charity proviso is to be enforced. He describes the proviso as giving the destitute an actual legal claim on assets held by others, but he does not go into much detail at all on how one is to go about securing this type of claim. It is as if, having established that the destitute have a sort of lien or nonpossessory claim on the good of others, the realization or actualization of that claim will just naturally follow. The many lawyers who work with liens, security interests, and the like would no doubt laugh at this naïveté. Yet there it is.

In reality, there are a number of issues that any legal system must resolve for liens and security interests to operate in practice. When, and under what circumstances, can the holder of such an interest exercise his or her rights, and gain access to some portion of the owner's goods? This is the crucial question, and it is unfortunately one that Locke for the most part dodges.

Perhaps this is intentional; maybe Locke did not mean to be specific. Maybe his talk of "title" in the description of the charity proviso is metaphorical—meant to convey simply a strong, durable claim, rather than a vague (and therefore easily avoided) interest. Even if this is true, it still leaves a social planner with a difficult question. Does the legal system require direct governmental action, for example, a redistribution of resources, to effectuate the charity interest? Or is charity to be understood as a general ethical duty, incumbent on all property holders morally, but having no concrete state enforcement mechanism? We will return to these important issues after a brief overview of charity as it relates to IP.

APPLYING THE CHARITY PROVISO TO IP

The charity proviso finds its greatest application in the IP world where IP rights intersect with issues of human health. Perhaps the greatest contemporary example is the case of patents for AIDS drugs. Although this is an exceedingly complex set of issues, I will take the time here to describe them briefly. Put succinctly, my argument is this: When it can be shown that IP rights are getting in the way of basic sustenance, those rights have to give way.[86] Destitute status is not a condition outside the institution of property rights that somehow weighs against the force of those rights. It is built into the fabric of the rights themselves.

When might this matter in the world of IP? When it can be shown that an IP right actually stands between the very poor and their sustenance. For example, it may apply with respect to patents on certain medicines.[87] And it may apply when patents over food products create palpably worse conditions for agriculture in poor countries. There are a lot of excessive claims about these circumstances and much speculation about how IP rights in one country, or potential IP rights, might create these conditions.[88] But in my view IP rights are limited only in actual cases where IP is enforced in a way that interferes with sustenance or survival. These are topics I explore in some detail in Chapter 9, on life-saving drugs.

I have talked about sustenance and survival. What about the broader topic of IP rights and cultural development (an important topic in itself, and one of special interest to broad-based development experts such as Amartya Sen)?[89] To begin, I understand that culture is important to human flourishing and development—development in the sense of growth beyond the realm of the merely physical. Yet even so, I think we have to differentiate between IP rights that interfere with actual sustenance and those that interfere with other aspects of development. The claims of those excluded by IP rights seem to me a bit weaker in the case of nonphysical or higher-order development. In Lockean terms, these excluded people do not have a viable claim under the charity proviso, strictly construed. If we are willing to expand it somewhat, however—to move from a position based squarely on Locke to a Lockean or even quasi-Lockean argument—we might conclude that those in cultural destitution may have a claim on some portion of the property of the well-off that could be used to facilitate cultural, that is, nonphysical human development. But not a strong claim. In assessing such a claim, we would be permitted to consider factors that are irrelevant when the stronger, strictly survival-based claim is at issue: the possibilities of cross-border trade, for example, or downstream effects from widespread copying of cultural goods.[90] This might sound vague, so let me be more specific: I think international IP law might permit copying of textbooks needed for cultural development in very poor countries (for example, history books, or sheet music, or novels, or books on how to organize amateur drama productions). But the claims on the other side—for example, claims by publishers that copies of these books are being exported from destitute regions into countries where they compete for sales with authorized copies—ought to be given more weight in this case than in the case of life-sustaining products.

Let me be clear: publishers' and authors' claims are not trump cards. They are considerations that count heavily. I understand that some people who might make good use of these books may sometimes come out on the losing end of this sort of balancing, and I regret that. But to allow these claims absolute supremacy over those of the authors of these books in all cases is to fatally undermine what it means for those authors to *have* rights. Cultural development (particularly education) is important; if it were not, the needs of the destitute would matter not at all in the calculus. But outside the realm of basic human sustenance, cultural development is not by itself important enough to *automatically* trump the rights of authors. Put simply, human sustenance ought never be balanced, but cultural development may be.[91]

Let me quickly add something to this. The developed world should make it as convenient as possible for authors and publishers to give away books and other material that helps with cultural development. This is not only the right thing ethically; it is also common (many property owners do give their works away, and decline to enforce their IP rights, in poor countries); and finally it makes good business sense.[92] Preventing arbitrage from destitute countries to the developed world then becomes perhaps the single most important policy that IP owners can promote to further cultural development. For with reasonable border protection in place, an IP owner can authorize or at least acquiesce in wide-scale copying to promote cultural development in poor countries, while maintaining reasonable financial returns where they are feasible. The IP owner can have her rights, and waive them too. Indeed, this ought to be the goal of all developed-world governments: to make the world a safe place for IP rightholders to acquiesce in extensive borrowing by poor countries of the products needed to encourage cultural development. And if my view of developed-world IP holders is too optimistic, a more muscular right to copy, not so dependent on widespread voluntary waiver, would make sense if borders are reasonably secure.

IP is connected to development issues in another way relevant to Locke's charity proviso. In a number of interesting ways today, developing countries can directly benefit from domestic IP rights. Here the issue is not how the interests of developing countries are served by inroads on IP-covered products from elsewhere. Rather, it is how IP rights over their own products can help in economic development and the promotion of cultural autonomy. For example, Ethiopian coffee growers have claimed trademark protection for indications of "authentic," traditionally grown coffee beans. (This is related to, but somewhat distinct from, the broader issue of "appellations of origin" in IP law.) These Ethiopian coffee growers can serve as a vital exemplar of an important theoretical point. The early post-TRIPs (Trade-Related Aspects of Intellectual Property) literature fashioned a narrative in which IP was associated with the developed world; opposition to IP thus aligned with the interests of developing nations. The case of Ethiopian coffee is not unique. Products based on native plant species, recordings of indigenous and indigenous-influenced music, and various works based on traditional myths, stories, and craft techniques are just a few of the many examples that might be cited. These instances inject a subversive twist into the earlier narrative: IP is now something that can help, and not only hurt, the interests of the developing world.[93]

From the perspective of Locke's theory, the point is this: if IP can be used more effectively to help the destitute achieve self-sufficiency, fewer inroads on others' IP rights may be in order. Increasing the autonomy and sustainability of the poorest will reduce their claim on the title of others who hold valuable IP rights.

The Provisos: Conclusion

In conclusion, I have reviewed work by other Locke students on the way to an understanding of how the Lockean provisos ought to apply to IP law. I found much agreement with Wendy Gordon's original account of the sufficiency proviso as applied to IP, but also much disagreement with Gordon's expansionist successors. I also found much to admire in Hull's argument that the spoilage proviso has important implications for principles of IP law, yet disagreed forcefully with Hull's handling of that principle as applied to actual IP problems. So for me, here's the rub: with respect to IP, the provisos live. Yet they lead a mostly closeted existence. Like a rare comet, they will be sighted every now and again, but they are not a steady and constant feature of the legal constellation.

Overall Summary: Locke and IP

Whatever the precise parameters of an operational charity proviso, one thing is clear. Locke's understanding of charity as an inherent limit on property rights maps quite well onto contemporary policy debates in the IP field. The same is true, as I argued earlier, of his description of initial appropriation. The presence of a "found" world of unowned things, the central place of effort, and above all the overriding concern with human thriving and flourishing—these are all well tailored to a theoretical account of what IP is all about.

With Locke, then, we are off to a very good start in the business of understanding IP rights. Yet these rights are complex enough in structure, and important enough in impact, to warrant an additional and supplementary account. To see why this is necessary, we must step back from the details of Locke's theory, to see it from a further remove.

In its basic outlines, Lockean appropriation involves plucking things out of the found environment and bringing them into a more personal zone, where they can be of use to the individual. Appropriation is a movement, in a broad sense, from outside to inside, from the external world to the internal or personal space. Though labor is added to the things that are found, the resulting complex moves items from the scattered and impersonal world of found things to the personal and useful world of property. Making things our own means taking them out of the public world.

In the next chapter we will see a vision of appropriation that turns this image inside out. From this alternative point of view, property is more about a move from the internal to the external. Property is an institution that helps transform personal and internal qualities and characteristics into things that are capable of functioning out in the world. The characteristic movement is from internal to external, from the personal to the public. Ownership from this point of view allows the isolated individual to project his talents, opinions, and unique personality into society at large. It allows the individual to stamp himself on something that can walk about freely in the world, sometimes generating revenue for the creator in the bargain. Property in this context contributes greatly to a sense of individual self-determination, or autonomy: purely internal qualities are projected out into the broader world. The personality is enhanced by interaction with objects in the world, while profit from creative work brings greater creative freedom. Because so many creative works include a personal dimension, we will see that this idea of property as externally-directed self-empowerment—this Kantian theory—adds an intriguing dimension to our understanding of IP rights.

CHAPTER THREE

Kant

Introduction

We turn next to the property theory of Immanuel Kant. Despite having made fundamental contributions to epistemology, ethics, and a wide range of other subjects, Kant is often excluded from the list of the preeminent philosophers of property. However, I hope to show that Kant's ideas about property are as stimulating and useful to the IP field as those of Locke.[1] The Kantian concepts I emphasize—individual will, appropriation (or "possession"), and personal freedom (or autonomy)—are welcome additions to our understanding of the role of property in general. But they are particularly welcome to the task of understanding intellectual property, where the relationship between people and the things they claim to own is far more complex than the one between Locke's survivalists and the food they gather. As we shall see, Kant's highly conceptual approach to property provides an excellent starting point for understanding IP, that most conceptual species of property rights.[2]

Orientation: From Locke to Hume, the Functional Approach to Property

In Chapter 2 we took a long look at Locke's property theory as it applies to IP rights. In its day, Locke's account was widely respected in part because of its solid footings in the natural law tradition. These footings were challenged, however, over the course of the eighteenth century. During that time, a novel understanding of human institutions emerged, one that emphasized observable facts and regular patterns of human behavior. To some degree, Kant's approach to property sought to both integrate and push back against this new empirical approach. As a consequence, to understand Kant's thinking, we need to first review briefly this empiricist turn in the theory of property rights.

One of the leaders of the skeptical empiricists was the Scottish philosopher David Hume. Hume emphasized observable facts, and from this empirical foundation he built his philosophical system. As Hume described it, property was an outgrowth of behavioral patterns such as reciprocity that began with the desire to avoid conflict over scarce resources.[3] Hume begins his account of the origin of property by describing man as a creature whose wants and needs far exceed what his immediate, individual capacities can supply. " 'Tis by society alone," he says, that man "is able to supply his defects," and bring himself up from his original desperate state to the level of other animals.[4] The founding norms of society have their roots in human nature, but are in themselves nothing but "artifice" or "conventions" that grow out of mutual advantage and acceptance rather than a formal promise or social contract.[5] The animating force behind property is the need to prevent harm from conflicting passions over objects of mutual desire—to keep the peace. In human societies, a regular pattern of mutual forbearance with respect to the claims of others develops over time, Hume said. And out of this repeated pattern comes a social custom, and thence, with the founding of civil society, the institution of property. Thus property is desirable and good not for any intrinsic reason, but because it well serves the purpose of promoting social concord. Its spirit is utilitarian, efficient, and practical—in a word, functional.[6]

Hume's ideas were joined over time with those of other theorists, notably Jeremy Bentham.[7] Slowly, this custom- or norm-based view infiltrated property theory, which had been, since Roman times, mostly organized around fixed conceptual categories and traditional taxonomic debates.[8] The "functionalist" heirs of Hume, Bentham, and others received a big boost in the early part of the twentieth century, with the academic movement known as legal realism.[9] The realists linked together two major threads: an empirical interest in operational norms and customs, and a political agenda centered on overthrowing the formalistic and conservative doctrinal structure of property law.[10] In the wake of the widely celebrated realist movement, lawyers and legal scholars became accustomed to thinking of property as a social convention that furthers important goals, such as stability, efficiency, and self-determination. Modern legal theorists have taken the concept of property apart and put it back together in a number of ways, often with the plan of better understanding how it works as an institution, a set of rules and procedures for directing control over assets and governing disputes that arise out of their use. We have come to see property as a set of rules attached to things but aimed primarily at regulating the affairs of people who contend for the use of those things.[11] It is essentially interpersonal in nature: property rules govern relations between individuals or groups with competing or conflicting economic interests. The assets themselves are the focal points around which property revolves; but the real purpose of property is to regulate the interactions of competing groups of people.

Hume versus Kant on People, Things, and Conflict

This functional approach forms the core of most modern theorizing about property. Kant's approach is very different. Like Hume, Kant starts with the observation that people want and need to make use of resources or objects they find in the world.[12] But Kant immediately moves to a discussion of these wants and needs not as a possible source of conflict with others in (proto-) society, but strictly as a matter of importance to the individual. To make full use of things, to impose their will on things and thereby do the sorts of projects they need to do, people must be free to use all sorts of objects in all sorts of ways. Implicit in this is that people will often have objects under their authority or control for a considerable period of time. To be free, people must be able to set all sorts of goals or ends for themselves. And to pursue the ends that they set for themselves, people need stable, durable claims over objects.[13] Out of people's desire to carry out individual projects on particular objects, according to Kant, the idea of legal possession is born. What follows is, first, the institution of property, and later, civil society.

For both Hume and Kant, the opening scene in the origin of property has at least two protagonists, plus an object that each would like to control. For Hume, the scene opens with both protagonists on stage. One or the other may have exercised some control over an object, or both may be eyeing it possessively; it does not really matter who holds the object at the start of the scene, as long as they do not kill each other. The tension in the scene comes from the conflict between the two would-be possessors. Its resolution—the birth of property—grows directly out of the need to regulate the potential conflict between the two people. The protagonists need some sort of convention that will govern who has access to the object and under what circumstances. The denouement comes when the protagonists recognize this. A convention emerges; conflict is averted; peace reigns. Hobbes, down in the front row, smiles knowingly. Fade to black.

Kant's version of this scene moves toward the same resolution, but it has a very different feel. Kant starts the scene with a lone individual, on stage with a single isolated object. Much of the initial drama is internal, as the protagonist struggles to locate and express his desires with respect to the object. To pass it by, ignore it; or, instead, to take it up, handle it, work on it, transform it—the protagonist struggles with the weight of this choice: for Kant, it is all about freedom and choice. If the choice is to take up the object, the protagonist immediately signals attachment and connection to it, as if the very act of choosing has invested the thing with significance.

Only after the lone individual works this out will other people come onstage. At this point, a secondary drama ensues, centering on this issue: how can the one individual keep the others from taking the object, from interfering with his plans for it (and thus for himself)? Only at this stage will the question of competing demands enter the scene. Only then is a durable claim like property necessary.

The difference between Hume and Kant can thus be stated quite simply: for Hume, society comes first, the property rights of individuals second. For Kant, it is just the opposite: the individual's need to control an object leads to the concept of property, and society follows as a way of translating this concept into actual operation. For Hume, property is unthinkable without society. For Kant, the individual act of free will leads to the desire to appropriate an object, which in turn gives rise to the need for social institutions.[14]

In this chapter, I leave behind the now-standard Humean script in Anglo-American property theory and turn instead to explore Kant's alternative. Though the Kantian narrative winds a bit, I find it a journey well worth taking. The payoff is this: the return of our attention to the individual person whose effort and insight produce the creative works at the core of the IP system. Kant's insistence on the dignity and worth of individuals delivers a timely message to the IP field today, a most important corrective to the current emphasis in IP theory on the Humean topics of conflict, efficiency and utility. There is no doubt that these have their place. But Kant helps us to see that their place is in service to something larger, the creative individual. This is the person whose act of will is at the heart of Kant's conception of property. And individual creators are for me the genuine impetus behind IP law.

From Possession to Autonomy

As a legal right, the essence of property for Kant is this: other people have a duty to respect claims over objects that are bound up with the exercise of an individual's will. Property is an amalgamation of duties owed to an individual. It is, in the strictest sense, an individual right. The contrast with much of modern property theory is stark, and very illuminating at this moment in the history of IP law.

Kant believed that any object onto which a person projects his or her will may come to be owned. Kant seemed to consider ownership as a primitive concept whose roots run very deep in human consciousness. This is evident from the language he uses. The origin of property, he says, is in a deep and abiding sense of "Mine and Yours." "That is *rightfully mine*," he writes, "if I am so bound to it that anyone who uses it without my consent would thereby injure me."[15]

But what is the point of this? Why do people want to be bound to things? In essence, Kant says, to expand their range of freedom—their autonomy.[16] People have a desire to carry out projects in the world. Sometimes, those projects require access to and control over external objects. The genesis of property is the desire of an individual to carry out personal projects in the world, for which various objects are necessary. For Kant, this desire must be given its broadest scope, to promote the widest range of human choice, and therefore human projects. Kant accordingly refuses to accept any binding legal rule that makes some objects strictly unownable, because the rationale for such a rule would conflict with the basic need for maximal freedom of action. Freedom to appropriate is so basic, so tied to matters of individual will and personal choice, that Kant finds it unthinkable to rule out large categories of things from the domain of the potentially ownable. As Kant scholar Paul Guyer says, for Kant, "The fundamental principle of morality dictates the protection of the external use of freedom or freedom of action, as a necessary expression of freedom of choice and thus as part of autonomy as a whole. . . ."[17] This captures it in a nutshell: freedom of action, including the right to possess, as a necessary expression of freedom of choice, or autonomy.[18]

Autonomy and possession are big concepts. A simple example may help to clarify them. Consider Michelangelo, approaching a large block of marble. He may have a plan, a mental picture of what he wants to do, what design he wants to impose on that chunk of rock. It will take a long time to bring this to completion, to fully impress the idea he carries onto the actual rock he has to work with. To fully realize his vision, to work out his plan for the marble, he needs to know that he can count on two things:

continued access to it, and noninterference by others. If he is to carry out his vision, free of unwanted interruptions in access or unauthorized contributions from others, he needs to be secure in his right to possess the marble. Possession, in the full Kantian sense, permits Michelangelo complete freedom over how to sculpt the marble. Secure possession also excludes interlopers from coming along and altering or adding to the sculpture. In short, ownership as Kant understands it means that Michelangelo, and only Michelangelo, has complete freedom over what to do with the block of marble. Thus does stable property contribute to individual autonomy.

Kant's Concept of Possession

At the heart of Kant's understanding of property is the notion that possession is an abstract concept, rather than an empirical fact or event. People need to control objects in the world to do the things they want to do. For control to be effective, it has to be robust, lasting beyond the time when a person has an object in his physical grasp. Michelangelo, in our example, should be able to eat, sleep, rest, take a walk, and so forth, secure in the knowledge that when he comes back to his block of marble it will be as he left it. This need for control to persist, to be effectively broadened beyond the circumstances of mere physical holding, supplies the force that drives us to think about possession conceptually, instead of as just a physical fact.

All manner of important implications follow. To carry out this more conceptual type of possession, we require an enforcement mechanism—some sort of legal system. Since this is unthinkable without a government of some sort, we call into existence civil society. And to permit civil societies to flourish and coexist, we need an international legal order. As all this makes plain, it could be said that for Kant property—or, more accurately, an appropriately nuanced conception of property—lies at the heart of nothing less than civilization.

Conceptual-legal possession, possession that is noumenal rather than phenomenal, cuts through the murk and fog that swirls around conventional theories of intellectual property. In the schematic account we find in Kant, people just naturally want to work their will on objects they find in the world. It is in their nature as beings steeped in freedom to do so. Kant lays out the basic building blocks of objects, will, and freedom in a clean, schematic way, uncluttered by numerous examples.[19] As befits his emphasis on reason and thought, Kant goes long on conceptual description and categorization, and short on real-world application. We are therefore free to apply Kant's idea to the building blocks of intellectual creations, just as we do for other assets such as blocks of marble or land. Many people in the modern world may choose to express themselves in intangible media. From Kant's point of view, these choices are no different from those Michelangelo makes as he crafts his block of marble. Property status is not a matter of marble versus electrons, chisels versus keyboards, trombones versus synthesizers. The medium is *not* the message; the individual is. By omitting a clutter of detail, and supplying instead a rich conceptual tableau, Kant's approach to property is marvelously relevant to the era of intellectual property.

By comparison, consider Locke. Because of the parable-like nature of his theorizing, we need to ask how books and invented machines are like or unlike apples, acorns, and rabbits on the run. Locke's great virtue is that he grounds his account of property in prosaic examples. But this ground-up approach has its limitations, the limitations inherent in working upward by analogy from concrete examples. Kant, by contrast, starts with the abstract. As we have seen, Kant starts with an individual person, with a unique and distinctive will and vision—a refreshing change of perspective, and one with special applicability to IP law.

I want to acknowledge how very strange the Kantian perspective may seem to us. IP doctrines and scholarship are so steeped in functional logic and rhetoric that we are often unaware of just how deeply this perspective grounds (and limits) our thinking. For the most part there is nothing wrong with this basic orientation. It serves us well and helps guide society's thinking about how to structure the operational details of our IP system. Usually that is enough. But now, given the many changes sweeping through the field—technological, social, and economic—it is important to revisit the normative roots of this area of law. Kant's stripped-down approach gives us some very useful tools along these lines. In the next few paragraphs, I will show why.

The Individual Will—and Why It Matters

Of chief importance to Kant is the contrast between objects and people. Objects may embody free will (or rather, the effects of free will), but only people can have free will.[20] This is an essentially oppositional way of defining "things": the essence of a thing is that it is not a person. A definition like this manages to put human agency at the center of attention, even in a conversation about things.[21] It is as if Kant wanted to "keep objects in their place," so to speak. In a world in which digital objects and other semiautonomous things are becoming more and more common, this is a very appealing feature in a philosophical framework.

THE ROOTS OF PROPERTY

Kant's understanding of property as a relationship primarily between people and objects will be jarring to those familiar with modern property theory. To those steeped in this field, it will seem an anachronism. The standard account of property these days says that it is an institution that primarily mediates relationships between people. The object-centered view of property was thoroughly discredited by the legal realists and their heirs; the revisionist, more "sociological" view so thoroughly dominated the property conversation that until recently there were few alternatives to be found.

That has changed somewhat in recent years, now that a new generation of scholars led by Thomas W. Merrill and Henry M. Smith has rediscovered the importance of objects to property law. The "thingness of property," as one scholar put it,[22] has reentered the conversation. Most of this recent literature explains property's object orientation in economic terms, arguing for example that property efficiently organizes access to assets.[23] It does this, these scholars argue, by delimiting rights over discrete assets so as to minimize the costs of acquiring information about those assets and how they may be used. Scholars writing in this vein focus on the logic of ownership, how owners have wide discretion over what may be done with assets they own, while outsiders have few rights in this respect. The interpersonal or social dimension of property is deemphasized, except insofar as property serves as a sort of membrane, separating the internal private sphere of the property owner from the rights and actions of everyone else. To access owned assets, outsiders must contact owners and transact with them. In this way the rights and duties associated with an asset are tied up with, or concentrated in, a single person, the owner.

The rediscovered emphasis on the relationship between owners and assets places this body of theory in the same neighborhood as Kant, though not quite on the same city block. Owners in the new theory are treated a bit too instrumentally for Kant's taste, I would think. They are important as legal entities, in that they serve as a convenient focal point for rights over assets; but these disembodied owners are seen simply as the repository of decision and use rights. Their personal, individual plans and goals are not really the heart of the story, as they are for Kant.

STAMPING THE WILL ONTO OBJECTS

It is clear enough at this point that Kant thought reliable expectations about ongoing possession of objects enables something positive to take place. Stable possession permits the imprinting of some aspect of a person, what Kant called his will, onto objects so as to enable the person to more fully flourish. Though nuances abound, Kant's basic idea regarding the will[24] is simple enough: Will is that aspect of a person which decides to, and wants to, act on the world.[25] It has three distinctive qualities: it is personal, autonomous, and active. It is highly individual, a function of each person's preferences and desires; Lewis White Beck says that will is "bent upon the satisfaction of some arbitrary purpose." It is this aspect or feature of ourselves that we imprint or stamp on the world through our choices and the resulting actions that carry out or manifest these choices. Right here, in this foundational element, we see a radically individualistic and autonomous view of humans. Although this is balanced by a universalizing, transpersonal sense of reason in other parts of his philosophy,[26] a highly individual will is nonetheless central to Kant's view of human thought and action, and thus an essential aspect of what he thought it means to be human.[27]

WILL AND OBJECT IN THE WORLD OF IP

It is tempting to get caught up in the terminology and conceptual complexity of Kant's ideas of persons, will, and objects. To prevent that happening, it seems wise at this point to talk about some specific examples. How exactly does Kantian autonomy work? What does it look like in the context of IP rights? After we have a better grasp of these ideas, and of how they relate to Kant's rationale for property, we can turn to an equally important topic: the limits on individual autonomy that Kant built into his theory.

Our earlier example of Michelangelo showed how stable possession is required for a creator to fully work his will on a found object—in that case, a block of marble. The same basic logic applies in all sorts of cases. Individual farmers and landowners generate and then bring to life a vision for the lands they work on;[28] inventors transform off-the-shelf materials into prototypes, rough designs, and finished products; and artists work in media such as paint and canvas, paper and pen, textiles and wood, keyboard and iPad, and so on, to give life to a concept or mental image. Wherever personal skill and judgment are brought to bear on things that people inherit or find, we see evidence of the Kantian process of will imprinting itself on objects.

It even happens when the objects at hand are themselves intangible. A composer working out a new instance of a traditional form—a fugue or symphony, blues song or tone poem—is working on found objects just as surely as the farmer or inventor. Even in our earlier example, some of the objects that Michelangelo works on in the course of carving his sculpture are intangible: received conventions about how to depict an emotion; traditional groupings of figures in a religious set piece, such as the *Pieta*; or accepted norms about how to depict athletic grace or youthful energy. He may take these pieces of the cultural tableau and refine them, or he may subtly resist or transform them. However he handles them, these conventions are just as much objects in his hands as the marble itself.[29]

As with found physical objects, extended possession of these objects-in-transformation is required to fully apply the creator's skill and judgment. And because of this, Kantian property rights come into play with intangible objects as well.

Let me say a word about this complex, and perhaps controversial, possession of intangible objects. It has often been argued that this feature of IP, the control of copies of an intangible work, constitutes a form of "artificial scarcity,"[30] that it runs counter to an ethically superior regime where information is shared freely—and is maybe even counter to the nature of information, which, some say, "wants to be free."[31]

According to Kant, all property rights have this element of artifice, because they define a conceptual type of possession. Property is not just a matter of physical contact between person and object; it describes a relationship that is deeper and goes well beyond the basic acts of grasping and holding.

I can hear one objection to this right away. Yes, Kant speaks of legal ownership as a special relation between a person and an object. But, the objection might run, in his writings he refers only to physical objects, for example, an apple (à la Locke). So maybe the ownership relation is limited to that sort of thing?

No. I give no weight to the fact that Kant uses only examples of tangible, physical property in most of the sections of the Doctrine of Right (DOR).[32] Kant describes an additional type of possession that makes it crystal clear that the idea is not in any way limited to physical things—the expectation of future performance under a contract. He posits that one could not properly be said to "possess" a right to performance under an executory contract (one that has been signed or agreed to, but not yet performed) unless "I can maintain that I would have possession . . . even if the time of the performance is yet to come."[33] With that legal relation established, however, "[t]he promise of the [promisor] accordingly belongs among my worldly goods . . . , and I can include it under what is mine."[34] The synonymous use of "possession," "object," "belonging," and "mine" in the case of a tangible, physical thing such as an apple and an intangible thing such as a promise of future contractual performance is too clear to require much comment. "Object" is very abstract for Kant, and can of course therefore include IPRs.[35]

Kant's ideas about ownership and intangibles are sometimes called into question by virtue of an essay he wrote about the rights of authors and book publishers.[36] In this essay, he defends the right of an author to prevent counterfeiting of his books by unauthorized publishers. Near the beginning he states: "For the author's property in his thought (even if one grants that there is such a thing in terms of external rights) is left to him regardless of the unauthorized publication . . ."[37] The main body of the essay is taken up with a sort of agency argument, whereby Kant contends that a counterfeiter who buys a copy of a book cannot copy it and sell copies, because to do so implicitly (and falsely) represents that the author has authorized the new copies. Kant in this essay closely identifies the author's interests with those of his publisher, and characterizes the author's core right as the right to authorize a single, chosen publisher of a work.[38]

Though much has been made of the structure of this argument, with some scholars finding in it evidence of Kant's rejection of a property claim to authorial works, the introductory passage cited earlier seems clear enough to me. Eliminating the parenthetical, it says, plainly enough, "For the author's property in his thought or sentiments . . . is left to him regardless of the unauthorized publication." Some see in this essay a normative statement that property rights ought not be granted over authorial works.[39] But for my part, the only hint of a qualification is the parenthetical in the passage cited above, which says "even if one grants that there is such a thing in terms of external rights." This is not much of a problem for my interpretation, however. Kant appears to be saying "*even* though" external (positive) law does not provide for copyright, the author's property remains, that is, it survives the act of counterfeiting. Not every country had true copyright protection when Kant was writing, and a lively debate was raging throughout Europe on the desirability of adopting strong copyright protection for books. Kant was saying, in effect, "even if copyright is not in force in a given jurisdiction, counterfeiting is still wrong." And it is wrong, he says, by virtue of the "author's property in his thought."[40]

KANT'S EXPANSIVE NOTION OF AUTONOMY

The right of authors to assert continuing control over their works, and hence to develop their distinctive authorial voices, is entirely consistent with larger themes in Kant's philosophical system. Over and over, Kant returned to the topic of human freedom in all its dimensions. He seemed hardly ever to encounter a topic that did not touch on some aspect of this central theme.[41] Freedom is certainly the unifying principle behind Kant's views on creativity, possession, and property. By examining some of Kant's statements on these topics in light of the freedom principle, we can better understand how we might apply Kant to the body of IP law, and even to a number of vexing contemporary problems in this field.

We will consider creativity first. In the *Critique of Judgment,* Kant said that art is to be defined as an act of the will: "By right we should not call anything art except a production through freedom, i.e., through a power of choice that bases its acts on reason."[42] Several of Kant's statements on creativity support the idea that the image of a creative work is presented to the human cognitive faculty in the same way as a maxim of behavior. Just as concepts of right and wrong join with specific situational inputs in the making of moral decisions, the abstract aesthetic sense joins with specific creative images or ideas when an artist chooses to produce a work of art. It is therefore reasonable to say that images from the free imagination may become a spur to action in the same way as a moral precept. Indeed, the entire topic of genius-level inspiration can perhaps best be thought of as a special case of rational creativity, one that illuminates particularly well the generous conceptual space Kant allows for the idea of a free rational will. The best way to sum it up might be to say that while the idea of a brilliant work of art may strike the mind as a pure inspiration,[43] the individual artist must choose to carry out this vision through mental toil and perspiration if the work is ever to be realized in the world. Pure inspiration may account for the first step, but only the freely applied action of an individual, willing person can carry out the second.[44] Putting aside highly improbable instances of completely serendipitous creations, then, creative production for Kant always involves some act of will or purpose, even if it begins with a sudden inspiration.

Just as individual will is expressed in creative acts, it is also central to Kant's ideas about freedom. In particular, he wanted to preserve as much individual freedom of action as possible, believing this allowed the fullest possibility of human development. This leads to a very expansive understanding of the range of things that can be appropriated. As Kant himself puts it, "an object of my will is something that I have the physical power to use." If use of it were prohibited by a voluntarily enacted law, "freedom would be robbing itself of the use of its will in relation to an object of the same will, inasmuch as it would be placing useable objects outside the possibility of use." This would, in other words, "constitute a contradiction of external freedom with itself."

To this end, Kant thought no category of object ought to be absolutely excluded from the possibility of human possession:

> The principle of external acquisition is as follows: That is mine which I bring under my *control* (in accordance with the law of outer *freedom*); which, as an object of my choice, is something that I have the capacity to use . . . ; and which, finally, I *will* to be mine.[45]

He added:

> [I]t is possible to have any and every object of my will as mine. In other words, a maxim according to which, if it were made into a law, an object of will would have to be in itself (objectively) ownerless (res nullius) conflicts with Law and Justice.[46]

This expansive conception of what might be owned gives the human will the broadest possible canvas on which to operate. And given that, for Kant, creativity always involves an act of will, Kant's ideas about claiming objects opens the way to ownership of a very broad range of creative products. We will see shortly what this means for IP law.

Before moving on, however, it is important to pause for a moment to note that, despite the broad terms he uses, Kant was no absolutist when it comes to property and possession. He was as concerned with the freedom of others—with third parties not directly involved with a specific possession—as he was with the freedom to make original acquisitions. In the passage just above, he condemns any law that renders "an object . . . in itself ownerless. . . ." His point is not that anyone should be able to possess and claim anything; far from it. As the Universal Principle of Right (described below) provides, my property claims are only valid insofar as they take into account the freedom of all others as well.[47] Kant is concerned in this passage with the relative status of people and objects. There is no class of objects, he says, that ought to be off limits when it comes to human possession. That would constitute an illegitimate restriction on human freedom. No object—no thing "in itself" as he puts it—can put forth a claim that trumps the value of human freedom. But when such a claim would conflict with the freedom of other people, Kant tells a very different story. Again, we take that up shortly when we address his Universal Principle of Right.

How far does Kant's solicitude for human freedom extend? What scope of rights, beyond mere first possession, does his approach to property suggest? Are there any limits to the autonomy interest of a possessor in Kant's philosophy? Because these issues all bear on important topics in the world of IP today, I consider them next.

We can paraphrase Kant's earlier statement: whatever I can bring under my control, and have the ability to make use of, I may own. The ability to make use of an object is important here. The purpose of the more extended or complex type of possession is to facilitate some further use of the objects involved. There is more going on here than maximizing freedom to grab or freedom to gather up, for its own sake. Gaining possession is not typically the end of a person's plans or goals with respect to objects. Objects have a purpose and a use, which are central to the possessor's reason for grasping them in the first place.

To put this more concretely, for possession to really further human will it must be expansive enough to embrace the plan, purpose, or goal of the possessor. Michelangelo's rights over a block of marble must include continuing access while he is working on it. But the point of this extended right to possession is to further his purpose or goal in carving the statue, that is, the end to which he applies his will. Note that this might very well include the right to control what happens to the statue after he finishes it. Obviously, if his plan in carving it is to place it in a church, it would seriously thwart this plan if some stranger could take the completed statue and place it on a street corner instead.

Even more, I would argue that Michelangelo's autonomy interest in the statue should extend to include a more expansive right to alienate. This even includes a right to try to make some money from selling it. A robust understanding of the role of Kantian will and autonomy must include not only a general right to alienate the statue, but more particularly the right to alienate it at the price he sets. That is, full realization of his autonomy interest in the statue includes the right to make a living from carving and selling it. His plan or purpose extends not just to possessing and carving a piece of marble, but well beyond. It includes a desire to develop his talent, to earn a reputation as an artist, and ultimately to make a living as an artist. Any conception of property that does not extend this far is therefore deficient. It fails to fully reflect and encourage an expansive sense of the creator's autonomy.

BEING FAITHFUL TO THE VALUE OF AUTONOMY TODAY

This wide-ranging notion of autonomy has some very practical ramifications for contemporary issues in IP policy. First, as I said earlier, it takes our attention off the themes that dominate current debate—technologies of distribution, and technological systems generally—and brings it back to the individual creator. It renews our interest in the people behind the systems, the creators of all this "content." Second, because it is couched so straightforwardly in talk of property as a right, it implicitly elevates the interests of creators to a very high level. This way of thinking about property removes creators from the realm of jostling interests and utilitarian trade-offs; it makes of them a class of special concern. And in the process, it points toward a general reorientation in policy, as well as a number of more fine-grained adjustments.

The general policy suggested by Kant's writings has to do with encouraging a larger number of smaller creative entities, as opposed to a smaller number of larger ones. (I speak here of creative entities because, as I discuss in Chapter 7, small creative teams offer many of the advantages of purely individual creativity, and because strictly individual production is often unworkable in the context of many contemporary creative works.) At the outset, it must be understood that speaking strictly in economic terms, there is nothing inherently superior about economic activity that is broken down into a greater number of discrete units of production. Disaggregation, as a mode of producing economic goods, has no moral superiority over the alternative of integrated production. Net cost is all that matters— whether, when transaction costs are added to the mix, creating things with many independent producers costs less than integrating many producers into a single big company. The benefits of independence, from this point of view, are reduced to economic terms. Typically, they revolve around greater concentrated effort on the part of independent producers. The economist Oliver Williamson calls this "high-powered incentives,"[48] by which he means the greater effort that can be expected when an independent producer makes an input and then sells it, via contract, to a buyer who uses it in some larger production process. The idea is that the same input will be made with greater care when it is produced by someone who has to sell it via contract. Part of the story is that an explicit contract can spell out quality and cost criteria with greater precision than the more informal, bureaucratic process by which one unit in a large firm acquires inputs from another unit in the firm. But another part—the important part, for our purposes—is that an independent producer will work harder and with greater focus.[49]

Again from a strictly economic point of view, this is desirable only because it leads to lower net production costs (assuming of course that the higher transaction costs of independent production are outweighed by improvements in the quality of the input, or lower costs). There is nothing inherently *better* about independent input production.

But from a slightly different perspective—a Kantian perspective— independent production *is* inherently better. Independent production serves important personal and social values beyond efficiency, which means that we as a society ought to bear slightly higher transaction costs than might be dictated by a strictly efficiency-based viewpoint. Such a policy reorientation is necessarily general, so a few specific applications are in order to show what I am talking about.

An understanding of IP that embraces creator autonomy directs us to resolve close cases, those where the costs and benefits of IP protections are in doubt, in favor of creators. This comes into play in a wide range of situations. One example is a class of cases where the creator of a protected work licenses the work for use in a certain medium, such as feature films, and then later challenges exploitation of the work in new media technology such as videotapes or DVDs.[50] Sometimes contractual terms resolve these cases cleanly, sometimes not. When they do not, when there is doubt whether the later-generation media technology is covered in the original contract, a policy interpreting the contract to exclude the new media would be in order. This interpretation, which would free the work's creator to sign a new contract for use of the work in the new media, favors creator autonomy and is therefore to be preferred. A policy that "the tie goes to the original creator" permits greater freedom of action, greater flexibility in exploiting a work after its creation, and thus it promotes autonomy.

A second detailed policy change suggested by an orientation toward creator autonomy has to do with the scope of IP rights, in this case particularly patents. I have shown in some earlier work that robust property rights can, under some circumstances, enhance the independence of highly skilled people who make a specialized technological input—something that is incorporated into products made by other (usually larger) companies.[51] Examples might be a specialized biomolecule used in making pharmaceuticals, a touchscreen for cell phones, or a piece of testing equipment for industrial machinery or semiconductor manufacturing. Property rights that cover inputs such as these allow the makers of the input to set themselves up as a separate, independent firm and sell their input in an arm's-length transaction with other companies. As compared to the alternative arrangement, under which the input makers work as employees of a larger company, their ability to work in an independent firm gives them more say over their work, more control over their professional fate—more autonomy.[52]

A third detailed policy is the requirement for permissions in the online world. It has been argued that permissions of this kind might well be more burdensome than is worthwhile from the perspective of wealth maximization.[53] Some permissions, as a class, might not be worth the cost they impose on would-be licensees. There is an argument, based on the autonomy of online creators, that society ought not to be so quick to this conclusion.

Efficiency might here be an inadequate basis for policy. Something deeper, more fundamental, signals a different outcome from the one suggested by simple utilitarian calculations. Those of us who are drawn to the writings of Kant have seen that his perspective can help us identify and flesh out values that go beyond the mere utilitarian. If IP rights are real, true rights, they will sometimes trump what have been called "mere interests," such as efficiency. Online permissions may be just such a case.[54]

The Importance of Waiver

The centrality of freedom in Kant's thinking about property shows up in a number of passages, many of which we reviewed earlier. I want to touch on one more here, to illustrate the importance of the concept of waiver in the Kantian tableau. The source is obscure, but the thought is important for today's issues. It deals with a crucial aspect of a creator's choice: the right to voluntarily surrender, or waive, property rights in something one owns.

In a book review he wrote in 1785, Kant considered and rejected an argument about freedom and coercion. The work in question was a book on natural law, with Kantian overtones, authored by the German legal scholar Gottlieb Hufeland.[55] Hufeland's book, entitled *Essay on the Principle of Natural Right,* had argued that a person faced with a potential violation of rights has a separate natural right to use force to prevent the violation.[56] Kant demurred, on the grounds that the very idea of a right already includes within it the possibility of coercing others not to violate it. What bothered Kant about Hufeland's argument was that it was premised on a supposed obligation to improve oneself, to increase one's own perfection. This was absurd, Kant argued, because it meant that a person would always have to maximally enforce his rights in order to fulfill this duty of self-perfection.[57] The natural right to enforce, as Hufeland had framed it, implied an ironclad *duty* to enforce—always. In rejecting this, Kant implied that it was important to leave open a rightholder's freedom of action. Kant said any definition of a right that includes the necessity of full enforcement becomes thereby a straitjacket, and this makes no sense at all. Kantian rights are meant to extend individual freedom, to enhance autonomy. Mandatory enforcement has no place in such a scheme.

The essence of Kant's objection is this: Hufeland's idea of rights did not include the concept of waiver. To waive a right is to choose to relinquish it, to elect not to enforce it. Given Kant's support for wide-ranging rights in support of human dignity and personal freedom, this is an important point. Kant obviously thought it essential to separate the grant of rights from their enforcement. As we saw from Kant's description of property, the function of rights is to further the reach of, and provide security to, individuals who wants to work their will in the world. But a right that constrains its holder to maximal enforcement works against these goals. Put differently, rights are meant to extend the range of personal freedom, not constrain it.

How would Kant's ideas regarding waiver apply specifically to property rights? Recall that for Kant, the state is to be quite liberal in granting rights over the many objects on which a free individual might want to project his or her will. But liberality of enforcement is another matter. Enforcement is a matter to be decided not by the state but by individual rightholders. Here individual freedom takes on a new and important dimension: the instrument of personal dignity and autonomy, a property right, is not permitted to become a straitjacket, restricting the freedom of the rightholder. Freedom of choice in the "postgrant" stage of the property right is to be preserved by placing the enforcement decision in the hands of the rightholder. The state may be obligated, in Kant's view, to permit a wide range of property claims, but it is at the same time prohibited from determining the conditions of their enforcement. Once again, maximizing autonomy—individual choice—is the organizing principle. And in the case of property, the instrument that makes this possible is waiver.

Why It Matters Now

Theoretically, waiver is an interesting aspect of autonomy: the freedom to give up one's rights. Practically, it has never been more important. This component of Kant's thought has deep and immediate relevance for problems we face today.

Waiver slices cleanly through a knotty set of issues at the intersection of individual property and collective efficiency. Waiver helps answer a serious conundrum: how do we reconcile a tradition of individual property rights with the need for ready access to all sorts of widely scattered information? Waiver holds incredible promise, because it remains true to the bedrock belief in the rights of creators to control what they create, while facilitating access to a large volume of works. When waiver is encouraged and implemented broadly, and especially when it is incorporated into large scale technical-legal systems designed to promote sharing, it can reduce transaction costs without sacrificing respect for individual ownership. Autonomy with flexibility: this is the magic combination we as a society should be looking for.

Or perhaps I should say, this is the combination we as a society often actually have in practice. Many critiques of the growth of IP espouse an overpropertization thesis.[58] This is for me a critical conceptual error. These accounts mistake the "law on the books" for the "law in action" in one crucial respect: they fail to account for the fact that in many cases, sometimes in the vast majority, IP rights are neither fully enforced nor effectively enforced at all. Critiques of the overexpansion of IP fail to understand the ubiquity of waiver in today's IP environment.[59] To be sure, a partial explanation is that enforcement costs in IP can be very high; so it is often financial constraints that prevent holders of IP rights from enforcing them. But even if this variety of waiver is something less than ideal, it is an important part of the IP landscape. And of course a fair number of decisions not to enforce rights are driven not by finances, but by a spirit of altruism,[60] or a desire to "seed the market" by giving away creative works now in hopes of selling more later.[61]

Because of high enforcement costs and waiver, the de facto zone of freedom for consumers of IP—the zone of participatory culture, if you will—is really quite large. An overly formalistic focus on the "law on the books" (as opposed to "the law in action") often obscures this. There is no better proof of this than the growth of large-scale sharing initiatives, which are built on the legal principle of waiver, combined with a norm of reciprocity.

The Voluntary Information Commons

Large-scale sharing initiatives range from formal institutions such as the Creative Commons championed by Larry Lessig, and the Public Library of Science (PLoS) movement, to many less formal efforts of individual creators.[62] Each organization or person contributing to these efforts publicly disclaims at least some property rights, thereby increasing the information available for free access by at least some users.

Consider one example. The Creative Commons disseminates standard-form licenses that allow creators to waive some or all of their legal rights over digital content (including text, music, photos, films, and the like). As the Creative Commons website makes clear, complete dedication to the public domain is only one option. For example, a creator can license all noncommercial uses, reserving the right to exclude (and earn compensation from) commercial users. This is in effect a partial dedication to the public domain, rather than a complete one. The user selects some of the sticks in the metaphorical bundle and waives the right to enforce them, dedicating those particular rights to the public. The various Creative Commons licenses can thus be seen as a menu of waiver options from which creators themselves select. While not every work subject to a Creative Commons license will fully enter the public domain, certain attributes of every work will. It is therefore a potentially powerful force for adding to the aggregate of works that are freely available to various users and various uses.[63]

Market forces encourage widespread waiver as well. Consumers like freedom. Businesses try to give consumers what they like. So if people prefer cultural products with a little extra freedom thrown in, some enterprising business is likely to give it to them.[64] Those who sell cultural products that significantly restrict freedom will either have to make those products especially attractive (to offset the loss of value to consumers occasioned by the greater restrictions), or change their policy on restrictions.[65] Simple as that. Put another way, there should be plenty of content available for remixing, mashing up, or otherwise using quite freely. Some will come from commercial companies, some from amateurs who like remixing and want to promote it. Not all content will be freely given out, but a fair amount of it will be.[66]

What about content that is not given away? In these cases the IP rights will not be waived, they will be retained. And this will by definition restrict the actions of others. This is but the flip side of waiver, so to speak. Autonomy has to include the right to enforce one's rights, or it is just a sham. I understand that some people feel that if they cannot physically mess with content and put their stamp directly on it, they are deprived of an important form of freedom. But I believe that forcing them to work around IP-protected creations, to comment on them without directly copying elements of them, is not too high a cost. It is the cost of recognizing the rights of creators. Rights always come with burdens. Autonomy means freedom, but is not itself free: it comes at a cost. In my view that is just a necessary corollary of protecting IP with actual, meaningful rights.

Kantian autonomy is thus best promoted by a combination of policies. Property rights ought to be widely available. It should be easy to waive rights. But waiver ought to be a strictly voluntary measure.

Kant and the Community of Individual Creators

I have been dropping hints throughout this chapter that despite his emphasis on individual freedom, Kant is no absolutist when it comes to property. As with Locke, significant limits on property are not just sprinkled on top of a theory of initial appropriation; instead, they are baked in, as a basic ingredient. Kant locates the legal rights of ownership in a broad web of duties that apply to all citizens. This section explains these limits and shows how they contribute to a bounded and therefore liberal theory of property.

Kant's theory holds two values dear: the dignity and worth of every individual, and the importance of the community of humankind. As with so many issues Kant writes on, he is concerned always with reconciling and balancing these two seemingly irreconcilable claims to freedom. So Kant, the quintessential integrator, would not be content to construct a legal philosophy as one-sided as, say, the modern pure form of libertarianism.[67] Indeed, one of the most important aspects of Kant's writings on property, and one that we will come to see is very useful in the context of intellectual property, is the notion that ownership must be so structured as to not interfere with the fundamental freedom of any other person. What does he mean by this, and does it have any possible application to contemporary questions of IP policy?

Property: From a Web of Duties to a Right

The place of others, of third parties, in Kant's property story is determined by the concept of duty. Kant begins by acknowledging that when one person (A) takes possession of something, everyone else then has a duty not to injure A with respect to that thing. When the duties of all others (that is, everyone but A) are pulled together and looked at in a unified way, they constitute a property right. In other words, property is the summation of the duties of everyone else toward A.[68] Kant scholar Kevin E. Dodson explains the principle this way:

> I am authorized to use coercion against anyone who would act unjustly toward me, just as others are authorized to use coercion against me so as to prevent me from doing them an injustice. Thus "strict justice can be represented as the possibility of a general reciprocal use of coercion that is consistent with the freedom of everyone in accordance with universal laws." We find, then, freedom and coercion combined in the same concept, that of justice, or of a right: "the concept of justice (or of a right) can be held to consist immediately of the possibility of the conjunction of universal reciprocal coercion with the freedom of everyone."[69]

Notice that appropriation, described so far in this chapter in terms of freedom, can also be discussed in opposite terms: coercion, or mandatory compliance—the implied force behind an obligation or duty. In a just society we take on this duty willingly, according to Kant, because others take it on as well. Thus appropriation—an individual, unilateral action—always takes place in a spirit of mutual respect and reciprocity. In the context of property claims, reciprocity means simply that individual acts of appropriation always and inherently take into account the full spectrum of others' needs, others' freedom. Because the IP system struggles mightily to reconcile individual appropriation with third-party freedom, Kant's ideas hold great promise for understanding and advancing this area of law. As Kenneth Westphal puts it:

> Kant's justification of rights to possession involves no unjust unilateral obligation of others because, in obligating others to respect our possessions, we also obligate ourselves to respect their possessions. This is not unilateral obligation because we recognize others to be like ourselves: finite rational agents living in sufficient proximity to interact with us and the things we use on a finite globe with finite resources.[70]

The interlocking duties that result constitute what I call "the community of owners."[71]

The duty-property connection is thus the basis for a consideration of third-party limits on appropriation. To understand this connection at depth, we need first to get a handle on the nature of the duty owed a right-holder. For this we have recourse to the principles of restitution.

The taking of what someone else has rightfully claimed is an injury that is central to the concerns of the law. Stated this way, there is a very strong affinity between Kant's ideas about duty and property and Professor Wendy Gordon's classic writings on restitution and intellectual property. Gordon, like Kant, sees the essence of property as consisting of the duties of others to refrain from using what someone else rightfully claims. In the traditional language of restitution, this takes the form of the principle that B must not be unjustly enriched at the expense of A. Unjust enrichment is at the heart of Kant's view that property is a necessary expression of the shared duty of everyone else to respect the prior legitimate claim of an original possessor of something. Likewise, Gordon's restitutionary theory of IP shows how a simple duty not to take wrongfully can serve as the footing for a true property right, good against the world. Gordon's theory, seen this way, has a thoroughly Kantian spirit.[72]

There is more to the duty-property connection than this, however. To see this, we need to turn things around. Restitution is based in a duty that is owed to a rightful owner. What about the duties of the owner himself? What does Kant have to say about that? Plenty, as we will now see by examining Kant's Universal Principle of Right.

The Universal Principle of Right

The movement from collective duties to an actual right is something Kant thought through very carefully. Early on in the Doctrine of Right (DOR), under the heading "The Universal Principle of Right," he states: "Every action *is right* if it can coexist with everyone's freedom in accordance with a universal law, or if on its maxim the freedom of choice of each can coexist with everyone's freedom in accordance with a universal law."[73] There is clearly some affinity here with Kant's famous Categorical Imperative, which he laid out in the *Critique of Practical Reason*. As with the Categorical Imperative, rightful individual action must accord with rational, universal principles of right and wrong.[74] Because of the symmetry between the concepts, a quick summary of the Categorical Imperative will help us here. Robert Paul Wolff writes:

> Kant argues that when [a person] gives reasons to [him]self, [he] implicitly commits [himself], as a matter of logic, to the proposition that such reasons are equally good reasons for any other agent similarly circumstanced. This requirement of consistency in willing can be expressed quite generally in the

form of a command, which reason gives to itself, to adopt only those rules of action ("maxims" in Kant's terminology) [whose rationale would be] equally compelling . . . for any rational agent. . . .[75]

The logic Wolff attributes to the Categorical Imperative is also at work in what Kant called his Universal Principle of Right (UPR).[76] The UPR can be thought of as the same sort of "universalizing" principle as the Categorical Imperative, except that it operates in the realm of positive law rather than moral constraint. Under the UPR, "laws secure our right to external freedom of choice to the extent that this freedom is compatible with everyone else's freedom of choice under a universal law."[77] It is not surprising, in light of the fact that Kant believes the need for robust property drives the formation of civil society, that property is subject to this "universalizing" constraint. Under the operation of the UPR, property rights must be granted, because they are necessary to enhance human freedom. But at the same time, these rights are constrained: they must not be so broad that they interfere with the freedom of fellow citizens. In a Kantian state, property, we might say, is both necessary and necessarily restricted.[78]

There are two interesting features of this for our purposes: (1) it turns what is perhaps the ultimate self-regarding act (the choice of individual acquisition) into one bounded by rational principles of justice and equality; and (2) it subjects the exercise of the will in this area to an implicit constraint—a sort of "community conscience" that operates as a check on one's self-regarding behavior. This is more than a large-scale proviso, or king-sized caveat; it is a pervasive, thoroughgoing, and highly constraining principle perpetually informing and influencing the legitimacy of individual appropriation.[79]

WHILE THE UPR certainly shares some kinship with Locke's provisos, it sets even more rigorous limits than they do. After all, it is certainly possible to conceive of individual acts of appropriation that would leave "as much and as good" for others (qua Locke) but would nevertheless fail to satisfy Kant's "universal law" criterion. This is because Locke would limit appropriation only when it affects others' opportunities for appropriation, whereas Kant would do so whenever it affected their overall freedom. Freedom includes, but of course is not limited to, the ability to appropriate. It also includes the opportunity to associate with others, to express oneself, and to move and act in all sorts of ways. An appropriation that interfered with these broader interests would run afoul of Kant's principle, even while satisfying Locke's provisos. For this reason, the internal logic of

Kant's theory of property fits comfortably with First Amendment limits on appropriation, better even than the labor theory of John Locke.

By virtue of the provisos, Locke made sure that an appropriator would not take more than his fair share of resources. And this undoubtedly contributes to the building up of community. By taking follow-on appropriators into account, an appropriator is not acting in a strictly self-regarding fashion; the needs and future claims of others count in the equation as much as the appropriator's own needs. This is the basis of Jeremy Waldron's very insightful discussion of the strong, theistically motivated, egalitarian streak in Locke's two treatises.[80]

Kant's "community of owners" achieves very much the same effect. Just as with Locke, Kant requires that an appropriator take others into account from the outset, from the moment of first appropriation. And Kant does so for a very similar reason: because he considers the needs and potential claims of others just as important as those of the owner.

The Social Face of Genius-Level Creativity

All Kant's talk of the individual is sharply at odds with prevailing views of creativity today, particularly those of intellectual property scholars.[81] A primary emphasis in recent scholarship is the highly social nature of creative production. The general idea is that the creative person swims in such a rich and stimulating sea of ideas that it is wrong to celebrate the backstroke or crawl of the individual racer. It is easy to see from what I have written so far that Kant could be expected to reject this approach out of hand, in favor of an agenda that puts the spotlight back on the swimmer, rather than the sea. This change in perspective casts our attention back to an older intellectual property scholarship that emphasized the importance of individual creative contributions.

At the same time, it would be wrong to say Kant's interest in the individual implies a lack of interest in the larger community. He shares with today's scholars the belief that creative people influence each other profoundly. But, unlike contemporary IP theorists, he spent more time thinking about the flow of influence from the individual to the community, rather than the other way around. In the *Critique of Judgment* where he talks about these issues, Kant says this about what we might call the social effects of a particularly interesting class of works, creations of genius:

> Genius, according to these presuppositions, is the exemplary originality of the natural endowments of an individual in the free employment of his cognitive faculties. On this showing, the product of a genius (in respect of so much in this product as is attributable to genius, and not to possible learning or academic

instruction) is an example, not for imitation (for that would mean the loss of the element of genius, and just the very soul of the work), but to be followed by another genius. . . . Yet, since the genius is one of nature's elect—a type that must be regarded as but a rare phenomenon—for other clever minds his example gives rise to a school, that is to say a methodical instruction according to rules, collected, so far as the circumstances admit, from such products of genius and their peculiarities. And, to that extent, fine art is for such persons a matter of imitation, for which nature, through the medium of a genius gave the rule.[82]

Milton C. Nahm, in his influential study of Kantian aesthetics, calls this "a brilliant interpretation of the function of the original genius," in which "Kant argues that the work of fine or free art produced by a genius awakens another genius."[83] The emphasis on the individual contribution here is unmistakable. But notice: a great original contribution does not create a dead end; it "awakens another genius." Like a many-sided flint, sparks fly off a work of genius, igniting other minds, other individual creators, who are inspired to stretch themselves and thereby reach their potential. This is a decidedly social phenomenon. The original creator does not work in a vacuum, and those who follow are in turn inspired by a genius-level work of creativity.[84]

Interpersonal influence, and not isolation, is the thrust here. Influence along these lines requires that multiple people are capable of appreciating the same aesthetic features of a creative work, an element of "the intersubjective validity of aesthetic judgment."[85] To be inspired, follow-on creators must first comprehend and appreciate the original creation. Those who are inspired validate the transpersonal nature of aesthetic judgment. For Kant, as Richard Eldridge argues, the fact that great works of art can be appreciated by many people shows the dual nature of aesthetic judgment: it is common among people, based on a common human foundation; and at the same time it is capable of recognizing novelty and innovation. As Eldridge says, for Kant a work of genius "makes new sense."[86]

This shared sense allows those who follow a genius to build on his or her work. A shared body of work accumulates as a cultural inheritance, available to everyone and appreciated (at least potentially) by everyone. Thus, the shared, innate faculty of aesthetic judgment creates the conditions for a shared body of work (that is, a shared culture). This same shared faculty then creates the possibility of an innovation within the culture that will be recognized by and built upon by others.[87] It is just this aspect of Kant's thought that leads Eldridge to speak of "Kant's subtlety in balancing the competing contributions of individual and culture, nature and craft, to the work of art."[88]

Chicken and Egg, Property and State

For Kant, protection of property interests is the central motivating factor that brings people in the state of nature to unite and form a true government or civil society. This position puts him at odds with Locke on an issue loaded with implications for IP rights. Locke famously understood individual rights—beginning with property rights—as belonging to people in the "state of nature." For Locke, civil society is instituted voluntarily by individual rightholders because it is a superior way to protect their rights.[89] Not so for Kant. In some of the most important passages of the DOR, Kant argues forcefully that rights are only possible under an established legal order; for him the idea of a "prepolitical" right, a natural or inherent right that precedes civil society, makes no sense at all. Indeed, according to Kant, rights in the full sense are not possible without a functioning state to back them up. Kant understood full, formal rights to be constituted simultaneously with the establishment of a legitimate government under the "general will." Rights and governments; governments and rights; these were an inseparable pair in Kant's political thought.[90]

So we might say that Kant believed the state, or civil society, precedes (or at least coincides with) the development of property, whereas for Locke, as we saw in Chapter 2, property comes first, with the state arising largely to secure and protect the property rights that people rightfully acquired in the state of nature.

In this matter, with respect to IP, Kant supplies the more appealing theory. The Kantian sequence of state first and property rights second seems more useful for a theory of intellectual property, because when it comes to IP, if we are to have any sort of effective enforcement, the state is absolutely essential. While various theorists of real property have analyzed why state enforcement emerged as a superior alternative to self-help or "small circle" mutual forbearance,[91] these accounts are hardly necessary in the case of IP. Despite some interesting work on social norms as a substitute for state enforcement, the literature on what I have called "private IP systems" recognizes throughout that these are rare exceptions and that in the main, IP law depends on a robust central state for real viability.[92] In the IP universe, the chief characteristic of a property right—that it is "good against the world"— is its central, crowning virtue, because it is so easy for "the world" to find and in many cases copy valuable information. In the case of tangible property, informal arrangements with those physically proximate to valuable assets can in some cases do an adequate job of protecting those assets from theft. But in IP, it is very difficult to make effective arrangements along these lines. The enforcement technology of a central government apparatus has always been essential to any functioning system of IP protection. Because of this, Kant's emphasis on the state seems completely apt.

The State, Rights, and Utilitarian IP Law

This discussion of the role of the state now allows us to join an important issue involving the theory and history of IP law. A series of eighteenth-century cases in Britain and the United States pitted statutory copyright protection against common law theories of protection.[93] The cases are widely viewed as representative of a conflict between natural law and statutes as the fundamental source of IP protection.[94] Indeed, the widely shared understanding of these cases is that they rejected once and for all the idea that IP protection was a natural right. After these test cases, the common view has been that IP rights are contingent creatures of specific states. Creators have no inherent rights to IP protection; governments can grant these rights if they see fit, but there is no absolute right to them. Many associate this outcome with the victory of a utilitarian—and distinctively American—perspective on IP law. This vision is usually contrasted with the European natural law tradition in IP law. Although careful historical work by Jane Ginsburg and others has long pointed out the deficiencies of this rather superficial view of things,[95] in everyday IP scholarship the labels have largely stuck: the United States is the home of a utilitarian brand of IP law; in Europe a rights-based, natural law vision predominates.

Kant's analysis of property rights, and specifically the role of the state, poses a most stimulating challenge to this superficial dichotomy. For Kant, the terms of this debate would make little sense. The American-utilitarian view is wrong because property is not something to be left to the whim of a particular legislature. If it is commanded by universal rationality, it must be enacted into law. Legislative discretion has nothing to do with it; or rather, the discretion of any reasonable legislature is constrained by universal reason. The demands of the Universal Law remove the discretionary and, one might say, arbitrary aspect of the American-utilitarian view, that governments can establish or remove property rights at their whim. A properly constituted government must obey the principles of rational justice. Because this includes some form of property—including of course intellectual property—then these rights simply must be established. True, there may be room for discretion in the details of the system. But the existence of such rights, where principles of reason and justice dictate, are not discretionary.

At the same time, Kant would reject at least some elements of the European natural law vision of IP rights as well. The reason circles back to the role of the state. Under conventional natural law theory, natural rights precede the establishment of the state. The state's job is to enforce these rights to the best of its ability. But there is no place for such prepolitical rights in Kant's thinking. The existence of rights and the establishment of the state go hand in hand. Rights are the expression of the general will, or a properly constituted legislature. They are not something to be confirmed or ratified by the state but rather are purely a creature of the state. Rights are in an important sense codetermined by the state: the state is the vehicle that carries them into being. They are not really conceivable without a state, so they cannot in any sense precede the state, at least not in their final, mature form.[96]

There is a further point that comes with this. As the eighteenth-century test cases argued, rooting IP protection in natural law strongly implies that these are perpetual rights. While temporally unlimited rights are not, strictly speaking, a necessary adjunct of the natural law view, they have often been treated as a logical outgrowth of that theory. Indeed, the American-utilitarian view described a bit earlier was developed at least in part to counteract this argument. If IP rights were merely creatures of state discretion, it followed that the state has the power to establish them only for limited times. (The power to grant limited rights is implied in the power to withhold IP rights altogether.) Given the pragmatic reasons favoring limited IP rights, this added up to a powerful brief in favor of the utilitarian perspective.

A major point in favor of Kant's understanding of property is that it allows us a way out of this traditional binary choice. We can argue, with Kant, that agreement with universal rational principles produces IP protection, but that the same rational agreement would require that the rights be time limited. The heart of the difference with traditional natural law principles is that for Kant, the universal rational will implies that the needs of others are incorporated into rational thinking about all rights, including property rights. Because property covers scarce resources, and thus mediates between the economic needs of many people, compromise and conciliation are built into its very fabric. Kant scholar Paul Guyer says it this way: because property rights depend on conventions and mutual agreements that are rationally acceptable to all, restrictions—such as state regulation aimed at equitable distribution—can be required as a matter of justice.[97] This rational-convention feature of Kant's thought is of course the foundation for John Rawls's ideas of the "Original Position" and "Veil of Ignorance" (which I apply to the choice of IP regime in Chapter 4).

Kant's universal rationalism retains some attractive features of both halves of the prevailing dichotomy in IP theory. From the natural rights half, we retain the idea that IP rights are really rights: they represent claims too important to be swept aside in the face of competing interests. The small literature on constitutional "takings" in the IP field is a move in this direction, and thus can be said to reflect at least partially a Kantian dimension.[98] At the same time, the social-conventional half of the equation permits us to hold that IP rights ought to generally be limited in time rather than perpetual, and that states have fairly broad discretion in crafting and applying IP rights. Property rights can only exist within a defensible framework, as Kant's universal principle requires, if they take into account the freedom of others. Although it is conceivable that this freedom might be accommodated in various ways other than temporal limitations, temporal limitations are an exceedingly effective way to protect both rights and third-party freedom—hence their very widespread presence in actual IP systems. The actual details of specific legal systems do not *necessarily* comply with universal a priori principles, but by the same token we should not be surprised if actual legal rules do often reflect and embody those principles. In addition, widespread adoption of a principle such as temporal limits on IP rights may give strong evidence for the existence of a shared sense of what is fair.[99]

To summarize: we might say that for Kant, it is equally wrong to argue (1) that important rights such as property are merely discretionary (they would not in that case truly be rights), and (2) that those rights somehow precede the formation of civil society, an actual government. His writing would lead us to conclude, instead, that IP rights are fundamental, but that they also of necessity must account for the needs and rights of others, because they are the product of an idealized set of social conventions, and that positive legislation will often reflect this other-regarding face of property.

This is not the same, however, as saying that IP rights are the product of a utilitarian calculus of costs and benefits. For Kant, "net social benefits" do often flow from actual property institutions, but this is a side effect rather than a motivating principle.[100] Rationally egalitarian property rules would still be called for even if the social welfare came out negative. Again, this is simply what it means to have a right, rather than merely an interest.

Case Study: The Right to Publicity

Kantian theory can get awfully abstract. This is a virtue, as I have argued; but it can also be a bit bewildering. Because I think the theory is really quite useful, and because examples and applications can help to clarify complex theory, I turn now to a real-life issue in IP law, the origin and nature of the right of publicity.

The right of publicity protects the persona of a famous person. It may manifest as a prohibition on the unauthorized sale of pictures of the person; or on copying the famous person's voice to use in an advertisement, so people believe it is the famous person singing when it actually is not; or on duplicating other recognizable features of a famous person's persona.[101]

Even though my main interest here is on the development of this somewhat exotic IP right, I need to pause for a moment to address the nature of the right. It might seem at first blush a poor example of some of the themes from Kant that I have been emphasizing. A persona is not really an object that one finds and then imposes one's will on. It cannot in any sense be possessed. Indeed, it may seem an odd candidate for IP protection, under Kant's theory or any theory.

Actually, though, it turns out to embody Kantian ideas fairly well. Start with the idea of an object, something outside oneself. I said that for Kant, objects are important because they serve as a sort of palette or platform on which people can impress their will. In right of publicity cases, we can think of the object as some raw talent or feature that a person just innately has. For an actor or actress, it may be a profile, a voice, a set of inborn mannerisms; for an athlete, some natural physical endowments, such as a strong throwing arm or a sturdy pair of legs. In most cases, it takes effort—great effort—to turn these natural endowments into the elements that make up a successful and famous performer or athlete. This effort represents that combination of self-discipline and imagination that in Kantian terms we call the will.

To fully develop these talents, a budding performer requires a number of things. One is consistent control over training and education. If some authority figure is in a position to dominate the performer's development, or interrupt it with forced service in another field, or otherwise direct or control it, the aspiring performer's ability to chart his or her own professional destiny will be thwarted. To put it another way, to fully realize one's aspirations requires that one be able to steer as thoroughly as possible by one's own lights.

Extensive self-direction of this type is a species of Kantian possession. The development of one's skills must not be interfered with; the unfolding of one's life plan must not be interrupted or distorted by someone else's vision. The human capital required to one day be famous is often built up over time. During this process of building up, it must not be taken, torn down, depleted, or redirected by any external force or person. Kant says that an object, once taken up by a person for the purpose of impressing the individual will upon it, is off limits for other people (consistent with the UPR, and so forth). It is just so with the human capital that one begins to accumulate on the way to becoming a famous performer. Consequently, even though that human capital cannot be physically grasped, it can be—and should be, if society is fairly structured—possessed by a person.[102] When this robust possessory right is properly recognized in a legitimate legal system, it becomes a property right. The property comes to protect the embodiment of the accumulated human capital, in the form of a famous person's persona. And so we have the right of publicity.[103]

The resulting IP right over one's persona is in fact an outstanding example of an "object" deserving of property in a Kantian (and also Lockean) sense.[104] And it is also an excellent example of the need for a nonphysical concept of possession. One cannot physically hold one's persona; it is by definition a transcendent set of qualities. The persona may be captured or signified in a photo (think of any Hollywood legend, self-aware of his or her "movie star-ness" and captured by a talented photographer: Betty Davis, Humphrey Bogart, Katherine Hepburn, Harrison Ford); but the essence of the actor (or athlete, or other famous personage) will always transcend any particular embodiment. To control that image, to prevent others from profiting from or distorting it, requires a form of property that goes well beyond the brute facts of physical possession. IP is that body of law. And so the right of publicity, the branch of IP law that protects just these personas, is in a sense the most Kantian of property rights.[105]

History of the Right of Publicity

Given what I said earlier about the complex relationship between Kantian ideals and the real world of positive law, it is interesting to trace the history of the right of publicity against this Kantian backdrop. Beginning in the late nineteenth century, legal scholars first pulled together a handful of disparate torts doctrines into "the right to privacy."[106] The doctrines, not much more than scattered cases, centered around the right of individuals to keep others from prying into their lives and publishing embarrassing images or otherwise private facts. These cases clearly established a duty on the part of third parties to respect the privacy interests of individuals.

In the 1950s, privacy doctrine was applied in a series of cases involving images of famous people, mostly baseball players.[107] The players' images were typically used on baseball cards sold along with bubble gum; then and now, these cards can be collected, traded, and pored over by fans. There was no violation of copyright in the cases, as the playing card companies were not copying photos or drawings done by others. Yet the courts sensed that it was unfair for the players to have no say in the sale of or profits from the playing cards.

In the leading case, *Haelen Laboratories v. Topps Chewing Gum, Inc.,*[108] the Haelen company held exclusive contracts to use certain baseball players' photographs. Haelen sued to prevent the defendant, Topps, from using pictures of the same players on competing baseball cards during the term of Haelen's contracts with the players. The legal complaint involved a creative mixture of theories, one of which involved the New York state right to "privacy." The case is noteworthy because it marks the precise legal moment when the duty to guard another's privacy was converted into a (quasi-property) right. The shift takes place in this passage, which begins with consideration of the Topps Company's argument that the right to privacy cannot support Haelen's claim because that right is strictly a protection against the unwanted publication of something private, a strictly negative duty not to invade someone's privacy:

> A majority of this court rejects [Topps's] contention. We think that, in addition to and independent of that right of privacy . . . , a man has a right in the publicity value of his photograph, i.e., the right to grant the exclusive privilege of publishing his picture. . . . Whether it be labelled a "property" right is immaterial; for here, as often elsewhere, the tag "property" simply symbolizes the fact that courts enforce a claim which has pecuniary worth.
> This right might be called a 'right of publicity.' For it is common knowledge that many prominent persons (especially actors and ball-players), far from having their feelings bruised through public exposure of their likenesses, would feel sorely deprived if they no longer received money for authorizing advertisements, popularizing their countenances, displayed in newspapers, magazines, busses, trains and subways. This right of publicity would usually yield them no money unless it could be made the subject of an exclusive grant which barred any other advertiser from using their pictures.[109]

The court here overturns the idea that the ballplayers have only a limited right not to have their feelings hurt. The intuition is that this limited right cannot support the activity the court is seeking to protect. In technical terms, it is not fully alienable, in the way a true property right is. The most one can do with this limited right is to release someone from a tort claim for invasion of privacy. A release such as this is a contract that says, in effect, "you have injured me, but I will let it go; I will not sue you." And if a famous ballplayer from the 1950s, say Willie Mays of the Giants, or Ted Williams of the Red Sox, had entered into such a release with Haelen, but not Topps, he could sue Topps if Topps began selling unauthorized baseball cards. But (here is the key point) *Haelen* could not sue Topps. The right to privacy, the right not to have one's feelings hurt by unauthorized publications, is a personal right, a limited right not to be injured. Without a true property right, all Haelen would have is a bundle of personal rights, in the form of releases from liability. Haelen would not have a true property right because the players would have no such rights to give Haelan.

This is what the court means when it says that "[t]his right . . . would usually yield [the ballplayers] no money unless it could be made the subject of an exclusive grant which barred any other advertiser from using their pictures." The tipoff here is the phrase "exclusive grant," which is classic "property talk." To succeed in its lawsuit, Haelen must hold some legal right—a grant of property rights rather than a mere contract—from the players that "bar[s] . . . any other advertiser from using their pictures." Without such a grant, Haelen does not have much (and so it would not pay much).[110] In other words, Haelen has to receive something from the ballplayers that allows it to bar others from using the players' pictures. And this "something" can only be a property right. The very definition of a property right is a claim "good against the world," often described as a "right to exclude others" from the particular legal interest involved (here, the use of the players' images).

The motivation is largely pragmatic, but the legal innovation at issue, creation of a property right, requires an important conceptual step in keeping with the Kantian theme of this chapter. From a practical standpoint, busy baseball players cannot be bothered monitoring and bringing a lawsuit every time one of Haelen's competitors starts selling unauthorized baseball cards. Haelen is in a far better position to do that. But legally, Haelen cannot protect the ballplayers' interests if the players' only rights are merely personal rights not to have their privacy violated.

Merely personal claims would only create a series of bilateral duties. What the ballplayers need is a legal right that transmutes all these personal claims into a single, alienable right that they can grant (that is, sell) to companies such as Haelen. This alienable right would "bundle together" all their potential personal claims against third parties, turning this collection of personal rights into a single legal "thing"—a property right. Such a right also makes it much easier for companies such as Haelen to get a bank loan or attract investors, because these rights give Haelen much more practical enforcement power against competitors, again without the need to rely on individual players to monitor the baseball card market for unauthorized competitors. Property rights concentrate economic power in Haelen's hands, making it a more viable focal point for enforcement.

It was precisely this felt need that the court in *Haelen* was responding to. It was a small step, logically and historically. But at the conceptual level it was much bigger. It is not every day, after all, that our legal and political institutions create new property rights. Given the importance of property, its centrality to our legal practice and everyday thinking, this was indeed a bold and significant move. After this move by the court, the duty on the part of third parties not to "hurt the feelings" of the players had been expanded and formalized into a general right to exploit their images: a simple duty had been converted into a full-blown property right.

The evolution of the right of publicity thus demonstrates an important Kantian theme. For these duties to fully transform into property rights, an elaborate enforcement mechanism was surely required. A simple series of self-enforcing bilateral deals would not have done the trick. Contracts with known baseball card companies, for example, would do nothing to keep an upstart company from taking a few player photos, copying them onto cards, and going into business. Some way to prevent this, to secure rights even against strangers and upstarts, was called for. What is necessary, in a word, is property.

Conclusion

The right of publicity displays all the Kantian themes we saw in this chapter. This novel right illustrates two basic concepts central to Kant's thinking about property: the object, and possession. It also highlights the centrality of the state in Kant's theory, for without generalized state enforcement such an abstract right would be difficult to define and virtually impossible to enforce. In its application, moreover, the right of publicity is limited by various doctrines, such as the First Amendment. As we have seen, such limits are easily described in terms of the overarching third-party constraint Kant called the Universal Principle of Right (UPR).

Both initial appropriation and the application of limiting principles are therefore dependent on the viability of a functioning state. Indeed, these are the only state roles mentioned explicitly by Kant in his discussion of property rights. In other settings, however, he contributed to a wider set of debates concerning the role of the state in allocating and redistributing resources. Kant's ideas about the dignity of each individual and the proper role of a rational collective power echoed down through the years and were joined with those of other philosophers ranging from Aristotle to Thomas Aquinas to Jean-Jacques Rousseau. This body of thought reached its culmination in the late twentieth century in John Rawls's work on social justice. To see how the individual right to property squares with this modern thinking about social justice, and to examine IP rights in the context of social justice theory, we must turn next to Rawls.

CHAPTER FOUR

Distributive Justice and IP Rights

PROPERTY AND REDISTRIBUTION are ideas that, at least in most accounts, pull hard in opposite directions. Property, as we have seen, means at heart individual control over discrete assets, while distributive justice (the fair distribution of resources in society) is often associated with redistribution, which requires state redirection of economic resources. Property, taken to its logical conclusion, means total individual control: it's mine; no one (especially the state) can take it away. Redistribution, pushed to its limit, means everything belongs to everyone (as mediated by the state), everything is fair game for state seizure and allocation. Nothing is "mine," everything is "ours," it belongs to society collectively.

In Chapters 2 and 3 I described how Locke and Kant tried to account for the third-party effects of individual property claims. Locke's provisos and Kant's Universal Principle of Right both limit property rights when they impinge heavily on the activities of others—a crucial first step in the direction of distributive justice. Yet compared to modern theories of distributive justice, this is only a very modest step. Locke and Kant take as their main theme the individual appropriator, which means they recognize third-party interests in the form of boundaries on individual property claims. But in contemporary philosophical thought, distributive justice requires more than this. Particularly in the work of John Rawls, the starting point for discussion is not fairness *within* the institution of property, but the fairness *of* property itself, considered in its overall social and economic context. For Rawls, the key question is whether, and to what extent, the very existence of private property promotes a fair distribution of resources among the members of society. From this modern perspective, the relevant question for this book is whether IP rights have a place in a society that aspires to a fair distribution of wealth.

Only if IP can be justified at this systematic level can we return to the topic that occupied Locke and Kant, the handling of fairness concerns within the institution of property. If property as a whole cannot be justified, there is no point looking into the detailed structure of individual property rights. But if I can show that IP rights have a place in a fair society, I can then turn my attention to a discussion of how fairness considerations might be embedded within the structure of particular, discrete rights—the detailed mechanisms through which the distributive impulse is applied in IP law. These mechanisms describe, at the operational level, how considerations of society-wide fairness limit, modify, and otherwise affect individual IP rights. They include, but go well beyond, the general sorts of third-party limits described by Locke and Kant. These two topics, systemic fairness and distributional mechanisms within individual IP rights, comprise the main tasks I take up in this chapter.

Systemic Distributive Justice and IP Institutions

And so we begin with the question whether IP rights and the economic institutions that surround them are basically fair. On this important topic, let me lay my cards on the table right up front: IP has a place—an important place—in the basic structure of a fair society. I believe these rights and institutions help allocate wealth fairly. But unlike Rawls, who had a highly abstract understanding of property, I believe fairness considerations not only surround or transcend individual property rights; they are also *built into* the structure of individual property rights. The distributional features of IP—the rules and doctrines that reflect third-party interests and general fairness in the scope and impact of particular IP rights—go a long way toward justifying IP institutions as a whole. No discussion of private property is really complete without reference to the details of specific property rights. So while I will begin at Rawls's starting point and consider the systemic fairness of IP rights at the abstract level, I return later in this chapter to a discussion of how distributive justice concerns are woven into the detailed structure of individual IP rights.

Rawlsian Principles of Justice

Rawls's great life work was to figure out moral principles for structuring a fair and just society. His system of thought begins with a Kantian focus on the rights of each individual, but then integrates this with an emphasis on the fair distribution of resources. This confluence of Kantian individualism and collective concerns, together with a highly analytical way of thinking, marks Rawls's major contribution to the theory of social justice.

The clearest statement of the twin considerations at the heart of Rawls's project appears in his two principles of justice, which he states as follows:[1]

First Principle
Each person is to have an equal right to the most extensive total system of basic liberties compatible with a similar system of liberty for all.[2]
Second Principle
Social and economic inequalities are to be arranged so that they are both:
   (a) to the greatest benefit of the least advantaged, consistent with the just savings principle,[3] and
   (b) attached to offices and positions open to all under conditions of fair equality of opportunity.

The first, or liberty, principle includes what are considered essential civil rights in modern constitutional democracies (freedom of speech, freedom to exercise one's religion, and so forth). What is distinctive in Rawls's thought is the thorough and systematic understanding that these abstract rights are of little practical value for people who are destitute. Thus his second principle, which addresses inequalities in society. The idea is that once basic liberties are established, resource equality serves as a moral baseline, and deviations from it must be justified. In particular, Rawls stipulates that inequalities are permitted only when they benefit the least advantaged.[4] This is often labeled the "difference principle," because it serves as a criterion by which to measure permissible differences in the resources available to people in a given society.[5] Rawls's specific formulation is often described as the "maximin" principle (short for maximizing the minimum):[6] inequalities are tolerated only insofar as they maximize the minimum level of support in a society, that is, the support of the least advantaged. The second part of the difference principle deals explicitly with equality of opportunity; it is meant to broaden the scope of Rawls's egalitarian project. To this end, it ensures that society is as concerned with the distribution of future opportunities as it is with fairness in access to current resources.

Both of Rawls's principles are relevant to a discussion of intellectual property. The first principle includes among the protected liberties the right to hold at least some property.[7] This is a very restrictive aspect of basic liberty, however. Rawls limits the right only to items of what he called "personal property," and he excludes from this right all forms of "productive property."[8] In his later book, *Political Liberalism,* Rawls gave a somewhat more detailed account of "personal property":

> Among the basic liberties of the person is the right to hold and to have the exclusive use of personal property. The role of this liberty is to allow a sufficient material basis for a sense of personal independence and self-respect, both of which are essential for the development and exercise of the moral powers.[9]

Personal property thus appears to mean those belongings that are essential for an effective private, personal sphere—one's toothbrush and basic clothing, certainly; dishes, cookware, basic tools, and the like, almost for sure; but a personal dwelling, means of transportation, and more elaborate possessions, possibly not.

Whatever the specific limits, Rawls's "personal property" is not an expansive concept. Thus a broad right to property is not among the essential liberties Rawls says must be provided at the outset for a society to qualify as fair under his theory. It is not that Rawls believed property should always be severely limited. To the contrary, he thought that citizens of a society founded on his two principles might well establish a wide range of property rights.[10] He simply held that these rights were not basic liberties essential to a legitimately constructed state. For Rawls, wide-ranging property is entirely *consistent* with principles of fairness, but it is not *essential* to them.[11]

"Primary Goods" and Beyond: Expanding Notions of What Is to Be Distributed

I have been vague so far about what is meant by the term "resources"—the things whose fair distribution is the main topic of social justice theory. Rawls himself started with a fairly expansive list of things he identified as "primary goods": "rights and liberties, powers and opportunities, income and wealth."[12] Despite this, most discussions of distributive justice have centered primarily on material goods.[13] A number of post-Rawlsian theorists have subsequently expanded the list to include a broader conception of human capabilities. In particular, Amartya Sen and Martha Nussbaum have argued that conceptions of development ought to include an emphasis on human capabilities for fulfillment and not simply the acquisition of basic economic goods.[14] Social justice, in this view, requires that society provide each person a full opportunity to flourish. Basic physical sustenance, and even freedom from coercion, are not enough.

If Sen and Nussbaum critique Rawls as too narrow, another viewpoint holds that Rawlsian redistribution operates too broadly. The basic objection from this other direction is that Rawls's egalitarian baseline suffers from many of the problems exhibited by real-world socialism and communism—in particular, too much emphasis on slicing up the economic pie fairly, in neglect of the fundamental importance of rewarding those who make the pie in the first place. Widespread redistribution of economic resources simply creates massive disincentives for people to work hard and improve their individual lives. Though fairness is a laudable goal, it comes at too high a price in terms of overall social welfare.

One response to this objection is to take refuge in old-fashioned laissez faire: let markets operate, keep redistribution to a minimum, and be reconciled that though things are unfair, it is the best we can do in this world. A more creative response borrows a page from the Sen-Nussbaum critique, while also recalling an older liberal tradition. The best way to a fair society is to maximize occasions for advancement and self-fulfillment. The emphasis is less on outcomes—on equality in the physical resources people have—than on opportunities for individuals to achieve those outcomes. More on chances to do and become, and less on what people actually have and hold.[15] The goal, put simply, should be to maximize the number of, and equalize access to, what might be called "tickets to an autonomous life." I have already explored the relationship between property rights, and IP specifically, in Chapter 3. It was implicit in what I said there that ownership represents a societal reward for effort and creative work. To paraphrase, hard work, done creatively, should be enough to punch one of those tickets to an autonomous life. In this chapter, I make this point more explicit. To do so, I have to go back one step. I have implied so far that the capacity to work hard and be creative is something that a person just naturally possesses, and that the actual hard work, and its fruits, thus belong rightfully to that person. But this sidesteps an issue of critical concern to Rawls. The place to begin then is with an exploration of *why* the products of hard creative work ought to be enjoyed primarily by the individual who happens to possess the talent and who actually expends the effort. And thus we are led to the challenging topic of the role that desert plays in distributive justice.

Property and Desert

Let us return to Rawls's framework. Note first that his two principles of justice are meant to be satisfied in order. Thus, something that is a basic liberty under the first principle cannot be sacrificed to promote resource equality under the second. One of Rawls's boldest claims is that neither the place in society we are born into nor our natural talents are things we inherently deserve. This justifies the state in taking from us some, or even much, of the fruits of these initial advantages. In other words, Rawls does not see natural endowments and social advantages as basic liberties to which we have inalienable rights. They are contingent advantages, conferred on us by random luck. As Rawls puts it: "It is one of the fixed points of our moral judgments that no one deserves his place in the distribution of natural assets any more than he deserves his initial starting place in society."[16] It follows that the fruits or proceeds from these lucky endowments are fair game for redistribution under Rawls's second principle. According to this principle, inequalities in resources are to be permitted only insofar as they serve the interests of the least well-off. So unless the proceeds from a lucky endowment happen to help the destitute, those proceeds can be taken and given away to people in greater need. As a practical matter, Rawls recognizes that it is sometimes necessary to allow favorably endowed persons to keep more than an equal share of their earnings. But this is permitted only insofar as it is necessary to encourage such people to develop and deploy their endowments so as to increase overall production and thus indirectly help everyone (including the most disadvantaged).[17] Insofar as property rights follow endowments, property claims are permissible only if, and only to the extent that, they tend to ameliorate the condition of the destitute. Again, Rawls starts with egalitarian fairness and adjusts for property rights, in contrast to Locke and Kant, who (roughly speaking) begin with property and then adjust for collective fairness.

WHAT WE DESERVE

Many observers agree with Rawls that people do not morally deserve inherited wealth. Indeed, the intellectual historian Samuel Fleischacker has said that the development of this attitude is perhaps the single most prominent event in the emergence of the modern conception of distributive justice.[18] Rawls is definitely on to something here. But when he extends his insight to the realm of natural talent and hard work, his thinking meets serious resistance. Fleischacker, for example, has said:

> [I]f we invoke "distributive justice" to express our dismay about lazy heirs living high on the hog while hard-working people live in penury, it is surely true, as Rawls supposes, that we implicitly have a general principle according to which luck should not determine one's life chances. But it may or may not be true, as Rawls also supposes, that we therefore regard people's talents and

willingness to work hard in the same light as their inherited wealth ...
[Rawls] needs to provide an argument to move us from our shared intuitions
about the arbitrariness of inherited wealth to his own intuition about the arbitrariness of inherited skills. He should not merely assume, as he does, that
we share his intuition.[19]

Beyond inherited wealth, then, the philosophical consensus about desert
fractures. An appreciable number of philosophers have argued strenuously
in favor of the idea that desert, in one form or another, can indeed form
the basis of moral claims in a distributive context.[20] Because IP rights are
tied particularly closely to notions of desert, we should take a real interest
in these ideas.

The philosopher Joel Feinberg makes some very useful basic points about
desert.[21] He begins with the concept of a desert basis, some ground on which
a person is said to deserve something. He then explores the connection between the desert basis and the thing that is deserved. First prize in the long
jump event in a track meet should go to the person who jumps the farthest;
high grade in a math class to the person who does best on the tests; and so
on. Most importantly, he differentiates between true desert, a moral concept,
and what he calls qualifying conditions. The formal rules of a contest or competition describe qualifying conditions, and often—but not always—the person who satisfies the qualifying conditions is also the person who, in a moral
sense, deserves to win it. But sometimes, the best long jumper, the one with
the most talent who has worked the hardest to develop it, suffers an injury;
sometimes the most deserving math student is sick on the day of the final
exam. Feinberg's general point is that there are legitimate reasons to separate
our concepts of desert from the operation of official, formal institutions designated to apply qualifying conditions.[22] Though there will often be much
overlap, they are not coextensive. This injects a pragmatic, institutional note
into the highly theoretical discussions of moral desert. And in addition, it is
obviously extremely relevant to discussions of desert in the IP system. All
manner of IP rules attempt to approximate assessments of desert yet also reflect an understanding that, given myriad practical limitations on evaluations
of desert, the system must rely on proxies, shortcuts, and other "qualifying
conditions" to do the practical work assigned to it.

In this connection, it is noteworthy that for some philosophers such as
Wojciech Sadurski, desert is linked closely to Locke's concept of labor. Sadurski argues that "effort is the only legitimate basis and measure of desert."[23] Others echo the thought, with wrinkles. For example, Julian Lamont
in general defends effort-based distribution norms but argues for some
refinements in the way desert is normally discussed, to take account of the
fact that effort and outcome may not always be tightly connected.[24]

Despite differences, theorists of desert such as Sadurski for the most part agree on a few main points. One is that desert is different from entitlement. Desert is a moral statement; entitlement has a more legalistic tone, meaning what one can validly claim under duly enacted laws or policies.[25] Generally, philosophers believe that desert ought to be reflected in entitlements as often as possible. But as the earlier discussion of proxies shows, there is also agreement that practical difficulties may sometimes make this impossible. Another point of consensus is that insofar as effort is taken as the ground for desert, the effort involved must be voluntary or purposeful effort.[26]

IP in the "Original Position"

For me to make my case that IP is a defensible basic right, I have to show that reasonable people who were setting up a social and economic system would agree to establish an IP system as a matter of right. In Rawlsian terms: I must show that IP rights emerge out of deliberations in the "original position."[27]

To do so, I will have to take issue with Jeremy Waldron.[28] Waldron argued that no right-thinking group of people would agree to a conventional arrangement of property rights in the Rawlsian original position.[29] By conventional, I mean "more or less parallel to Western societies as they exist today." And while I leave it to others to assess Waldron's general point, I want to focus (naturally) just on the IP system. My basic argument is simple: I think the current IP system in many if not most of its particulars is basically fair, and therefore I believe there is a good chance that rational people in the original position might agree to it, or something roughly like it.

Waldron bases his reasoning on the notion that strong property rights necessarily mean potential exclusion from food, clothing, and a place to live—the basic necessities of life.[30] Per Waldron, no one in his right mind would agree to to support an arrangement that might some day cost him his life. One never knows if one will be born needing these essentials. If agreement to respect property leads to the possibility of dire deprivation, it would be wise not to agree. As it is stated, without qualification or softening of any kind, he has a point. But of course no actual property system requires the rigid trade-off Waldron proposes. Every real-world property scheme—certainly every one with any kind of claim to fairness—comes equipped with at least a minimal set of tools for dealing with gross disparities in the distribution of resources. It is not necessary today to choose between respecting property and providing for the neediest. Put differently, only if property is *defined* as a hard-edged libertarian institution would people refuse to acquiesce in the foundation of property rights. If on the other hand private property rights are understood to be integrated in a larger system that includes provision for the destitute and other social needs (e.g., via taxation), people might well be attracted by the benefits without fearing the worst-case scenario. In the end, then, Waldron's distaste for property rights is based on a stark trade-off that seems utterly unrealistic.

Whatever influenced or motivated Waldron, I believe he was wrong when it comes to IP rights. People who find themselves in an original position would be quite reasonable to agree to a conventional IP system. In the original position, no one knows what his talents and tastes will be.[31] Thus anyone might potentially be a creative professional whose best and highest employment, and whose personal happiness, would lie in a job in which IP protection would give much greater freedom than is possible without these crucial rights.

The argument flows from Rawls's first principle: IP is a basic liberty for those who would most benefit from creative independence and the career fulfillment that follows. Everyone in the original position faces the possibility that he or she will have the talent to enjoy these benefits.[32] A similar argument might be made with respect to other types of property, but I will stick to IP here.[33]

I need to call attention to one feature of my argument. The benefits of IP protection fall disproportionately on a group I call "creative professionals." What do I mean by this term? Basically, these are the people who have the raw talent, and the potential to develop it, that makes it possible to be employed in one of the creative industries.[34] However, even with a broadened view of the likelihood of becoming a creative professional, it should be apparent that most people will never have these jobs, that the class of creative professionals is a small one. If we are to defend IP rights, which by design bring special benefits to creative professionals, we must do so in a way that justifies the unequal distribution of benefits that they necessarily entail. In other words, we must confront the fact that rational people in the original position will ask how IP can be justified given that they have only a small likelihood of benefitting directly from this special legal privilege.

This can be seen as an instance of the more general problem of special incentives to engage in certain occupations. Rawls says that in some cases it may be necessary to provide incentives that draw well-positioned people into socially beneficial activities.[35] Rawlsian scholar Michael Titelbaum uses the example of medical researchers and health care workers generally.[36] Some egalitarians have taken Rawls to task for this view, arguing that the general cooperative spirit that characterizes a society constituted along Rawlsian lines—called the Rawlsian "ethos"—would require that highly skilled people perform socially desirable tasks without the need for special incentives.[37] It is relevant here that Rawls intended the difference principle to apply to society's basic structure, and not individual decisions. Yet it is also evident that a certain amount of other-regarding behavior is expected of citizens in a Rawlsian society.[38] Even so, Titelbaum says, this egalitarian ethos is not so strong that it must dominate all of our work-related decisions. Citizens of a Rawlsian society will internalize not only the egalitarian spirit of Rawls's second principle, but also the spirit of the first principle as well.[39] This full Rawlsian ethos permits individuals much more latitude in decisions about their working lives. And it is this fuller version of a Rawlsian ethos that provides solid justification for an IP system, and the individuals who take advantage of it.

Our work is such an important and personal domain that people in a Rawlsian state would understand that individuals are not required to maximize social welfare with respect to their "productive decisions."[40] Reasonable people would agree, Titelbaum says, that personal values are so important they might very well inform one's choice of work. He gives the example of a social worker whose services are most needed in a large city, but who chooses instead to work in another town, closer to family, where his services are valued but not as highly.[41] This deeply personal decision does not, under the circumstances, maximize social welfare.[42] But it does reflect an important set of interests that everyone in the original position would agree may be allowed to modify a strict application of Rawls's second principle.

The justification for the resulting distribution is that the social worker's liberty interest in autonomy outweighs the operation of the "difference principle." This is the same justification I am arguing for in the case of creative professionals and IP rights. People in the original position would permit the "inegalitarian" distribution resulting from the incentives offered by an IP system, because these incentives are necessary for a creative person to achieve career fulfillment. These incentives give creative people career options, which in turn affect the overall distribution of society's resources. As Titelbaum puts it, IP creates "productive latitude":

> A worst-off individual who understands the reasoning behind the basic structure of his society will accept certain exercises of productive latitude by others as justified, for both he and they will see the actions in question as more important to the exerciser's plan of life than the marginal economic status involved is to the worst-off's good. It may be that by demanding a higher salary to work in the city, our social worker is taking money away from his

agency that could be distributed to the worst-off if he would do the same job for a lower wage. Yet the social worker could make a case to the worst-off that whatever extra goods they might buy with that money would be less significant to their plans of life than the opportunity to spend time with his family and friends is to his. This strikes me as a plausible justification one member of a democratic society could offer to another for an exercise of productive latitude.[43]

In the IP context, this translates as follows: even if the special incentive of an IP right leads to a somewhat unequal distribution of resources, as between a creator/owner and a consumer, the right may be justified. It may enable someone to pursue her most cherished career goal, and to do so independently. The freedom to do this might well be worth the loss of some social value that would be provided if the creator worked for less money, or under less autonomous conditions.[44] And finally, people in the original position would understand that creative freedom and autonomy are important enough values that they should join the list of essential liberties. This ensures that even if IP protection leads to some distributional unfairness, society should still include it among the basic rights to which all are entitled.

CAN I INTEREST YOU IN SOME DESERT?

At this point, I want to return to the topic of desert, and the role it might play in deliberations in the original position. Philosopher Margaret Holmgren argues, contrary to Rawls, that some notion of desert would very likely be built into the basic structure of any fair society.[45] For Holmgren, it is unthinkable that a fair society would be devoid of notions of desert. People's ideas about desert would inevitably be integrated into judgments about how to establish a fair society. Put another way, desert concepts are in part constitutive of the basic structure of a reasonably fair society. Holmgren presses this argument by showing, convincingly in my view, that it is very likely that people in the original position would agree on desert as an important principle, and on the need for institutions to make judgments about desert and hand out rewards accordingly. And she makes the explicit point that those in the original position would see that desert and desert-based institutions were fair even for the poorest members of a society. Others echo this theme.[46]

For purposes of defending IP rights, it is telling that Holmgren mentions incentives to invent as an example of desert-based policies that people would likely agree to in the original position.[47] This comes in a general discussion of the division of resources as decided in the original position.

She begins by assuming a radically egalitarian division of resources: every citizen would get an equal share of all resources in the society. She goes on to explain the frustration that would be felt by a certain citizen, Jones, who is intrinsically motivated to work hard toward a goal that was important to him:

> [C]onsider the individual (Jones) who wants to develop himself or his own life in ways which are very important to him, but which require more financial resources than he has been allocated. If income and wealth are to be distributed equally, Jones will have virtually no opportunity to pursue these goals. Working extra hours, working more intensely, turning out higher quality work, developing more efficient ways to get his job done, inventing new products, etc., are all to no avail. Whenever he manages to generate more resources, they will be distributed equally among all the members of his society.[48]

Holmgren points out that citizen Jones is here being deprived of "a fundamental interest that could be secured for him compatible with like benefits for all."[49] This she describes as "the opportunity to make the most of his life through his own efforts."[50] So long as opportunities such as this can be supplied without canceling completely a level of basic support for the needy, it appears very likely that people in the original position would agree that society should supply them.

IP, SERENDIPITY, AND DESERT

Even accepting that desert has a place in the foundational principles of a just society, one objection remains to the idea that IP rights would emerge from the original position. IP rights, and the profits that may flow from them, do not always seem to be deserved. Recall the idea of a desert basis or ground—some behavior or attribute that anchors or justifies a claim to deserve something. Not everyone believes that IP rights are always awarded to people with a legitimate desert ground or basis. If the award of IP rights is based on something that is not a legitimate basis for desert, then those rights are not themselves deserved in a philosophically defensible sense. Consequently, under these circumstances IP might be rejected by those in the original position. If desert is the key, in other words, IP rights must be shown to be based on grounds that constitute a real basis for desert.

Probably the most common argument along these lines is that creative works are in essence primarily collective works, developed by many different people, often over a long period of time. According to this theory, most movies, novels, nonfiction books, inventions, and product designs are the result of group creativity that accumulates over many years. From this perspective, IP rights are seen as artificial legal constructs that often assign individual ownership on the basis of incomplete and inadequate understanding of the real essence of the creative enterprise. Individual vision and effort are at best overrated, and at worst nothing but dishonest conceptual constructs employed to serve the interests of powerful industries.

I address this attack on the idea of desert at various places in this book, and will not attempt a comprehensive rebuttal here. Instead, I limit myself to one primary point. The universal experience of creative people is that fashioning something new and distinctive almost always requires sustained attention, effort, and personal vision. It is far more than simply dipping into the collective well and warming up a new version of something old. But having said that, it is also true that virtually every creative work draws on the contributions of a wide array of predecessors and contemporaries. That is why I take pains, later in this chapter, to construct a model of the creative work that recognizes both the ineluctable contribution of the individual and the inevitable contributions of peers and predecessors—the social contribution to each creative work. Any accurate understanding of creative works requires that both of these elements be integrated and balanced. Only in this way can individual desert be both honored and placed in its appropriate context.

IP rights and notions of desert fit together well at the conceptual level; this much I have established so far. But at the operational level, at the level where most IP doctrine actually does its work, there is still one issue to be resolved. I noted earlier that according to theorists such as Joel Feinberg, effort must be purposeful to ground a legitimate desert claim. As it happens, this issue is one that IP theorists have argued about over the years. How well does IP law accommodate the notion of purposeful effort as the basic grounding of an IP right/desert claim?

A classic problem along these lines in IP law is the purely serendipitous discovery: the researcher, for instance, who spills just the right ingredients in the laboratory, accidentally creating a valuable medicine.[51] Some might argue that purposefulness is lacking here, and therefore that no IP right should be awarded in such a case. But others would argue—and I would tend to agree—that working in the lab and assembling the ingredients are purposeful enough to merit a desert claim to the lucky invention. Purpose in this example operates at a higher conceptual level to be sure, but it is still present. One works in a lab and assembles ingredients in order to make discoveries. The fact that a *specific* discovery was serendipitous is irrelevant if it results from a larger project that is intentionally and purposefully pursued.[52]

Serendipity raises a more general issue about desert and its proxies. When the design of an IP system is under discussion, one has to decide how much effort to expend on examining each proposed IP right. Is it worthwhile, for example, to spend substantial social resources assaying for the presence of real, purposeful labor in a work whose creator seeks IP protection? If some fairly reliable indicator is readily available, and if this indicator will usually serve as a fair proxy for the expenditure of substantial purposeful labor, then this reliable, accessible measure should be used in place of a detailed analysis. Desert theorist Julian Lamont has made just this point in arguing that increases in productivity are an efficient proxy for labor, and therefore a defensible grounding for a desert-based system of entitlements.[53]

Similar objections can be made that other desert proxies—"originality" in copyright, "nonobviousness" in patent law, and so forth—do not always reflect true desert. We can dispense with these quickly, I think, on grounds similar to those discussed already.

First, we can say that although in a particular case these standards are poor measures of desert, they are good approximations in the general case. Within the practical limits of administrative efficiency, the actual standards that have developed do a reasonably good job of testing for desert. Testing for actual desert—the real thing, and not a proxy—would be difficult in some cases and would add unnecessary expense in many cases.[54] To see why, consider a few brief examples.

A famous hypothetical case in copyright involves a squiggle created when a person holding a pen is startled by a thunderclap. The squiggle so created is original enough to qualify for copyright protection. The example expresses, through an admitted reductio ad absurdum, just how little "creativity" is required for copyright law, and by extension, just how little the courts are permitted to inquire into the type or degree of creativity under the standards of copyright law. The hypothetical is meant to illustrate just how thoroughly courts have been taken out of the business of judging the merits of copyrighted works.

We can put aside the jarringly commonsense question of who would ever register or try to enforce a copyright in such a work, and instead home in on the element of desert. There is obviously almost no effort expended here, and therefore only the thinnest possible desert claim. So why should federal copyright law permit a valid right in the accidental squiggle? The answer is that the number of cases in which protection is sought for a completely accidental work like this can be expected to be vanishingly small. But if the law requires some element of effort-based desert to be proven, it will place a burden on creators, which could be exploited by copiers or other infringers in some cases. Proving up the circumstances under which an abstract painting was conceived and executed—that the painting was just a series of random, undirected marks inspired by a series of

thunderclaps—may place a burden on the creator. She will have to produce sketchbooks or witnesses, to corroborate her story that the work in
question was produced with some effort and as the result of an intentional
series of acts. This procedure would produce some benefit to be sure; it
would eliminate the rare case where copyright protection was sought for
an essentially effortless creative work. But the cost would be very high, as
the example shows. The legal system has made the commonsense choice
to avoid the necessity of this proof, on the grounds that it is rarely worth
the cost.

Consider a variation on this story: the case of the purely serendipitous[55]
discovery for which a patent is sought. I alluded to a classic instance of this
earlier, where a lab worker spills random ingredients in just the right combination to create a valuable chemical or pharmaceutical product. Under a
desert theory based on effort, why should society grant a patent in this case?

The copyrighted squiggle discussion above provides one answer: administrative efficiency. It might simply not be worth the cost to require proof of
intentionality or nonserendipitous discovery in every case. As an empirical
matter, it might just be the case that random lab spills almost never result in
valuable chemical or pharmaceutical products. So it might therefore not
make sense to build into the law a test for this highly unusual scenario.

There is another reason to dispense with the idea that serendipity bars a
patent, however. Serendipity leading to invention is often the result of
prior painstaking work that paves the way for the final, "lucky" event.[56]
The history of technology is filled with stories that bear out the old apho-
risms "chance favors the prepared mind" (from Louis Pasteur)[57] and "the
harder I work the luckier I get."[58] The fact is that serendipitous events are
in fact common in the history of invention—but luck by itself, luck with
no prior spadework or subsequent elaboration, almost never accounts
fully for the creation of important discoveries. In every case I am aware of,
either long and painstaking work led up to the lucky moment, or long and
painstaking development was required to flesh out and prove the work-
ability of a lucky insight or inspiration.

Let me give a few examples. The discovery of penicillin is often said to
have sprung from a serendipitous moment, when the researcher Alexander
Fleming noticed that bacteria in some sample plates he had stored had
been killed, through the action (he later discovered) of the airborne mold
penicillium.[59] But it took years of subsequent research, much of it by
Howard Florey and Ernst Chain, to show clinical effectiveness and to perfect techniques for administering what came to be known as penicillin.[60]
The Nobel Committee recognized this when it awarded the prize to all
three researchers, and not just Fleming.

Another oft-told tale, at least in the patent world, revolves around a New York City inventor named Bert Adams.[61] One night, the story goes, some ash from Bert's cigarette fell into a chemical paste he had been mixing up—and the result was a remarkably effective dry cell battery. The truth of Bert's tale is that he experimented with hundreds of candidate mixtures for his battery; and while the cigarette ash did help point the way, the true tale is of a long and painstaking process of invention that started in his kitchen and ended only when his patent was validated by the U.S. Supreme Court.[62] These stories hardly support the idea that patents are awarded for essentially effortless, and thus non-deserving, acts of invention.

IP Rights and the Most Disadvantaged: Defending IP Inequality

Here is what I have argued so far. Property, including IP, forms a much larger part of the "total system of basic liberties" than Rawls himself believed. Because at least some form of property is essential to the development of a person's unique individual life projects, or overall life plan, it forms part of the system of basic liberties that any fair society must guarantee. Even if the broadest and most sweeping types of property are not required under Rawls's first principle—even if, that is, only a subset of all potential property rights are truly essential for the sake of fairness—IP surely forms part of the subset of property rights that *are* basic and essential. This is due to its more personal nature, and its close relationship to individual personalities and the need for individual autonomy.

To sum up, I have been arguing that IP forms part of the "basic system of liberties" of a well-ordered society. Or, in Rawlsian terms, IP complies with the first principle of fairness. On strictly Rawlsian grounds, if I am right I can stop here. Basic liberties take precedence over egalitarian considerations in Rawls's system of thought. Put differently, there is no need to justify the distributional consequences of a basic liberty if it is truly basic.

I am not going to stop here, however. You may not be convinced by my argument that IP is a basic liberty. And, more importantly, I think a case—a *good* case—can be made that the distributional effects of IP rights are fully defensible on fairness grounds. So for these reasons I am going to traverse Rawls's second principle, and argue that the inequality created by the IP system is a justifiable form of inequality when viewed from the perspective of society's most disadvantaged citizens.

Recall that Rawls's second principle requires that all deviations from equal distribution be justified with reference to the poorest members of society. The "differences" in resource distribution that result from a given social arrangement must be defensible on the grounds that they provide "the greatest benefit to the least advantaged" of any such potential arrangement. As I said earlier, this has been summarized as the principle that society ought to be designed to maximize the minimum support provided to the very poorest members of society—the maximin principle.

HOW DO IP INSTITUTIONS HELP THE
POOREST PEOPLE?

A fair number of the products of IP-intensive industries confer direct benefits on the poorest members of society.[63] IP rights are part of the scaffolding that supports various key industries such as entertainment and consumer electronics. The products of these industries are highly valued by, and bring a great deal of benefit to, the people who make up the least advantaged class, those who are the object of Rawls's second fairness principle. So the extremely high salaries at the top of the entertainment industry, the profits of consumer electronics companies, and the like, may benefit the poorest members of society enough to justify the way these industries are set up—including, of course, the availability of IP rights and the profits that flow from them.

Here is an example of what I mean. Many people in the lower income distributions of the United States are big fans of television shows. According to data from the nonprofit Pew Foundation, 66 percent of people making less than $30,000 per year (roughly the bottom third of the U.S. income distribution) who responded to a survey said that television was "essential" to them; 32 percent said that cable or satellite television was essential.[64] An ethnographic study of relatively poor, elderly people in the United States found that a significant number of elders valued television as an empowering medium that gave them a chance to explore issues and gather information even though they were at a life stage in which their mobility was limited and their informational horizons were restricted.[65] Interestingly, almost twice as many low-income as high-income respondents in a recent survey reported that a flat screen television was essential to them.[66] And extensive research has documented the popularity and impact of U.S. television programming on all levels of society in the developing world.[67] Moreover, because of its penetration and popularity, television has proven to be a highly effective medium for communicating public service messages to the poor.[68]

The data for movies appear a bit more mixed, at first glance. Only 6 percent of moviegoers surveyed in 2007 fell into the lowest income bracket (those making less than $15,000 per year).[69] This would seem to under-represent this group, given that roughly 12.2 percent of U.S. residents belong to families that make less than $15,000.[70] It is important to remember that these are figures for first-run movies only. Virtually all films are eventually released in various formats suitable for viewing on TV, from direct television broadcasts to DVDs to VHS tapes to various on-demand and online viewing options. So the popularity of television ownership may give some evidence that low-income audiences watch a significant number of movies.

In addition, movies have been seen as an important source of entertainment for immigrants and other people in lower income groups.[71] The early twentieth-century social reformer Jane Addams commented at length about the popularity of the "five cent theaters" among Chicago's poor in the 1920s.[72] And among major art forms, films (particularly independent films) are most likely to take a sustained and engaged look at life among society's least advantaged. From *The Grapes of Wrath* to *Slumdog Millionaire,* and especially in a host of lesser-known independent films,[73] a steady stream of feature movies depicts details of life at the lowest rungs of the socio-economic ladder.

A similar story can be told for patented technologies. Many successful inventions have been aimed squarely at saving money for poor consumers. Consider for example the telephone, which permits those who are travel-restricted to stay in touch with family and friends at a reasonable cost, and so is highly valued by less-advantaged people.[74] The widely recognized revolution in agricultural technology beginning in the 1940s has lowered the worldwide cost of food significantly.[75] Air-conditioning is another technology that revolutionized life among the poorest citizens of the United States.[76] The same might be said of more advanced technologies such as cell phones.[77] So too with the introduction of advanced pharmaceutical products. Longevity has increased across the globe as a result of these products, for which patent protection is often considered crucial.[78]

Of course, all these data establish is that many people in lower income brackets enjoy certain entertainment products or have benefited from certain technologies. They suggest on the whole that these industries and innovations have been a net positive in the lives of the poorest people. This is good as far as it goes. But it is another thing entirely to conclude from these anecdotes that IP rights and the industries they enable represent an arrangement that is of "the greatest benefit to the least advantaged." A critic would argue that other social arrangements might produce innovations and entertainments of a similar quality but with less resulting inequality. Salaries and profits might be lower in these industries, resulting in lower prices and thus more money left in the pockets of the poor. I think there is good reason to doubt this critique; one lesson of various experiments with communism and systematic socialism is that it is exceedingly difficult to isolate the good parts of capitalism (innovation, growth) from the less-good (inequality). So while we do not know for sure that there is no better way to get innovations and desirable entertainments to the poorest members of society, we do know that the system as it is produces numerous benefits for these people. That may be as close as we can come at this point to showing that IP-based industries comply with Rawls's second principle.

SUMMARY: IP AND THE DIFFERENCE PRINCIPLE

Treating IP as part of the "basic system of liberties" sidesteps distributional considerations. Basic political rights are prior to distributional concerns in Rawls's theory. So the benefit of fitting a right in under the first principle is that it forms part of the basic structure of rights on which resource distributions are then built. But some readers may not be convinced that IP (or property generally) belongs on the list of rights that form the total system of basic liberties. For this reason, and because I believe there is a solid case for the distributional effects of IP institutions, I have in this section tried to defend the skewed resource distribution produced by IP rights on the grounds that it is of great benefit to the least advantaged. The overall thrust of my argument, therefore, has been this: IP and the institutions these rights support do result in economic inequality, but this inequality provides significant benefits to the least advantaged.

As I said, this is not quite the same as concluding that IP institutions satisfy Rawls's difference principle. To reach this further conclusion, it would have to be shown that the IP system has been arranged such that it produces the minimum inequality necessary while providing benefits to everyone, including the least well off. While it is a tall order to show that the current system is ideal from the point of view of distributive fairness, it is a clear sign of fairness that our overall economic system does include mechanisms designed to mitigate the skewed distributions that result from powerful rewards for the highly successful. In the IP context, two mitigation mechanisms stand out. One, specific to IP, is the structure of the legal entitlements themselves, which includes numerous exceptions and limitations designed to benefit certain classes of IP users and consumers. The other, more general in our system, is the taxation of proceeds from successful economic projects, including IP-based products. I consider both in the sections that follow. To set up this discussion, however, I need to first revisit some earlier material from Chapters 2 and 3. In light of the detailed discussion of individual desert and the appropriateness of private IP rights, how can redistributive policies be justified? That is the question I take up next.

How IP Law Embeds Distributional Concerns in Each IP Right

It is time now to look at distributional concerns at the level of individual IP rights, so that we can place them in the overall context of a fair society. How are distributive fairness issues built into or embodied in the structure of individual IP rights? How are fairness considerations taken into account in the microstructure of IP rules and doctrines? These are the topics we turn to in this section.

Individual Desert and Social Obligation: Core and Periphery

The way I conceive things, every IP right includes two separate components: an inviolable individual contribution, which I call the "deserving core" of the work covered by the right; and a component that can best be thought of as owing its origins to social forces and factors, which I call "the periphery." Because the periphery is attributable to social forces, it represents the part of the work that society itself has a claim on, by way of its redistributive policies.[79] The periphery itself can be subdivided, roughly along the lines of the three redistributive stages I describe later in this chapter.[80] Figure 4.1 shows the core/periphery concept graphically.

Let me say a word about the diagram. The relative proportions of individual and collective in each part of the diagram were chosen with care. I want to depict the idea that the preponderance of each creative work

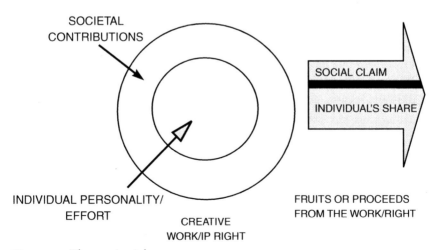

Figure 4.1. The core/periphery concept

comes from the unique talents and contributions of an individual (an argument I make in more detail later). The social contribution is smaller.[81] This of course means that the social claim is smaller and therefore that the maximum degree of redistribution is capped at a moderate level. But although the magnitudes are suggestive, the depiction is nonetheless rough. I do not want to suggest a false sense of precision. This is a conceptual drawing, not a scientific graph or accurate cartographic representation. I might simply have said "not to scale" or something along those lines. The point is not to get hung up on the details of the diagram, the specific dimensions, but to take in the essence of what I am saying.

Generous readers might see that this maneuver of subdividing each property right conceptually addresses two sets of issues that have caused many a scholarly row. One is the question of how deeply redistributive claims may intrude on the legitimate property claims of individuals. The other, of special interest to IP scholars, is whether to locate the source of creative works in the inspiration of individuals or the vast treasure trove of society's collective know-how and knowledge. Both questions are important. But even a generous reader may pause at my insistence that these two issues have to be tackled together, in one sweeping conceptual move. Why not take them on separately? Why not discuss first how broad IP rights should be based on individual and collective contributions to each work, and then, as a separate matter, ask what level of redistribution makes sense where IP rights are involved? Why insist that somehow the answer to the second question must be entwined with the first in some unholy tangle? To put it another way, what good does it do to combine the tug-of-war between individual and social inputs into creative works, together with arguments about individual versus societal claims on resources?

The benefit is this: my approach uses a keystone of modern IP theory to gain leverage on distributional aspects of property rights. Most IP scholars recognize that forces beyond an individual creator go into virtually every creative work, and that therefore IP rights ought to be permeable enough to permit extensive access by third parties as a limitation on the creator's exclusive rights. My approach ties this conventional concern to classic questions of distributional fairness. The basic idea is to use the "social quantum" that goes into each work as a justification for societal/distributional claims on the proceeds or fruits of the work. Social influences go into the making of creative works, so societal claims deserve to be thought of as integral to the rights that cover those works. This is a kind of input-output model: social influence in, societal claim out.

Yet this understanding of IP also captures the importance of the individual contribution. Individual initiative in, ineluctable property claim for the creative person, out. The two-part conception of IP rights preserves the centrality of individual contributions and individual control of assets. The social contribution that enters into the right is mixed and intertwined with the individual initiative required to make a protected work. Likewise, the social claim that emerges when the state grants a property right is attached to an inviolate private right. That private right is the immoveable substrate that supports and carries the social claim. Without the individual right, the social claim does not exist.

To me, this model captures the essence of property, certainly as it manifests in IP. Property rights map individuals to specific assets; they represent individual control, control that is warranted because of an individual contribution. Yet property—classically said to be a claim "good against the world"—cannot exist without the backing of the state. In granting a property right, the state confers a small dollop of its coercive power on an individual. The individual is then permitted to invoke the power of the state against the actions of strangers who have invaded the right. The state is constituted of all its citizens; so the property owner in effect deploys the power of the collective citizenry when enforcing his property right.

There are collective contributions to virtually all works covered by IP. And once an IP right is granted, its enforcement is an inherently collective act. This is especially true for IP. Private enforcement is virtually impossible in most cases, because no owner can police everyone who might employ or copy the owner's works. There is a kind of symmetry then to the origin of creative works and the structure of the rights that protect them. Society helps to shape the works; social institutions are required to effectively protect the works; so by rights society retains a stake in every work. Seen this way, IP law encodes the deeply symbiotic relationship between an individual creator and the larger society he calls home.

There is a lesson here for property in general. I think it shows that distributive justice is internal to the law of property, not an external value. Redistribution is not layered on top of property, like frosting on a cake. It is baked in, part of the essential ingredients, integral to the recipe from the get-go.[82] For me, this is the only way to reconcile the deep justification for both individual property rights and redistributive policies that affect and modify those rights.

IP RIGHTS AND THE VESTING OF
DESERT OVER TIME

Aside from its basic fairness, philosophers have shown an interest in another aspect of desert, this one temporal. Though most discussions of desert are conducted in the past tense,[83] an interesting wrinkle changes this assumption, with salutary effects for the discussion of IP rights.[84] Philosopher

David Schmidtz, writing in this vein, begins with the idea that to deserve something is an ultimate state that requires a number of "inputs" over time. According to Schmidtz:

> Everyone is lucky to some degree, but there is a big difference between being lucky and being merely lucky. The bare fact of being lucky is not what precludes being deserving. Being merely lucky is what precludes being deserving, because to say we are merely lucky is to say we have not supplied inputs (the effort, the excellence) that ground desert claims. To rebut a desert claim in a given case, we need to show that inputs that can ground desert claims . . . are missing in that case.[85]

Schmidtz here supplies a useful vocabulary for the idea that, although life situations are in many ways fortuitous or contingent, it is possible for a well-situated person to supply the inputs that render him deserving at some point. Sometimes hard work or diligence are added to or mixed with a fortuitous starting point. In such a case, the hard work or diligence is an input into the final success, and may as a result form the basis or ground for a claim of moral desert.[86] In Schmidtz's setup, timing is important; some initial endowment such as raw talent may not make us deserving ab initio, but, when a talented person adds inputs over time, such as hard work to develop the initial talent, she may become deserving. In such a case, the person has then done all she could to show worthiness.[87] Desert in this account is not a binary variable, either on or off at a given moment; it vests over time, so to speak, as the initially talented person works to refine and enhance her talent. This understanding of desert means that we cannot speak as if desert were a binary state—either we deserve or we do not. Instead, at any moment in time we may be "coming to deserve," that is, we may be in the act of earning our way into a valid desert-claim.[88] It is interesting in this connection to note that the common linguistic construction that one is "perfecting one's talent" is closely related to the legal concept of perfecting a claim, a property right, or a legal interest. This shared construction highlights the common linguistic heritage of ethics and the law.

The view of desert as vesting over time is precisely the sense in which I believe creative talent is often "deserved." You deserve at least some fruits of your talents if you have proven desert for the talents themselves. And you show this by developing those talents over time, coming to deserve them through your actions. And in an important way, this notion of "earning desert" requires that we be given a chance to show that we deserve our initial endowments.

Desert that vests over time makes for a very interesting dual role for IP rights. An IP right can be one way that society recognizes desert; it can be a "badge of desert" attached to a specific work. But IP rights can be something more as well: they can be the basis of a system that permits people to show that they are deserving in the first place. IP rights can provide a platform on which a career is built, and that career can be a vehicle for working out and fulfilling an initial set of endowments. In this way, IP rights can be more than emblems of desert; they can help bring about desert. They can permit us to come into full ownership of our creative gifts, and thus show that we deserved them in retrospect.[89]

MORE ON CORE AND PERIPHERY

Even if you have come along with me this far, you may well see that a general defense of desert is not enough to establish the basic fairness of IP law, let alone the IP system as currently constituted. You may agree that some people, because of their efforts or actions, deserve some rewards, but you may have serious questions about the nature and level of those rewards. Someone who creates a valuable work covered by IP may indeed deserve something; but if, as is often true, part of the work's value is a result of background material in the culture, or other public domain resources, how large is the desert claim in light of society's contribution to the work? That is, you may question whether desert is a slender reed that supports only a minimalist claim to control creative works, or whether it supports a full-bodied claim to those works and all the fruits and proceeds from them. Finally, you may question how desert claims, in the abstract, should be modified in light of the fact that for property rights—and especially IP rights—rightholders must rely on social resources such as patent and copyright offices and courts if they want their rights to make any palpable, material impact.

Put simply, the issue is this: how do we balance an individual desert claim with two facts: (1) social input at the front end, when a work is created; and (2) the need for social resources at the back end, to help secure and enforce an IP right? What we need is a conceptual model of the creative work/IP right that captures the need to balance these two factors. This brings us back to the core/periphery model introduced at the beginning of this chapter.

The Making of Creative Works. Behind every IP-protected work is a creator or creative team. In addition, every creator is himself the end result of a host of influences and life experiences. There are two basic ways to view the creator at this level. One is as a self-contained and self-motivated entity: a person whose own talents and willpower are part of his unique identity.

Creativity on this view is a question only of natural talent and the self-discipline to develop and direct it. The creator's works are the end product of a highly individualistic exercise of personal training and personal effort.

This viewpoint brings to mind the most widely criticized aspect of Rawls's influential theory of fairness, his ideas on individual desert. Rawls tried heroically to counteract common intuitions about the role of the individual, but for many he was never able to do so. As we have seen, there is a large body of philosophical debate over desert and its place in distributive justice, but I think the ultimate appeal here is often to personal experience. We all know people who have native ability combined with every conceivable "positional" advantage—wealth, education, training in self-discipline, and so on—and yet who do not work hard to develop their talents at all. This is especially true in fields where a talent for creativity must be combined with discipline and a desire to cultivate one's natural endowments. Knowing this, when we see someone, even someone with all these "positional" advantages, who does work hard to develop his or her talent, and who as a result achieves substantial success, it is very difficult not to conclude that such a person deserves a reward. It is crystal clear in such a case that something beyond social factors, or positional advantage, is required for success. This something extra, an act of the individual will and not some preprogrammed response to societal "inputs," entitles people like this to the benefits of what they work to create.

At the same time, most people at some time or another see a picture of famine victims, or see a picture of children suffering from a debilitating (and perhaps treatable) disease, and wonder: is one of these children a potential Mozart, does one possess the expressive capabilities of a Wynton Marsalis, is there a great inventive mind behind that suffering face? We know intuitively at that moment that one's birth situation is a huge factor in determining whether one's talent will ever be realized. Social situation obviously matters a great deal. And for anyone who values each individual person's opportunity to develop fully, to experience real freedom or liberty, this means one thing: we need to compensate for deficient social situations where necessary, to give every person a chance to bring out his full potential.

A comprehensive and balanced theory of IP rights ought to account for both these intuitions: the importance of individual will in expressing talent, and the influence of society in the recognition and development of that talent. In the next section, I describe one important conceptual building block of such a theory, the idea of "the core."

The Anatomy of the Core. The basic idea is this: we can imagine that there is a portion of every creative work that is the product of individual discipline and will. Call this portion "the core." Conceptually speaking, it is the central, ineluctable, and essential component of every intellectual creation—the central nugget. The idea of the core symbolizes the key insight that every creative work involves an act of will on the part of an individual. Even though a person has all sorts of training, and benefits from wonderful situational advantages instilled by friends, family, and society at large, to create something of value that person still has to apply himself to the problem at hand. The idea of the core honors the creative work that goes into any intellectual creation. It represents the component of creative impulse that cannot be attributed to society—the part that is the expression of an individual's own unique combination of talent, discipline, and hard work. Because of this, it represents the part of a creative work that the individual owner deserves to control and benefit from. The core represents a creator's deepest and most defensible claim to a creative work. The individual will creates the core, so the individual deserves to own the core.

By contrast, again at the conceptual level, we can imagine that some of the intrinsic value of a given creative work is attributable to the creator's situational advantages—to "social factors," broadly construed. To keep our ideas straight, we can refer to this as "the periphery." The point is not that we can make some sort of exacting analysis of every creative work, to arrive at some precise measure of the core and the periphery for every discrete creative act. The idea is rather to start with a mental image of the intrinsic value of each work, and then to refine this image by breaking it into two constituent parts. One part, symbolically at the center of the image, represents the core, the product of the act of individual will. The other, surrounding this, represents the periphery, the residue of situational advantage or social factors that gave the creator a leg up in creating the work. Figure 4.1, reproduced earlier in this chapter, shows one way to represent this image, though certainly not the only way.

This is all highly inexact. That much is obvious. It is very difficult to assign certain aspects of creativity to one of the two rough categories I have constructed, (1) individual will and (2) social/positional advantage. To cite just one example (from Rawls): the willingness to undergo training may be the product of socialization. At the same time, the discipline to push that training in new directions may be a uniquely individual trait.[90] Things can become complex indeed if we consider the special case of disadvantage. Because initial disadvantage can spur efforts beyond the norm, in some cases the "advantage" of initial disadvantage might be counted a social contribution to success. Even if we could tease out each individual component that led to a successful creative work, the mix of factors in each case would vary widely across individuals and across individual works. A poor young author might write a first novel that requires Herculean self-sacrifice to complete; later works might benefit from the peer input and privilege that come with literary success. Thus, that author might experience two quite distinct types of situational advantage. The first, grounded in deprivation, is an odd sort of advantage, but not implausible. The second is the more common one: the author accrues more conventional situational advantages over time, by dint of success and the contacts and life experiences that accompany it.

Again, the point is not to look for too much precision. The core/periphery model is not a detailed analytic device. Its purpose is to provide a mental construct that justifies the assignment of a strong claim to the creator of a work. A claim like this goes conventionally by the name of a property right, of course. So what we really have is an explanation of why the creator of an original work deserves a true property right over that work. The concept of the core is thus meant to counter the excessively social orientation of Rawls's theory of (non)desert. From the general idea that creators truly deserve some sort of property right comes the further point that it is appropriate to include well-deserved IP rights among the list of basic liberties that people are entitled to in a just society.[91]

The Periphery: Justifying Redistribution in the Presence of Property Claims. As I have been saying, there is a component of every creative work that is not the product of individual effort and will.[92] The periphery, as I have called it, can be conceptualized as the product of a host of social factors. It represents that part of a work over which society, as opposed to the individual creator, has a legitimate claim. The idea that there is some portion of every work that is not within the core justifies redistributing some of the proceeds from that work.

The concept of the periphery engages directly with Rawlsian rationales for redistribution. If the core represents the scope of legitimate desert claims over a given work, the periphery stands for that part of a work's intrinsic value that is a proper subject for redistribution. Put simply, the core may not be invaded, at least not under normal circumstances. But the periphery is fair game for society's claims.

What kinds of claims may society make on "its" portion of a given creative work? I can answer in terms of three stages of redistribution I identified at the start of this chapter: (1) the initial grant of rights; (2) the deployment stage of works covered by IP rights; and (3) the time period after profits have been earned from sale of IP-covered works.

Stages 1 and 2 are internal to IP law, while stage 3 is external. By internal I mean internal to the structure of IP law, forming part of the rules and doctrines of IP law. The most obvious example of these sorts of IP-internal claims is the stage 1 rule, typical of IP systems, under which the term of protection for an IP right is limited. Property rights last only for a limited time for patents and copyrights, and this limited time can be thought of as a sort of temporal core—a portion of the lifetime of an intellectual work that belongs exclusively to the work's creator. After the right expires, we can think of the right as having passed into the periphery: the creator's desert claim having been satisfied, the public at large now has free access to the work. An example of a stage 2 issue is the set of rules that permit third-party use of and access to a creative work. Fair use in copyright law, experimental use in patent law, and nominative or nontrademark use in trademark law are exemplary.[93]

Distributive Mechanisms in the Details of Actual IP Law

The core/periphery model brings the highly abstract considerations of Rawlsian theory down to the level of the individual IP right. Under the rubric of this model, we have seen that a quest for fairness and balance pervades IP law, and becomes manifest in the basic structure of that law.[94] But whatever its contribution to conceptual clarification, the notion that each work has a core and a periphery is still somewhat removed from the detailed rules and doctrines that make up the workaday substance of IP law.

So now, down to brass tacks. What are the detailed mechanisms through which the distributive impulse is applied in IP law—the operational rules that embody the core/periphery concept I have been discussing? This is the question we address in this section. To make the analysis here more tractable, it will be helpful to describe in more detail the three stages in the life of a typical IP right at which distributional mechanisms come into play.

The first stage is the one that figures in the theories of Locke and Kant, that is, the initial property grant. Limits based on the needs of others, of third parties, form part of the grant; they are built into the fabric of the IP right. The second stage takes place after an IP right is granted and an IP-covered work is made available to the world. Rights that are fair when granted may turn out to harm third parties, for example when circumstances evolve such that the rights end up conferring disproportionate leverage on the rightholder. At this point, various rules and doctrines operate to police the way an IP right is *deployed*—what the IP owner is permitted to do with it. Because these rules protect third parties from the harmful effects of already-issued IP rights, they provide a second opportunity to assess the distributional impacts of IP law. The third stage comes after a right is granted, and after an IP-protected work is deployed. Profits earned from the sale of IP-protected works may be taxed, just like other economic activity. Because taxation is traditionally the most common mechanism of government redistribution in modern economies, it must form part of our analysis as well.

FAIRNESS AND THE INITIAL GRANT OF RIGHTS

Down in the details of the various statutes that embody IP law, all sorts of minor distributional compromises can be found. Many IP rules are so old, and so deeply embedded in the law, that their distributive role is almost invisible. But they are there nonetheless. The best example is the limited terms that attach to most IP rights—patents, copyrights, and publicity rights, to name three important examples. Time limitations effectuate distributional goals by ensuring that IP rights do not last forever, and that the benefits of the creative works they cover will eventually be freely available to the general public. A rich and deep public domain develops over time and benefits everyone, no matter how situated in society.

IP law is rife with all sorts of other distributional bargains, woven into the legal fabric in many different ways. Public television broadcasts and church services receive special exemptions from some copyright rules, for example, as do works for blind people. Likewise surgical procedures are excluded from patent coverage, and the international Olympic symbols receive special protection under trademark law. These technical details, which largely occupy the time and efforts of many practitioners of IP law, are the repository of all manner of intricate judgments about IP rights, about the scope and reach and impact of those rights. They show that distributional issues are addressed not just at the structural level, where the existence and basic framework of IP law is set, but at each progressively lower level of IP law as well. The fabric of IP law is shot through with distributional policies, of all levels of granularity.

In Chapter 6, on the proportionality principle in IP law, I offer a general principle that pulls together a large number of distribution-oriented rules scattered throughout IP law. There I describe the idea of proportional reward as one of the essential conceptual building blocks of IP law. Proportionality carries an inherent distributional element: each creator should obtain rights commensurate with and proportional to the value of his contribution. Proportionality has a sort of secret twin, however. Because rights are limited to a proportional reward, this leaves the residue for others, for the public in general. A work whose author is entitled to modest rights leaves much for others when it is released to the public. There is a distinct and identifiable distributional component here. Users of a work receive as much of its benefit as exceeds the author's proportional reward. Though there are some loose ends that must be accounted for, the way I see things, the proportionality principle performs much of the distributive function of IP law that others have identified.

THE DEPLOYMENT STAGE: FAIRNESS IN THE POSTGRANT ENVIRONMENT

The second stage in the life of an IP right is what I call the deployment stage, after the right has been granted. The owner of a work protected by an IP right will typically sell copies of the work outright or embody instances of the work in some larger product, by for example including a patented component in a complex, multicomponent commercial product. Distributional questions often arise at the deployment stage, and various IP rules and doctrines have evolved to answer them. Indeed, some of the most difficult problems in the IP field arise when a right that has been legitimately granted is deployed in a context in which it confers far greater power than was contemplated at the time the right was granted.

It is at this stage that the proportionality principle does some of its most important work. In Chapter 6, I consider in detail several representative cases along these lines.[95] Among them are copyrights for very short software codes that prevent unauthorized access to computer game console systems, such as the Xbox. Several cases have held that although these codes are fully copyrightable, they may be reverse-engineered by third parties seeking to gain access to a game console system. In effect, these rulings depend on the notion that enforcing complete exclusivity in these short codes would give disproportionate leverage to game console makers. The short snippets of code are the key to a large market; so to prevent this code from effectively locking others out of the market, the courts refuse to enforce the copyright in the code. (Technically, they find that copying the codes is fair use.)

Another example concerns patents. Some patentees have learned to acquire patents over potentially lucrative technologies, and then play a waiting game. The idea is to hold the patents while other companies invest in developing a technology, and then when the market is mature and manufacturers have incurred significant sunk costs, spring the trap by asserting the patents. The Supreme Court has caught on to this strategy. To prevent patent holders from exerting disproportionate leverage, the Court gives lower courts the discretion to deny injunctions in these cases. This effectively lowers the economic returns from the strategy of springing the trap, thereby reestablishing the rough initial value of the patents in question.

In cases such as this, courts constrain the deployment of IP rights to prevent those rights from exerting disproportionate leverage in a specific commercial context. From our perspective, what is important is that this impulse has its source in distributional concerns. Courts police how an IP right operates out in the world, after the right has been granted, to ensure that economic returns from the right do not become excessive in relation to the original contribution it represents. Courts protect, in other words, against overreward in certain circumstances. In so doing, they are striving to maintain the distributional balance embodied in IP rights at the time of grant.

TAXATION OF IP-PROTECTED WORKS

Beyond these internal rules, other aspects of the IP system represent the portion of a work's value that is subject to the claims of society at large. The most obvious example is taxation, a classic stage 3 distributional regime. Taxation is of course external to IP law. But in principle, some share of the proceeds from creative works may be taxed without any invasion of the creator's core ownership right. One aspect of the periphery, in other words, is the social claim—in the form of taxes—on the proceeds that flow from an IP-protected work.

This part of the model runs head-on into some objections that originate with libertarians such as Robert Nozick, who vigorously oppose redistributive taxation. Nozick wrote that if resources are (1) fairly acquired at the outset of a society's existence, and then (2) transferred and accumulated in a series of voluntary transactions, society and its political institutions have no business interfering with the subsequent distribution of resources.[96] Fraud, crime, and nonvoluntary transfers may be handled under the principles of corrective justice, but beyond this, the state has no authority to redistribute assets that have been fairly acquired. Nozick's libertarian theory has been attacked from a number of directions,[97] but here I will limit myself to one obvious point. IP rights depend heavily on the functioning of the state, a collective entity.[98] As I emphasize throughout this book, IP rights are virtually impossible to enforce without the assistance of a state apparatus. It only makes sense, then, that the proceeds from these rights may be taxed to address the needs of the state's citizens. These needs begin with the courts and justice system directly related to IP enforcement. But they also extend, I would argue, to much that goes beyond IP enforcement. The background culture out of which new works arise, educational institutions that train creators and their audiences, even the keeping of civil order necessary to maintain a class of highly specialized creators—all these are relevant collective needs. And taxes on the proceeds from IP-protected works can and should be used to help pay for them.[99]

Two quick points about taxation. The idea that the state has broad power to tax property owners, though not (in the United States particularly) the right to invade ownership per se, is obviously not unique to IP law; it is a feature of all forms of property.[100] Second, at some point, tax rates climb so high that, in principle anyway, the state may be seen to overstep the proper bounds of its authority.[101] In terms of the core/periphery concept I am describing here, this would mean that the tax rate has become so high that the state is in effect claiming part of the value of a work that it has no legitimate claim to. That would be to invade the core, which it may not do.[102]

From Rawls to Rowling: A Case Study in Distributive Justice and IP Rights

Many of the themes I have been talking about are well illustrated by the story of J. K. Rowling. Though in some ways her career is exceptional, it nonetheless provides an excellent case study in issues of distributive justice and IP rights.

Ms. Rowling came from a middle-class family of professionals. Her mother was an avid reader who imparted by example a deep love of books and stories. Rowling attended public (in the U.S. sense, that is, nonprivate) primary and secondary schools, and then the public Bristol University. In an interview she credited one inspirational English teacher in particular as a key influence.

Rowling wrote the first book in her famous seven-book Harry Potter series shortly after a divorce, while she was caring for a new baby on her own. She received state assistance during this period, in the form of general unemployment insurance and then a grant from a public arts council.

The book, as we all know, was a great success. Jo Rowling, as she was known, has now become the rarest of writers, a billionaire on the strength of her own creative efforts. Having achieved this staggering success, she now pays millions of pounds annually in taxes to the British government—giving, in effect, to people who are today where she was only a few decades ago.

The story of J. K. Rowling captures several points I have made in this chapter. Rowling has often told the tale of her heroic struggle to get the first book down on paper. She would walk her baby in a stroller until it was nap time, then rush to a café where she could get some good coffee and write a few pages of the manuscript. Rowling was unemployed, depressed, and often anxious about her future, but she felt a strong calling to write down the story that had first flashed into her mind on a long train ride several years before.[103] In Rowling's telling, the conventional steps required to get the book published—finding an agent, then a publisher, then editing and finalizing—are far less compelling than the epic struggle to get her well-formed characters and plot ideas into written form.

Despite her difficulties, Rowling had many advantages that others do not. She was from a stable, middle-class family; had received a good basic education; had attended a solid public university; and had the support of family and friends during her early days as a single parent. Even so, it undoubtedly took a great deal of personal initiative to finish that first book. Her friends were amazed at her persistence and commitment. Looking back, she describes the drive required to push through her difficulties and complete that first book. The simple fact is that during this trying time, none of Rowling's "situational advantages" were sufficient to ensure that the book would be written. She was born with innate talent, to be sure. And her parents, teachers, neighbors, friends, and fellow citizens may all have had a hand in shaping and helping her. But she had to write the book herself. It could not spring forth from her natural talent. Nor could the people who shaped her write it for her, nor could "society." So it is, I think, with almost every worthwhile product of the imagination. There comes a time when hard work and drive are necessary to get the thing done, and that is all there is to it.

To sum up, there is a part of the Potter books that comes from J. K. Rowling as an act of individual will and commitment. This is the part I call the core. Speaking conceptually, we can imagine another part, which represents the residue of all Rowling's family influences, training, and other situational advantages. To keep things straight, I have called this the periphery of the works. Contrary to Rawls, and in league with some of his critics, I contend that Rowling deserves to own and control the core of her Potter books. Her claim to this aspect of her work is in my view very deep: she has really earned it, she really deserves to own it—she has a *right* to it, with all that implies. This right is something more than the sort of claim that follows from a system of utility-maximizing incentives. Even if it were proven beyond question that she would have produced one or more of her books for less money than she has received, or in exchange for a weaker copyright, she would still retain this core right. And because of this, the state may not claim so much of her works, or so much of the proceeds that flow from them, that it effectively eviscerates this core.

The metaphor of the core extends beyond the idea of a zone that may not be intruded upon. It also implies a counterpart, something lying outside the core that is still a part of the creative work. This zone I have called the periphery. In the case of the Harry Potter books, the periphery is that portion of the books that represents all of society's investment in and support for the author J. K. Rowling—all her influences, all her situational advantages. As I have said, it is impossible to quantify this area, or to contrast it in an arithmetically meaningful way with the core. All that is required is that we understand that there is, conceptually speaking, such a zone, outside the core but still a part of the creative work.

It is this idea of the periphery that justifies Britain's Inland Revenue Service—the British IRS—in taking a chunk of the proceeds from the Harry Potter franchise and distributing it to others. The claims of society, represented by the fairly assessed tax on Rowling's works, can justly be said to reach the periphery of Rowling's works, because this is the part that embodies society's contribution to those works in the first place. British society helped shape and nurture J. K. Rowling, so that society has a claim on a portion of her works. Society, loosely speaking, has earned this claim and deserves to exercise it in the form of taxation on Rowling's works. This tax is the fair and just counterpart to the strong claim she has to the core of those works. Some of Rowling's own tax payments can be thought of as supporting other underemployed single parents, struggling to make a living (maybe even some as writers). Thus is the circle closed: out of the proceeds of her highly personal works, society claims its share, thus supporting others who are in need as she was.

Conclusion

At the beginning of this chapter I said that I was going to talk mainly about distributive justice as it is understood by legal philosophers, and that is what I have tried to do. Throughout, what I have been after is a precious commodity in the precincts of these discussions: balance. When it comes to property and distributive justice, most theory is concentrated at the extremes. Typically, philosophers whose primary concern is distributive justice tend to tolerate property rights, rather than embrace them. It is easy to see why. Individual control over individual assets will often interfere with a vision that requires moving resources from person A to person B. Especially if equal distribution of resources is the goal—as it was at least sometimes for John Rawls, the most well-known theorist of distributive justice—then property rights must clearly be de-emphasized. On the other hand, supporters of property rights typically show at best tepid appreciation for redistribution. Social claims, enforced by a collectivist state, intrude into the zone of private control that is the driving force behind private property. The typical advocate of property rights therefore wants to keep to a minimum the redistribution of resources via government decree. A more atypical view, the libertarian perspective, may show up less in the conversation but is vociferously expressed; it is usually more or less absolute—individual claims are the only legitimate ones, and *all* redistribution is theft.

As I said, I have aimed here for balance. I started with the comprehensive distributive justice theory of John Rawls, defending IP rights under both of Rawls's dual principles of fairness. The arguments ran like this:

1. IP is a primary right that may not be invaded by fairness considerations: it forms part of the "total system of basic liberties"; and
2. IP benefits the worst off to such an extent that its special rewards have a net positive distributional effect, in Rawlsian terms. Put simply, the poor benefit so much from things covered by IP rights that the products covered by those rights more than make up for the excess distributional shares that wind up in the hands of rightowners.

Beyond Rawls's detailed system, however, there is another sense in which distributive issues have entered the conversation about IP rights. In this chapter I also addressed these IP-specific rules and doctrine, demonstrating how this body of law systematically embodies distributional concerns. In all three stages in the life of an IP right, I found a lively distributional impulse and showed how it operated. I have also tried to emphasize that though Rawls provides the basic structure for discussions of social justice, in many ways (e.g., an emphasis on equality of opportunities rather than material resources, and a greater appreciation of the role of desert) our understanding of these issues has moved well beyond his original conception.

PART TWO

PRINCIPLES

CHAPTER FIVE

Midlevel Principles of IP Law

I START THIS CHAPTER by describing "midlevel principles" in legal theory—concepts that run through and tie together disparate doctrines and practices, and that provide a common policy vocabulary that bridges different foundational viewpoints such as Kantian and utilitarian. I then describe what I see as the four primary midlevel principles in IP law: *non-removal* (that is, the public domain); *proportionality; efficiency;* and *dignity.* The remainder of the chapter is devoted to a brief explanation of each of these principles, with some supporting examples. Chapter 6 is devoted to an extensive discussion of one principle, proportionality.

What Are Midlevel Principles?

Midlevel principles are basic concepts that tie together a number of discrete and detailed doctrines, rules, and practices in a particular legal field. In tort law, for example, legal doctrines such as negligence and strict liability, together with practices such as accident insurance, constitute the gritty detail of the field. What ties these disparate details together, according to the legal philosopher Jules Coleman, is the principle of "corrective justice": the ideal of putting an injured person back where he or she was prior to a harmful event.[1] According to Coleman,

> I prefer to begin . . . in the middle, by asking what principles, if any, are embodied in the legal practices we are presently engaged in. . . . We do not begin

with any presupposition about the moral status of the principles we will find. Rather, we simply seek to identify the normatively significant elements of the practices and to explain them as embodiments of principle.[2]

Identifying midlevel principles is an inductive exercise: one looks for the common conceptual threads in a field and treats them as instances or manifestations of a more complete principle.[3] The idea is to start with ground-level practices and abstract "upward," toward a unifying principle that explains and rationalizes the practices.

If detailed doctrines and practices come first, and midlevel principles arise from or are embodied in them, what lies beyond those principles; what is at the top of this hierarchy? For Coleman (and others), the answer is a set of "upper-level" principles, which correspond roughly to deep or foundational ethical values. In Coleman's words, "The principle of corrective justice . . . occupies a mid-level between the practices of tort law and an upper-level principle of fairness in allocating the costs of life's misfortunes."[4]

In this book so far, we have of course already seen a good deal of the "upper-level principles" Coleman speaks of. Chapters 2 and 3 covered fairness in ownership, through the vehicles of Locke's and Kant's theories of property. Chapter 4 was dedicated directly to fairness, to distributive justice as it applies to IP law. As I said in the Introduction, I believe in the independence of these foundational normative principles from the operational details of the field, as well as from the midlevel principles that arise from and are shaped by those details. By "independence" I mean that there are a number of foundational normative commitments that may serve equally well to anchor the principles and practices of IP law. I offered the ones I did, in Chapters 2 through 4, because those are the ones I believe best justify the structure of IP law. But other foundations might serve as well. As I put it earlier, in my view there is "room at the bottom," at the foundational level of the field, for various justificatory principles, including perhaps utilitarianism and various alternative ethical theories.[5]

Midlevel principles engage foundational values in a number of ways, but they do not depend on any particular set of values for their validity. They spring from doctrine and detail, from the grain of actual practice. It is at the level of midlevel principles, therefore, that much normative debate in the IP field takes place. From a certain point of view, in fact, this is their role exactly: they enable normative debate—debate above the detailed doctrinal level—without requiring deep agreement about ultimate normative commitments. Because of this, they are the common currency of most debate over IP policy. They are the equivalent in the IP world of the shared "public values" that permit normative political debate in a pluralistic society. Individual citizens may differ radically in their ultimate ethical values (think fundamentalist Christian, committed atheist, and devout ·Orthodox Jew) yet agree enough on certain basic values to share a "public space" permitting deliberation over policy issues, such as freedom of religious worship or freedom of speech. In the same way scholars and practitioners with very different ultimate convictions may come together to debate appropriate IP policy. Midlevel principles supply the common tongue for this debate.

I will put the idea in the form of a story: a Kantian, a utilitarian, and a skeptical positivist (who believes IP law has no ethical foundation at all) walk into a bar, the Midelevel Bar and Grille. The Kantian grumbles, knowing he will not be able to order his favorite, an obscure German heffeweitzen. The utilitarian joins in, and bemoans the absence of a hand crafted English Stout on the beer menu. Even the skeptical positivist commiserates, because he too cannot have his first choice (a Pabst Blue Ribbon). A bit reluctantly, they order the standard Budweiser—the only beer on the menu. The bartender takes their order, and says, "You ought to be grateful you can get anything at all. Don't you know this is the only bar in town that will serve all three of you together?" They continue the conversation, not without more grumbling, deep into the night.

Stories aside (where they undoubtedly belong), the idea of midlevel principles may well be familiar. My version of it derives, as many will recognize, from John Rawls's conception of pluralism in a modern state.[6] For Rawls, "public reason" plays much the same role as midlevel principles do in my approach to IP. He calls the shared deliberative space created by public reason an "overlapping consensus," and this is very much in the spirit of what I am describing in this chapter. Midlevel principles create an overlapping consensus among people with differing beliefs about the ultimate normative foundations of IP law. These principles provide a common conceptual vocabulary for conducting policy debates. They bracket, and in a sense transcend, disagreements about ultimate issues, while tying together disparate strands of doctrine and practice.[7]

Where Do Midlevel Principles Come From?
Nonremoval/Public Domain as a Case Study

To illustrate how these principles can be identified out of a welter of doctrines and rules, let me start with the example of nonremoval.[8] After describing the various sources for this principle, I briefly review how it differs from the deeper normative theories I described in Chapters 2 through 4. The general idea is to focus in on the "mid-ness" of a midlevel principle: to show how such a principle can be identified out of a welter of ground-level rules, doctrines, and practices, and to show its simultaneous consistency with and independence from various foundational theories (Lockean, Kantian, distributive justice, and so on).

Not all information can be protected with IP rights. For example, in copyright law historical and other factual information cannot be copyrighted.[9] So too for patents: no one can obtain exclusive rights over basic mathematical or scientific formulas or laws of nature (such as Newton's law of gravitation, or Boyle's laws relating to pressure and volume of gases). And in trademark law, merchants cannot appropriate widely used words as brand names. In each case, the information in question is seen as inherently public, as being beyond the bounds of individual appropriation. It helps form the stock of common knowledge that all are free to draw on and no one may privately own.

Other legal rules limit the duration of IP rights.[10] At the end of the statutory term of protection, or earlier if protection is not renewed, every IP right lapses. At that moment, the work becomes freely available to everyone in perpetuity. Thus, in a strict sense, appropriation under IP law is always a temporary phenomenon. All works, even those subject to stringent protection, are inchoately public. It is only a matter of time until all can use them. So although a creative work can be removed from free public availability for a limited time via IP protection, once the right lapses it can never again be removed from circulation. In IP, property is temporary; free availability, permanent.

There is also an implicit zone of expansion surrounding all freely available works. Nothing in this zone can be privately appropriated. The expansion zone is different for different types of IP. In copyright law, a work must be "original" to secure protection. The originality requirement protects against someone who wants to reclaim something in the public domain—an already-published book or movie.[11] It further protects against private appropriation of broad plot elements or standard motifs that have come into common usage—so-called *scenes a faire*.[12] These standard "building blocks" are as much a part of the public domain as are specific unprotected works such as out-of-copyright books or never-copyrighted films.[13]

Patent law has even more elaborate protections against appropriating anything that is already available in "the prior art." To begin, an invention must be "novel" to be patentable. This highly technical doctrine protects against the granting of patents for anything that was previously available in any publicly accessible form. This rule has a highly technical, almost scholastic, feel; for example, in one case a single copy of a student thesis in a German university library spelled the death of a patent for an industrial researcher in the United States.[14] Likewise, an article in a Russian metallurgy journal rendered unpatentable a useful industrial alloy developed by an American research team.[15] These are extreme examples, but they are by no means unusual in the annals of patent law. The rules in that field are so solicitous of preserving access to the prior art that they can seem almost absurd. There is no inquiry into in the practical accessibility of the prior art; once it is public, even marginally, and only in one obscure place or one obscure form, the game is over—no patent. Period.

As with copyright, patent law too protects a "zone of expansion" around what is already available. This takes the form, primarily, of the famously cryptic "nonobviousness" requirement. Under this rule no one gets a patent on something that is obvious in light of the prior art. The fear of encroaching on what is already available extends, through this doctrine, to all those inchoately available things that emanate easily and predictably from what is at any moment actually available. Even if an inventor does something new, something "novel" in patent parlance, this is not enough. It must be significantly new, nontrivially new. The insignificant, the trivial—these are already available to all, even though they have not yet been brought into being.

There are similar rules in trademark law, and even trade secrets. In each case, in each area of IP, the central doctrinal thrust is the same: to prevent appropriation of that which is already possessed by people working in a field. And these doctrines are applied and enforced by other institutions in the IP landscape—by the patent, trademark, and copyright offices, and by the courts. They form a set of behaviors or practices that run throughout the definition and application of this entire body of law.

LOCATING PRINCIPLES BY GENERALIZING FROM PRACTICE

These rules from IP law can help us clarify Jules Coleman's idea of midlevel principles. For Coleman, the task at the conceptual level is to see each rule, each practice, as the embodiment of a broader principle. We are to understand that the principle is latent in the detailed rules; the rules are not self-consciously deduced from the principle a fortiori. The job of the conceptual analyst is to induce the principle from the details of the specific rules and practices.

The IP rules I have been describing make up the principle of nonremoval from the public domain. This principle ties together and explains each of these rules in terms of a broader conception. However, the various doctrines I described were not deduced from some Olympian starting point; no one said, before any actual IP protection was ever granted, "there shalt be a public domain." Instead, each doctrine grew organically from a specific set of problems, and each developed and evolved over time in response to new conditions. My own detailed studies of the nonobviousness doctrine bear this out, and there are parallel studies for each of the doctrines I described.[16]

What is the point of this exercise—where is the payoff? The answer for me has two parts. First, constructing a midlevel principle permits a more sophisticated understanding of the rules, in particular the way they work together, the interactions between them. This is a distinctive contribution of contemporary property theory; we are mad to organize, categorize, and identify principles and themes that run through the fabric of specific property doctrines, and I believe the result is a much clearer understanding of the conceptual structure of property law. This has all sorts of benefits, beginning (but not ending) with greater clarity and precision in our thinking.

Second, discourse at the level of midlevel principles provides all these advantages without the need for agreement on normative foundations. We can see this again with the IP doctrines I described. It is quite possible for someone with Kantian intuitions or Lockean commitments or a strong utilitarian grounding to discuss the public domain in IP law. The very idea of nonremoval as a basic principle invites and channels this sort of discussion. And the theme of nonremoval allows the discussion to take place at a high level, at the level of policy, and not just at the level of individual cases, controversies, or doctrines. The conversation is more productive—and a lot more civil!—than it would be if participants tried to conduct it at the ultimate normative level.

Take the example of originality in copyright law. Some scholars see this as a utilitarian or at least consequentialist rule, designed to maximize expression or even overall welfare.[17] In this view it is all about costs and benefits. The cost of acquiring information that already exists is presumably lower than the cost of recreating it. This is certainly true as a general rule. So a property system, to be efficient, must prohibit appropriation of that which is already known. This ensures that society will not overpay for information.

A committed Lockean might say that the modicum of originality required to establish copyright is a good proxy for effort or labor, and that without evidence of some original contribution there is no solid grounding for a property right.[18] A Kantian might argue that even minor evidence of the will projecting itself onto an object or thing ought to qualify a resulting work for copyright protection.

COMMON GROUND

Principles such as nonremoval emerge from the analysis of a number of doctrines and rules. They are therefore theoretical or policy-oriented; yet because they are not rooted in any specific normative framework, they avoid what might well be a fruitless debate if conducted at that level. I describe some of the reasons for this in the Introduction to this book. For utilitarian justifications, the data are just not there.[19] For some, including IP scholar David McGowan, the upshot is clear: we must stop pretending to argue on instrumental grounds, in favor of a more straightforward debate along explicitly ethical lines.[20] I think this proposal is overly optimistic regarding the chances for agreement in such debates. With Rawls, I am willing to concede that ultimate ethical commitments may be so divergent that they obviate all likely grounds of agreement. The best we can hope for in such a situation is a shared normative language, which can be used to conduct debate on a nonfoundational level. Again, midlevel principles serve just this purpose.

When the IP rules I discussed are thought of in a unified way, they define something that courts and scholars have come to call "the public domain."[21] This domain, this conceptual space, is the end product of the nonremoval principle. Because it is the product of many disparate doctrines, and was not itself launched as a unitary concept, we should not be surprised to see a great diversity in conceptions of it. For example, the IP scholar Pamela Samuelson counts no fewer than thirteen distinct "public domains." These differing conceptions diverge primarily with respect to the sources of the public domain that they identify: (1) information that cannot, by its nature, ever be protected by an IP right; and (2) information that could have been protected but was not; could yet be but is not protected; or was but is no longer protected.

Another perspective, associated with IP scholar David Lange, challenges what he sees as the prevailing presumption that the public domain represents a sort of residual afterthought of the IP world—that which is left over after the behemoth of IP rights has rolled through, granting protection as it goes.[22] Lange says that this conventional way of thinking about IP rights places property in the foreground, even when the topic turns to the public domain. This follows from a definition of the public domain as that part of the IP landscape characterized by the absence of IP protection. Thinking of the public domain as a "hole in property space" still centers the conversation on property. Lange wants to take the public domain out of this background, residual state and place it squarely in the foreground.[23] This means conceiving of public domain status as a positive attribute, and an affirmative right, rather than that part of the IP landscape defined by the absence of property.

I agree with some of what Lange says, particularly about the need to recognize an affirmative right for groups of creators who work collectively to contribute value on top of a preexisting proprietary work.[24] At the same time, some of this literature elevates the concept of the public domain to too high a status; the principle of nonremoval moves so far into the foreground that it obscures the fundamental purpose of granting IP rights in the first place.[25]

Notice something about the disagreement between Lange and me. Because it is conducted in the typical language of IP scholarship, we argue about how prominent the public domain should be in our thinking, and about the ideal scope and dimensions of the public domain. If it were conducted in the IP scholarly literature, the argument would probably have several other features. First, we would each trade empirical claims, for example about whether the public domain is shrinking or growing in response to new technologies of content distribution and new legal developments. These we would mix with nonempirical claims, or at least overtones: I might emphasize the importance of incentives for creators; Lange, the importance of a well-stocked public domain for free and full opportunities for expression. We would both cite cases and other legal commentary to show support for our positions. The same style of debate would prevail if a particular controversy were at issue or if we were just arguing at a more general level. If a specific case were at hand, the court deciding the case might well engage some of the same themes as the scholarly debate; it might even cite some scholarship in its opinion. If so, it would likely speak in terms of the well-worn balancing metaphor. In the end, one side or other of the balance would have to win out, and the case would be decided. It would then feed in immediately to the scholarly discussion, which would digest, comment on, and critique the decision. A legislature might get involved at this stage too, though this is less common. In any case, the normal course of IP scholarship and jurisprudence marches on in just this fashion.

My point here is to notice how the day-to-day business of IP law and policy are served by midlevel principles such as the idea of nonremoval from the public domain. The public domain—as a concept—permits scholars such as Lange and me, and courts too, to engage important policy issues without having to agree on fundamental precepts. I have no idea what are the fundamental normative commitments of David Lange, or of any of a number of other scholars who have influenced the public domain conversation. Some may be utilitarians, others devoted Kantians; others may believe that IP law is nothing but glorified power politics—a sort of deep-rooted Hobbesian-materialist worldview. The point is, for purposes of this debate, the diversity of ultimate commitments is irrelevant. IP scholars, lawyers, and judges can engage one another on important policy issues surrounding the public domain without needing agreement at this level.

The Pragmatism of Principles

Midlevel principles bridge conflicting worldviews, which makes them extremely useful. But the way they do this has an additional benefit as well. By moving attention from the level of ultimate normative commitments to a more functional, pragmatic level, they can, and should more often, call attention to practical features of the IP system that are easily ignored in arguments over foundational theories. These practical issues are crucial to the operation of the IP system. What is more, they have the potential to enliven and deepen the understanding of theoretical issues as well.

We have an excellent example of this in the context of the public domain: the issue of enforcement costs. Specifically, practical questions of how many rights are actually enforced may influence our understanding of the effective size and scope of the public domain, and hence inform our views on what policies to adopt. Looking at the practicalities of enforcement may affect some of our deep theoretical commitments.

There are all sorts of IP rights, and they are issued to all sorts of owners operating in all sorts of environments. And since enforcement contexts differ radically, it is impossible to tell a single, unified story about the practicalities of enforcement. Thus, to illustrate the effect of pragmatic considerations on IP policymaking, we will have to single out one particular instance: digital content.

By this I mean creative works of all kinds (text, images, music, video) that are distributed in digital form, usually online, over the World Wide Web. IP scholars have worried about the shrinking public domain in the online world—a result, they say, of stronger copyrights and changing business models enabled by more effective technological protection. I have much to say about the creators of digital content and critiques of IP policy in this area in Chapter 8. Here I want to limit myself to one point, pertinent to midlevel principles: enforcement costs in the digital domain.

My basic argument is that once enforcement costs are taken into account, much of the scholarship on IP protection for digital content begins to look overblown, if not downright alarmist.[26] The larger point, of course, is that one need not buy into any particular foundational theory to understand my argument or even to agree with me. I can conduct the conversation at the middle level, using the vocabulary of IP policy to bridge and transcend different fundamental conceptions of IP law.

I can illustrate my argument with two diagrams, as shown in Figure 5.1. Each one is a spatial representation of various legal rights as they apply to digital content. The first one, shown at the top of Figure 5.1, shows the legal situation as it existed roughly in the 1980s and early 1990s—the pre-Internet regime. The shaded areas show the different sets of rights that apply in this space. Notice that users have some affirmative rights (they are represented by the shaded area to the left); creators have some rights; and because it is costly to enforce rights, some of those creators' rights are left "on the table" for others to use. Those rights make up the "waiver space" in the diagram. This space represents the group of creative works that are covered by IP rights in a legal sense, but that are for practical purposes not enforced by right owners.[27]

Now look at the diagram at the bottom of Figure 5.1. This shows the rights space after the rise of the World Wide Web in the mid to late 1990s. Notice two things. First, the scope of legally protected works has expanded significantly. This is due to legal changes, including the adoption of the Digital Millennium Copyright Act in 1998, the broadening of musical copyrights to cover short digital sound snippets ("samples"), and a host of other developments (many discussed in Chapter 8). Second, notice the radical increase in the scope of theoretically protected works that are not actually enforced—the large expansion of the "waiver space." We see evidence of this in all sorts of free, online content—everything from "effectively free" material on fan websites, news websites, and the like, to free music websites, free video (on YouTube and many other websites), free samples to promote interest in for-pay content, and so forth. In all sorts of forms, the expanded waiver space is a very prominent feature of the digital environment today.

Let me be clear about what I am and am not saying about midlevel principles with this example. I am not saying that enforcement costs have no interesting theoretical implications, or that they do not support various ultimate normative commitments. In fact the real-world enforcement environment is a very rich source of insights for foundational theories of all sorts. What I am saying is that the practical realities of enforcement costs are especially important for discussions centered on midlevel principles. Information about enforcement costs bears heavily on the operation of IP policies, and on the real-world impact of doctrines and institutional practices. These are the sorts of policy discussions that are often conducted under the rubric of midlevel principles—the sorts of pragmatic, fact-intensive issues that occupy much of the bread and butter of IP policy argumentation. Tentative and conditional agreement on policy solutions depends on a common language of principles that both transcends the lowest-level details of discourse (individual cases, doctrines, and the like) but falls short of deep-seated foundational issues such as the nature of IP rights and their ultimate justification. Pragmatic facts about the operation of the system, such as information about enforcement costs, thus fit especially well into policy debate at this level.

TRADITIONAL RIGHTS CONFIGURATION

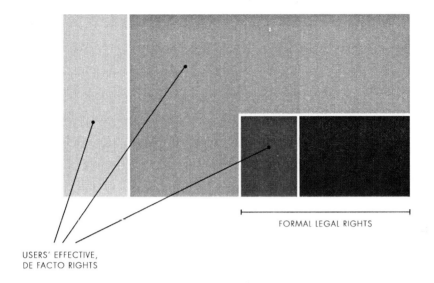

FORMAL LEGAL RIGHTS

USERS' EFFECTIVE,
DE FACTO RIGHTS

DIGITAL ERA RIGHTS CONFIGURATION

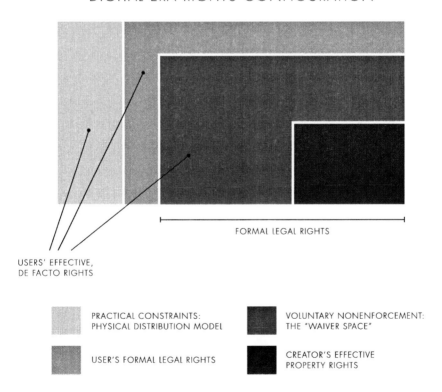

FORMAL LEGAL RIGHTS

USERS' EFFECTIVE,
DE FACTO RIGHTS

PRACTICAL CONSTRAINTS:
PHYSICAL DISTRIBUTION MODEL

VOLUNTARY NONENFORCEMENT:
THE "WAIVER SPACE"

USER'S FORMAL LEGAL RIGHTS

CREATOR'S EFFECTIVE
PROPERTY RIGHTS

Figure 5.1. Traditional rights and digital-era rights

The Midlevel Principles of IP Law

So far in this chapter I have introduced the idea of midlevel principles and given a detailed case study of one—nonremoval from the public domain. Let me now list the other midlevel principles I see at work in IP law. In addition to (1) nonremoval, they are: (2) proportionality, (3) efficiency, and (4) dignity.

I take each in turn, describing the principle itself and giving examples from the main areas of IP law. I cannot here give anything like a full treatment for each one. Instead, I offer the basic idea, followed by some examples, in the hope that this will give the flavor of each.

Proportionality

The size or scope of an IP right ought to be proportional to the value or significance of the work covered by the right. This is the proportionality principle. It is important and complex enough that I devote all of Chapter 6 to explaining and applying it. So for now, I give just a brief sketch and a short discussion of how it relates to the other midlevel principles.

I am not the first to see the importance of proportional reward in IP law.[28] And as we saw in earlier chapters, there is firm support for the concept in both Locke and Kant.

In past work, I have called attention to occasions when legal entitlements give a party "excessive" or "disproportionate" leverage—power beyond what that party rightfully deserves in a certain situation. For example, I opposed patents for small snippets of genes, a hot issue in the 1990s when sequencing technology first made these viable. I also thought that some patent owners were taking advantage of complex technological landscapes and the large-scale investments of technology companies in a way that necessitated the denial of permanent injunctions when those patents were infringed—a serious inroad on one of the classic appurtenances of a property right. I have also seen in copyright law that at times, courts are reluctant to permit a "small" right to be used as strategic leverage to control a large market.

Indeed, this same basic concept informs many doctrinally distinct areas of IP law. A patent claim must be commensurate with what the patent specification teaches; failure to adhere to this basic symmetry results in an invalid patent. Patent scope is also traditionally adjusted to take account of the significance or importance of the invention at issue through such avenues as the "pioneer patent" rule under the doctrine of equivalence.

As interesting as the various doctrinal issues were (at least to a student of the IP system, like me), I felt they raised a deeper problem. They threatened to confer more economic power on their holders than I thought they deserved. Only recently has it become clear to me that a common principle runs through these examples: the principle of disproportionate reward. The basic idea is very simple. Beyond the statutory requirements for the grant of an IPR, or, to put it better, embedded in these requirements, is a transcendent principle that ties together all manner of disparate situations. To state it simply, an IPR must not confer on its holder leverage or power that is grossly disproportionate to what is deserved in the situation. If an IPR would effectively confer power or control over a much larger market than is actually deserved in light of the work covered by the IP right, that right must be limited or annulled in some way.

Of course, it is easy to use broad strokes in describing disproportionate leverage and the proper deserts of an IP owner. It is much harder to fill in the corners and details of such an idea. This I do, or try to do at any rate, in Chapter 6.

Efficiency

Efficiency means getting things done as cheaply as possible. A fair number of IP scholars believe efficiency both explains (in a positive sense) and guides (in a normative sense) the shape and direction of the field. In the Introduction I explain why I believe this is misguided. When it comes to providing convincing foundations for the field, utilitarian accounts of IP law are not yet up to snuff and they may never be. The rich and robust ethical traditions of Locke, Kant, and others provide a much more solid grounding for the field, in my opinion—as you can see from Chapters 2 and 3. Yet as I also explained in the Introduction, efficiency is still quite relevant to the field in a number of ways. It is a principle—an important one—but it is not the only one we need to explain and guide the field.

My goal here is to show how efficiency works as a midlevel principle. But I would like first to explain in just a bit more detail how efficiency at this midlevel differs from a full normative theory of IP law based strictly on the concept of optimal efficiency, that is, a utilitarian account.

WHY EFFICIENCY IS NOT FOUNDATIONAL

There is a long tradition of attempts to ground a full-blown foundational theory on the Pareto principle in economics, which holds that resources should be allocated such that no transfer of them would leave anyone better off without simultaneously leaving someone else worse off. This state of affairs is referred to as Pareto optimality. A slightly less demanding standard begins with the idea of Pareto superiority; under it, all transfers should occur whenever someone is left better off and everyone else is either indifferent or also better off. These technical definitions of efficient allocation are similar to commonsense ideas about efficiency, but not precisely coextensive.[29] Attempts to use these principles to form an ethically sound foundation for resource allocation have often been condemned. One commonly cited reason is that theories of ethically ideal resource allocation via market exchange depend critically on assumptions about the fairness of initial resource endowments.[30] Pareto allocation depends on prices—prices are the signals that transmit information about parties' relative valuations. Resources can only move to higher-valuing people if those people signal their higher valuation by greater willingness to pay. But ability to pay depends, obviously, on more than subjective valuation. It also depends on ability to pay—which in turn depends on the initial allocation of money, property rights, and legal entitlements. If these initial (pretrade) allocations are unfair, market exchange cannot overcome this.[31] Even the pioneering law and economics scholar Richard Posner concedes this basic point in some of his later writings.[32]

So fairness depends on the initial structure of ownership. A grossly unfair distribution of resources cannot be magically remedied in every case by a series of voluntary transfers. We have seen this idea already in Chapter 4 where distributional justice was discussed. However, a narrower, more limited version of the idea surfaces in other areas of IP. This narrower set of cases demonstrates why efficiency alone cannot fully justify and support a system of IP rights.

Sometimes an observed pattern of market exchanges appears to be absurd in light of well-known facts about the actual value of economic assets. An asset with a fundamental valuation that is quite reasonable may be changing hands at what appears to be a grossly inflated price. When the conditions of the exchange are brought to light, it may turn out that a particular set of circumstances is causing the inflated valuation.

For example, party A may have sunk enormous costs in putting together a product design incorporating hundreds or thousands of individual components. If, after A's costs are sunk, a late-arriving person, party B, announces that one crucial component is subject to a property right that B owns, all of A's sunk costs may be at risk. If B's position is strong enough, he can demand a substantial chunk of the value of A's entire complex product—even though B only owns rights to one small component. In this situation, A may well argue that the prevailing market price for B's component is grossly disproportionate to the fundamental value of that component. Economists say that B has "holdup power" over A. For our purposes, what matters is that if a court or other outside agency does not intervene to redress the holdup situation, the market price paid by A to B will be out of all proportion to the fundamental value of B's component. The court will be asked to intervene to bring the price of B's component back into line with its fundamental value.

This example shows that to maintain the fundamental fairness of market exchange, courts must be willing to look at whether actual transactions in some extreme cases are indicating dysfunction in the underlying entitlement structure—a problem that needs to be fixed by adjusting IP rights. It will not do for courts to say simply, "this exchange was voluntary, so it must be efficient, and therefore fair." Efficiency follows market exchange only if the entitlement structure is working properly. In some extreme cases that structure loses its connection with economic reality; market exchange in such a case is therefore not an indication that all is well, all is fair. Fairness is maintained only because courts have the ability to look behind bizarre market valuations in search of dysfunction in the way entitlements are being deployed. Put simply, voluntary market exchange is not a universal proxy for bilateral fairness.

This is a situation I explore in much more depth in Chapter 6. There we will see that this is but one of many instances where the IP system strives to align intrinsic merit with the scope and strength of IP rights. For present purposes my point is simply this: voluntary market exchange does not always indicate a fair result. Thus efficiency—which requires that goods move by market exchange to their highest-valued users in all cases— cannot serve as the foundation for an IP system. If we need on occasion to go beyond efficiency to reach the right result, efficiency alone cannot serve as the universal touchstone for our system.

THE PROPER ROLE FOR EFFICIENCY

I have argued so far that efficiency is not capable of serving as a stand-alone foundation for IP rights. What role does it play then? What is the function of efficiency as a midlevel principle?

The answer is simple. Efficiency guarantees that whatever entitlements the legal system starts with, they will be allocated to their highest-valued use as cheaply and quickly as possible. Efficiency cannot explain or justify the foundations of IP law, but as an operational principle it can guarantee that this body of law works smoothly and at the lowest possible cost. Although not an ultimate value justifying the existence of this system, this is nonetheless a hugely important role.

Efficiency as a working principle brings all sorts of benefits. The economic historian Deirdre McCloskey, in a broader defense of capitalist economies, explains it this way:

Private property and unfettered exchange—in a phrase, modern capitalism—
is not the kingdom of heaven, Lord knows. But for allocating scarce goods
and especially for making more of them, well . . . it is the worst system, except
for all those others that have been tried from time to time. And its ethical
effect, I have been arguing, is by no means entirely bad. . . . [33]

Amartya Sen defends market exchange along similar lines:

The freedom to exchange words, or goods, or gifts does not need defensive
justification in terms of their favorable but distant effects; they are part of the
way human beings in society live. . . . We have good reasons to buy and sell, to
exchange, and to seek lives that can flourish on the basis of transactions. [34]

To summarize: efficiency is that principle which takes starting points as a
given and strives to reduce the costs of fostering voluntary exchange. To
see how this general principle applies to aspects of IP law, large and small,
we will consider a few examples.

EXAMPLES IN IP LAW

Like all property rights, IP rights map individual owners to specific resources. This serves the goal of efficiency because when someone wants or
needs a resource, she knows where to turn for access to it: just find the
owner, and strike a deal. The great advantage of property rights is that
they correlate assets and owners, thus setting the starting point for deal
making and ultimately the moving of resources to their highest-valued use.

IP theorist Scott Kieff identified and described this virtue. Kieff writes
often of the way IP rights serve the needs of those who want access to information. He ascribes a "beacon effect" to IP rights, under which potential information users are attracted and drawn to the source of needed in-
formational assets. [35] Users seek out owners, knowing that it is owners who
have the power to grant access to things that users want.

The property theorist Henry Smith writes of IP in a similar vein. For
him, an IP right—like property of all kinds—creates autonomous zones
around assets. [36] This serves two purposes: inside the zone, owners have
wide discretion to develop the asset and use it as they wish. And outsiders,
third parties, know with whom they must deal when it comes to accessing
and using the asset. In Smith's terminology, IP rights are a good example of
exclusionary rights that are highly "modular." [37]

In my own work I recognized some of these same advantages in the
structure of IP rights. I have argued, along with economist coauthor Ashish Arora, that IP rights under certain circumstances permit the producer
of a complex component to form an independent company to make and
sell the component. [38] The idea is that when the component is an "input"

into a multicomponent product made by another, typically larger firm, IP rights help protect the component maker from the risk of being taken advantage of. According to our model, without IP protection, those skilled in making the component might find their only choice is to work for a large company. What is lost in this case is the advantage of smallness—nimbleness, focus, and autonomy. IP rights thus serve these values by making it possible for the component experts to constitute themselves as a separate, independent firm.

In some other work, I look at the way IP rights facilitate information transactions.[39] In particular, I argue that a property right in information—intellectual property—yields dual benefits for someone who wants to market information to a buyer: an IP right (1) protects the information seller during the sensitive period leading up to the signing of a formal legal contract, which facilitates "precontract disclosure" and thus supports market exchange; and (2) gives the information seller more legal options, including stronger legal remedies, in the event of a dispute or conflict over an information transaction.

It is apparent then that IP rights can serve as the starting points for negotiations and exchange, setting in motion the great resource-allocating machinery so heartily lauded by theorists such as McCloskey and Sen. But efficiency is a broader principle even than this. Sometimes in IP efficiency means not granting a property right in the first place. The application of efficiency in this context often overlaps with the nonremoval principle. One long-standing justification for the requirement that an invention be nonobvious is that this conserves social resources. An obvious invention will likely soon be made even without the award of a patent right. So why award the patent? Society will get all the benefit of the invention soon enough without the cost and bother of a patent to go with it. Patents cost society something, and if society only gets in return something it would have gotten for free, why grant the patent?[40]

Sometimes efficiency is invoked after rights have been granted. This is one now-classic explanation for the fair use defense in copyright. Invoke fair use, the theory says, only when a market for copyrighted works fails to take shape.[41] At the core of this market failure theory of fair use is efficiency: enforcing copyrights makes no sense if a market will not form anyway. Authors gain nothing without a market, and those who would use the works lose their chance to do so.

The originator of the market failure theory of fair use, Wendy Gordon, recognized from the outset that there is more to the doctrine than simple efficiency.[42] She pointed out that there are times when fair use should be invoked even though an efficient market may take shape. Overriding societal interests may be more important. In so arguing, Gordon engaged in just the sort of analysis I am advocating in this chapter. She recognized that efficiency is an important principle in IP law, but not the only relevant principle. So she argued for an efficiency theory that also admits of cases where efficiency is not the operative principle, and where something more like distributional issues, or basic fairness, can better explain and guide the law. At the same time, Gordon did not attempt to ground her theory in any ultimate normative framework, such as utilitarianism or Lockean property theory.[43] She operated instead on the basis of midlevel principles. This implicitly left room for people holding diverse and divergent normative commitments. Her theory tied together a range of actual cases, while tacitly bridging deep normative disagreements. In this sense, Gordon's market failure theory of fair use provides a very solid model of how midlevel principles work.

The Dignity Principle

The dignity principle lies behind many rules and cases in IP law. It is the principle that says the creator of a work should be respected and recognized in ways that extend beyond the traditional package of rights associated with property: the right to exclude, to alienate (sell or license), to use as one wishes, and so forth. There is often a nonpecuniary dimension to situations where this principle is relevant, and indeed the interests it protects are often said to continue after a creator sells the rights to a given creative work. Thus, the issues in IP law where dignity is relevant are often the closest the formal legal system comes to recognizing an ineluctable personal imprint placed on a work by its creator—familiar elements of Kantian and Hegelian property theory.[44]

There is an old convention in the IP field that the U.S. IP system is formed along utilitarian lines, while in Europe the system is based instead on natural law principles. Certainly, there are indications throughout the IP law of each region that there is something to this point. Even so, it has a tendency to be wildly overblown. Careful historical work has shown that both IP systems are a complex mix of natural law, utilitarian considerations, and other influences.[45] The idea that creators ought to be recognized for their works, which have intrinsic value to society, surely forms part of the fabric of both IP systems.

This is easiest to see in copyright, where the dignity principle has both a long history and a secure doctrinal home, particularly in Europe but also in the United States. Even patent law—supposedly the purest refuge of utilitarian IP theory—bears the imprint of the dignity principle. Historically, it appears that natural rights concepts did make their way into the basic structure of patent law, despite traditional accounts to the contrary.[46]

But let us return to copyright. Moral rights—the right of an author to continue to get credit for, and control the presentation of, her works—are perhaps the classic example of the dignity principle at work.[47] The right to continuing credit means that an author cannot have her name removed from copies of the work; credit for having created it continues, even after the creator has sold all other legal rights over the work. In other words, the buyer of rights cannot purchase the right to remove the creator's name, and certainly cannot legally substitute his own name. The fact of authorship is inalienable; it cannot be sold by the actual creator, and cannot be purchased by a third party.

Although moral rights such as authorial credit are well established in European law, they have traditionally been severely limited in the United States.[48] To be sure, there are some flickers of recognition for the dignity principle in the United States,[49] such as in the rules permitting authors to terminate licensing agreements signed at a time before the authors may have had bargaining power, or before the value of the work became established. For authors, these termination-of-transfer rules create an ongoing, inalienable interest in a creative work that cannot be bargained or signed away, and that may as a matter of right always be reclaimed later. The inalienable quality of this right—the fact that it cannot be given away by contract, no matter how voluntary the deal nor lucrative the compensation—shows it to surely be at least in part a manifestation of the dignity principle.[50]

Aside from the termination provision, there are other scattered corners of copyright law that bear the imprint of the dignity principle. In one celebrated case, creators of the Monty Python TV show prevented a butchered version of some episodes from being broadcast in the United States.[51] Often however, given perceptions about the utilitarian orientation of U.S. IP law, this principle hides covertly behind other legal rationales. For example, the songwriter and musician John Fogarty won a long-running battle with the company that came to own copyrights in some early Fogarty songs. The copyright owner had sued Fogarty for writing and performing new songs that were stylistically similar to some of his earlier hits. Although the court held the later songs noninfringing under conventional copyright doctrine, there was a strong sense in the opinion that it would be fundamentally unfair for the earlier copyrights to preclude Fogarty from creating and performing subsequent works in what had become his unique personal style. As a reviewing court phrased it, the lower court had "vindicated [Fogarty's] right . . . to continue composing music in the distinctive

'Swamp Rock' style and genre and therefore furthered the purposes of the Copyright Act. . . ."[52]

The moral right to credit exists in patent law as well. An inventor has a right to have his name on a patent. Even where no pecuniary interest is at stake (for example where he has already preassigned any interest to an employer), this right survives.[53] As with copyright, the status of author or inventor cannot be bought and sold. There is a right to be recognized for one's creative work, and this right transcends and survives economic transactions involving other rights to the work. In some countries, this principle finds expression in rules giving an inventor—though employed by, and having signed away the invention rights to, a big company—the right to be separately rewarded in the event of a major, highly lucrative invention.[54]

Conclusion

So now, if I have been effective at all in this chapter, the idea of a midlevel principle is at least somewhat intelligible, and four plausible candidates in the field of IP law have been sketched out. More—actually, much more— could be said about each of these. They form major themes across and through a massive body of law, so obviously a short description of each will hardly exhaust the discourse. There are also other plausible candidate principles in addition to these four. In a field as large as IP, there is room for a diversity of organizing and explanatory principles, not just four. One chapter cannot do it all.

At the same time, one of the four principles seems to me so important, and so poorly understood as a principle, that it deserves extensive treatment. This is the proportionality principle, the topic of the next chapter.

CHAPTER SIX

The Proportionality Principle

Introduction

In Chapter 5 I described four midlevel principles of IP law. All are basic, all are important, and all encompass a wide range of detailed rules and doctrines; these are the features that *make* them principles. But of the four, I want now to home in on one, the proportionality principle.

I have chosen to emphasize proportionality for two reasons. First, it is the most undertheorized of the four midlevel principles. A huge amount has been written about the public domain, which I describe under the principle of nonremoval. Efficiency, the second midlevel principle, is in a sense the animating force behind an entire school of thought in IP scholarship, the law and economics approach. As for the dignity principle, it is the cornerstone of the massive literature on moral rights, and forms the backdrop for the many studies that compare the American and European traditions in IP law. Proportionality is rarely identified as a stand-alone principle, though I think it is at least as important as these other principles.

Second, I believe the proportionality principle illustrates exceedingly well what a midlevel principle is. Proportionality sits solidly between lower-level principles, or foundational theory, and the detailed practices of IP law—the rules and institutions that apply this body of law to real-world problems. At the lower level, the notion of proportionality is built tightly into the foundational theories of IP we considered in Chapters 2 and 3.

Locke's justification for initial appropriation depends, as we saw, on a basic symmetry between labor expended and property right claimed. And the provisos are almost explicitly formulated in terms of due proportion: they apply when property rights would exceed what is fair for the original appropriator to claim. The same is true for Kant; the best way to understand the universal principle of justice as applied to property is to see it as a constraint that prevents an appropriator from making claims that are disproportionate to his deserts, and hence overly burdensome to society.

At the same time, looking "upward" in my conceptual hierarchy, the proportionality principle ties together all sorts of disparate rules and institutional features in the IP landscape such as the scope of rights, limits on those rights, and remedies for violating them. All these doctrinal areas, in all major branches of IP law, embody notions of proportionality. The contribution made by the creator of a work, its relative magnitude and importance, drives much of the detailed application of IP law. Beyond this, proportionality shows well what Jules Coleman meant when he said that midlevel legal principles do more than *describe* large swaths of doctrine.[1] As Coleman said, doctrine actually defines and shapes the principle; that is, the meaning of a principle can be understood only by looking at the detailed body of practice out of which the principle arises. In this sense, we can talk meaningfully about proportionality in IP law only if we understand some of the details of enablement and infringement in patent law, fair use and misuse in copyright law, and a host of related operational rules.

What Is Proportionality?

Our legal system recognizes that there are times when legal entitlements give someone "excessive" or "disproportionate" leverage. By this I mean power beyond what a person rightfully deserves, or beyond what makes sense, given the circumstances. An illustrative example involves patents for small snippets of genes made possible by modern sequencing technology.[2] In the 1990s, companies seeking patents for gene snippets had a creative strategy: they were randomly patenting hundreds of short snippets, without any real knowledge of whether those snippets were part of useful genes or not. Then they planned to wait until someone else figured out that a certain gene generated a protein actually useful for humans, at which point the appropriate patent on a snippet of that gene would be deployed to gain a share of the resulting revenues. The short snippet patent, intrinsically worth very little when granted, might come to generate very substantial revenues. This strategy seemed to be working for a while, until the courts shut it down.[3] But what bothered me about it was a sense of disproportion: these very minor patents on essentially random gene snippets could, if they were fully enforced, have been worth huge amounts of money.

More recently, some patent owners have found a way to leverage the large-scale investments of technology companies in a way that strikes me (and many others) as quite unfair. Patent owners in these cases use a combination of companies' sunk costs and the "automatic injunction" rule to extract unfairly large payments from technology companies. Often, this grows out of a patent on a single component of a complex product. Such a patent can generate excessive leverage if the patent is discovered or asserted after the design for the complex product is fixed—at which point the costs to switch to another design may be very steep. For some years, the Federal Circuit, the chief patent court, had a rule guaranteeing that a patent owner who had won a patent infringement lawsuit could get a permanent injunction against the infringer, the losing party in the suit. When applied blindly, this rule sometimes gives patentees enormous bargaining leverage, especially where the infringer would suffer huge economic losses if the injunction means shutting down a profitable product line. When large sunk costs and a mechanical application of the injunction rule are combined, a patent on a minor component of a complex product can generate immense, and immensely disproportionate, leverage.[4]

Proportionality shows up in other places as well. For example, I have written extensively about a legal standard that is applied for patentable inventions, the nonobviousness requirement.[5] Under this test, an invention is patentable only if it represents a nontrivial advance over what came before (the prior art). The award of a patent is in this way calibrated so that only significant inventions are rewarded. A property right is handed out only when a technical contribution is proportional to the legal right at stake.

The same logic can be seen at work in the patent doctrine of enablement, which is often couched in the language of proportional reward. Under this rule, an inventor must disclose enough information in his patent to teach others in the field how to make and use the claimed invention. The disclosure must, according to cases in this area, be commensurate with the scope of the patentee's claims.[6] A patent that claims too much compared to what it teaches is invalid because its potential economic power is disproportionate to what it actually teaches the field.

Roughly similar rules operate in the field of copyright law. The copyright infringement test of "substantial similarity" serves a function similar to that of nonobviousness. And under a series of doctrines courts are reluctant to permit a "small" copyright to be used as strategic leverage to control a large market. Three distinct doctrines have been applied to achieve this result: fair use, copyright "misuse," and a refusal to apply anticircumvention law. In the fair use cases, for example, sellers of video game hardware attempted to use copyrights over very short "lockout" codes to exclude other companies from making video games compatible with their hardware. The courts turned them back, holding that competitors had a "fair use" right to copy the code so as to make compatible games.[7] These very minimal copyrights were deemed inadequate to command the kind of market leverage the video game makers claimed for them. The leverage they gave was disproportionate to their intrinsic value, so they were not enforced.[8]

I have come to see that a common principle runs through these examples: the idea of *disproportionate reward*. The basic idea is very simple. Beyond the statutory requirements for the grant of an IP right, or, to put it better, *embedded in* these requirements, is a transcendent principle that ties together all manner of disparate situations. To state it simply, an IPR must not confer on its holder leverage or power that is grossly disproportionate to what is deserved in the situation. If an IPR would effectively confer power or control over a much more vast market or set of markets than what is actually deserved, in light of the work covered by the IP right, that right must be limited in some way.

The Parable of the Bridge

The principle can be illustrated with a simple story and diagram (see Figure 6.1(a)). Suppose that there is a town on the west side of a large river. From time immemorial, people have crossed the river in boats, but the river is swift and the crossing dangerous. Although the land on the east side of the river is fertile, it is not valuable, since it is too far to the nearest bridge for anyone to commute to the city. Furthermore, any produce grown on the east side would spoil before it could be brought to market, and would be too expensive to transport all that way in any event.

Al, a resident of the town, owns a stretch of land along the river near the narrowest point for many miles in either direction as shown in Figure 6.1(b).

One day, some entrepreneurs decide to build a bridge across the river. Because the land title situation in this part of the river country is confused and it is not clear where Al's property line is really located, the entrepreneurs obtain permission from a number of local landowners, but not Al. The entrepreneurs build the bridge, at great expense and risk, overcoming a number of difficult logistical problems in the process (see Figure 6.1(c)). At the same time, Al petitions the local land court for guidance on the boundaries of his property line.

Meanwhile, the bridge turns out to be a great success, opening up vast new markets on the east side of the river. There are crops to be planted and money to be made, and these markets grow rapidly. Everyone has faith that the system will eventually sort out the land title situation. Meanwhile, energetic people jockey for position in the newly lucrative area on the east side of the bridge. Figure 6.1(d) shows the situation.

Being rational businesspeople, the entrepreneurs who built the bridge slowly raise the bridge toll over time, to take advantage of the valuable markets they unlocked.

Then one day the land court issues its ruling: the foot of the bridge is clearly within the boundaries of Al's land claim. Indeed, the court holds that Al owns 5 percent of the total area necessary to support the bridge. Al immediately opens negotiations with the entrepreneurs who had built the bridge. He wants to maximize his income, so he calculates the total value of all the produce that could be grown on the east side of the river, the total value of the homes that might be built there, and the cost people had been paying to cross the river at this spot before the bridge was built; he then sets his asking price accordingly: 40 percent of total expected profits from all economic activity on the newly opened (east) side of the bridge. The entrepreneurs are nonplussed: the price is very high indeed. Figure 6.1(e) shows the contrast between the size of Al's landholdings and the share of economic activity he is claiming.

When the entrepreneurs protest profusely, Al responds, "But the bridge is my property. You can't trespass without my permission, which I sell in the form of a lease to the land under the bridge footing. So I have the right, by virtue of my property, to set the price wherever I want."

In general, Al is right. *In general.* One of the true incidents of a property right is the right to exclude others. Another is that it is alienable (and partible, and alienable in parts). All this adds up to a strong case for Al, built on the general principles of property.

But is there nothing to be said for the entrepreneurs? Is their sense of outrage just a misunderstanding, a failure to think through their otherwise thorough commitment to the concept of private property? I don't think so. I think there is another general principle that can come into play here, the principle of *proportionality.* In that rare case where a property right confers truly disproportionate leverage, the proportionality principle comes into play in one form or another as a limiting factor. I can and will (beginning in the following section on the *eBay* case) point to numerous examples of this principle at work in IP law generally. But for present purposes, it amounts to this: Al may not be given complete, unfettered freedom to set his price at whatever level he wishes. He is probably going to have to

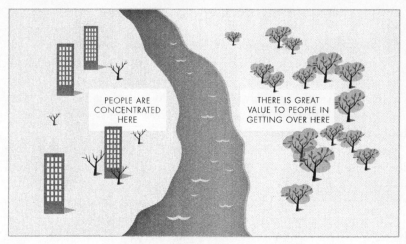

(a)

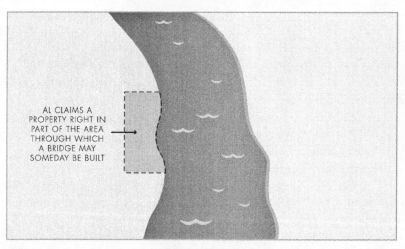

(b)

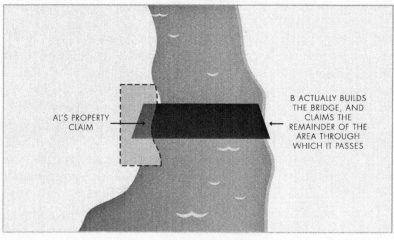

(c)

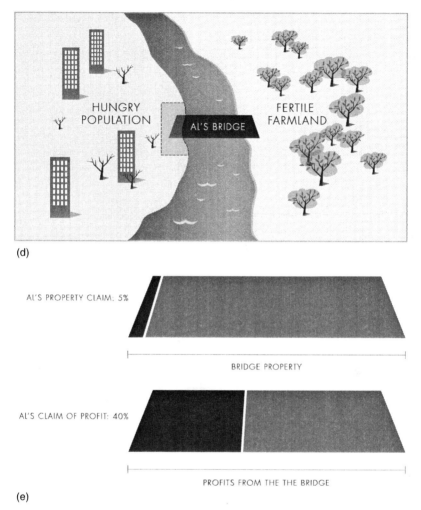

Figure 6.1. The parable of the bridge: in the beginning (a), Al's property claim (b), the bridge is built (c), after the bridge (d), dividing the spoils (e).

moderate his demands so they approach something closer to a fair return for building the bridge partly on his land. The law may limit his return to something approaching a fair rental rate. If it does, the property right will be effectively limited by the counterprinciple of proportionality.

AN EXAMPLE FROM PATENT LAW: THE *EBAY* CASE

Proportionality is the principle behind the *eBay* case in patent law.[9] The topic of this case was the "automatic injunction" rule I mentioned earlier in this chapter. In the case, the Supreme Court directed the lower courts to abandon the automatic injunction rule and instead rely on traditional principles of fairness—as expressed in the branch of law called equity—in deciding whether to grant injunctions at the conclusion of patent infringement trials. A strong concurring opinion in *eBay* called specific attention to the excessive leverage that injunctions can sometimes give patentees. According to the concurrence,

> An industry has developed in which firms use patents not as a basis for producing and selling goods but, instead, primarily for obtaining licensing fees. . . . For these firms, an injunction, and the potentially serious sanctions arising from its violation, can be employed as a bargaining tool to charge exorbitant fees to companies that seek to buy licenses to practice the patent. . . . When the patented invention is but a small component of the product the companies seek to produce and the threat of an injunction is employed simply for undue leverage in negotiations, legal damages may well be sufficient to compensate for the infringement and an injunction may not serve the public interest.[10]

As many amicus briefs in the case explained, delay in the specification of property rights often drives the tactics of these patent holders. There are so many patents that potentially cover or "read on" components of complex products that sellers of these products cannot identify all the patents they might infringe. Companies specializing in identifying these patents and asserting them in litigation have emerged to take advantage of this.

These companies are much like Al in the parable of the bridge. They hold property rights that turn out, after a period of time, to be valuable. Like Al, they themselves contribute little to actual economic value. You will recall that Al's property right is not a major factor in the building of the bridge; it is in fact irrelevant to the initial investments by the entrepreneurial bridge builder. In the same way, a productive company that builds a valuable product, composed of many components, garners little value from a patent that lies latent until the product becomes successful.

If the latent or dormant property right is enforced to the hilt, it confers economic power far beyond its intrinsic value. This is what Justice Kennedy recognized in the concurrence excerpted just above. As he said, in such a case "the threat of an injunction is employed simply for undue leverage in negotiations." It is this idea of undue leverage, of economic power beyond what is legitimate, that lies at the heart of the proportionality principle.

OF SMALL RIGHTS AND BIG LEVERAGE

The alternative view takes the property right as a fixed fact, and treats any economic leverage it creates as a natural and intended consequence of granting such a right. The Court of Appeals for the Federal Circuit, whose opinion in *eBay* was reversed by the Supreme Court, stated this position in the following passage:

> If the injunction gives the patentee additional leverage in licensing, that is a natural consequence of the right to exclude and not an inappropriate reward to a party that does not intend to compete in the marketplace with potential infringers.[11]

The key difference between the Federal Circuit view and the one adopted by the Supreme Court is this: the former implies that any leverage generated by a properly-granted property right is legitimate, while the latter believes that this is not always so. The Supreme Court takes the position that it may in proper cases look behind the leverage created by a property right. This inquiry, though itself rare, reveals the heart of the proportionality principle. In this somewhat extreme case, the basic logic of the principle is revealed. The contribution of the property owner is weighed against the economic leverage the right provides in actual market transactions. Where this relationship is out of balance—where a "small right" provides "very big leverage"—the Court intervenes to reset the balance.

One point to emphasize is that Al did little that was admirable in attaining the situation that conferred so much leverage. He did not take a risk, or invest inordinate time, effort, or other resources in acquiring his parcel of land. He did not, as I told the story, invest substantial resources to locate the small parcel of land, and he did not incur exceptional costs or take exceptional risks to litigate the title issue.[12] If any of these facts were different, the parable might push in a different direction. If Al had incurred significant investments for a socially constructive purpose, for example, the intuition of undue leverage might not be so strong. The sense that the leverage is "undue," in other words, depends on the fact that Al has done little in the way of work, risk, or investment to deserve it.[13]

Variation on the Parable:
Value Building or Rent Seeking?

The parable and the examples have these elements in common. Assume A acquires an IP right at time To. At the time of acquisition, the asset covered by the right has some "baseline" value, but no special value. Later, at T1, the asset becomes more valuable—as a result of clearer property rights, some change in market forces, the effort of others besides A, or other events not attributable to A's effort, skill, or even foresight. Should A be able to reap the reward—one is tempted to call it a windfall—that will

now accrue to the owner of the IP right? IP law, through a number of inge-
nious rules and doctrines, often says no. Though at the doctrinal level,
courts do not relate these disparate rules to a central animating principle,
there *is* a unifying principle at work: the proportionality principle.

Now let's vary the parable's facts a bit. Suppose that there are many
crossing points along the river. Suppose further that many people have
discussed the possibility of a bridge being built across the river, to tap the
valuable land on the other side. But no one has yet stepped forward with
explicit plans to build the bridge; no one knows exactly where it will be
built. Al sizes up the situation and decides on a strategy. He decides to
purchase a series of small parcels of land all up and down the established,
settled side of the river. But there are complications. Securing property
rights in this area is tricky, because title information is not easy to find and
because the local recording office is not very efficient. So Al puts a good
deal of time and effort into "working the system." He becomes a fixture at
the recording office, poring over old maps and studying old land grants.
He becomes friendly with the people who work at the recording office,
and even contributes to the political campaign of the county recorder, who
runs for office every two years.

Because of his connections at the recording office, Al is able to buy and
record a number of parcels along the settled side of the river. No single
parcel is very big, but Al tries to buy parcels that include every place where
there is solid ground on which to build a footing for a bridge. Because re-
cordkeeping about who owns which parcels is fairly spotty, it is not easy
for anyone to discover what Al is doing, or even to find out who is the
current owner of any particular patch of ground. After Al acquires the
land parcels, each costing an average of five gold pieces, he waits.

Sure enough, a few years later a group of entrepreneurs announce plans
to build a bridge. They look along the riverbank and decide on a specific
location to begin building. Lawyers for the entrepreneurs do their best to
search the records to figure out who owns the parcel, but it is very difficult
to tell. So they advise the entrepreneurs to set aside a reasonable amount
of money to pay the owner if and when he is located. The amount is determined by looking at comparable land sales along the river in the preceding
few years. The comparable sales are all in the range of five gold pieces, but
to be safe, the lawyers advise that the entrepreneurs set aside ten gold
pieces to pay for the land. This they do, and then they begin to build the
bridge.

After the bridge has been completed and has proven to be a huge
success—generating 10,000 gold pieces in revenue in the first year
alone—Al approaches the entrepreneurs and shows them his deed to the

small parcel on which the bridge footing was built. He demands 2,500 gold pieces for a permanent lease of his land parcel. The entrepreneurs are outraged. But their lawyers tell them, after investigating the situation at the recording office, that Al's deed is probably valid, and that if the entrepreneurs file suit against Al seeking to invalidate his title, a court may issue a temporary injunction during the litigation, effectively closing the bridge. The fear is that Al would insist on a larger share of the 10,000 gold pieces in annual revenue as the price for putting aside the injunction and allowing the bridge to remain open.

This version of the parable has some things in common with the first version. One is the issue of timing: the property right is not asserted until after the entrepreneurs' costs are sunk and it is too late to change the location of the bridge. Another common factor is a wide disparity between the price Al paid for the land and the ultimate price it eventually commanded in a market exchange with the entrepreneurs.

Even so, I want to emphasize a different element in this version of the parable. Al bought a number of parcels, hoping that one would eventually be chosen for the bridge location. In economic terms, he made a series of bets, expecting that one might pay off in the end. Put simply, in this version of the story, Al was a speculator. There is nothing wrong with this, of course; being "ahead of the curve," as Al was, is central to entrepreneurship, and hence to economic growth in general. The tricky part is the *way* Al speculated—his particular form of speculation. His speculation involved a good bit of time and effort invested in "working" the legal-political process. The question we must answer is whether this sort of activity is the type of thing we want our society to promote. Put simply, we have to decide whether or not Al's crafty use of the legal/political process contributes to economic growth.

WHAT IS RENT SEEKING?

It will be helpful at the outset to acknowledge that in economic terms, speculation is a broad concept, covering a range of activities. On one end of the spectrum, almost all investments that involve any sort of risk could be classified as speculation. Everything from buying shares on a stock exchange to selling insurance contracts to buying commodities futures contracts might qualify. There is little doubt at this stage that these are all, in general, productive activities. They permit large pools of capital to be formed; disparate risks to be aggregated, their costs regularized and controlled; and various risks to be offset or hedged by taking financial positions that will soften the blow of a costly event. These are all positive contributions to a functioning modern economy. The linguistic root of the word *speculation* bears this out; according to the *Oxford English Dictionary,* it derives from the Latin *speculari,* to spy out, watch, examine, or observe.[14]

Although there is a consensus that speculation is efficient, it has met with condemnation when it depends on direct governmental action—land grants, regulatory decisions, legislation, or the like. In general, economists often refer to extraordinary investment returns as "rents." When used in this neutral sense, rents or "supernormal profits" can be productive and even virtuous, in which case pursuing them, as Al arguably did, is a good thing. But rents can also be unproductive. The prospect of government action that yields large rents can lead to inefficient behavior as entrepreneurs invest in working the governmental system in one form or another. In the economic literature, this is commonly called "rent seeking"—a term with a distinctly negative connotation. Typical examples of rent seeking include bribing public officials, spending lavishly on lobbying or other behavior meant to influence officials, or more generally spending money to position oneself advantageously in the governmental process. All these expenditures are contrasted, implicitly at least, with more directly productive activities: investing in real assets such as raw materials and machinery, or spending money to make existing assets more productive. Rent seeking is bad because it results in a simple wealth transfer, usually from taxpayers (via the government) to a private firm or individual. When too many resources are drawn into transferring wealth, instead of creating it, society is in trouble. It is this contrast between investing to create wealth and rent seeking to simply transfer wealth that is at the heart of the rent-seeking concept.

To be honest, economists can be painfully vague on the line that separates an inefficient rent from a good or virtuous rent. By convention, good rents are rarely referred to as rents. They are instead called positive incentives, investments in innovation, or supracompetitive returns. Some years ago, the economist Deirdre McCloskey wrote an intriguing book on the ways economists communicate implicit moral messages through the use of this kind of terminology.[15] In the context of rents and positive incentives, the typical account has it that when people seek to obtain rents through some sort of illicit or at least questionable activity, this is a bad thing for the economy. Professor and Judge Richard Posner distinguishes between supracompetitive returns (which some might call rents, and which are morally neutral) and "artificial" rents, such as those obtained through monopoly power in a market or through some special government grant that excludes others from entering a market.[16] Others use the word rent to mean any government-mediated wealth transfer.[17] However it is defined, rent seeking is usually considered a bad thing. To return to the theme of rhetoric, one seeks a rent, but responds to or follows a positive incentive; or one creates an innovation. Rents are bad or inefficient; rent seekers are a blight on society. Investments and innovations are efficient, even virtuous; investors and innovators are a great boon to society.

APPLYING PROPORTIONALITY:
THE RENT-SEEKING RATIO

With these conventions in mind, the question we must consider in the parable of the bridge is this: is Speculator Al a virtuous entrepreneur, following positive incentives and doing good for the economy; or is he a scurrilous rent seeker, somehow manipulating or misusing the rules of the game to garner an illicit advantage that is costly to society? This can be a difficult question to answer in a given case. But getting it right is extremely important. As the economist William Baumol has observed, entrepreneurs are typically amoral. They will seek gain wherever they can, as long as it really is a net gain, given their preference for risk.[18] Thus from a strictly entrepreneurial point of view, there is no difference between trafficking in illegal bomb-making equipment or leading the way in the market for AIDS therapies or religious statuary. It is up to society, particularly the legal system, to set things up so that entrepreneurial energy is channeled into socially useful directions.[19] From this perspective, strict criminal laws, and a willingness to enforce them, lower the returns from trafficking in bombs and presumably therefore raise the relative returns from participating in markets for socially useful things such as AIDS therapies. As Baumol and others recognize, entrepreneurial energy is a fact of human nature. The only question is how will it be channeled?

To return to the parable of the bridge, the first question before us is this: how exactly did Al secure the property rights to the land parcels he bought? Is there any value in Al's activities with respect to the recording office? If not, we might consider this if and when it comes time to enforce Al's rights. We might even consider a limited restriction on the most egregious attempts to influence or "game" the recording process. The entire inquiry is an exercise in applying the proportionality principle. In particular, we should pay attention to the ratio of investment in the legal-bureaucratic process to investments of various kinds related to the land itself. These might include time, effort, and resources invested in determining which land parcels might be especially good prospects for a bridge footing (for example, land surveys, geological surveys to determine stability of rock formations), as well as direct investment in the land parcels themselves, such as clearing land and exposing solid footing areas so as to demonstrate the suitability of the land for a bridge footing.

We can express the overall sense of this proportion with a ratio. Where $Invest_{LB}$ is the investment in legal and bureaucratic costs, and $Invest_{AD}$ is investment in asset development, the ratio is

$$Invest_{LB}/Invest_{AD}$$

This leads to a simple way to apply the proportionality principle. If this ratio is too high—greater than $1:1$, for example—that should be a warning to courts and regulators that rent seeking may be going on. When the ratio is low (less than $1:5$, for example), by contrast, we can be sure that the legal-bureaucratic process is not driving the investment decision, and presumably therefore at least this form of rentseeking is probably absent.

SOME EXAMPLES FROM HISTORY

When the rent-seeking ratio becomes too heavily weighted on the socially unproductive side, institutions need to exert a course correction to bring it back into balance. From an economic point of view, governmental institutions are a means to an end. Rentseeking becomes a problem when they become instead an end in themselves, when governmental interaction is seen not as assisting productive investment but as an investment unto itself. If governmental relations serve a profit center, the business is probably productive. But when governmental relations *become* a profit center unto themselves, that spells trouble.

Historically, in high-growth economies, rent seeking is limited by legal and political institutions when it gets out of hand—when the ratio just described begins to send warning signals. The modern language of rent seeking emerges from these episodes. The concept of rent seeking pulls together and explains the disparate, scattered episodes of state-oriented speculation that have been condemned throughout history. The common ingredient is expenditure of resources on securing government property grants at the expense of socially valuable investment in developing real economic assets. Many of these episodes historically center on land speculation schemes of one sort or another. After a quick tour through some historical examples, we will return to the parable of the bridge, armed with tools that can help determine whether Al's land investment should be condoned (as meritorious, beneficial speculation) or condemned (as speculation of the rent-seeking variety).

Consider an early example, land grants in the Massachusetts Bay Colony in the 1630s. The Massachusetts General Court—the colonial legislature—distinguished early between two classes of large-scale landowners.[20] Absentee owners who held title without expending any effort to develop land were condemned, and the titles in question were withdrawn. But active speculators, who recruited settlers and invested in improvements, were lauded and rewarded. It is well understood that many speculators in the colonial era, and in the federalist period just after American independence, were politically well connected. And there was a premium on speculators who knew how to work the legal system to advantage.[21] Often, the race went to the swift, and not necessarily to the one who was punctilious about legal niceties and ethical standards. (See, for example, George Washington.)[22] Yet even so, most of these speculators did more than play the legal-political system. The earliest among them explored and surveyed land on the frontier of European settlement, promoted development and occupation, and in some cases occupied a portion of their holdings and invested directly themselves.[23] Then there was the additional "investment" of putting themselves at risk in a direct military confrontation with the British. When the nation's founders agreed in the Declaration of Independence to "mutually pledge to each other our lives, our fortunes and our sacred honor," the middle term—which took the form primarily of landholdings—was not a trivial matter. Postrevolutionary speculators also prospered best when they did more than buy and hold land. A detailed case study of William Cooper, speculator and developer of Cooperstown, New York, showed him living among his settlers, extending them credit, and encouraging their investment of effort and resources into their farms.[24]

The same pattern held into the nineteenth century. Early in the century, a federal committee headed by Thomas Jefferson devised a sales and surveying system that was designed to thwart the efforts of rent-seeking speculators.[25] The legal historian J. Willard Hurst, in his monumental study of the role of law in the development of the timber industry in Wisconsin, found that later in the nineteenth century antispeculator rhetoric was aimed primarily at minimizing land accumulation by large and politically powerful companies. Speculation on this scale, and by these interests, was thought to be at odds with the goal of maximizing immediate economic development:

> In this context, one may fairly read the criticisms of "speculation" in timberland as aimed at those who would profit merely by holding the land for a rise in value without undertaking to put it to work. Condemnation of forest "speculation" in itself evidenced the preference for valuing fixed natural capital for its utility in fostering the productivity of scarce mobile capital; the point of criticism was that the "speculator" did not acquire land to make it part of production.[26]

A similar theme is apparent in the law relating to mining claims in the western United States. Legal rules in this setting started out as informal norms, developed by miners themselves in the absence of a formal legal system.[27] One of the problems miners grappled with was overclaiming—staking claims over a very wide area. To prevent this, groups of miners developed a rule that limited the scope of claims to a size that a normal work party could develop.[28] Retaining the claim required that it be worked. As with most of these informal norms, this rule was later codified in federal mining law, which required staged investments for a claimant to "perfect" an inchoate claim.[29]

These examples are not meant to demonstrate that legal systems always root out rent seeking, or even that they keep it under some semblance of control. To the contrary, the institutional economist Douglass North once expressed the sentiment that it sometimes seems miraculous when societies do get things right when it comes to specifying property rights.[30] And many a historical study of societal stagnation, decay, and collapse features tales of rent seeking on a grand scale. In the United States, economic historians have pointed out some of the many occasions when societal incentives became skewed. Examples include the Homestead Act of 1862, which led, some have argued, to overinvestment in "land races" and claim staking, to the detriment of orderly and timely investment in real economic development.[31]

REINING IN RENT SEEKING: A SERIES OF SMALL ADJUSTMENTS WORKS BEST

We have seen two things so far in this section, and I want to recap them before moving on to our final variation on the bridge story. First, economic speculation is an essential and usually efficient form of economic activity. Society needs a first wave of investors to blaze a trail, or settle a frontier, whether we mean this literally, in a new geographical location, or figuratively, with a new technology or business idea. Second, the forward-looking speculative attitude, being concerned only with potential future gains, does not distinguish between investments that are socially useful and those that are not. That is the job of the branch of government dedicated to regulating and maintaining the basic conditions of economic competition, and economic activity in general.[32]

In our system, this job falls in the first instance to courts, though the executive branch also frequently has a hand in things. Legislatures too come into play. But typically in the first instance, courts are involved in more discrete, particularized disputes arising out of the economic system. So they will often see the signs of emerging rent seeking before the other branches.

This is certainly true in patent law. An excellent example from the past few decades is the rise of a large patent holder named Jerome Lemelson.

The story of his rise, built on the creative use of patents, is a classic case study in the emergence of a new set of practices that are at first tolerated, then treated with some concern, and ultimately reined in when it becomes evident to all that they are witnessing an episode of rent seeking. Lemelson amassed a large number of patents across a wide range of industries. He was an inventor, to be sure, but his real talents were foresight and determination. He filed hundreds of forward-looking patent applications, which he kept "alive" in the patent office for many years while entire industries formed and developed.[33] Then, benefiting from a distinctly pro-patent environment in the late 1980s, he sprang his patents on a whole series of unsuspecting industries. The result was a billion-dollar licensing empire, often built on patents that legally covered large and important industries (such as bar code technology) but to which Lemelson had never really contributed. His "insights" were buried in secret patent applications that no one ever read until he caused the patents to issue and promptly sued everyone in sight.

Lemelson eventually met with defeat in a case involving a patent application filed in 1954 and issued only in 1994. He asserted this forty-year-old application against the bar code technology industry, and in this, as in many other cases, the courts were inclined to find the patent valid and infringed. However, the court in this case dipped into history to rediscover a doctrine prohibiting this sort of blatant misuse of the patent system.[34] That it took so long was of course not ideal. But at least in the end the courts put a stop to this particular rent-seeking ploy.

Another example is the requirement of utility.[35] This has been described as a legal rule that tries to optimize the timing of a property rights award. Building on the seminal work of David Haddock,[36] students of the utility requirement have shown that it is designed to prevent rent seeking on the part of those who would obtain a patent before a new technology has been adequately described or understood. The obvious rationale for this requirement is that it prevents the dissipation of legitimate rents by requiring those who obtain a patent to show real technological progress. The award of a patent at too early a stage in the innovation process would clearly lead to excessive expenditures of resources in an attempt to draft an early and broad patent instrument. The utility requirement in patent law prevents these wasteful expenditures by requiring that an innovator achieve actual technical milestones prior to receiving a patent. Investment and effort are therefore directed toward the socially useful goal of developing the technology, rather than simply racing to the patent office. This is a perfect example of a patent doctrine that prevents rent seeking before the grant of the patent—at the ex ante stage.

Another Variation: Winning on the Strength of the Crowd

Here is the third and final variation on the parable of the bridge. Imagine the same basic setup—a thriving population on one side of a river, and the chance to unlock great economic potential if only the other side can be reached by a bridge. This time, imagine that there are many potential bridge crossing sites, all equally good. Now imagine that Al owns one plot along the river. It is a nice plot, in a good location, but no better and no worse as a river crossing site than many other locations.

Now imagine that one or two people gather on Al's site to begin the process of building a bridge footing. Each person brings a few rocks and drops them in the river off Al's site. The same thing happens at other sites along the river that are not owned by Al. Before long, word gets out, and slowly the crowd of people placing rocks off of Al's site begins to grow. The other sites see some participation along these lines, but not quite as much as Al's. Before too long, the word spreads that Al's bridge site is the place to be. More and more people begin to come, and the bridge begins to take shape in earnest: first the footing is completed, then supports go up, then work begins on the span. By now the other sites where people had started work are slowing to a crawl. People who want to meet people who are interested in developing a business on the other side of the bridge begin to congregate at the work site on Al's property. Through no real planning—through chance, in some ways—Al's site is clearly "it." This is the place where the bridge is going to be, so it has become "bridge central" to anyone with an interest in the bridge or in things that will be built or developed on the other side.

As the bridge nears completion, Al begins to get a sense that his property right on the site of the footing might become very valuable indeed. The people who have worked on the bridge, and who are now nearing completion, are hoping that Al will recognize all their contributions. They trust that because they have all worked so hard to build the bridge, Al will be reasonable if and when he decides to assert his property right.

Maybe Al will be reasonable, on the theory that he does not need to charge too much in a lease to the bridge builders to still do well. After all, once the bridge is complete and the traffic on it begins to grow, there will be a high volume of people and goods crossing the bridge. So Al can probably do quite well without getting too unreasonable about the rate he charges, especially if he asks for a (small) percentage of the tolls on the bridge, or on the revenue generated via the bridge.

PROPERTY RIGHTS, NETWORK EFFECTS,
AND GROUP LABOR

What I am trying to capture with this version of the parable is something called "network effects." From an economic perspective, this is the simple idea that in some cases, other people's choices can affect how much you value something, and therefore your own choices. The simplest example is an old-fashioned landline phone network. Your choice of which network to join was heavily affected by the network chosen by your friends. Under this kind of system, a telephone and a calling plan are much more valuable when the people you want to talk to are on the same network. Thus, assuming a number of competing networks, your choice of which network to join was heavily affected by which network your friends have joined. (In actuality, this dynamic was so strong that landline phone systems were often considered "natural monopolies," because in truth a network was most valuable when *everyone* shared a single one.)

In this version of the parable, once a critical mass of people started to build on Al's site, network effects began to kick in. It was obvious at some point that the bridge starting on Al's site was going to be the winner. The story is skewed a bit to show this point, because in truth the network effects that flow from building physical infrastructure are usually not as strong as those flowing from participation in technical standards. Although it may be handy that everyone with an interest in the building of a bridge gathers at Al's site, someone who doggedly set out to build another bridge would not by virtue of that choice be excluded from interacting with other bridge builders. Compare this to technical standards, such as a choice of computer operating system. It may be that if the vast majority of people have chosen System X, someone who chooses System Y will be frozen out. She might not be able to exchange documents, graphics files, or computer programs with users of System X. The value of System Y in such a situation is very low indeed. One has to be a sort of virtual Robinson Crusoe, content never to interact with other users, to find much value at all in a system that no one else adopts.

One thing the story of Al's "crowd sourced" bridge gets right, however, is the randomness of winning. There really seems to be no particularly good reason why Al's site won out over the others. It was not superior in any way, nor was Al more diligent or prescient. What he was, in fact, was just lucky. From what we know about the emergence of technical standards, this is often the case. The winning design or standard is often no better by conventional measures than one or more alternatives. Something happens to tip things in its favor—and that's it. Game over for the other would-be winners. Markets that exhibit strong network effects are often referred to as "winner take all" markets.[37] The parable shows why this label is apt.

So a certain amount of good fortune is part of the parable.[38] Another aspect is the contribution of many people to the ultimate success of the bridge. This feature is present in differing degrees across different network markets. Sometimes the user effort is limited merely to learning a certain system—a user interface like Microsoft Windows, for example. At other times a great deal of user effort goes into making the ultimate market winner. I tried to capture this aspect of network effects by describing the huge collective effort of many individual people to build the bridge. By including this, I wanted to show that the presence of large-scale effort by many dispersed users adds an extra dimension to the network effects story. Although it is true that, in any network market, the choices of the individual users are what create a "winner," the making of a choice in and of itself does not necessarily entitle the users to much of anything. The aggregated choices make up the winner, but the person or company that designed and sold the winning product—the phone system or operating system that won out— obviously contributed much more. Where users contribute not only their choice, but also effort, the story is more complex. In fact, the contribution of significant effort by widely dispersed users may form the basis for important limits on the rights of the owner of the winning system. To hold otherwise would be to treat the effort of the dispersed users as less important, less worthy, than the effort of the system owner. Although these limitations may themselves be subject to caveats and restrictions, they are in theory at least required if we are to stay true to the Lockean principle that labor or effort ought to ground claims to property.

EXAMPLE: USER-GENERATED ENHANCEMENTS

In a case from the mid-1990s, a U.S. appeals court denied copyright protection to the menu command structure of the Lotus 1-2-3 spreadsheet program.[39] The effect of the decision allowed Lotus's rival, Borland, to sell a spreadsheet that incorporated a Lotus-compatible menu structure. The majority's holding was straightforward and came right out of the statute. But there was a concurrence in the case by Judge Michael Boudin, which suggested that he was aware of the imperative to recognize user contributions in the setting of rights for network products. In the concurrence, Judge Boudin wrote on the importance of maintaining a "common" space hewn out by the many users of the Lotus spreadsheet who had written their own mini-programs or "macros" that ran with their Lotus spreadsheets. Despite the language of the commons, however, his logic stressed that much of the value of Lotus's menus was created by the efforts of those who used and wrote macros for the 1-2-3 program:

> Requests for the protection of computer menus present [a] concern with fencing off access to the commons in an acute form. A new menu may be a creative work, but over time its importance may come to reside more in the investment that has been made by users in learning the menu and in building their own mini-programs—macros—in reliance upon the menu. . . . A different approach [to resolving this case] would be to say that Borland's use is privileged because, in the context already described, it is not seeking to appropriate the advances made by Lotus' menu; rather, having provided an arguably more attractive menu of its own, Borland is merely trying to give former Lotus users an option to exploit their own prior investment in learning or in macros. The difference is that such a privileged use approach would not automatically protect Borland if it had simply copied the Lotus menu (using different codes), contributed nothing of its own, and resold Lotus under the Borland label.[40]

The idea that the users' collective efforts, their labor, should count in the analysis of the original program owner's property rights is a striking note.[41] It seemed to build implicitly on the idea that property has to do with labor; that central to a legitimate property claim is the expenditure of labor. But it defied conventional—that is, Lockean—thinking in contemplating a role for users' efforts in the analysis of the owners' rights, or maybe even the assignment of some sort of property right to the dispersed users themselves. At any rate, the concurrence recognized the efforts of the dispersed users as a relevant consideration in the overall property calculus relating to the 1-2-3 program.

In an essay I wrote about this case, I explored the possibility of awarding some form of IP to large groups of dispersed creators. My argument was that dispersed user effort is not well accounted for in our legal system, which is organized around the idea of a single highly centralized creative entity (usually a person or corporation). In the essay I also spelled out a few suggestions about how to bring dispersed creators' contributions into the mainstream of IP policy. The simple idea was that these users' efforts merit the attention (and protection) of IP law, using the property rights theory of John Locke. I described two primary types of collective creativity: "add-on" and "purely original." Add-on works are those that are based in some way on a preexisting work, typically owned by a single proprietor. These include fan websites where users contribute original material; user-generated game characters and scenarios in online games; user-generated software add-ons, such as macros, program modifications, and the like; and even user efforts to learn a standard technology (such as an operating system) and adapt their work to it. "Purely original" works are those, such as Wikipedia, created by dispersed users from the ground up. Each type of collective creativity has its own features, but a common thread unites them: they invite some sort of group property claim to honor the labor that goes into them.

The fact of collective creativity is hardly news. Lots of people have remarked on it in recent years. For the most part, however, observers have talked about this form of creative work as falling well outside the traditional models—organizationally, socially, and even legally. From the perspective of law, collective creativity is seen today as a challenge to conventional mechanisms of encouragement, protection, and recognition. Intellectual property in particular is said to be a poor fit with this new form of creative work. Although there is a good deal of overstatement in many of these accounts, I have come to see that some of the charges do stick. Chief among these is the idea that IP law is too attached to an outdated model of creativity, whose centerpiece is the lone creative individual. To be sure, this model has a long way to run; we are very far from the day when the lone creator is a rare and unusual island in a vast sea of collective creations. Even so, I think the emerging model of collective creativity is something new, at least in its current mass form. As such, it poses a challenge to conventional thinking in the IP field. This is the challenge I take up here.

Put simply, the challenge is this: how do we adapt a system of property rights, conceived and designed for individual creators and the organizations that have traditionally employed them, to a new model of creativity where creators are widely dispersed? How do we move beyond the traditional dichotomy of rights/no rights, IP/the public domain, or exclusive rights/the commons, to craft a new set of entitlements that recognize a middle ground—exclusive (or semiexclusive) group rights? A detailed answer to this will come over time, and it will involve all sorts of microadjustments in doctrine, rules, and institutions.[42] But here, almost at the outset, it seems useful to set out some of the conceptual ground rules that ought to guide this process of adjustment.

The best way to proceed is to return to first principles. For IP law, as for property rights generally, that means the work of John Locke. When we look for a Lockean approach to the problem, as we did in Chapter 2, we find some straightforward principles that can help structure our thinking about the problem generally. The principles are these: (1) labor ought to be rewarded with a property right—a claim good against others, justified by the exertion of effort that transforms starting materials into something useful; (2) laboring on an asset already owned by someone else may create some rights in the laborers, but this depends on the "terms of employment" under which the labor is expended; and (3) collective property claims are subject to the same caveats ("provisos") as other such claims, all of which are designed to reconcile the rights of individual creators with the larger claims of society in general.

Restoring and Maintaining Proportionality

A quick summary: proportionality is the idea that a property right ought to be reasonably related to something socially useful and valuable. Where the unregulated market price of a property right moves radically out of alignment with underlying social utility, an institutional response is called for. In the preceding section we looked at three scenarios where property rights had, for various reasons, come to bestow disproportionate economic leverage in comparison to their underlying social value. I sketched some examples drawn from IP law, such as the component patent holders discussed in *eBay* and the code-writing macro users in the *Lotus* case. I tried to show through the examples that the bridge parable captured something important, that the elements of the parable correspond to important aspects of real-world IP conflicts.

At this point, I want to dig more deeply into one aspect of the examples I described. The Supreme Court in *eBay* spoke of the patents there as conferring "undue leverage." This was, as I said earlier, the main point of disagreement with the Federal Circuit, which had resisted any attempt to second-guess the market price for patents that resulted from application of the traditional strong-injunction rule. The Federal Circuit's commonsense, and widely shared, view was that once the basic legal entitlement was set—in that case, once a valid patent had issued—courts had no business meddling in the market-making process. Whatever price a patent commanded because of the injunction rule was simply a normal consequence of the fact that patents are property. But the Supreme Court disagreed. It listened to the complaints of the petitioner, eBay, and the other companies that filed briefs in the case. These complaints boiled down to a charge of disproportionate leverage—a charge the Court took seriously.

The Court therefore demonstrated a willingness to look behind the entitlement structure that was driving market-making for component patents. Starting with this prominent example, I want to review some other occasions when courts have been willing to make this move. What I am after is to understand when courts feel comfortable modifying the entitlement structure of already-issued IP rights to correct for undue leverage. As I said earlier, there is a connection between these instances of postgrant correction and requirements for the grant of rights in the first place. Both postgrant correction and pregrant requirements aim to enforce the principle of proportionality. This is easier to see—and less controversial—in the case of pregrant requirements. Instances of postgrant correction are fairly uncommon, due to the legal system's strong presumption in favor of stable entitlements and enforceable agreements based on them.

Beyond eBay: Postgrant Proportionality

The key to understanding postgrant correction is that it is usually an attempt to reestablish proportionality after unforeseen developments effectively increase the leverage attendant upon an IP right. Just as with the three scenarios in the parable described earlier, disproportionality often does not become apparent until after some time has passed. Often, undue leverage is a matter of changed circumstances, when the application of legal standards that were logical and effective at some initial time becomes, due to changed circumstances, unreasonable. Courts are of course especially well suited to assess these sorts of changes and to adjust legal rules accordingly. They have shown a propensity to do this in the IP system, as many of the examples described in this chapter show quite clearly. Just to recap a few:

- The application of fair use to prevent undue leverage by computer game makers
- The revision of injunction standards to prevent disproportionate leverage by patent holders in *eBay*
- The updating of the utility requirement in patent law to obviate the patenting of gene snippets aimed at capturing the value of later-discovered genes
- The revision of patent damages doctrine to bring financial awards back into line with technological contributions where small component patents are asserted against complex, multicomponent products

These are all situations where courts have intervened to correct for disproportionate leverage.

PROPORTIONALITY THEORY: EX ANTE VERSUS EX POST

I have, in the spirit of Chapter 5, identified proportionality as a midlevel principle in IP law. What I have not done—and what the courts that apply proportionality never really attempt to do—is to provide some theory to back it up. I will try to remedy that now.

At the outset, we need to deal with a potential objection to applying proportionality after initial property entitlements have been set. There is a considerable intellectual tradition that is deeply opposed to such a move. Resistance to meddling with established property rights is often associated with libertarian theory. The fear of unrestrained governmental power let loose to grab private holdings and destroy private security forms a potent motif in this brand of political philosophy. At the level of legal rule and policy, these concerns are often expressed in strong claims about the imperative of government respect for established property holdings. Governments may change the parameters of property rights before they are granted, at the ex ante stage. But woe unto any governmental official who tries to seize property or even rejigger property rights after they have been granted.

Despite the sharpness of the ex ante/ex post distinction, there is reason to be skeptical about this dividing line. One of the most important contributions of law and economics methodology has been to call attention to the way a legal decision in a discrete conflict today influences and shapes private activities in the future.[43] The resolution of an existing dispute after it has arisen gives a legal rule that shapes and structures bargaining and other behavior in the future. Ex post shapes ex ante. As countless observers have argued, if there is a pervasive understanding that property rights can be adjusted after the fact and at the margin to take account of changed circumstances or urgent social needs, this understanding will naturally be incorporated into the settled expectations of all property holders. If the fact of occasional rebalancing is built into expectations, it cannot be argued that an actual instance of rebalancing radically undermines settled expectations.

This is a controversial issue in the literature on constitutional "takings."[44] But one does not necessarily need to take sides in that contentious and long-running dispute to accept my argument regarding IP rights. IP rights are complex and multifaceted, and IP doctrine is subject to a never-ending pattern of ebb, flux, and flow. Courts can change literally hundreds of small details of IP doctrine over the life of a copyright, trademark, or even a patent. Everyone knows at the outset, when the right is first granted, that this is the case. All sorts of uncertainties attend the initial acquisition of an IP right—uncertainties as to validity, coverage, and especially ultimate economic value. Because these rights are so subject to the vicissitudes of doctrinal flow and flux, it cannot be reasonably argued that expectations regarding them are rigid, fixed, and comprehensive. Owning an IP right is in some sense an adventure—and every experienced IP owner knows this. The adventuring spirit that is built into each owner's expectations is thus thoroughly inconsistent with the notion that the slightest change in IP doctrine or policy will somehow destabilize the well-ordered expectations of IP owners everywhere. If any class of owners is used to zigs and zags in the fortunes of a property right, this is it. It is a class of owners that knows better than to count on unchanging doctrine, unwavering policy. To argue otherwise, to argue that all aspects of IP rights must be fixed and frozen at the outset and never varied or altered, except upon payment of full compensation for the cost of the alteration, is an exercise in folly.

PROPORTIONALITY THEORY: REGULATING MARKET EXCHANGE

And so, in my view anyway, it is perfectly legitimate to impart moderate adjustments to IP entitlements to correct for radical imbalances that may emerge. The question now is: where can we find guidance about when and how to do this? What theory can we employ to do the job properly, well, and not to excess?

The answer begins, as so often, with Locke. In Chapter 2 I pointed out that there is extensive support in Locke's writings for the idea of limits and restraints on property. We have seen already numerous examples of micro-adjustments in IP rights: a change in the injunction standard in *eBay,* or a disqualification of gene snippet patents in the *Fisher* case, or the application of copyright fair use to cover reverse engineering of computer game interfaces, to name a few. All these adjustments fit comfortably into Locke's thinking on property, for several reasons. One is that they represent small adjustments that seem implicit in the grant of initial rights. It is not possible, in a complex field such as IP, that all third-party effects of a given appropriation of resources can be foreseen at the time of initial appropriation. So it follows that some of the provisos I discussed in Chapter 2—sufficiency and charity, especially, but possibly spoilage too—would at times need to be applied at the ex post stage, after the initial grant of rights. In addition, recall that Locke understood that his basic theory of appropriation supported the founding of civil society, but that he understood there would be a fair degree of discretion in the details of property regimes as implemented by a fully functioning state. For these reasons, postgrant rights adjustments seem entirely consistent with Locke's concept of property rights as strong but nonetheless bounded.

Kant is relevant too. He has his own set of limits on property rights, both at the initial claim stage and, implicitly anyway, at the application or deployment stage. The key restraint for Kant is his Universal Principle of Right, which says that property should be granted to enhance individual autonomy but only when consistent with the freedom of all others as well. Though this may be interpreted only as a constraint on initial grants—to grant rights only when all others are subject to the same conditions on grants—it may also be used in support of ex post property adjustments. There is nothing in Kant that suggests that the conditions of freedom may not change over time. And because he leaves so much room for the operation of actual legal systems after the founding of a civil state, it is reasonable to suppose that microadjustments of the type I have described fit comfortably within his overall views on property.

What about the lessons of Chapter 4, on distributive justice? There is a rich literature in this general vein that is quite relevant. It deals with the questions of the fairness of market outcomes, and also the related problem of when and how states may intervene to undo or adjust the results of market exchange. Questions of proportionality touch on this sort of theory, because the impulse to correct disproportionate leverage always involves changing a property entitlement in a way that necessarily alters market exchange. If we think back to the *eBay* case, when the Supreme Court spoke of "undue leverage" it meant simply that under the existing injunction rule patent owners were demanding a price that seemed out of all proportion to the intrinsic value of their patents. When the Court changed the injunction rule in response to this perceived imbalance, what was this but a resetting of the entitlement structure in a way designed explicitly to affect the entitlements being exchanged in the shadow of the injunction rule? Buried deep in the logic and rhetoric of the Court's action was the idea that if the Court did not intervene, patent owners would continue to get more in the market for patents than they intrinsically deserved.

Put this way, the holding in *eBay* stands in for all those occasions when courts feel that property rights have come to exert "undue leverage." The implicit premise, of course, is that there is another, lesser, degree of leverage—that which is intrinsically "due" the patent owner. Applying this logic in specific cases is, therefore, a limited, covert application of the ideas of fairness or distributive justice in economic exchange relations, a topic we considered in some depth in Chapter 4. Small adjustments to patent doctrine are not of course on the same scale as sweeping redistributive schemes such as the one embraced by John Rawls. But under the surface, the basic logic behind cases like *eBay* does occupy some common ground with broad theories of distributive justice.

The common ground I am talking about centers on the impulse to look behind voluntary market exchange when conditions seem to warrant it. Market exchange, based on existing entitlements, is not always to be taken as an ineluctable sign of fairness. Nor is it to be treated as a process so sacrosanct that it may never be tampered with or adjusted. Indeed, it is right at the point where a sense of disproportionality, stemming from existing entitlements, meets microadjustments in doctrine that the spirit of distributive justice finds practical application.

ON THE SURPLUS VALUE DEBATE—AND STAYING OUT OF IT

What we are bumping up against is the edge of a messy and complex topic—the problem of "surplus value." The basic issue is whether the sellers of goods in a market economy deserve—are strongly entitled to—all the surplus value they can capture through the market price.[45] Surplus value has a number of definitions, but the basic intuition is that goods sold on the market have some sort of natural or normal value and that, at times, due to various market dynamics a seller can charge more than this amount. The question in this area is, do they deserve to keep the portion of the market price that exceeds the natural or normal price—the surplus value? The conflicting and cross-cutting answers to this simple question form one of the longer-standing quarrels in the intellectual world.[46]

One corner of the debate is dedicated to John Rawls, discussed in Chapter 4, and some of his critics, most notably the prominent libertarian philosopher Robert Nozick. In his book *Anarchy, State and Utopia* (1974), Nozick argues that the only relevant criterion for judging the fairness of resource distribution is the fairness of initial acquisition and subsequent transfers. Nozick says that if people voluntarily transfer some of what they have to others, and these transfers accumulate in the hands of one individual disproportionately, there is no reason to question the resulting distribution. Any effort at redistribution would undermine the legitimacy of the initial acquisition. In addition, redistribution would require constant interventions by the state to adjust the distribution of property to keep it within the parameters of what was deemed "fair." This amounts to the argument that people are entitled to the full economic value of their property—the price it commands in a fair market exchange—so long as they come by that property honestly. This has been called the "historical" account of entitlement. It is one justification for the position that sellers deserve to keep the full market price of anything they sell. As long as the seller has a valid legal title to what he or she sells, no one can claim any portion of the sales price. This is a broad-ranging argument, embracing a strong antitaxation message, but in the present context I want to stick to just one aspect of it: the notion that it excludes any opportunity for ex post adjustment in the property rights over the things people own, regardless of any societal intuition about the "intrinsic" value of those entitlements or the unfairness of the market price that the entitlement commands. Thus, if valid title implies the right to all surplus value, there is no such thing as "undue leverage" as that term was used in *eBay*, and hence no place for the broader principle of proportionality.

The literature on fairness and surplus value is large and diverse; this is an issue that shows up in many forms in a society based on a market economy. We touched on one aspect of the surplus value debate in Chapter 4, in a discussion of whether creative people deserve the fruits of their talent. A good illustration of this issue is a famous illustration employed by Nozick to explain his "historical title" theory. Nozick—in response to Rawls's argument that no one in a strong sense deserves the natural talents he is born with—describes the willing transfer of money by fans eager to see a game starring the basketball player Wilt Chamberlain. According to Nozick (again, contra Rawls), Chamberlain deserves his talent, and because of this deserves to keep all the money he makes from the fans who pay to see him display his talents. The idea is simple: fans own the money they pay to see the game—no one has a superior claim on the money. So the aggregation of all the money in Chamberlain's pocket is unquestionably fair. The fans come by their money honestly; Chamberlain comes by the fans' money honestly. For Nozick, case closed.

A critique of Nozick's Chamberlain story by the legal scholar Barbara Fried says, in effect, "nice try."[47] Fried contends that Nozick's story is a sleight of hand, drawing the reader's attention to the uncontroversial idea that people may rightly transfer what they own, and in the process hiding a classic controversy: whether one who receives something of value in a transaction is morally deserving of the full exchange price. The old and controversial question of surplus value, in other words, is lurking just below the surface. Fried does not attempt to resolve the surplus value puzzle (probably no one can do that to complete satisfaction), but she argues persuasively that Nozick's approach of hiding it—"smuggling it out" of the discussion, in her words—is not the answer either. Fried's position is that each fan having title to his or her money, and then transferring that money to Chamberlain, does not *automatically* establish the fairness of the total market payment to Chamberlain. Assuming that it does just begs the question of fairness, assumes it away. So for those who take Fried's side in her argument with Nozick, the state might tax Chamberlain's earnings, perhaps even aggressively, because Chamberlain has no impregnable desert claim to all of his income.

Fried's critique of Nozick's theory can be invoked in defense of the proportionality principle. The same rigid adherence to status quo entitlements that drives Nozick's theory can be identified in the view that property entitlements must never be tampered with, must never be adjusted, to redress perceived instances of undue leverage. And the same critique applies: to say that all market outcomes are per se valid and fair because they are based on entitlements as they existed when a deal was struck is to beg the question of fairness, not answer it. To put it slightly differently, it is a thin and shrunken picture of fairness that requires us to turn away from the outcome of a market exchange because we are permitted only to examine the preconditions of that exchange. If unfairness seems to appear at the aggregate level—Chamberlain makes a mint and pays no taxes while others starve, for example—we should not be prevented from looking into and even adjusting aggregate-level outcomes.

If our approach did prevent this, it would signal a misplaced commitment to looking only at initial endowments or entitlements. If our hands are tied at the level of large-scale outcomes, we will be prevented from reaching out and performing many acts of justice. True, each fan who pays to see Chamberlain may have a right to the money used to buy a ticket to the game. Even so it might be fair to tax Chamberlain for the great windfall that has come his way by virtue of his talent and the fans' interest in the game. By the same token, it might seem perfectly legitimate for a property owner to extract as much as possible from users of his land, based on the starting conditions—actual legal ownership, and a given set of market conditions. Even so, it might be fair to modify the owner's rights slightly to correct for the unintended and unforeseen windfall that attends changed circumstances that permit the owner to charge much more for the asset covered by the property than that asset was intrinsically worth. Implicit in the judgment that in each case market exchange produces a windfall is the notion that this form of exchange is not always unquestionably and unalterably fair.

We also see echoes of some of the distributive issues covered in Chapter 4. In each of the three scenarios of the bridge parable, forces outside the control of the owner contribute significantly to the market value of the property right. The disproportionality this produces is a result, we might say, of social forces. This has a familiar ring, when we recall the discussion in Chapter 4 of social versus individual contributions to a creative person's success and achievements. Just as I defended a bifurcated notion of desert—distinguishing between the deserving core attributable to the individual and the peripheral contributions of society in general—I would argue that proportionality relies on a similar bifurcation. A judge, looking at a case in which a property right appears to have accrued undue leverage, must assess whether the market power of the right still bears some plausible relation to the intrinsic value or contribution the right represents. The deserving core addressed in Chapter 4 is close in spirit, therefore, to the idea of a property right's intrinsic value. Both concepts are expressions of some deep sense of appropriateness or fitness.

An Important, but Modest, Principle

This business of court intervention into private market ordering is and should be a highly unusual event. The various legal doctrines courts employ in disproportionate leverage cases are all hotly contested and narrowly limited. And they should be. In the right case, it makes perfect sense to short-circuit the operation of a market. In these rare cases, markets are thrown out of whack because the property rights underlying them are subject to manipulation and misuse. Meaning, in the case of IP, that because of unusual circumstances the market price a property right can fetch has been distorted out of any sane relationship to the intrinsic value of the underlying work.

In these rare cases, the usually reliable market mechanism misfires and courts have to step in. This is of course one of the primary assignments of the court, to maintain stability and regularity, and to intervene when fundamental fairness demands it.

Here is the distributional point: in these cases, the market cannot be relied on to set an appropriate price for the relevant transaction. Or, perhaps more accurately, intervention is required to reset the market. Until things are reset, the market cannot be relied on to achieve its proper purpose. Property owners who have achieved disproportionate leverage will be overrewarded in light of the intrinsic merits of the creative works they own. The result—an unearned economic rent, a supernormal return—will then draw investment and resources away from other projects that are more productive. A court is needed to recalibrate the starting point for market negotiation and transactions.

Two points are in order about the limited nature of the intervention this principle requires. First, while the doctrines that embody this principle involve a judgment by the courts that the default market valuation is out of proportion, it does not require that courts substitute their own valuation. The only real valuation required is a comparison between two values: the "intrinsic" value of the right and the price the right in question would fetch in a market transaction. In other words, the valuation is rough, and strictly comparative—ordinal, rather than cardinal, in the mathematic sense. The judge need only ask: is the intrinsic value of this right utterly disproportionate to the price it is commanding in the market? This is a much easier decision to make than a finding of specific (cardinal) value. By eschewing the need for explicit valuation, and by burying even the implicit valuation it does require in the preliminary steps of a complex analysis, the proportionality principle saves judges from the scrutiny and criticism that typically follow when judges explicitly substitute their judgment for that of a market.

A second advantage of the valuation implicit in the proportionality principle is that it is subsumed—hidden or submerged, really—in a doctrinal determination or ruling. The valuation need never be explicitly stated, and indeed a judge need never make a discrete dollar valuation at all. The end result of a proportionality analysis is not stated in terms of valuation. In fact, unless you look carefully, you won't see any valuation going on. The judge says, "this injunction should not issue," or "this is fair use," or "this patent does not meet the utility requirement." The formal structure of these rules carries a great virtue. It is very easy to attack judicial valuation in our sociolegal system, which for so many purposes uses market exchange as the legitimate benchmark. Rules operating under the proportionality principle reflect a clever form of social wisdom. They disguise not only the specific valuation of a particular right, but also in many cases the very *fact* that a valuation has been made at all.

Even so, explicit recognition of undue leverage is a slippery slope, and a steep one. Taken too far, it leads to a rock-strewn abyss. I know that well-intentioned intervention designed to "correct" all manner of "market failures" is the opening wedge into many a dystopian policy backed by many a well-intentioned socialist reformer or power-mad despot. I realize all that. And still I say that though it is dangerous, it is *more* dangerous to allow market distribution even though its outcome is absurd or manifestly unfair. If Rawls teaches anything, it is that attention to fair distribution at the systemic level bears tightly on political legitimacy. It is hard to defend a legal system that permits grossly distorted transactions, even if they grow out of arrangements that were originally voluntary. Unfair and unreasonable economic arrangements are after all the ultimate weapon of the despot.

Conclusion

The essence of the parable of the bridge, and the IP cases it was drawn from, is that a small property right winds up controlling a large market. This violates an implicit principle of IP law: that property rights ought to be proportional in their intrinsic value to the market they control. A whole host of IP doctrines operates to regulate this relationship of proportionality.

This principle has a strong affinity with the property theory of Locke and Kant. It is a perfect application of the kinds of prudential limitations these theorists built into their theories. And, because it reflects a judgment that property owners are reaping more than they deserve in a certain situation, it is also an expression of some of the distributive justice concerns we examined in Chapter 4.

Our in-depth exploration of the midlevel principles of Chapter 5 now comes to an end. Referring back to the hierarchy diagram in the Introduction, we are ready to proceed to the top tier, the domain of detailed rules and policies. The plan is now to apply and extend the concepts developed so far to some complex IP-related issues, starting with the general problem of corporate ownership. How do we understand the relevance of IP rights, justified and granted on the basis of individual effort, individual desert, and individual autonomy, in a world where collective organizations like corporations actually own and control so many of these rights? That is the general problem we take up next.

PART THREE

ISSUES

CHAPTER SEVEN

Creative Professionals, Corporate Ownership, and Transaction Costs

I HAVE SPENT A LOT OF TIME so far justifying IP law at a foundational, theoretical level. I argued in Chapters 2 through 4 that IP law is fully consistent with, and made good sense in terms of, foundational ideas about property rights and the basic organization of society. In Chapters 5 and 6 I laid out what I see as the essential principles of the field: Nonremoval/public domain, efficiency, dignity, and proportionality. I devoted Chapter 6 to a detailed consideration of the last principle. I hope it is well established by this point that IP law deserves a place in a just and rational modern state. If it is not, I have done my best, and leave whatever is missing for others to fill in.

Having done what I could to put in place the conceptual building stones, I turn now to the more visible parts of the structure that is IP law. Rewarding effort and promoting autonomy—these are the deep designs that find expression in IP law, along with a concern that individual property rights always be squared with the interests of others. In the above-ground world of wind and weather, how are these designs put into practice?

The fundamental answer is simple; its working out, complex. Reward means payment: those who create works worthy of IP protection ought to have a shot at decent compensation. Autonomy means freedom of choice and action: IP ought to give its owners the chance to develop talent and thereby make a solid living as creative professionals. So the hallmarks of this structure we call IP law should have these two features, evident from every angle and viewed in every light: reward and autonomy.

Creative Professionals

I want in this section to give some general information about creative professionals—how many there are, who they work for, and, roughly, how much money they make. The goal is to take a diverse class of people, often discussed abstractly if at all, and provide some basic information about their economic situation.

Before doing so, however, I need to first defend the idea that creative professionals ought to be a special object of interest for IP law and policy.

Why Special Solicitude for Professionals?

There was a time when IP protection and the nurturing of creative professionals were ideas so deeply intertwined that they might well have been thought to be coextensive. In that era, making a living from creative work was the central function of IP law. Though there have always been noteworthy amateurs and altruistic contributors to the storehouse of creative works, the livelihood of the creative class was thought central to what IP is about. In my view, it still is.[1]

That this claim today not only needs defending, but is positively contrarian in many circles, shows how much has changed in our discourse over the years. Today many voices speak out in favor of "bottom-up" creativity. The rise of the amateurs, the democratization of culture, the leveling effect of ubiquitous technologies of creation and dissemination, the contributions of "users" as against official creators—these are the prominent themes today. Any defense of the professional creator must confront the dominance of these themes in contemporary IP discourse.

My defense has two parts. Professionals and the high-quality work they do are still crucial to the industries that rely on IP rights; I start there. But the further point is this: solid respect for IP rights is also the most flexible and accommodating policy, one capable of supporting a thriving bottom-up cultural movement as well. Nurturing the careers of creative professionals via strong IP protection thus does the most for *all* varieties of creative work—professional and amateur alike. This policy has the advantage over a policy of weak IP that might help amateurs a little, but could deal a crushing blow to professionals. By contrast, stronger IP—despite what many say—does little harm to amateurs while providing a crucial lifeline for professionals. The reason strong IP does not stand in the way of amateur, bottom-up creativity is that IP rights are often not enforced. Technical infringements are undetected or overlooked, or rights may be formally waived through a variety of mechanisms (contract, notice, or dedication to the public). Thus the common notion that stronger IP inevitably interferes with amateur creativity is wrong. Any policy designed to weaken IP rights in order to promote bottom-up culture is therefore unnecessary. The harm it would do to professionals is simply not justified.

IP AND THE PROPERTIZATION OF LABOR

Though what I have written so far may seem self-evident, it is worth a moment to go into more depth about how IP serves the interests of creative professionals ("creatives"). What we need to understand is the mechanism by which IP rights are connected to the care and nurturing of the creative class.

Put simply, the answer is that IP on average increases the incomes of creative professionals. It enhances dignity as well, as we saw in Chapter 6; but augmenting income is its main contribution. The *way* it does this is not always completely understood, however, so that is the topic at hand.

Picture someone whose job involves creating or performing: a computer programmer, for example, or a musician. Suppose the programmer specializes in writing code for a specific set of problems faced by a specific industry—inventory and sales tracking software for auto dealers, for example. And maybe the performer writes songs and plays the guitar.

People with jobs like this can and often do get paid "by the hour." Their income is capped, in effect, by the number of hours available for work. When not writing code or playing music, they earn no money.

What does the coder or musician need to break free from this limit? Two things: a way to capture the effort of a moment in a manner that allows it to be copied and replayed; and legal protection. The need for the first is obvious. You have to put a performance "in the can" to be able to replay it at will. The second requirement is fairly apparent too. At the limit, if there is no way to protect against copying a performance that has been captured, the coder or musician will sell only one copy.

Ideally, the legal protection over the captured performance will be powerful and flexible. It will apply not only to audience members who enter into contracts but to complete strangers as well. This means of course a property right—a right good against the world. A property right over the captured performance permits the creative person to earn money on a given quantum of effort even after the effort is finished. It protects the captured work from being copied without authorization, converting the effort from a static, one-time event into a dynamic, productive asset—converting *work* into *a work*, an asset or thing. This is what I mean by the propertization of labor.[2]

When the person who exerts the effort owns the asset, the advantages are obvious. A creative person with IP rights over an asset has a chance to earn money from it in many different ways. Most basically, a creative person can earn money from a given effort multiple times. The capacity to earn lives on after the effort has been expended. But propertization can still help the creator even when she does not own the asset. A creative professional who works as an employee adds more value to the employer when effort can be propertized. Enhanced prospects for the employer, made possible by propertization of employee effort, can translate into enhanced earnings for the creative employee. There is also evidence that the possibility of IP rights may, under prevailing legal rules, increase the share of profits that will be allocated to a creative employee.[3]

BRIEF HISTORICAL DIVERSION:
PATRONAGE AND ITS DISCONTENTS

An example from history can help illustrate how IP rights enhance income while increasing creator autonomy. Before the advent of workable IP systems (roughly, before 1800), there were people employed as creative professionals (though of course many of the jobs discussed so far did not yet exist). But by far the most common employment pattern was what we call today patronage. Under this system, an independent composer, author, scientist, or scholar was employed directly, typically by a person of wealth and noble birth. Creative professionals served at the whim of their patron. While there was some mobility—professionals with greater talent typically, though not always, migrated toward wealthier patrons—there were also significant constraints. Creative people had to please their patrons and, more generally, serve their patron's purposes. They also had to produce new works constantly to keep their primary audience happy; it was not possible to "recycle" old works when a patron or group of court favorites constituted the sole revenue-generating audience. Patronage thus provided a living for creative professionals, but working conditions, and especially the conditions required to foster creativity, were far from optimal.

A common narrative about the rise of IP rights in the nineteenth century (associated perhaps most closely with the work of Stanford professor of law Paul Goldstein)[4] is that these rights allowed creative professionals to *directly engage* a mass audience for the first time. They provided a way to bypass patronage and connect a creative person directly with a large audience. This resulted in an explosion in the ranks of creative professionals, as direct connection between creator and audience replaced the limited and constraining market for patronage. Perhaps surprisingly, in at least some cases the result was also a more relaxed pace on the part of creative professionals. We can see evidence of this, and some of the other points I have been making, in the history of some great composers in the nineteenth century.

Like other pre-eighteenth-century creative professionals, composers worked under the patronage system.[5] To be a creative professional, one had to find someone who would pay for creative output. Patrons, usually members of the nobility, and often kings and other sorts of political rulers, could add to their prestige by employing composers and others to write music for performance at court or in similar settings. (Wealthy churches also employed composers.)

Joseph Lowenstein, in a study of the literary marketplace in history, makes note of the difficult situation of premodern authors: "Technically, however, the situation of authors was extremely stark: a Renaissance author never quite *owned* a literary work, or at least not a literary work as we now somewhat abstractly conceive it. (The development of such an abstract notion of literary work was a slow process: it depended on— among other things—the expansion of authorial rights within the seventeenth-century literary market. . . .)."[6] This lack of control bothered composers as much as the struggle to earn a living. As the eighteenth-century Italian composer Luigi Boccherini said: "But remember that there is nothing worse than to tie the hands of a poor author, that is to say, to confine his ideas and imagination by subjecting him to rules."[7]

Scholars generally agree with this assessment: things began to change in the eighteenth century. Owing to a combination of factors—changes in political structures in many countries, growing wealth and appreciation of music by nonnobles, and, not least important, stronger IP rights for musical compositions—creative professionals began to earn at least part of their income through direct contact with a mass audience. Small payments from many anonymous consumers replaced one large payment from a single wealthy patron.

Those who lived during the transitional period of the eighteenth century were attuned to the advantages and disadvantages of patronage versus mass-market participation. A trenchant comparison comes to us from the famous writer and wit Samuel Johnson, whose views on this (and many other matters) were preserved and transmitted by James Boswell. A review of a nineteenth-century edition of Boswell's *Life of Johnson,* written by the eminent nineteenth-century essayist and historian Sir Thomas Carlyle, surveys Samuel Johnson's experience with eighteenth-century patronage:

> At the time of Johnson's appearance in the field, Literature . . . was in the very act of passing from the protection of Patrons into that of the Public; no longer to supply its necessities by laudatory Dedications to the Great, but by judicious Bargains with Booksellers. . . . At the time of Johnson's appearance, there were still two ways, on which an Author might attempt proceeding:

[patronage and commerce with booksellers]. To a considerate man it might seem uncertain which method were the preferable: neither had very high attractions; the Patron's aid was now well nigh *necessarily* polluted by sycophancy, before it could come to hand; the Bookseller's was deformed with greedy stupidity, not to say entire wooden-headedness and disgust . . . , and barely could keep the thread of life together. The one was the wages of suffering and poverty; the other, unless you gave strict heed to it, the wages of sin. In time, Johnson had the opportunity of looking into both methods, and ascertaining what they were; but found, at first trial, that the former would in nowise do for him. Listen, once again, to that far-flamed Blast of Doom, proclaiming into the ear of Lord Chesterfield and, through him, of the listening world, that Patronage should be no more![8]

IP Rights and the Birth of the Mass Audience. At the theoretical level, there is a clear relationship between stronger, clearer IP rights and the viability of writing, composing, and the like as real professions. IP, like all property, is all about the making of markets: rights are granted over a thing so everyone who might want to use that thing knows whom to contact, and whom to pay for its use. Without a property right on the thing one produces, there is no direct market for that thing. There may be other ways to get paid for making it—as an employee, for example, contributing something to a larger product but paid only for the labor spent in the process. But only if some form of property right covers what one makes can one confidently sell one's output on a mass market, to a large number of strangers.

This basic logic played an important part in the growth of the market for writings and compositions, and hence the emergence of non-patron-supported professional options in these fields. It is no coincidence that the professional composer, supported in part at least outside the traditional patronage system, came of age at the same time the copyright system was explicitly recognizing the rights of composers. For example, in a celebrated eighteenth-century British case involving C. P. E. Bach (son of Johann Sebastian) and challenging the rights of composers to claim copyright in their written music, the eminent jurist Lord Chief Justice Edwin Mansfield ruled in favor of Bach after hearing oral argument from Bach's attorney:[9]

> The words of the Act of Parliament are very large: "books and other writings." It is not confined to language or letters. Music is a science; it may be written; and the mode of conveying the ideas, is by signs and marks. A person may use the copy by playing it; but he has no right to rob the author of the profit, by multiplying copies and disposing of them to his own use . . . [W]e are of opinion, that a musical composition is a writing within the Statute of the 8th of Queen Anne.

This expansion in the rights of composers was not limited to Great Britain. Throughout Europe, courts and legislators in the nineteenth century came to grant copyrights for musical compositions. The question that scholars have tried to answer is, did these changes have the anticipated effect; was professional composing a more viable, more rewarding career after these changes took effect?

The economist F. M. Scherer has gone the furthest to answer this question. Scherer's statistical analysis tries to estimate the effect of stronger copyright protection on the career choices of Europeans in the eighteenth and nineteenth centuries.[10] His findings are best described as mixed. On a strictly quantitative basis, he concludes that it is impossible to demonstrate that increased copyright protection definitively increased the number of composers in Europe during the period under study. At first glance, this strikes a blow against the idea that copyright protection matters for composers of music—that it is an important factor in making composing a viable career choice. Before accepting this, however, two pertinent points must be noted. First, despite the importance of copyright during this period, composers still usually made at least part of their income from non-copyright-related sources. This means that the marginal effect of increased copyright protection may not have been significant enough to draw more people into careers as full-time composers. However, it does not mean that copyright was irrelevant. As the case of Giuseppe Verdi shows, copyright allowed at least some composers greater control over their professional lives.[11] So the relevant issue may not be whether people chose to become composers; those with talent may have seen that it was possible to make a living at it even when copyright was weak or nonexistent. It may instead be what mix of activities professional composers chose to undertake. All the qualitative evidence here points to an important conclusion, which comprises Scherer's second main contribution. Scherer shows that the strengthening of copyright gave composers greater control over what kinds of works they could compose while enabling them to make a living as professional composers. Thus, in the end it is clear that stronger IP protection did in fact give a major boost to the viability of composing as a rewarding career.

The best evidence here is the statements of composers themselves. Consider this impassioned statement from musical composer Arthur Sullivan, of Gilbert and Sullivan fame, in a packed New York theater on the U.S. opening night of the now-famous musical comedy *The Mikado:*

> It may be that some day the legislators of this magnificent country . . . may see fit to afford the same protection to a man who employs his brains in literature [as to a mechanical inventor]. . . . But even when that day comes, as I hope and believe it will come . . . we . . . shall still, . . . trust mainly to the unerring instinct of the great public for what is good, right, and honest.[12]

Sullivan was referring to the fact that in 1885, when he was speaking, patent protection in the United States was considered robust and effective. (This was in contrast with Sullivan's native England, where the late-nineteenth-century patent system was said to be quite behind that of the United States at the time.)[13] He might also have been referring to international protection: when he spoke, international patent protection was already in place in the United States (thanks to its adherence to the Paris Convention of 1883, during the first wave of international interest in patent harmonization), but the United States was much slower to adhere to the Berne Convention, not becoming a full member until the late twentieth century.

A brief word on state patronage is in order, by way of contrast. At one time it was thought that official state support for creative work might be a better alternative to both traditional patronage and "capitalist" IP-based models.[14] There is essentially no evidence to support this hypothesis, and so it is largely a dead letter today. While modest state support lives on, it normally takes the form of grants and subsidies, rather than direct commissioning and support for full-time creative professionals. Even these small gestures in the direction of full state support still raise concerns, however—strong evidence that full-on state patronage is recognized as perhaps the worst of all possible worlds.[15]

Of course, one example from history cannot make a lock-solid case. Yet the move from patronage to individual ownership certainly illustrates how IP rights can facilitate and enhance creative autonomy.[16] Though economic conditions have changed in many ways, and though ideal IP policy is not simply a matter of strengthening rights and leaving the market to do the rest, there is nonetheless a valuable lesson in this episode from history. With proper handling and an appreciation of nuance, we can continue to reenact the success story of the move away from patronage. IP still holds the potential to make working conditions better and to enhance the creative freedom of individual creators.

A Just-So Story? Even for those who agree that creative professionals deserve special attention in IP law, there may be doubt that strong IP, or even any IP in some cases, serves this goal. Some would argue that there are other, superior, ways for creative professionals to profit from their work. Others might say that even if IP effectively rewards these professionals, it does so at a very high social cost—that in effect the IP game is not worth the candle. I will take on both objections later in this chapter. For now, I want to sketch out who we are talking about. How many creative professionals are out there, what kinds of jobs do they have, and how much money do they generally make? Until we have an idea of how many people we are talking about, and some general characteristics of their working lives, we cannot talk intelligently about how best to help them.

The Professional Creative Landscape

I turn now to a description of exactly who these creative professionals are. I want to give an overview of the types of jobs they hold, the types of work they do, how many work alone, how many work in companies, and how large those companies are. (A major theme here is that the abstract goal of individual autonomy translates into a practical preference for independent workers and "small creative teams," usually smaller companies.) Where possible, I also want to give a sense of how much money creative professionals make in the jobs they hold.

I will divide my treatment into three sections. The first covers what are sometimes called "the copyright industries": entertainment, publishing, and the like. The second covers a very diverse group, technologists who work in jobs where inventions are common. The third covers a smaller and also diverse group, people who specialize in trademark and brand promotion work. The idea is to give an extremely abbreviated snapshot of the creative professionals, taken as a whole.

ENTERTAINMENT

We will start with some basic information about employment in the arts, entertainment, and recreation industries (see Table 7.1).

Table 7.1 Employment in arts, entertainment, and recreation by detailed industry, 2006 (employment in thousands)

Industry segment	Employment	Percent
Arts, entertainment, and recreation, total	1,927	100.0
Performing arts companies	121	6.3
Promoters of performing arts, sports, and similar events	83	4.3
Independent artists, writers, and performers	47	2.4
Agents and managers for artists, athletes, entertainers, and other public figures	17	0.9

Source: U.S. Dept. of Commerce, Bureau of Labor Statistics, current data at http://www.bls.gov/oco/cg/cgs031.htm#emply.

One important point to note: according to these data, there are only 47,000 "independent artists, writers and performers" at work in the U.S. economy. Though many others work in what might be called the "creative professional ecosystem," as some of the other tables in this chapter will show, artists, writers, and performers are the core of the system. And it is a very small core. At the same time, the stated figures clearly understate employment in this sector. As the report says, "Most establishments in the arts, entertainment, and recreation industry contract out lighting, sound, set-building, and exhibit-building work to firms not included in this industry."[17] We learn something else from these data: most companies in this sector are small. Figure 7.1 tells the story.[18]

A more detailed look at the figures for employees (as opposed to independents) shows again the small creative core at the center of the entertainment industries.[19] There are 84,200 "art directors," 79,000 multimedia artists and animators, 23,600 fine artists (sculptors, painters, illustrators), 13,100 "craft artists," and 21,500 "other" artists. By contrast, landscapers

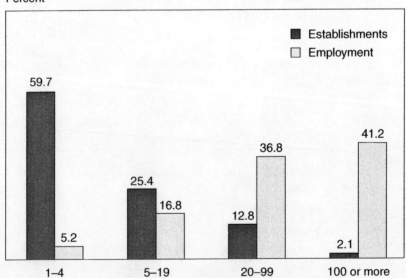

Eighty-five percent of establishments in the arts, entertainment, and recreation industry employ fewer than 20 workers.

Percent

Number of workers employed by establishment,
March 2006

Figure 7.1. Firm size in arts, entertainment, and recreation industries, 2004. *Source:* U.S. Bureau of Labor Statistics, *Career Guide to Industries, 2006–2007* (Washington, D.C.: Government Printing Office, 2006), at 246.

and amusement park attendants number 113,000 and 166,400 respectively.[20] A small group of creative professionals, then, supports a large ecosystem of related workers.

Looking specifically at writers, we can get a sense of earnings. Table 7.2 shows employment estimate and mean wage estimates for this occupation, while Table 7.3 shows percentile wage estimates for this occupation. Table 7.4 presents the top-paying industries for writers, along with the number of writers employed in each of those industries, while Table 7.5 shows the main industries that employ writers.

Table 7.2 Writers' employment estimate and mean wage estimates

Employment	Mean hourly wage	Mean annual wage
43,390	$31.04	$64,560

Source: U.S. Bureau of Labor Statistics, Occupational Employment Statistics, 27-3043: Writers and Authors, http://www.bls.gov/oes/current/oes273043.htm.

Table 7.3 Writer's percentile wage estimates

	10%	25%	50% (Median)	75%	90%
Hourly wage	$13.47	$18.34	$25.51	$36.08	$51.26
Annual wage	$28,020	$38,150	$53,070	$75,060	$106,630

Source: U.S. Bureau of Labor Statistics, Occupational Employment Statistics, 27-3043: Writers and Authors, http://www.bls.gov/oes/current/oes273043.htm.

Table 7.4 Top-paying industries for writers

Industry	Employment	Hourly mean wage	Annual mean wage
Independent artists, writers, and performers	2,550	$44.91	$93,420
Motion picture and video industries	2,040	$41.07	$85,420
Advertising, public relations, and related services	6,380	$35.19	$73,200

Source: U.S. Bureau of Labor Statistics, Occupational Employment Statistics, 27-3043: Writers and Authors, http://www.bls.gov/oes/current/oes273043.htm.

Table 7.5 Industries that employ writers

Industry	Employment	Hourly mean wage	Annual mean wage
Newspaper, periodical, book, and directory publishers	8,630	$25.51	$53,050
Advertising, public relations, and related services	6,380	$35.19	$73,200
Radio and television broadcasting	3,090	$31.41	$65,330
Motion picture and video industries	2,040	$41.07	$85,420
Independent artists, writers, and performers	2,550	$44.91	$93,420

Source: U.S. Bureau of Labor Statistics, Occupational Employment Statistics, 27-3043: Writers and Authors, http://www.bls.gov/oes/current/oes273043.htm.

As with the entertainment industries, when we take a close look at employment in the publishing industry, we see a small core of creative workers supporting a larger corporate ecosystem: there are 32,810 reporters and correspondents, 61,820 editors, 9,130 writers (listed separately from reporters—a bit of a slight to all reporters, I might think), and 4,950 photographers.[21] Some of the same negative-employment trends are evident in the projections for professional writers as a whole, as shown in Table 7.6.

For musicians, things are a bit different. As Table 7.7 shows, there are two salient facts about employment of musicians: (1) those who are employed are scattered over a wide variety of industries; and (2) just about exactly half of them (119,000 out of 240,000 total) are self-employed, with no fixed or permanent employer.[22]

Again, the key points are that in the entertainment industries, a small group of creative professionals form the core of a large economic structure or ecosystem, and that many of these professionals work in small companies or on their own.

PATENTS AND SMALL CREATIVE TEAMS

The general story in the patent world is similar. Creative professionals are a small but vital core group in a larger economic context. As with entertain-

Table 7.6 Employment by industry (ind), occupation (OCC), and percent distribution, 2008 and projected 2018 (employment in thousands)

Industry	2008			2018			Percent change
	Employment	Percent of ind	Percent of OCC	Employment	Percent of ind	Percent of OCC	
Total employment, all workers	151.7	0.10	100.00	174.1	0.10	100.00	14.81
Information	16.1	0.54	10.60	15.4	0.50	8.86	-4.00
Publishing industries (except Internet)	9.1	1.04	6.02	7.4	0.88	4.24	-19.17
Newspaper, periodical, book, and directory publishers	8.6	1.39	5.67	6.7	1.34	3.84	-22.26
Newspaper publishers	4.2	1.30	2.80	3.3	1.34	1.88	-22.69
Software publishers	0.5	0.20	0.35	0.7	0.20	0.40	30.68
Motion picture, video, and sound recording industries	2.4	0.64	1.61	2.8	0.66	1.61	14.56
Motion picture and video industries	2.3	0.63	1.51	2.7	0.65	1.54	17.20
Sound recording industries	0.2	0.81	0.11	0.1	0.84	0.07	-23.23
Broadcasting (except Internet)	3.2	1.02	2.12	3.6	1.06	2.06	11.87
Radio and television broadcasting	3.0	1.31	1.99	3.4	1.43	1.93	11.03
Radio broadcasting	0.4	0.42	0.29	0.4	0.45	0.26	0.68
Television broadcasting	2.6	2.07	1.70	2.9	2.16	1.67	12.81
Cable and other subscription programming	0.2	0.22	0.12	0.2	0.22	0.13	25.41

(continued)

Table 7.6 (continued)

Industry	2008			2018			Percent change
	Employment	Percent of ind	Percent of OCC	Employment	Percent of ind	Percent of OCC	
Arts, entertainment, and recreation	3.0	0.15	1.95	4.0	0.18	2.29	35.07
Performing arts, spectator sports, and related industries	2.7	0.65	1.75	3.6	0.78	2.09	36.45
Performing arts companies	0.3	0.28	0.22	0.4	0.30	0.22	12.94
Spectator sports	0.1	0.08	0.07	0.1	0.08	0.07	15.67
Promoters of events, and agents and managers	0.1	0.09	0.06	0.1	0.09	0.07	23.12
Independent artists, writers, and performers	2.1	4.22	1.40	3.0	4.65	1.73	41.76
Museums, historical sites, and similar institutions	0.3	0.20	0.17	0.3	0.20	0.19	23.89
Self-employed and unpaid family workers, all jobs	105.5	0.90	69.54	122.2	0.99	70.15	15.82
Self-employed workers, all jobs	105.2	0.91	69.37	121.9	1.00	69.99	15.84
Unpaid family workers, all jobs	0.3	0.21	0.17	0.3	0.22	0.16	8.11

Source: U.S. Bureau of Labor Statistics, Occupational Outlook Handbook, 2010–2011: Authors, Writers, and Editors, http://www.bls.gov/oco/oco320 .htm (projections data, detailed statistics, XLS file, visited 12.30.2010).

Table 7.7 Musicians, singers, and related workers, 2008–2016 (in thousands)

Musicians, singers, and related workers	2008		2016 (Predicted)	
	Number	Percent	Number	Percent
Total employment, all workers	240.0	0.16	259.6	0.16
Total wage and salary employment	120.3	0.09	133.7	0.09
Information	1.2	0.04	1.2	0.04
Motion picture, video, and sound recording industries	0.8	0.21	0.8	0.18
Motion picture and video industries	0.4	0.10	0.4	0.10
Sound recording industries	0.4	2.26	0.3	2.31
Broadcasting (except Internet)	0.2	0.05	0.2	0.05
Radio and television broadcasting	0.2	0.07	0.2	0.07
Radio broadcasting	0.1	0.11	0.1	0.12
Educational services, public and private	3.9	0.03	4.9	0.03
Arts, entertainment, and recreation	34.4	1.75	36.7	1.61
Performing arts, spectator sports, and related industries	33.4	8.22	35.6	7.61
Performing arts companies	29.1	24.73	30.3	23.95
Promoters of events, and agents and managers	2.2	2.02	2.6	1.99
Independent artists, writers, and performers	2.1	4.07	2.7	4.12
Full-service restaurants	0.4	0.01	0.4	0.01
Drinking places (alcoholic beverages)	0.2	0.06	0.2	0.06
Other services (except government and private households)	78.4	1.42	88.4	1.42

Table 7.7 (continued)

Musicians, singers, and related workers	2008		2016 (Predicted)	
	Number	Percent	Number	Percent
Religious, grantmaking, civic, professional, and similar organizations	78.4	2.64	88.3	2.63
Self-employed workers	119.7	1.03	125.9	1.03

Source: U.S. Bureau of Labor Statistics, Occupational Outlook Handbook 2010-2011 edition (current data), Projections Data, http://www.bls.gov/oco/ocos095.htm.

ment and publishing, we see a variegated industry structure or ecosystem, within which creative inventors work in several different settings. There are some large companies with extensive R&D divisions; IBM and Microsoft are two good examples. But these large companies indirectly support a network of smaller firms, many of which are highly innovative. In fact, research on innovation has in recent years consistently emphasized the increasing importance of smaller innovative companies in the overall corporate landscape.[23]

The "rise of the little guys" represents the reversal of a long trend.[24] From the latter years of the nineteenth century to almost the end of the twentieth, economic power was concentrated in the hands of ever-larger corporations in most industries.[25] This had profound effects on the professional lives of the inventive class. The growth of large corporate research and development departments, and the concomitant increase in corporate patenting since the late nineteenth century, are well-documented facts of economic history. In 1891, 71 percent of patents were issued to individuals;[26] by 1999, 78 percent of all patents were issued to corporate owners.[27] For many years, economic historians seemed to believe that this trend was largely irreversible, and that the great bulk of innovation was destined to come from large, vertically integrated companies drawing primarily from their own in-house R&D divisions. Though independent inventors continue to make valuable contributions, it was long thought that most serious innovation was destined to originate with large corporate R&D groups.[28] Certainly the data on patents owned by individuals versus companies support this view; even data from recent years shows a continuing increase in corporate ownership, at the expense of individual inventors (see Table 7.8). (The data are for U.S. entities only; the distribution of ownership by foreign entities is even more skewed toward corporate ownership.)

Table 7.8 Ownership of U.S. patents

	Pre-1995	1998	1999	2000	2001	2002	2003	2004	2005	2006	2007	2008	Total
U.S. corporations	1,101,870	66,052	69,389	70,887	74,329	74,154	75,327	73,021	65,207	78,925	70,498	69,962	2,032,622
U.S. government	43,417	1,028	984	928	957	913	882	842	698	792	724	676	55,737
U.S. individuals	352,680	16,407	16,698	16,129	15,203	14,116	13,536	12,172	10,358	11,857	9,898	9,021	537,603

But corporate ownership is not necessarily the same as large company dominance. Recent years have seen significant revisions in the conventional wisdom that large companies are destined to dominate the landscape of innovation. Two developments in particular have received attention: the resurgence of small companies as a major source of new technologies, attributed in part to renewed awareness of the advantages of small firms;[29] and the growing understanding among large companies that they need to look outward, including to smaller companies, for new ideas.[30]

For creative scientists, engineers, and inventors of all stripes, this has meant new opportunities to own and participate in small companies. IP rights are one key to the success of these companies.[31] Scholars have demonstrated repeatedly that small, specialized technology companies are especially reliant on IP rights because, compared to larger companies, they have fewer ways to capitalize on research and development investments.[32] Large companies can often earn back R&D investments by incorporating new technologies in complex, multicomponent products, by beating other firms to market with innovative products, and with other techniques that rely on large scale and size. Small companies seldom have this wide palette of choices. For them, IP is more important because they must often sell a specialized component to other companies for incorporation into a larger product.[33] These transactions come with risk; larger trading partners may sometimes copy new technologies, and without patents the smaller company has little effective recourse. In some of my own research, I have shown that patents help facilitate supply transactions involving new technologies. And in related work, a coauthor and I have shown the benefit of patent protection for specialized supply firms that must deal with large companies as buyers of technology.[34]

This line of research, while rigorous in an economic sense, touches on a theme that goes beyond pure economics. Though couched in terms of assisting the viability of small, specialized companies, IP rights in these scenarios serve a deeper goal: autonomy. By making small companies viable as separate, stand-alone entities, IP rights permit more individual inventors to form freestanding creative teams.[35] Free from direct supervisory control by a large employer, skilled technologists have on average greater freedom of action in their working lives. They have more freedom to specialize in the areas that interest them and to choose the projects they will work on. If we think of their body of work as a sort of object, we can glimpse in this career freedom a Kantian theme. As we saw in Chapter 3, property permits stable expectations over time; people know that an object under their legal control will persist over time without outside interference. In just this way a small inventive team can build up its technological knowledge and skill base without interference from corporate supervisors, relying on patents to maintain independence. An IP portfolio does not of course guarantee that the team will succeed. But it does give it a chance to succeed on its own terms.

This is all premised on the idea that small creative teams allow individual participants more leeway than they would have as employees in large companies. This should not be a controversial claim; social science research consistently shows that one of the strongest motivators for entrepreneurial activity is the drive to exercise more control over working conditions and work life.[36] Even though small companies have hierarchies, and typically a single CEO, they are by nature far less bureaucratic, far less hierarchical than large companies.[37] It is their more nimble structure, in combination with technologies and organizational practices that permit networks of small firms to sometimes duplicate the advantages of large companies, that has pushed small firms into the forefront of technological advance.[38]

IP rights—in this case patents—therefore support the goal of autonomy in this setting, just as they do with creative professionals in the entertainment industries. Though the effects may be mitigated somewhat by the fact that many inventors work in teams, and thus not strictly autonomously, and that large corporate customers can exert significant pressure notwithstanding the nominal independence of a smaller company, the fact remains: smaller teams do permit more personal autonomy for each of their members. To the extent IP rights make smaller companies more viable, then, those rights contribute to autonomy. This is an important but often overlooked contribution, and a subtle reflection of the normative foundations we explored in Chapters 2 and 3.

DESIGN AND BRAND-BUILDING PROFESSIONALS

Trademark protection has often been thought to fit uncomfortably in the same conceptual basket as copyright and patent. The basic purpose of trademark, we are often told, is to protect consumers from fraud, not necessarily to induce people to come up with more or better trademarks. Though the normative foundations of trademark are now understood in a slightly more robust way than this conventional view would dictate, one thing has not changed: the idea that trademark law is somehow basically different from other IP rights.[39]

There is something to this, to be sure. Yet it is also easy to overestimate the differences. One way to see that there is more similarity than difference among patent, copyright, and trademark law is to pay attention to the creative communities that each area of law is meant to serve.

I would argue that, when viewed this way—in terms of the role IP plays in the creative community that relies on it—trademark law is not so different from patent and copyright. In the world of the creative design and brand professionals, trademark law serves much the same function as copyright for authors or patents for inventor/entrepreneurs. It allows them to exist, to function, and sometimes to flourish. And even where trademarks are generated within large firms, legal protection for them draws resources to this function and therefore supports a cadre of trademark professionals.[40]

Industrial designers rely on various forms of IP protection to secure rights in their works. To be more accurate, for the most part their clients do. Industrial design shops typically do not make and sell products; their "output" is sleek designs, attractive and functional packaging, and catchy yet informative logos and trademarks. But clearly industrial designers' clients value the ability to secure rights over the designs and marks they commission from the designers. And again, as with copyrights and patents, the availability of a property right over designs and marks makes pure design houses more viable than they would otherwise be. In the extreme, if no design protection were available, designers would be obliged to work for large integrated producers. Only with the other investment-recouping strategies open to large firms would an investment in sophisticated design pay off.

Though there is as yet no definitive study, the notoriously low pay of design professionals may be tied not only to corporate attitudes about the value of design, but also to the relatively weak IP rights that attach to designers' work product.[41] To be sure, designers often work independently; as one source puts it,

> Most of the designers I know work as consultants rather than (as is common in the auto industry, for example) as employees of the business they design for. . . . Although there is no way to know the relative proportion of goods that come from these consultancies compared to in-house designers, in terms of innovation, technique, and product leadership—autos excepted—these outside offices are where the action is.[42]

Yet designers' low pay, and their lack of control, mean that even when independent they are less autonomous than they perhaps should be. Trademark law can help solve this problem. Usually, protecting against consumer confusion—the traditional touchstone for legal liability—will be coextensive with recognizing a property right in an original design. And when trademark protection is extended further, it should be done in a way that furthers the ability of independent designers and brand professionals to make a living doing what they do best.

It is important here to correct a potentially false impression. Not all trademark-related work relates to industrial design. Brand building, in the form of advertising and related promotional spending, is a massive worldwide industry, totaling some $653 billion in annual spending.[43] The professionals responsible for ad campaigns and promotional projects are surely engaged in work that is similar in some respects to writing, music performance, inventing, and the like; these people are not referred to as "creative talent" for nothing. There certainly are limits to how far traditional IP can be extended to protect the work product of these professionals. To take just one, it would be dangerous to stretch trademark law to protect the visual impression (or "look and feel") of an ad campaign created for Company X when to do so would undermine trademark law's traditional imperative to protect consumers. So for example there would be no trademark liability for an ad campaign that is cleverly reproduced by Company Y to sell its products, so long as it does not lead consumers to believe that Y is selling X's products.

Even so, even with limits, there is room in trademark law for some solicitude for brand and design professionals. Where consumer confusion and professional reward do coincide, there is no reason why trademark law should not be assimilated into the conceptual structure of IP law. As compared to copyright and patent, the policy rationale for trademarks may be more multidimensional. But it need not be completely divorced from the pro-autonomy, creator-rewarding underpinnings of copyright and patent.

Dealing with the Transactional "Overhead" of More and Stronger IP

I have emphasized that designers and brand builders rely on trademark law to support their livelihood, just as entertainers and other creative talent rely on copyright and inventive teams rely on patents. But the IP rights that support these creative professionals come at a cost. Giving legal rights to the creative class helps them, but places a burden on those who use or consume the products of creative work. How to grant these rights, encouraging and doing right by creators, while minimizing the burden on users and consumers—that is both the imperative of the normative theories described in Chapters 2 through 4 and the practical challenge that IP policy must meet. The remainder of this chapter faces that challenge squarely.

As I said earlier, IP rights are often waived or not enforced; even so, there can be little doubt that a pro-IP policy adds costs. When rights have not been waived, it can be expensive to locate IP owners. After they are located, there may be negotiation costs. And then of course there may be licensing payments—often royalties—that add to the costs of selling a product. The simple fact is that more and stronger IP rights usually add to the transactional overhead that goes into producing things that draw on creative assets. To state the issue in terms of a pet theme, autonomy, stronger IP encumbers and drags down anyone who uses creative works as "inputs" into their own work. It reduces the autonomy of input users while enhancing the autonomy of those who make and sell inputs.

Is it simply then a matter of *whose* autonomy should count? Partly, yes. As I argued at length in Chapter 4, there are good reasons to believe that in a fair and just society, consumers and users of high-quality creative works should and would be willing to pay more. The distributional effects of IP can be justified, despite the concern with elitism that these rights necessarily entail. Audience members and users would gladly cede a tiny portion of their autonomy (in the form of payment, and restrictions on use) so as to confer a greater measure of autonomy on creative professionals.

But there is more to the story than this. An ideal IP policy would serve the interests of creative professionals *at the lowest cost to users.* Consistent with the efficiency principle described in Chapter 6, and with the autonomy interests of users, the idea is to benefit creative professionals without unduly burdening users and consumers. But isn't this impossible? Doesn't the cost of licensing always translate directly into benefits for creatives, so that lowering this cost necessarily reduces creatives' compensation?

Not completely. There is one component of licensing costs that does not benefit creatives at all—the pure transaction costs of clearing IP rights. These are the costs of locating rights holders, negotiating licenses, and running the mechanics of rights-related payments. They are a prime target for cost-cutting, because they serve no valuable purpose at all. They do not help any group of people worth helping. They are, to use a mechanical analogy, pure friction between different parts of the IP machinery. Figure 7.2 illustrates this concept. It shows that with proper attention to transaction costs, we can increase creator compensation without increasing the cost to consumers. The final panel in Figure 7.2 demonstrates that, when we take into account the "spillover" benefits of creative works (i.e., the benefits to future users and other non-consumers), the overall benefits of IP rights outweigh the costs even with robust creator compensation.

IP policy ought to reduce the proportion of a consumer's payment that goes to transaction costs. The aim should be to reduce friction as much as possible, while maximizing the compensation that flows to creative professionals. A smooth-running machine is good for everyone. If we as a society can minimize the costs of moving rights from owners to users, we will at

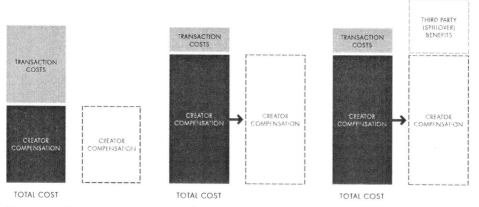

Figure 7.2. Creator compensation and transaction costs

least ensure that the burden of IP licensing serves a valuable end—increasing the autonomy of creative professionals. For all the reasons described in the early part of this book, this seems to me a noble goal. Minimizing money that goes essentially nowhere—that is simply consumed in the process of moving rights around—moves us toward the goal we want in the most efficient way possible.

The Integration Solution: Large Companies in the Creative Industries

In some cases, legal rights over individual creative works add to the cost of doing business. Consider a businessman wanting to start a company to make children's toys. This is an expensive proposition. He has to rent or build a factory, or at least identify a contract manufacturer somewhere who has some spare capacity. Packaging, distribution, sales, and promotions must all be paid for. In addition, if some of the toys he wants to make are covered by IP rights of one sort or another, this adds yet another cost. The owner of the IP right must be located, and a deal must be struck, most likely in the form of an IP license. The deal might include some information about how to make the toy, in which case it will in a sense go beyond mere IP to include production details and other valuable information. But it might also be a pure IP license: if the toy is already well known, or our businessperson is simply licensing a familiar logo or design (think Mickey Mouse), the only thing acquired in the deal might be the simple legal right to make the toy.[44] In any event, the point is the same: looked at from the perspective of our toy-making entrepreneur, IP rights over the toy are just another cost.

The cost of locating a rightholder and negotiating with her is a good example of what economists call transaction costs. A large body of economic theory and empirical research—pioneered by Nobel Prize winner Oliver Williamson—has been built up, dedicated to studying these costs and analyzing how businesspeople deal with them.[45] Stated in terms of this theory, my view is that IP policy should be about rewarding creative professionals while reducing transaction costs.

The literature on transaction costs is organized around one central trade-off, often described as "make or buy." The things a business needs may be produced "in house," that is, made. This has some obvious advantages, the most important for our purposes being that a manufacturer can eschew the costly process of negotiating and executing a contract with a separate firm. In a large company, if the manufacturing division wants to make toys designed in the toy department, there is no need for a contract. One executive issues an order, another prompts her team to respond, and it is done. This form of organization is called "hierarchy" by transaction cost theorists.

The downside of this arrangement is that big companies can be bureaucratic. The consequences of ignoring an order from another division may not be that great; or the impulse to respond may be muted. Each division may build up its own loyalties, its own practices, its own priorities. Hierarchy saves the cost of writing a contract, but it can also be slow and unresponsive.

A small company, by contrast, may be more nimble. One reason is that when small companies sell what they make to larger companies, they enter into contracts. Under a contract, detailed performance requirements may be built in, specifying for example that the small company will not be paid unless and until it fills an order to the complete satisfaction of the large company-customer. These specific contractual spurs to action are called "high-powered incentives." They are one of the great benefits of arranging production via contracts, as they form an implicit contrast with hierarchical or integrated production. It is easier to specify detailed performance requirements and make them stick, via contract, than it is to try to order performance from an affiliated division of the same company.

But there is another side to the theory. Contracts have costs too. First there is the cost of writing up a detailed set of performance requirements and negotiating them with the other party to the contract. One important insight from transaction cost theory is that sometimes these costs are very high, and sometimes, in the extreme case, it is virtually impossible to write an enforceable contract. The more amorphous the thing being transferred under contract, the more likely that an enforceable contract will be all but impossible to put in place. A good example would be a contract under which a small company performs research or works on a new type of product, one that has never been made or even tried before. How to specify performance characteristics for something when it is amorphous or little is known about it at the outset? Any contract written under these circumstances will necessarily be open-ended, and that creates risks. An unscrupulous contracting party can take advantage of this sort of looseness. For example, a small company might make a passable prototype of a new product and arguably satisfy a vaguely worded obligation to "use best efforts to deliver an adequate product." But then, after the contract is completed, the small company might roll out a much better version of the new product under its own label, or in a lucrative contract with someone else. It would be difficult for the buyer under the first contract to prove a violation of the original deal.

This sort of risk goes under the name of "opportunism" in transaction cost theory. One way to solve the problem, according to the theory, is to do away with contracts where the risk of opportunism is high. This means, in practical terms, a resort to integration and hierarchy. In simple terms, the maker of a hard-to-specify input will be acquired by a large firm that needs the input to make its product. Hierarchy wins out in these cases; the high-powered incentives of contracts are too difficult to achieve, so production of the input is internalized in the large firm.

Some scholars have introduced a twist into the transaction cost story, under which agreements about owning assets can resolve some difficult transactional conflicts. In cases where a contract would not be effective, the parties can agree to give one or the other ownership over some asset related to the transaction, and in this way create incentives for performance that benefit both parties. This variant on transaction cost theory is powerful, but limited in scope because it applies only when a specialized input must be made and sold.[46]

Both straight transaction cost theory and the asset ownership variant describe conditions under which components of complex products will sometimes be made by independent firms, then sold to other firms by contract. Sometimes these components will be creative works that form one component of a larger, integrated work—an entertainment product such as a movie, or a technical component of a complex product. I have argued throughout this chapter, and indeed this book, that IP rights support the viability of independent creators and small creative teams, and in so doing promote the autonomy of creative professionals.

Even so, large companies have a number of advantages that make them superior in a significant number of situations. Transaction cost theory describes one advantage: the high costs of a large number of separate transactions can make integration a superior alternative. This is especially true when the separate components that must be assembled for a product are closely interrelated. A feature-length animated movie, for example, may include thousands of separate drawings, a dozen or more musical compositions, and numerous other creative inputs. If each professional animator worked as an independent contractor, thousands of separate contracts would have to be executed for the entire film to be assembled and distributed. In this and similar situations, there are obvious advantages to keeping all or most of the creative team in-house as employees. Integrating all the relevant productive components inside a single firm has advantages in this setting, just as it does in others.

But what does this mean for the creative professional? Is the economic logic of large-firm production, where it holds, inconsistent with creator autonomy? When it comes to creative professionals, is there anything to be said for large companies? In a word, yes. In ways both direct and indirect, large companies serve important functions, making them essential elements in the commercial ecosystems in which creative professionals operate. Because the contributions these companies make are different for each of the major industry groups that employ creative professionals, I address them in the separate sections that follow.

LARGE MEDIA COMPANIES

Contemporary critics usually take a decidedly negative attitude toward the large entities that amalgamate huge numbers of IP-protected works. Walt Disney, large record labels, movie studios, and their counterparts are frequent targets. The prevailing view is that these companies are old, entrenched, and for-profit, and therefore decidedly not on the side of individual creative types. Wikis, fan sites, open source projects, and other collaborative organizations are the opposite: new, fresh, not-for-profit, unencumbered by old ways of doing things, and much more reflective of and responsive to the individuals who compose them. The contrast comes down to this: faceless, metallic corporations versus vibrant, organic communities.

Big companies, like most big organizations, are easy to pick on. And there is surely at least some truth to the idea that movie studios often churn out "formulaic" movies, and that big record labels produce a lot of "pop bubblegum." On the other hand, it is also crucial to remember that these big media companies employ thousands of people who have dedicated their careers to the delivery of highly creative mass-market works—movies, records, TV shows, graphic art, and the like. Thousands of amateur filmmakers post films to websites such as YouTube; but the major movie studios actually employ 270,000 people.[47] The same is true in publishing, where, as Figure 7.3 shows, a small number of companies (fewer than 2 percent of the total) employ over 40 percent of all people in the industry. Employees of large companies in all these industries—good examples of creative professionals—make substantial salaries by contributing to valuable and popular creative works. They make a living through their creativity. From the perspective of IP policy, this group is absolutely crucial. The ability to make a real living from creative works is what IP is all about. It is what ensures a steady supply of high-quality creative works to consumers—the real purpose of IP law. And it therefore cannot be irrelevant that so many creative professionals are employed by large media companies. Policies that favor YouTube contributors at the expense of big media companies must, in my view, account for the negative impact on this essential group of people.[48]

Even if we assume away the contributions of creative professionals in large media companies, we still might want to pause before crafting IP policies that harm them. That is because the health and welfare of large

Half of the establishments in the publishing industry have fewer than 5 employees, but over 40 percent of jobs are in establishments with 250 or more.

Percent

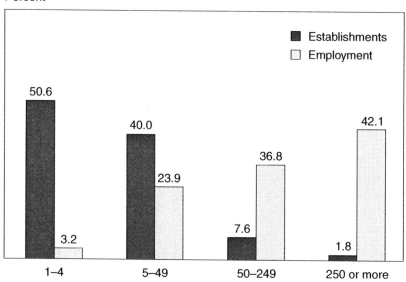

Figure 7.3. Size of establishments in publishing

companies affect individual creators and small companies in many significant ways. Large media companies, for example, are often incubators of
independent professionals and small companies.[49] Many creative designers of large theme parks, world's fairs, and the like got their start at Walt
Disney,[50] as did several small players in the animation field, such as Mira-
cle Studios, made up of people who want to preserve the hand-drawn animation tradition of the older Disney movies.[51] Even when small creative
companies are established independently from the beginning, they often
make deals with large media companies to distribute or market creative
content. Pixar's arrangement with Disney followed this model (until Disney
acquired Pixar in 2006), and independent record producers have made such
deals with the large, established record labels for many years.[52] In these
ways and many others, large, established companies provide resources and
give assistance to creative people and small companies. They are, to use
some business school jargon, an integral part of the "ecosystem" of the entertainment industry. Damage them, and it will surely affect small and independent creators as well.

Why all this emphasis on the importance of creative professionals, and
the necessity for large companies to support them? Because those who argue that IP should be downplayed, since it is harmful or irrelevant in the
modern era, frequently put forth a kind of three-part syllogism to defend
their views: (1) IP policy is made by big media companies, for big companies, with little or no concern for individual creators; (2) big media companies are bloated and outdated dinosaurs whose fight to preserve a dying
economic way of life—in part by means of ever-stronger IP rights—is both
pathetic and dangerous; and (3) policies that truly favor individual creators must necessarily oppose the interests of large media companies, in
part by reducing the emphasis on IP rights. An overstated simplification
might be: in the digital era, if it hurts Disney, it's good for the little guy.

My goal here is to break apart the logic of this syllogism. In my mind,
big media companies are not the sworn enemy of all those who contribute
to creative works. They are not even necessarily the enemy of "little guy"
creators, individuals and small groups working outside the confines of big
media.[53] My ultimate goal is to defend the idea of property rights in the
contemporary economy, to argue that a one-to-one mapping of owners to
valuable assets continues to make sense, even in the era of digital media.
To do so, I have felt it necessary to justify a continuing place in the creative
landscape for one of the key interest groups pushing for the maintenance
of IP protection—to, in a sense, defend the defenders of property rights. It
is not that Disney and its ilk are the greatest things that ever happened to
animators, writers, and musicians; it is just that they provide gainful em-

ployment to a lot of people who do these things for a living—a nontrivial consideration in an area of policy whose goal I take it to be to keep providing such a living to such people.[54] My next task is to turn away from questions of industry structure and to address more directly the central issue I see in digital IP policy today: making a case for a legal infrastructure that best facilitates the economic viability of creative professionals. As is obvious by now, I see a continuing commitment to individual property rights as a key part of that infrastructure. This has the effect of privileging one subset of creators, a policy I defended at length earlier in Chapter 4.[55]

A WORD ABOUT ALTERNATIVE (OPEN/COLLECTIVE) PRODUCTION MODELS

Because the academic literature on IP rights is now quite full of work praising the modern alternative to large media companies, I feel it important to state here my views on the relationship between big companies and the new models of cultural production so often championed today.

First, I should say that I take the participatory, democratic aspects of culture very seriously. I have devoted some effort to thinking through how the inherited legal structure of IP rights can be adapted and modified to encourage the many new avenues of participatory creativity—the wikis, open source projects, and other forms of what are called "crowdsourcing."[56] But—and here is where I differ from a fair number of contemporary IP scholars—I *also* believe that IP policy has a special obligation to promote and encourage creatives. Without the efforts of people devoted full-time to developing and expressing their considerable creative talents, and the large-scale organizations often needed to assemble their individual contributions into sophisticated, refined, and polished form, I believe our collective culture would suffer enormously. It is these creative professionals who bring us many of the products that become cultural icons and shared touchstones. Without them, we would have far less shared material to work with. True, we all in some sense "make culture," and some of what these professionals work with are received myths, legends, and ancient stories. But without high-quality contemporary products in accessible form, there would be a lot less material out of which we can construct our shared culture. This is why I see these professionals as so important. And because, when they are effective, their works appeal to a mass audience, I do not see this as a particularly elitist view. They operate, after all, in a market economy. So their works must (in many cases) invite acceptance from a wide audience. And given the rules of IP law, a wide array of participation is also open, from commentary and criticism to emulation (of ideas, not expression of course) and even parody. One can say a lot of things about popular culture in the United States, but "undemocratic" is not a label that too many would apply. If it is elitist to show concern for the care and feeding of creatives, it is a strange form of elitism: solicitude for the people so often accused of foisting low-brow entertainment on the American people!

Well, maybe it is not undemocratic. Maybe it is just wrong. Why do professional creatives deserve special protection? After all, protecting their works deprives other people of freedom: freedom to use those works as they see fit, to mash them up, incorporate them in new (possibly subversive) works, *appropriate them,* and make them their own. It deprives people of the freedom to participate in the making of their own culture. How can this deprivation be justified?

Two ways, I think. First, by recognizing the importance of high-quality content to a shared cultural experience. And second, by criticizing the claim that protecting this content makes major inroads on freedom. The first point I described earlier. A few words about the second point here.

Freedom is constrained by IP law, no doubt about it. But not as much as many believe. IP rights are not generally self-enforcing. So the first protection against serious inroads on freedom is the stubborn fact of high enforcement costs. This prosaic fact of life for IP owners has very important ramifications for the question of user freedom. The de facto zone of freedom for consumers of IP—the zone of participatory culture, if you will—is really quite large. An overly formalistic focus on the law on the books (as opposed to the law in action) often obscures this. But it is a fact nonetheless.

The second way freedom is protected is through the market. People like freedom. Businesses try to give people what they like. So if consumers prefer cultural products with a little extra freedom thrown in, some enterprising business is likely to give it to them. This means that those who sell cultural products that significantly restrict freedom will either have to make those products especially attractive (to offset the loss of value to consumers occasioned by the greater restrictions), or change their policy on restrictions. Simple as that. Put another way, there should be plenty of content available for remixing, mashing up, or otherwise using quite freely. Some will come from commercial companies, other from amateurs who like remixing and want to promote it. Not all content will be so freely given out, but a fair amount of it will be. Where certain works are so canonical that cultural participants feel they must reference the works—there are no available substitutes with fewer use-restrictions attached—IP law still allows criticism (for example, an essay or entire website devoted to "Barbie as Ideology"), commentary (an essay on "Countering the Limiting Vision of *The Little Mermaid*"), and even parody (a play lampooning

Hogwarts Academy and the Harry Potter stories). But commercial remixes of canonical works can be prevented by IP law. Does this restrict freedom? Yes, but for a good reason (to support canonical works) and in a limited way (one may always appropriate ideas from these works, and incorporate those basic ideas into one's own original work; criticize and comment on them; and parody them). In my view, these restrictions on freedom are limited, but insofar as they exist, fully defensible. I understand that some people feel that if they cannot physically mess with content, and put their stamp directly on it, they feel deprived of an important form of freedom. But I believe that forcing them to work around these canonical works, to comment on them without directly copying elements of them, is not too high a cost. It is the cost of recognizing the rights of creators of these works. Rights always come with burdens, and in my view these burdens are not so great as to justify undermining those rights.[57]

One final point about "bottom-up culture" returns us to the idea that IP is truly a legal *right*. This is of course the upshot of the idea of property extolled by Locke and Kant and described in detail in Chapters 2 and 3 of this book. Whatever form it takes, I have come to see that we cannot rigorously apply a utilitarian calculus to the question of optimal IP policy, so as to generate cultural outputs that perfectly balance the economic preferences of creators and consumers. With our current state of knowledge, IP is therefore best thought of as a question of rights. And in my mind, creative professionals deserve to hold and enforce IP rights—as a matter of first principles (à la Locke and Kant) as well as social agreement (à la Rawls, as described in Chapter 4). Any policy that significantly favors amateur creators at the expense of professionals is simply not defensible to my way of thinking.[58]

LARGE TECHNOLOGY-PRODUCING COMPANIES

As with the entertainment industries, while the ideal situation for promoting autonomy may be self-employment, or complete independence, large companies do contribute to the prospects for creative professionals. They do so two ways: first, by buying the specialized products that small firms sell, in turn selling consumer products that require small company add-ons or extensions, and thus forming the backbone of the ecosystem in which small firms can often thrive; and second, by employing large numbers of creative professionals, making their careers viable and sometimes training them sufficiently to enable them to exit large companies and start up new companies of their own. When we look at the bigger picture, then, we see that large companies are hardly anathema to the care and feeding of the creative professions. They are instead indispensable.

One way large companies indirectly assist small enterprise is as a training ground, a source of experience and know-how that entrepreneurs draw from in a number of ways. For example, studies of entrepreneurship show consistently that most successful start-up companies draw their founders from large, established firms. Studies of specific industries bear this out. Detailed research on the pattern of company formation in the disk drive industry, for example, traces the origin of most small, innovative companies to a handful of large companies. Historical accounts of the development of the Silicon Valley innovation culture demonstrate the same point; again and again, vital, small companies are shown to have their origins in a few large incumbents, most famously Fairchild Semiconductor.

Recent high-level accounts of the changing structure of innovative industries show a different but also important role for large, established firms. In the more variegated industry structure that prevails now, specialized components required by large companies are often supplied by small, highly focused companies. Though the themes of "modularity" and vertical "disintegration" are often featured in these accounts, they also recognize the importance of large companies. The Japanese auto industry, which relies extensively on outsourcing for many components, is often held up as a model of the new, "flatter" industry structure that prevails today, in comparison to an earlier era when virtually all parts of a car were manufactured in-house by the large auto companies. Yet even in this brave new world, Japanese auto companies continue to be very large. Industry dis-integration, in this field at least, is a relative term. Large companies are still at the core of the auto industry (and many others); they continue to be *large* companies no matter how one cares to measure that.

The general point is just this: the autonomy-promoting features of individual ownership and smaller companies may be in tension with an industrial landscape dominated exclusively by large companies, but at the same time an industry structure that would include smaller units of production is often assisted and facilitated by the presence of a healthy number of large companies. So while robust and enforceable IP rights may well promote a greater number of autonomy-supporting small companies, these rights will not lead to the withering away of all large companies. Nor should they, if we really value autonomy and independence. The ability of a small unit to make a go of it may well depend on the existence of one or more large firms in the landscape. So entirely apart from the benefits that IP rights may provide for large companies in and of themselves, these rights also allow small companies to stand apart from, yet participate with, large companies in the making of all sorts of innovative products. The upshot sounds paradoxical, but makes sense in this context. Large companies may often be a necessary link in the chain connecting IP rights to greater autonomy and the economic viability of small firms.

Back to Transaction Costs

As I said earlier, though, the more links in the chain, the higher the transaction costs. It may assist little companies to have a few big players in the corporate ecosystem, but there is no getting around the fact that more independent units of production often make for higher administrative costs. The solution I have emphasized is to accept this as a necessary cost, even a worthwhile one, and at the same time work to minimize it as much as possible. In this section I try to give teeth to this general admonition by suggesting some practical ways to reduce transaction costs among multiple, independent rightholders. My suggestions fall into two general categories: (1) to lower the costs of complete waiver, on the theory that making it easier to give rights away lowers the overall cost of the IP system; and (2) to lower the cost of exchanging rights, by encouraging multifirm consortia and centralized IP clearinghouses.

IP Waiver and the "Right to Include"

I want to talk first about making it simple and easy to give away IP rights. At first blush this might seem a strange topic for someone like me to pursue. Collaborative content, the leveling aspects of online culture, and the open source movement are themes central to the discourse of the digital revolutionaries. They all emphasize the contrast between outdated "proprietary" or "centralized" culture, and the newly dawning era of interconnected, highly democratic culture, which depends on widespread norms of giving away individual claims to facilitate interactive and massively collaborative "works." Why would an old-timer like me want to talk about gifting IP rights?

For two reasons. First, because the digital revolutionaries are right: the ability to instantly and ubiquitously share content is revolutionary, and people are doing exciting things with it. And second, because, unlike the critics of traditional IP rights, I do not believe that the new-style sharing undermines the rationale for traditional IP rights. Indeed, I want to argue that with a proper understanding of the legal context of this sharing, we can come to see it not as a threat or challenge to IP rights, but as proof of the flexibility of those rights in practice and of the still-relevant normative foundation for those rights. Put simply, the option to give property away is a central feature of any property system. We saw this in Chapter 3, among other places, when discussing Kant's attention to the idea of waiver and its relation to individual autonomy. That many potential owners of IP rights are surrendering their inchoate claims in favor of shared, collaborative participation does not in any way undercut the rationale for property in the first place. Instead, it supports it. And, as important, that many people choose this route does not in any way imply that others must make the same choice. For just as IP rights permit owners to contribute their works to collective projects, they also protect those who want to keep their individual creations from being integrated into large-scale collaborations. This freedom to either waive one's rights entirely, or else hold onto them for purposes of economic exploitation or simple aesthetic preference, is what property is all about. Kant says as much, and IP law reflects this basic insight. But the fact that complete waiver is easy and popular does not imply that this should become the legal default. To allow this basic element of property—the respect for individual autonomy—to be changed under the pressure of the digital revolution would be a grave mistake.

THE RIGHT (AND WRONG) WAY TO GIVE IT AWAY

The best way to facilitate sharing while retaining traditional respect for autonomy is to make it easy for owners to waive their rights. The wrong way to facilitate sharing is to curtail or eliminate those rights in the first place. The first approach retains the central place of individual choice in the structure of IP rights, while the second way steamrolls individual choice in the name of collaboration. If the IP system puts effort into retaining traditional rights, while making it simple and easy to share those rights, we get the best of both worlds: traditional ownership and easy sharing. But if rights are curtailed under the rubric of promoting sharing, the traditional respect for individual autonomy is lost.

Before I briefly describe some straightforward ways to promote sharing by waiver, let me deal with two objections to my approach. The first objection is that the extension of traditional IP protection into the digital realm amounts to a significant *expansion* of rights. This claim depends on several facts, especially the (theoretical) ability of rightholders to enforce their rights much more completely in the digital world, thanks to (mostly unrealized) technologies such as digital rights management (DRM). Because this general argument has been summarized under the heading of "the growth of the permissions culture" (a label associated with digital theorist Larry Lessig), I will address it in those terms. The second argument, also associated with Lessig (as well as William Fisher and others), says that what is wrong with IP law is not that it tries to provide compensation to creators, but that it allows *control by* creators. The solution these observers put forward is to separate compensation from control, typically, in the form of a (highly underspecified) compulsory licensing system for digital content. I will also consider this idea of ubiquitous compulsory licensing.

In my opinion the "permissions culture" idea is mostly wrong as a factual matter. It is quite evident that the online world is not one in which IP rights are easy to enforce, and is therefore one in which users of digital content are subject to all sorts of restrictive permissions and licensing procedures. The declining fortunes of many creative industries whose works are available digitally—from professional music to traditional newspapers—bears this out. If anything, we could use *more* automated permissions and compensation systems, not fewer. (The Google Book Search settlement offers some intriguing possibilities in this area, though control of the accounting and compensation system by a single dominant company is somewhat troubling.)[59]

The idea of ubiquitous compulsory licensing fails as well, in my mind, on both practical and theoretical grounds. Practically, the very difficult question of how to divvy up the potentially large stream of revenue from online activities among individual creators is one that must be addressed before the viability of this proposal can be realistically assessed. Based on past experience with compulsory licensing, I am not optimistic. At the theoretical level, the idea is, if anything, even worse. It is very difficult to effectively separate compensation from control; they tend to go hand in hand. And, crucially, some creators are willing to sacrifice some money in exchange for greater control. This is an important aspect of the autonomy that ought to accompany all property rights. While digital holdouts may look hopelessly out of date to some IP theorists, the right to hold out is part of what it means to have a property right.

SIMPLIFYING WAIVER

So how best to balance autonomy with the desire of many creators to share their works? The answer is simple: create a straightforward mechanism that allows individual creators to waive their IP rights. This is the essence of the Creative Commons organization, which promotes various licenses that have the effect of allowing creators to share their works widely. The problem is that these licenses are only contracts. A better mechanism would be to build the waiver mechanism directly into copyright (and patent) law, and to create a central online registry that would record waivers and allow them to be searched and verified easily. This would solve some of the technical problems that accompany the use of contracts to signal a waiver of rights (concerns with notice, privity, and so on).

The net effect would be to retain our traditional respect for individual decision as it relates to individual IP rights. A robust system of waiver would simply carry the principle of autonomy—so central to the IP system as we know it—into the era of shared content and collaborative creativity. Traditional legal structures, in service of desirable practices facilitated by the new digital technology—this sounds like a good combination.

Lowering the Cost of Clearing Rights: Multifirm Consortia

While it is important to make it easy to give away rights, it is also important to recognize that property rights are meant to bring economic rewards; this is of course the practical route through which individual works lead to greater individual autonomy. So we come face to face with the fact, mentioned earlier in this chapter, that robust IP raises transaction costs. Ideal IP policy starts here, but then goes further. It must recognize rights while minimizing the resources consumed in moving those rights around through the economy. Here is where multifirm consortia come into play.

Multiple IP holders come together in a number of ways. In technology-related industries, they may form patent pools designed to gather together patents held by different firms, make them available for licensing under a "one-stop shopping" arrangement, and then divide the licensing revenues according to an internal valuation procedure agreed upon by the members. Antitrust authorities will usually overcome their traditional objections to industry-wide cooperation where pools are concerned; the transaction cost savings will typically offset any worries over anticompetitive activity stemming from such an arrangement.[60]

Consortia are also well known in the entertainment industries. One of the earliest examples is the American Society of Composers, Authors and Publishers, or ASCAP, an organization that draws together a huge number of music composition copyrights and makes them available to radio and TV stations and other media outlets for licensing. Broadcast Music, Inc., a rival organization, performs the same function. Various organizations with similar charters have been formed to license other music rights as well as copyrights in written works.[61]

Despite a generally favorable reception from antitrust law, consortium building has not always received carte blanche from the regulatory authorities. ASCAP and BMI have been subject to court-supervised consent decrees for decades, in the wake of earlier challenges. And patent pools are routinely challenged under antitrust theories as well.[62] Though the law tends to be largely favorable, antitrust challenges are still deployed on a regular basis against these arrangements.

A newer generation of consortium building has brought new challenges. One important set of challenges emanates from the growth of technological "platforms" that can be used to distribute content. Apple's iPod is a technological platform in the music field, as are e-book readers such as Amazon's Kindle. Technological platforms become popular when they add value by making works available in a new form, but also when platform owners manage to attract a large number of content owners to the platform. For example, most major music recording labels have made their music available on the iPod. And most book publishers have agreed to place at least some of their authors' books on e-book readers such as the Kindle. The combination of multiple content owners and large, powerful technology companies holds the promise of real value for consumers, but at the same time poses serious risks.

One such risk, prominent in contemporary scholarship, is the potential anticompetitive prospects of platform-content combinations.[63] Some observers of the IP scene argue that IP rights ought to be restricted or regulated when they might promote platform-content combinations that threaten the competitive balance in a particular industry. This is the theory behind various European regulatory initiatives with respect to Apple's integrated music system that combines the iTunes content portal and iPod hardware platform.[64] Though a minority view actually champions policies that promote platform-content integration, on the theory that this will facilitate the optimal production of compatible content,[65] most observers express real concern over business deals that tie together content and platforms.

But I see little reason for ex ante concern with platform-content deal making. IP rights permit content owners to explore a wide variety of options: exclusive licensing with specific platform owners in some cases; time-limited exclusives; exclusives in some media but not others; and so forth. This competition, which IP rights makes possible, will resolve most concerns that scholars have shown with respect to content-platform deal making.

CASE STUDY: MUSIC DRM SYSTEMS

The controversy (especially in Europe) over Apple's iPod-iTunes platform, combined with its proprietary FairPlay DRM system, provides a good case study of some of the issues described in this section. I begin by describing Apple's IP position with respect to its platform, and then discuss how competitive forces in the music content industry have influenced Apple's overall strategy in this area.

Apple's iPod music player originally required all music sold for it to be encoded in Apple's proprietary FairPlay DRM system. Though FairPlay protected musicians and composers from having their music copied, it was also well understood that it had the effect of locking consumers into Apple products. Once a person's music was loaded onto an Apple iPod, it was converted to the FairPlay format, and no other music player besides an iPod could play that music file ever again. The power of this "lock-in" effect could theoretically be used by a format owner such as Apple to build a dominant position in the music player business. Various regulatory proposals were floated to address the problem, and by 2003 it was generally thought that antitrust intervention was going to be necessary to prevent single-company dominance.

But then came competition. According to one account,

> [O]nline music services have emerged that allow permanent music downloads in an unprotected format, such as, for instance, Amazon's music store launched in September 2007. Further, some of the major music labels announced that they would make parts of their music catalog available to online stores in an unprotected format for a premium. Arguably, these developments are a response to interoperability concerns voiced by users and illustrate the market dynamics in the field of DRM interoperability. . . . [66]

These developments suggested an alternative to regulation. The idea is simple: as long as there is competition *between* platforms for the distribution of content, consumers will be largely protected. Temporary lock-in, such as what we see with the iPod, may be a factor, but as competition among platforms intensifies, lock-in will decline. This is because lock-in is a direct function of the cost of the platform, and competition among platform owners naturally and necessarily tends to reduce the price of a platform. This dynamic is evident in the current market for digital music, as shown in an interview with Jeff Bezos of Amazon.com, a new entrant to the music market that has challenged Apple. Amazon's entry into the digital music business has been watched closely by the primary content owners—the big record labels—because it is seen as a crucial counterweight to Apple's dominance of the music platform market:

> [*Wall St. Journal:*] Are you [Amazon] benefitting from the fact that the content companies, at least some of them, are not always very happy with Steve Jobs [of Apple]?
> *Mr. Bezos:* I would frame it somewhat differently. I would say it is clearly in their enlightened self-interest to have a vibrant multitude of companies distributing their music. The music [intellectual property] owners are watching our growth rates very carefully. And I think they're very happy.[67]

This is in keeping with other commentators, who have observed that competition among platform owners (and among the makers of complementary products, such as music content) is (1) pervasive, and (2) often underestimated by regulators, who tend to be blinded by market share numbers taken as a "snapshot" in a long and dynamic competitive process.[68] It is easy to look at momentary market share numbers, in conjunction with information about the IP rights held by a platform owner, and quickly conclude that the IP rights are dangerous in the platform setting. But as the rapidly evolving digital music scene shows, it would be a mistake to make rash changes to IP policy here.[69] Competition, and not interoperability mandated by weakened IP protection, or blanket ex post IP regulation, will usually be the best guarantor of consumer welfare.

PLATFORMS AND CONSORTIUM BUILDING

This case study on music DRM illustrates the power of technological distribution platforms to serve as a focal point for content owners. In many content areas—music, books, and movies, to name three—ownership of rights over content is spread across many different entities. But the need to attract a critical mass of content to its platform leads the platform owner to take the lead in assembling a centralized clearinghouse for content, and the IP rights that cover it. In this way, platforms become a focal point for the creation of content consortia.

There were many skeptics who said that the major music labels would never come together to allow music consumers to buy digital music from a single source. It took Apple Computer, driven by the desire to draw content to its iPod platform, to prove the skeptics wrong. Book publishers too have been slow to create a "one-stop shop" for electronic books, but e-book sellers such as Amazon, Apple, and Google all had an incentive to bring the rival publishers together and invest in the transactional infrastructure to make such systems work.

There is good and bad in this arrangement. The good is that the platform owner serves the interest of content creators. Platform-centered content clearinghouses allow independent creators to *remain independent* while gaining access to new distributional technologies. This serves the traditional goal of fostering creator autonomy, and makes it possible for creative professionals to reach new audiences in an efficient way while continuing to produce their works individually or in small teams.

The bad part is that the very platform owner that creates the IP/content clearinghouse is in a position to exert significant leverage over content owners. Apple can argue, for example, that some substantial portion of music sales are the result of its investment in the iPod design, the iTunes distribution software and website, and other Apple-owned assets.[70] The resulting leverage reduces the share of revenue that is available to creators of content—the songwriters, musicians, and authors who are, I have argued, the dearest and fondest object of IP policy.

What to do? To some extent, part of the answer is not to panic and rush into ill-informed policy responses. As I have been arguing, competitive entry will often moderate the power of temporarily dominant platform owners. The same force that squeezes content owners—the platform owners' leverage—produces high profit margins, a surefire invitation to competitive entry. Even so, in some cases, market power may be large enough to make entry difficult or at the least very slow in coming. During this period, some countervailing legal pressure may be necessary. There is precedent that can help in this regard—for example, cases in the video game area (described in Chapter 6) where fair use has been invoked to prevent copyrighted lock-out codes from foreclosing video game competition. Courts in these cases have permitted entry by refusing to enforce copyrights designed to preclude sales of video games not authorized by a platform owner. Other doctrines, including IP misuse and antitrust theories, could also be brought to bear in appropriate cases. And if existing doctrines are not up to the job, some new ones might be developed to fit the case.[71] The point is that it only makes sense for IP law to show real solicitude for the creators of IP-protected content, and where this requires novel theories to offset the power of platform owners, the law should not be shy in responding.

But note the nature of the response I am calling for here. It is largely responsive, largely ex post. Only when conditions have proven consistently and perhaps intractably bad for content creators should the legal system step in to set things right. As in the earlier discussion of waiver, I would argue here that the basic framework of awarding individual rights over individual assets—the basic policy that informs the granting of IP—can be relied upon to best serve the interests of creators over the long term. Rushing to regulate the dominant platform owner of the day reflects the same vice as rushing to weaken IP rights out of concern for the supposedly crushing transactional burden of IP in the digital era. Policies of panic show a lack of trust. The same basic framework that has proven robust to changing conditions in the past will likely serve the creative community in the future as well. So long as platform owners are making efforts to enlist the support of content creators, and especially so long as there is competition among platforms, a policy of patience and trust makes sense.

Conclusion

This book presents a theoretical justification of IP rights. Though I try to accommodate a pluralist view of the field's foundations, I have not been shy about stating my own preference for a deeply normative approach. This chapter has been about the practical ways that our society's commitment to IP rights makes a difference in the working lives of creative people. I started with an overview of who these people are—a factual description of the professional creative class that IP rights are meant to nourish and sustain. I emphasized especially the way that autonomy—the rather abstract goal at the root of all property, including IP—is increased when creative professionals are given individual control rights over the assets they create. I had to recognize, of course, that in the industries where IP is important, large companies are a prominent feature of the economic landscape. I explained the paradox that these large companies support the conditions that make it possible for more creative professionals to work independently, or at least in small creative teams. One reason large companies thrive in some cases is that individual ownership creates significant transaction costs. Thus lowering transaction costs is an important corollary goal of any effective IP system. I argued that the autonomy IP confers includes the right to waive property rights freely, and extensive waiver thus demonstrates the flexibility of the IP system in action. Finally, I reviewed the current controversies over new technologies of distribution, that is, the problem of new platforms and their implications for creators. These platforms hold both promise and peril. The promise comes in the form of a single distributional chokepoint that necessitates the gathering together of many independent creators and IP owners, a natural focal point for aggregating content and lowering the cost of acquiring it. The peril is that platform owners may extract a good portion of the value of the aggregated content, by virtue of owning the technologies of distribution. Platform competition, I said, can go a long way toward ameliorating this concern, though some ex post regulation may make sense as well.

Throughout, I have argued that the goal of IP policy should be to award individual property rights, while making it easy to transfer rights, so as to serve autonomy while reducing social costs, all with the goal of carrying out the normative imperative of rewarding creators that is at the heart of IP law.

Much of what I have said so far in this book is highly general and is meant to describe what animates IP protection in contemporary legal systems. In the chapters that follow, I turn away from these generalities and to discussions of two complex and contentious problem areas in the life of

IP law today: legal protection in the digital era (Chapter 8) and the problem of IP rights in developing countries, particularly in the field of medicines and pharmaceuticals (Chapter 9). My goal now is to apply the thinking of these early chapters to some detailed policy questions that command perennial debate in the IP field, and in so doing, to show that the high-level abstractions of normative theory and conceptual principle can help us come to grips with some especially perplexing problems.

CHAPTER EIGHT

Property in the Digital Era

Introduction

Nowhere is the fate of creative professionals under more pressure than in the world of digital content. So in this chapter I continue to extend and apply the basic normative framework of Chapters 2 through 4, mixing in as well the midlevel principles of Chapters 5 and 6. My goal is to show that even in the part of the IP field undergoing the most rapid change, and even in a setting where most IP scholars believe IP rights often stand in the way of creativity rather than promoting it, robust IP protection is still the best and fairest policy.

This is most definitely a minority view today. Many IP scholars have emphasized the important benefits of "openness" with respect to digital media and identified IP as a major obstacle to this goal. The general idea is simple enough: digital media, driven by the internal logic of widespread availability and network effects, will better flourish and better serve the goals of the intellectual property system if digital content and the platforms that carry it are freed of as many restrictions on use as the law can promote. In a nutshell, the dominant idea is that in the digital age, the best IP policy is a minimalist IP policy.

In this chapter I aim to take issue with this now widely prevailing wisdom. In my view, robust IP protection is in no way inconsistent with the promotion of a flourishing environment for digital media. Quite the contrary: IP rights are essential to this goal. IP facilitates a wide range of effective strategies in the digital era, ranging from extensive control and enforcement to the promotion of widespread open access. IP as traditionally defined and understood permits private firms a very large degree of flexibility, which is just what is needed in the dynamic and challenging environment for digital media. As compared to the top-down, one-size-fits-all approach of the "IP minimalists," traditional, strong IP protection encourages and facilitates a wide variety of approaches—*including various degrees of openness*—without mandating or coercing any single approach.

So to me the traditional virtues of individual property ownership—autonomy, decentralization, flexibility—are in no way obsolete in the digital era; they are indeed just as prominent as ever. Even though we are surrounded by dynamic new technologies for creating and disseminating original works, individual control over individual assets, in the form of IP rights, still makes sense, and for the same reasons as always. IP rights reward and recognize individual achievement, and bring with them greater scope for individual autonomy. They permit individual decisions about how creative works may be used, and by whom. IP rights provide a fair and legitimate institutional setting for creativity in the digital era.

So I believe the basic case for property is still a very strong one. Digital technologies have eased the mechanical, repetitive aspects of creative work, but they have not in my opinion fundamentally made *creativity* any easier. You can sit in front of a notebook computer or an advanced computer workstation and sweat blood, trying to come up with a good idea or a good way to say or do something, just as easily as you can sit in front of a typewriter or drafting table.[1] And once having created something original, there is just as much at stake now—on both the individual and societal levels—in questions of who will reap the financial rewards of creativity, and who will control the creative work once it is loose in the world.

The long tradition of strong IP protection for creative works is under heavy fire these days in the academic literature. Which means that, while arguing for robust IP protection is hardly radical, arguing the central place of traditional property concepts in the current era, the age of digital technologies, does cut somewhat against the grain. On the theory that it helps to know what grain one is cutting against, before I get to my primary argument about the continuing viability of property rights, I want to briefly address some aspects of current IP scholarship.

Does Property Still Make Sense?
A Topography of Current IP Issues

The legal literature on IP rights is huge. It grows every day. It has become almost impossible to keep up with it. If you add blogs, e-mail newsletters, and web pages to the traditional definition of literature, the picture only gets worse. And it is not only big, it is highly variegated. The practitioner literature alone is staggering. Add to it the highly specialized academic literatures on the various IP topics—patent, copyright, trademark, and the like—and you have an extremely diverse set of writings to consider.

Out of this massive literature I propose to identify and then critique two major strands of contemporary thought, two important lines of argument. The first is what I call *digital determinism* (DD). This is the idea that the central driving force behind IP policy should be the technological imperatives of digital creation and distribution. The rallying cry for digital determinism might be, "network-friendly policies for a network-dominated world." That is, to those schooled in the DD logic, the goal of policy (in IP as well as other fields) is to get out of the way of the things that digital technology makes possible. Good rules from this point of view are those that permit maximum interconnectivity, maximum throughput of digital "stuff," and maximum latitude for each node or user on the network. For example, because it is now possible to download and distribute music from the Internet, even though such practices are generally prohibited without the content owners' permission, the DD proponent would argue that the law should be changed to accommodate this widespread practice that technology now enables. As IP scholar Lawrence Lessig sees it, for instance, since users won't stop despite recognizing they are breaking the law, it's time to change the system to accommodate inevitable real-world behaviors of those who "naturally do what new technologies encourage them to do."[2] The mindset behind this notion shows itself in the scholarly rhetoric used to describe it. Creative works are "inputs"; viewers and consumers of works are "users"; creativity and interconnection take place via "fat pipes" in the distinct domain of cyberspace. Especially with respect to the use of "inputs" to describe creative works, the rhetoric suggests the crucial influence of the technological systems that enable and shape the creation and dissemination of creative work.

A quick word on the pedigree of digital determinism is in order. This idea has some things in common with the general concept of technological determinism, which is defined as the notion that technology drives history.[3] The spirit of this line of thought is perhaps best captured in the motto of the 1933 Chicago Century of Progress world's fair: "Science Finds—Industry Applies—Man Conforms."[4] Sociologists and historians of science and technology since the 1980s have taken issue with the basic premises behind technological determinism, especially that people must conform to whatever imperatives are generated by the "inherent logic" of technology.[5] Many of them argue that social forces shape and determine many (some say almost all) aspects of technology. For these scholars, the concept of determinism masks numerous occasions for human intervention in technical systems.[6] In other words, these scholars reject the descriptive claim of determinism that technologies shape society. They counter with the idea that technologies do not develop along autonomous paths, and do not have an inexorable, internal logic. Instead, they argue, technologies are shaped and guided by human (social) forces.

On this view, the rallying cry of early cyberspace enthusiasts—"information wants to be free"—was at best naive. For historians of technology, the very idea that information "wants" anything is a form of determinism. But more importantly, and more germane to this book, is the normative thrust of this early claim by cyber-enthusiasts. For these folks, "information wants to be free" points directly to a normative agenda: we should help it! Society, in other words, should adapt to the possibilities of this technology by removing whatever obstacles stand in the way and prevent it from achieving its full potential. So while cyber-enthusiasts may not express full faith in technological determinism in the positive or descriptive sense, they do express a normative version of it through their policy proposals.[7]

The second trend is closely related. It is the idea that the distinctive feature of digital technology, and therefore the thing that policy should most seek to encourage, is *collective creativity* (CC). This is an idea that starts with the fact of greater interconnectivity, but goes beyond. Scholars writing in this vein are interested not so much in the technological logic of networks, but in the potential for human interaction and (especially) group-level creativity that this technology makes possible. Some of the claims that issue from this school of thought are really quite striking. According to its leading lights, we are in the midst of a hugely important cultural revolution. For the first time, far-flung individuals are connected in virtual communities that make possible all sorts of previously unthinkable collaboration. Creative works—music, writing, film, and the like—can be shared instantaneously with receptive people all around the world, without the need for large, self-interested "intermediaries" such as record labels, publishers, and film studios. Small contributions by many individuals can be aggregated seamlessly, making possible a new kind of "distributed creation" that is unlike anything the world has ever seen. With our new knowledge of the power of groups, of virtual creative teams, society is being transformed, and all sorts of "legacy" or "entrenched" interests are being replaced or threatened. Indeed, an entirely new way of doing work (maybe even a new way of being)—a social way, an open way based on sharing—is emerging, right before our eyes.[8]

Digital determinism (DD) and collective creativity (CC) obviously have a lot in common. Indeed, it might not be much of a stretch to say that they are merely two different ways of describing the same thing. DD looks into the wires and servers that power the interconnectivity that is the platform on which CC rests. CC looks at the virtual communities, the "distributed single brains," made possible by all this hardware. There are some distinctions, of course. The DD perspective might emphasize that *individual* creation and consumption/use of digital material are just as much a part of the network picture as collective work, while the CC school of thought might point out that collective interaction is strongly enabled by, but not necessarily dependent on, any particular technological infrastructure.

What interests me is the view of property rights common to the DD and CC perspectives. Whether the central idea is that technological systems should determine policy, or that society ought to be highly concerned with fostering collective interaction and production, individual property rights are usually seen as part of the problem, and not part of the solution. To technological enthusiasts, property rights just get in the way of the efficient flow of information through the network and out to the "nodes" (or people) that it connects. The same goes for those whose interest is in societal transformation through collective creativity. Property rights, associated as they are with *individual* firms or people, tend only to gum up the free sharing of information and the process of building upon it. Property is fundamentally at odds with the spirit of openness and creative humility (that is, no need for individual credit) that suffuses the virtual communities behind collective creativity.

Now most scholars in the DD and CC camps are far too good at what they do to advocate the complete elimination of property in the digital realm. They admit it is a useful institution in some, perhaps many, contemporary contexts. What they argue for is policies that minimize the effect of property rights on the technological imperative (DD) or group ethos (CC) of the digital era; or, at the conceptual level, strict limits on the intrusion of what might be called "property logic" into the digital domain. So as not to deal in straw men, let me be clear that these are the criticisms I will be addressing. I am not arguing that the DD and CC worldviews are completely anti-property in some global sense. The thrust of these perspectives is rather that property as an institution and as a concept gets in the way of important trends in the digital era. I recognize that their goal is not to eliminate property altogether, but to lessen its effect on the digital domain. It is this central idea of "property as obstacle," both practically and conceptually, that I take aim at here.

Property rights give individuals control over assets or resources. To hold property is to have the right to say what happens to an asset: who gets to use it, and on what terms. Although there is of course very wide divergence across property institutions, these are the core elements of property: (1) control over assets (with at least some degree of exclusivity), (2) by individuals. The basic idea is captured well by Jeremy Waldron, who as I mentioned in Chapter 2 speaks of property as a one-to-one mapping between individuals and resources.[9]

In the digital world, both these elements are problematic. Assets or resources are said to operate according to different rules in this world. And, as already described, individuals are less important; networks, collectivities, are the more essential unit of analysis. Let me describe these ideas a bit more fully, so that my response to them can be better understood.

The Fluid World of Digital Resources

An interesting article by philosopher Gordon Hull makes the point that it is now virtually impossible to tell the difference between a digital "original" and a digital "reproduction."[10] This quality of digital works leads other scholars to emphasize digital works' fluid boundaries.[11] It is very easy to add to, modify, or adapt a copy of a digital work, which makes it very difficult to maintain the original integrity of the work. According to a whole host of scholars, this is one of the great, revolutionary benefits of digital technology, and is indeed the hallmark of the emerging set of practices and norms that is rapidly taking shape—what is frequently referred to as "digital culture."[12]

Collectivity: The Essence of Digital Era Creativity?

For many, of equal importance with fluidity in the digital realm is the ability for many disparate individuals to contribute creative effort toward large, collective goals. Open source computer programs—many individual programmers contributing computer code to make a sophisticated end product such as an operating system or server software—were the prototype. But now the model has spread into all sorts of interesting pockets. Wikipedia, or wikis in general, are currently the hot examples. Dozens of disparate people, each with some useful knowledge about a given topic, pool their contributions in a single online source that is constantly edited, refined, and updated. The same dynamic is currently at work in many other areas as well: from fan websites (where people contribute stories, commentary, graphic art, and other kinds of content related to a common interest such a book series or movie), to recipe-swapping websites, to all sorts of travel advice websites.

The basic logic behind collective works such as these is of course quite old; "many hands make light work," "two heads are better than one," and many another cliché attest to this. But once again, digital enthusiasts point out that ubiquitous interconnection and a common (digital) medium have catapulted group efforts into a completely new dimension. Whatever analog predecessors there may have been, they offer only a dim comparison to the instantaneous, far-flung, and comprehensive aggregations that the Internet and digital technology make possible.[13]

The enthusiasts certainly have a good argument here. Bands of "amateurs" contributing small amounts of creative work to an impressive single work were not pioneered in the digital era, but they are certainly much more common now. So for example the individual instances of word usage contributed by the many amateur lexicographers who worked on the first edition of the *Oxford English Dictionary* added up to a magnificent whole, but this was long thought remarkable, and very rare, if not sui generis.[14] And "collaborative entertainments," from spontaneous musical jam sessions to role-playing games such as Dungeons and Dragons, while they did exist, were sufficiently unusual that they could be dismissed as out of the mainstream. Today, however, there are thousands of "little OEDs" and other collaborative communities online. This surely marks a major departure of degree, if not of kind.

There is no disputing that instances of collective creativity are now much more common. What I object to, however, is the idea that collective works will and should systematically replace individual works in the digital era. And, as a consequence of the continuing importance of individual creativity, I argue that property rights still make sense as a legal and social institution. More importantly, I argue that continuing to grant and enforce property rights does not threaten the viability of collective creativity, but that seriously *curtailing* property rights so as to further promote collective creativity *would* significantly undermine the conditions for individual creativity. I return to these themes in the "Updating Property" section below.

Creative Professionals and Legal Infrastructure

As explained in Chapter 7, the DD and CC perspectives have a decidedly negative attitude toward big companies that own large numbers of IP-protected works. The usual suspects include Walt Disney, large record labels, and movie and TV studios; established software companies such as Microsoft and Oracle are often thrown in as well. In Chapter 7 I argued that many of these critiques are off the mark. Big companies not only employ many professional creatives, they also, perhaps more importantly, occupy a crucial place in the overall ecosystem of the creative industries. They are purchasers of specialized products and services (animation, sound engineering, scientific and technical specialties, independent "talent," and so on), and they also incubate startup firms in these and other niches. As I said in Chapter 7, anyone concerned with the care and feeding of creative professionals should think twice before advocating the demise of all the "dinosaurs" and other big companies that support IP-based industries.

But of course all this presupposes that creative professionals are a class of people worth caring about—that they deserve some sort of special attention or recognition. Not everyone would agree. So before moving on to a broader consideration of the fate of creatives in the digital era, we must first review the rationale for favoring this class in the first place.

Privileging Certain Forms of Creative Expression

Recognizing a special class of "creative professionals" raises a number of problems. I will discuss two, one broadly ethical and one more pragmatic. The first is, what justification is there to privilege the contributions of one group over those of another? I will emphasize here especially the claims of "remixers"—people who express their creativity by modifying original works and mixing multiple original works together to create something new and distinctive. The second issue is why we as a society should take special efforts to protect creative professionals from the sweeping changes wrought by new technologies. If vacuum tube makers, telegraphers, horse drivers, telephone operators, and travel agents can be squeezed out of jobs by new technologies, why not writers, musicians, and artists? What, in other words, is so special about this class of people that we should take special care to preserve their means of economic livelihood?

Remixers and mashup artists do not just passively consume digital creations; they integrate preexisting works into new creative works. These people present a more difficult case than the mere user: they want to treat the digital creation as a starting point for a larger work on which they want to impress their own will. If the law recognizes creativity as an important goal, why should the claims of these remixers be treated with less respect than those of an "original" creator?

The answer, I think, is indicated by the language often used in these discussions. The original creation is said to be an "input" for the remixer. My response: if creative professionals do not want their work to be treated as an input, or want to exercise control over when and how this happens, the law should protect that preference. If some potentially object to having their original work, a vehicle of self-expression, characterized as a commodity to be thrown into the remixing assembly process (like so much creative slurry), they ought to have the right to insist on permission. To put it as bluntly as possible, the claims of remixers do not usually have the same weight as those of original creators, because they stand in a very different relationship to the original creators' works.[15] The law may enforce the creators' property claim here because that claim *is* more deserving of recognition.

At this point in the discussion, IP critics usually enter with the argument that creative work has always involved borrowing. This leads sometimes to the charge that powerful, entrenched interests manipulate the (fundamentally amorphous) concept of "originality" to serve their own ends,[16] and sometimes to the more benign argument that the law ought to get up to date and recognize the coequal contributions of remixers.[17]

In this matter, I have to agree with copyright scholar Doris Estelle Long, who comments on the argument that "creative people have always borrowed" by pointing to the difference between Shakespeare, Michelangelo, and some instances of "remix culture":

> [F]ew would dispute that the works which both Michelangelo and Shakespeare created ultimately enriched the public domain, laying down truly new works that have in turn inspired subsequent artists. Today, in light of the advances in reproductive technology, inspirational reproduction is push button easy and in many instances does not require the training or skill demonstrated by earlier reproductive works. I do not mean to suggest that works created using such reproductive technologies lack creativity or are unworthy of protection. I merely suggest that the level of reproduction allowed through such digital technologies has radically altered the nature of inspirational reproduction, requiring a renewed examination of the purpose and impact of copyright protection in the Digital Age.[18]

In other words: yes, remixers are original. But some works are more original than others. And yes, "originality" here *is* a socially constructed term.

But we as a society have so constructed it to reflect what we value. Originality that draws on ideas, rather than fixed and final creations, is to be privileged over originality that mixes together preexisting final works.[19]

INCENTIVES AS A FORM OF PRIVILEGING

This discussion of originality leads us to a related topic. One common theme in recent writings on copyright is that most authors are primarily motivated by intrinsic rewards.[20] This leads many an observer to conclude that the "incentive story" for IP protection is untrue with respect to many artists, and therefore that a major prop under the current IP system has been removed. The conventional response to this sort of argument is to either cite some general statements on the importance of incentives to particular artists or creators, or to cite some aggregate empirical studies showing a macrolevel correlation between rewards and creative output.

I would like to try something different. I am going to argue that there is more to the incentive story than a simple binary effect—that incentives either do or do not cause creators to produce new works. Incentives may well have more to do with the *quality* of creative works that are produced, rather than whether a certain person will produce at all, or even necessarily the total quantity of works produced.

There is very little solid evidence on these matters; indeed, when writing about it, one faces difficulty in avoiding a "battle of anecdotes." So, for example, authors often cite biographies of artists, or even their own experience, in support of the intrinsic motivation thesis.[21] And on the other side, hard-headed economists and those supportive of robust IP protection cite their own counterexamples.[22] With the issue stated in these terms, there can be little satisfactory resolution.

But with a slight reframing of the issue, we can make some headway on the question of extrinsic (incentives) versus intrinsic motivation. The problem with the conventional statement of the issue is that it is put so starkly. Artists who cite their intrinsic motivation may be saying only that yes, no matter what the reward structure they were faced with, they would create their art. The alternative—answering "no" to the question "would you create even in the absence of IP protection?"—requires people to negate a very large aspect of their identity. And it is true to our experience that "art will out," somehow; some writers at least kept writing in World War II concentration camps, artists of all kinds find ways to express themselves in prisons, in poverty, and in the absence of any kind of support or encouragement, as with many artists in the former Soviet Union. So there cannot be much doubt that many artists are indeed driven by a strong intrinsic motivation. Some will find a way.

So even if it is worthless to ask whether at least some artists will create in the absence of extrinsic rewards, we can ask a more refined set of questions. And with these, we may gain better traction on the real issues at stake in the debate over IP protection for works in the digital era, and the role that property rights might play. How *much time* will a creative person be able to put into his or her work; and can an artist work full-time, so as to grow to full maturity and become in a true sense a creative *professional* (a topic we considered in depth in Chapter 7)? Will an artist's work be carefully and meticulously edited, refined, and presented to the audience, so as to bring out its full potential and place it in the best light possible? To put it simply, what conditions will surround and shape the work of creative persons, and will those conditions allow the creators to fully flourish—to create works of the highest quality they are capable of?[23]

A CREATIVE ELITE?

There is no escaping the fact that I have framed the incentive problem in a way that may be uncomfortable for some. That is because I have implied strongly that there is such a thing as a "creative professional," that the care and feeding of this class of people is an essential—maybe *the* essential—function of the IP system, and that perhaps not everyone who wants to work creatively can attain membership in this class. Bound up with my discussion of extrinsic motivation, or the incentive effects of IP, in other words, is a sense of hierarchy, the notion of a creative elite. In short, I do believe that some creative works really do reflect higher quality than others.

This runs headlong into a broad and perhaps even dominant strain of thinking in contemporary observations of the digital world: the "democratizing" of creativity at the hands of the new digital technologies. Many who have looked carefully at the emerging digital landscape have noted the rise of "amateurs" or laypeople—nonspecialists, people outside the traditionally anointed elite—as a major force in digital creativity.[24] My solicitude for the class of people I have called creative professionals would seem quite at odds with the democratization trend. I seem to be implying, in fact, that there is some kind of close connection between respect for property rights and the presence and maintenance of a concentrated elite that excludes most amateurs. Even if I am right about the effect of extrinsic motivation, one might legitimately ask, is it worth the cost? Is the maintenance of a creative professional class worth the loss of democratization, of grassroots creativity? Do we as a society really want to pay that price?[25]

That at any rate is the question that I think some of the advocates of democratization would like to ask. It leaves people like me in a tough position. Stick to my guns, and argue for the exclusion of the "little guys" who contribute YouTube videos, new scenarios involving popular characters, new characters for online computer games. Or, alternatively, embrace the value of democratization as an important force in the digital landscape, at the expense of my cherished defense of property rights.

Does Digital IP "Discriminate Against" Amateurs?

Fortunately for me I reject this whole approach. I believe it presents a false choice. The simple fact is this: amateur culture in all its forms and all its myriad glories can and will thrive even in the presence of strong property rights that support a creative professional class. Of course, a continued commitment to property rights will cut down on *some* amateur creativity in the digital realm. (Because of enforcement costs, and voluntary decisions to waive many rights, the effect will not be nearly so severe as many IP critics fear.) But this marginal diminution in free digital culture is simply the price we have to pay to maintain the creative professional class. The cost of premium creative works, in other words, is a slight reduction in the volume of amateur works. To me it is worth it.

Note carefully that we do not have to choose between top-flight movies or music, and a plenitude of amateur content. We can have both. Indeed, as a quick browse through YouTube shows, we do have both. The *real* choice is between an IP policy that forces potential creative professionals to abandon their careers before they want to, or take those careers in undesired directions to survive, and a policy that permits (some) talented and creative people to move, at some point, into the creative professional class. Put differently, the choice is between (1) weakening IP rights (or acquiescing in their de facto weakening), and forcing *everyone* into the permanent amateur class, and (2) maintaining a commitment to robust IP protection.[26] The latter policy will necessarily keep some creative people out of the top ranks. But the former policy, in my view, is worse. It will prevent anyone from ever entering that class. It will in effect destroy the entire category of "creative professional" as we have come to know it.

It is also important to note that "digitally dependent creators" are not forever barred, en masse, from the ranks of creative professionals. Indeed, some have seen the voluntary submission of "fan" works, game characters, or open source software code as elaborate ways for people to "audition" for admission to the professional ranks. In a related way, robust protection of original, creative works may push people toward creation of such works, and away from creation of more straightforward digital creations. Enhancing more original creations with the imprimatur of a property right, in other words, may encourage people to push a little harder to create something that merits the label of legal originality.[27]

Fair Use for Remixers?

My discussion of the remix issue so far has emphasized the creators of original content. As with others who work to make something new, they deserve IP protection. That their works can be easily copied, distributed, and modified—these are of secondary importance in my view. They share with creators from the past the same need for autonomy in their work and the same hope to make a living doing what they do.

A new generation comfortable with digital technology has become adept at using original creative works as a starting point for all sorts of creative projects. These are the remixers. They take digital versions of original works and modify them, mix them with other works, sometimes in interesting and creative ways.[28] Because they draw from materials that are freely available, and because they add their own creative twist, they often argue that what they do is no different from "traditional" creativity.[29] Their argument leads to the conclusion that remixing deserves formal legal recognition—that is should be respected as a "fair use" under copyright law.[30] They would say that on the remix issue, I have placed the legal privilege in exactly the wrong place, with the creators of original content instead of the bold, misunderstood, and equally creative remixers.

To properly engage this debate requires that we traverse a bit of fair use doctrine. After doing so, I will try to relate the remixing controversy to issues raised in Parts I and II of this book. Drawing from Locke and Kant, and citing the principles of dignity and efficiency, I will justify why I believe that in general the privileged position in IP law belongs to original creators and not remixers. I will also describe how some well-known conventional limits on the rights of creators ought to apply in the case of remixed works.

TRANSACTION COSTS AND TRANSFORMATIVE USES

Fair use is a subject of nonstop contention in copyright law. This is partly because it is one of the few defenses to a charge of infringement that still applies after infringement has been proven. That is, it is in the nature of a justification or excuse: when the facts establish that a copyright has been violated, the infringer may still plead fair use and in some cases escape legal liability. In every case in which fair use determines the ultimate outcome, a valid copyright exists, and its infringement has been proven. So ethically, there is a lot of weight on this defense; it is a powerful doctrine that starts from the fact of a legal violation yet still lets the otherwise liable party off the hook.

A second reason for contentiousness is that, as codified, the doctrine is open-ended. The copyright statute announces an exemplary purpose for the doctrine, then lists four nonexclusive "factors" that courts may consider when applying it.[31] For creative litigants and motivated lawyers, the contours of the doctrine have appeared to be just so much putty; the doctrine can be shaped, molded, and smoothed in a thousand new and creative forms as the case at hand requires. This is as it should be, given the need for a flexible and open-ended "safety valve" capable of relieving the pressure that can build from overly technical application of the copyright law. Yet it is also a source of exasperation for people just trying to figure out what they are and are not allowed to do with a copyrighted work.

I do not propose to traverse the entire fascinating landscape of fair use in this section; a number of lengthy books do that already, and, if history is any guide, more are no doubt on the way. Instead I want to turn my attention to the two features of the doctrine that have risen to prominence over the past twenty-five years and can assist us in understanding the core dilemma of fair use as applied to remixes. These are (1) the market failure, or transaction cost, rationale for the doctrine, and (2) the concept of a transformative use. Getting a grip on these concepts will give us the tools we need to address the remix question.

Market Failure. Roughly thirty years ago a young, ambitious copyright scholar named Wendy Gordon surveyed the cases on fair use and hit on a revolutionary idea. Maybe what explained them, in all their seeming inconsistency, was the simple idea of market failure.[32] Maybe fair use was a proxy the legal system used when transactions between copyright owners and users of copyrighted works were too expensive or otherwise impossible. This was a radical concept at the time, because it deviated from the conventional idea that the key to fair use was to find an all-embracing notion of fairness. In Wendy Gordon's hands, fairness was not primarily a magic a priori concept that could resolve actual disputes; it was something that dropped out *after* the really important analytical work was done. And this work was all about the market for copyrighted works. If a marketplace formed, with the requisite conditions of willing buyers and sellers, there was no need to consider questions of fairness. It was only if a market did not form, but was in other respects desirable or logical, that fair use would be pulled out of the legal kit bag and applied to achieve the right outcome. Wendy Gordon was smart enough to know that sometimes the privileges of users necessarily trumped the interests of copyright holders, so she left room for a residual category of fair use that had nothing to do with the ready availability of a market. She also carefully formulated her approach to require courts to estimate the impact of a finding of fair use on the value of a copyrighted work—so that even in the absence of market failure, a case should be decided in favor of the copyright owner if the alternative, a finding of fair use favoring the infringer, would destroy or severely damage the value of the copyrighted work in question. But aside from these caveats, the key to putting fair use into practical effect for Gordon was to look for cases of market failure.

One difficulty in applying Gordon's revolutionary approach has to do with timing. Sometimes markets take a while to form. Especially when a new technology crops up, disrupting established patterns of commerce, it can take time for market incumbents to come to grips with the new reality. This has happened repeatedly in recent years, as when downloadable music burst onto the scene, or when Internet distribution of video content became a viable alternative to traditional broadcast and cable distribution. To paraphrase IP scholar Rebecca Eisenberg, it can be hard to tell whether markets are failing or forming.[33]

Consistent with my enthusiasm for individual IP rights, in this debate I take the side of those who would be cautious in finding a particular practice to be fair use. I worry that a rush to apply the fair use label will stifle the formation of a market. Once fair use is found, I think it unlikely that future developments will provoke a court to reverse course and find that an established fair use no longer qualifies for the defense. Because private parties will come to rely on the initial finding, structuring their decisions and perhaps even entire businesses on this basis, a later reversal could very well upset widely shared expectations about what is legal. Courts hate to do that sort of thing, and I do not think they would do it very often. Which means that an initial finding of fair use can come to have a sort of societal "lock-in" effect—depriving a copyright owner of a market for all time.

It will often be more prudent in a close case to deny fair use initially, to give markets a reasonable opportunity to form. (Obviously this does not apply when the infringing activity at issue falls into a sphere traditionally protected by long-established fair use cases, for example, parodies; see below.) If markets do in fact take shape, avoiding an early finding of fair use will have reserved an opportunity for creator compensation. And if they do not—if, after every opportunity for interested parties to take action, they still have not—it may be appropriate at some later time to find fair use. But this ought to be put off for a substantial period of time, as markets can take some time to get going.

A certain caution in making a definitive finding of fair use can be detected in several recent copyright controversies involving new technologies. In one case involving photocopying from the 1990s, a company with a large staff of research scientists was accused of copyright infringement for making numerous copies of selected articles in scientific publications. One argument the company made was that the market for individual copies of scientific articles was as yet not well established, that it was still somewhat unusual for publishers of scientific journals to offer pricing for the making of individual article copies. The Second Circuit Court of Appeals, speaking through Judge John Newman, rejected the thrust of this argument. The court looked instead to the nascent structures for per-article licensing that were taking shape, noting in particular that a finding of fair use would in effect strangle these initiatives in the cradle.[34]

A similar strain is seen in recent cases relating to online music distribution. Though they are centered on complex questions about the technologies of digital music sharing, the opinions in these cases exhibit a reluctance to completely insulate from legal liability the copying of individual music files.[35] Because viable online music licensing initiatives have been in the process of formation, the courts wisely avoided an irreversible declaration of fair use with respect to file sharing.

Of more direct pertinence to remixing, courts have also been reluctant to grant a broad exemption for the use of short copyrighted snippets in the creation of "mix tapes" and remixed music.[36] Though controversial, these rulings resisting a general exemption for digital "sampling" seem to me fundamentally correct. The cases have come in the still-early days of the practice. And at least some courts have found that a market may well be forming for the use of digital samples. As I have argued here, a fair use finding in this context would have the effect of eviscerating this market at the very outset. Better to wait, the instinct seems to be, giving institutions, mechanisms, trading practices, and norms the chance to take shape. If they do, the early fears of potential market failure will have been for naught; copyright owners will therefore have another outlet for sale of their works (an important consideration in light of the widespread concern that the digital music era is significantly undermining musicians' ability to make a decent living). And if markets fail to materialize, there is always room later for a finding of fair use. As I have mentioned, there are many obstacles to the formation of markets for IP-protected content. A definitive finding of fair use, early in the game, presents an obstacle that is unlikely to be overcome, and so should be avoided.

Transformative Uses. If market failure represents one half of the major recent innovations in fair use theory, the other half would have to be the idea of a transformative use. Beginning roughly in the 1980s, scholars began to reconsider the ways they might isolate infringing uses that significantly benefit society, and therefore were more worthy of the fair use justification.[37] They hit on the idea of the transformative use: an infringing use that added creative input from the infringer, brought the infringed work into a new realm or market, or simply produced an end product that so differed from the original that freedom from infringement liability seemed most appropriate. However it is conceptualized, at the heart of the idea of transformative use lies some noteworthy and socially beneficial contribution on the part of the infringer. Though never entirely free of controversy, this concept has become a recognized constituent of the law of fair use.[38]

The contrast with market failure is easy to see. Transformative use is all about what the *infringer* contributes, the value of what is added. Market failure envisions value-adding works, to be sure, but in the context of prior market exchange. The marketplace is the default institution that decides which deals get done, and on what terms. The specifics of what the infringer might add, and what the underlying work is worth to the infringer, are to be worked out between the parties.

At the same time, there is some common ground between the two ideas. Often in cases that accentuate the transformative aspects of an infringement, there is an undercurrent of market failure. That is, the courts imply, the infringer has used the work in a fashion or for a purpose that the copyright owner would not have contemplated. The infringing use is somehow foreign to the plans, designs, or conventions followed by the copyright owner or others similarly situated. The strangeness and newness of the infringer's use thus points in the same direction as the market failure analysis: this is an application or modification of the work that would probably not have been authorized by the copyright owner.[39] It is not perhaps quite accurate that a market has failed to form; it might be more accurate to say that a market was not seriously contemplated—the original creator never considered a voluntary exchange in the first place.

Where this scenario plays out, the underlying sentiment is one of unfair appropriation.[40] The thought is that the infringer has concocted a new and original application for the copyright owner's work—one undreamed of by the work's creator. It seems wrong in these cases to permit the copyright owner to gain the advantage of the infringer's original insight. It seems, in a sense, as though the copyright owner seeks to misappropriate the value added by the infringer's original insight. Because this seems wrong, the courts declare a fair use, and the infringement is permitted to stand.

Market Failure and Transformative Use for Remixes. Where does this leave us in the case of remixes? We have to decide which of these analytic concepts predominates: the idea that markets may form and ought not be preempted; or the idea that remixers add value in ways that copyright owners have not contemplated.

With some exceptions, I believe market failure predominates. Now that remixing is a well-understood practice, and now that various transactional norms and mechanisms are emerging to accommodate it, applying the market failure analysis is reasonable. An across-the-board declaration that remixing is fair use will shut down a nascent market, eliminate a potential revenue source for original creators, and therefore marginally reduce the scope of autonomy for creators of works in digital form. By the same token, although some of the earliest remixers might have employed copyrighted works in unforeseen ways, remixing is today a well-understood part of the creative scene. It is no longer possible for a remixer to argue that digital modification is an unexpected and surprising use for an original work. We are past the era of the pioneering remixer. Copyright owners are well aware of the remix phenomenon, and of the market for digital remixes, so no individual remixer can plausibly claim to have brought that market to the attention of a copyright owner.

Of course, individual *instances* of the remix phenomenon can be wonderfully creative and original.[41] But I do not see this as reason to establish a broad fair use privilege. Where there is a well-established market for adaptations of copyrighted works—what those in the field know as derivative works—originality is no defense. A marvelously creative film version of a copyrighted story will still infringe the copyright on the story. This rule has occasioned a fair degree of debate over the years, with perhaps the best rationale being that the copyright holder deserves to control the fate of her characters and story even when they are adapted to a new medium (an expression, in some ways, of the dignity principle laid out in Chapter 5). At any rate it is an accepted part of the IP landscape. And when applied to remixes, in light of the strong preference for market exchange, it means that the claims of even creative remixers must yield to the rights of original content creators.

LOCKE AND KANT, REMIXED

Superficially, the centrality of labor in Locke's theory might seem to provide support for the remixers' claim. It is hard work to take a digital file and slowly, painstakingly, transform it into something new. Shouldn't this be grounds for some sort of right on behalf of a remixer?

Of course not. Locke's theory goes well beyond simply equating labor and property rights. For one thing, Locke recognized that one who labors on an asset that is already owned by another does not thereby ground a legitimate property claim. So long as there are ample unclaimed objects around, laboring on something that has already been appropriated (or, a fortiori, created) by another constitutes "meddl[ing]" in Locke's schema.[42] In short, labor cannot justify an act of misappropriation. Second, Locke recognized that labor, and with it a claim to property, could be alienated by contract.[43] For him this meant that an employee could surrender property claims in exchange for an hourly wage. But it can also be read to support the idea that where a contract is the customary way in which labor is directed into a productive channel, potential property claims give way to the binding effect of contracts. Follow-on labor is commonly alienated this way in creative fields; examples such as film editing, literary editing, postfilm special effects, sound mixing for recorded music, and the like all illustrate the point. These are difficult, laborious tasks, to be sure, but traditionally they do not give rise to a separate property claim or a legal privilege. They are traditionally, and properly, considered subordinate forms of labor that stem from and depend on an initial creative work. Remixing is no different.

For both of these reasons, the hard work spent making a remix does not add up to a property claim. It is labor applied on top of labor, added over the labor of the original creator, whose earlier effort on a blank slate justifies a superior claim. And it is labor that often should be and typically could have been channeled by a contract between the original creator and the follow-on remixer. Both reasons point to a rejection of any Lockean claim here.

As for Kant, his Universal Principle also has something to say about remixes. As we saw in Chapters 3 and 7, the hallmark of this Principle is the concept of balanced autonomy. Property is granted to encourage autonomy, but is limited in cases where it impinges significantly on the freedom of action of other people. When it comes to remixing, the question is whether the remixers' freedom of action is so seriously restricted that the Principle would militate against full property protection for original works. I think not. While it is true that the art of remixing requires access to preexisting digital content, there is a good deal of content available for free. No particular or individual work is essential in most cases for the remixer to ply his craft. Thus nothing critical is lost if a particular work is placed outside the reach of the remixer. But something important *is* lost if an individual creator who does not want his works remixed is forced to make them available. So when the respective autonomy interests are weighed in Kantian fashion, the original creator prevails.

COPYRIGHT AND THE VOLUME OF REMIXING:
WHERE'S THE PROBLEM?

Another strong reason to resist broad fair use rights for remixes is this: there is no evidence of a remix shortage. The Internet abounds with creative, cheeky, fun, and sometimes bizarre remix content. And all of this has been achieved without a broad fair use privilege for remixers. How can we account for this?

Mostly it is because rightholders have, in various ways, acquiesced in the practice of remixing. Some have affirmatively waived their rights; well-known performers such as David Byrne, the Beastie Boys, and Chuck D have made selected works available for remixing.[44] Some newer artists have joined "open source record labels," which make their works freely available to others.[45] For aspiring musicians, giving away free samples is now a well-understood tactic in career building, and even established artists have learned the value of maintaining audience awareness and interest by selectively releasing free content.[46]

But formal waiver is only one source of content for remixers. More common is a less formal type of acquiescence. Content owners simply tolerate, without formally authorizing, a range of remixing activities. Partly this is a result of high enforcement costs; the large volume of amateur remixes makes it very difficult to effectively shut down remix activities. Partly it is strategic: amateur remix activity builds interest in proprietary content and can be a form of "viral marketing" spreading the word about the virtues of the original remixed content. Also, many content owners are reluctant to bring lawsuits against their own fans.

Finally, because remixing is popular, a good deal of remix-ready material is made available by amateurs, for amateurs. The Creative Commons organization, which disseminates information on open-sharing contracts and makes content available free of all or most use restrictions, participates in a website called ccmixter that serves as a major hub for content that is available for unrestricted remixing.[47]

A number of copyright experts have taken notice of widespread nonenforcement in the digital realm. They have used different labels to describe it, including "tolerated use" and expanded implied licensing.[48] Whatever the label, the basic idea is the same. Widespread nonenforcement has brought a new set of de facto rights to the users of digital works. These quasi rights are ubiquitous, since in many cases remixes will not be policed. They are not on a par with the true rights held by original creators, for reasons I have sought to explain in this chapter. Yet they are significant; users do take the quasi norm of nonenforcement into account when deciding whether making and distributing a remix is a good idea. Judging from the massive volume of freely available remixes, remixers have fully internalized the widespread norm of nonenforcement. As a consequence, it is not too much to say that today, amateur, noncommercial remixing falls somewhere between a quasi-fair use and an activity that is implicitly licensed by the vast majority of right holders.

The broad range of tolerated uses is critical to understanding the real-world effect of IP rights over digital content. As I stressed in the Introduction and again in Chapter 7, the postgrant environment is at least as important as the formal description of the rights "on the books." The de facto scope of rights over digital works is much narrower than it would seem from the formal expression of IP rights on the statute books. And this is so even though formal rights have undergone significant expansion in recent years. Figure 8.1 illustrates the point, by showing both the formal "rights space" created by IP law and the de facto "effective rights space" experienced by content owners in the real world. The overall point of the diagram is quite simple: to show graphically that the de facto rights of users of digital works, including remixers, have expanded significantly in recent years despite the contemporaneous strengthening of formal IP rights. (Figure 8.1 is identical to Figure 5.1 and is reproduced here for convenience.)

Nonenforcement and the "Rights Cushion." So systematic nonenforcement is a predictable feature of the digital IP landscape. As the diagram I just referred to shows, this in effect creates a cushion between IP law on the books and IP law as it is experienced by users and consumers of protected works. How should this rights cushion affect IP policy?

When practical conditions cushion the impact of handing out rights, there is less pressure to get the policy balance exactly right. There is also less pressure to grant rights to both sides in equal measure. The interests of consumers and users are taken care of not just through the formal rights they receive, but also (and primarily) through high enforcement costs and market competition between rights owners. The difficulty of enforcing rights, together with voluntary decisions to forgo enforcement, cushion users and consumers from the full impact of the rights as specified. And yet those who create valuable works do receive their proper reward, in the form of a property right sanctioned by the state. So when we take these two things together—the right to property in creative works, and the reality of a considerable cushion between formal rights and social practice—we arrive at something like an equilibrium. IP rights are rights, with all that entails; but we can expect that they will often be waived or not enforced due to the self-interest of the rightholder. That they may not always be

TRADITIONAL RIGHTS CONFIGURATION

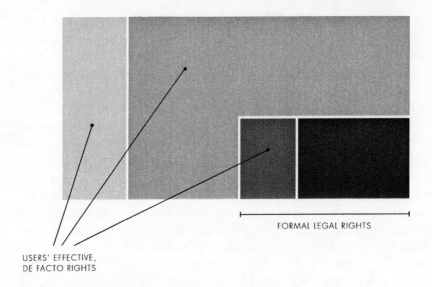

USERS' EFFECTIVE,
DE FACTO RIGHTS

FORMAL LEGAL RIGHTS

DIGITAL ERA RIGHTS CONFIGURATION

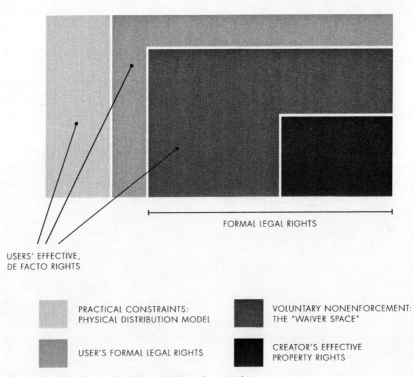

USERS' EFFECTIVE,
DE FACTO RIGHTS

FORMAL LEGAL RIGHTS

PRACTICAL CONSTRAINTS:
PHYSICAL DISTRIBUTION MODEL

USER'S FORMAL LEGAL RIGHTS

VOLUNTARY NONENFORCEMENT:
THE "WAIVER SPACE"

CREATOR'S EFFECTIVE
PROPERTY RIGHTS

Figure 8.1. Traditional rights and digital-era rights

waived is the cost we as a society must be willing to bear for having done the correct thing by those who make creative works. That rights are not always valuable enough to be enforced is the reality creators must face if they are to try to make a living being creative in the Internet era. Rather than embodying users' and consumers' interests in countervailing rights, we can recognize instead that those interests are often protected in a de facto sense by the enforcement environment in which IP rights are granted.

The rights cushion has a flip side that should be noted as well. Just as significant nonenforcement offsets the burden of IP on users, it may dilute the benefits of IP for creative professionals. Which means that IP rights may have to be strengthened for those rights to continue their traditional function of adequately rewarding hard-working creators. One might argue, in fact, that this is exactly what has been happening in IP legislation over the past fifteen or so years. IP law has been significantly strengthened in some respects; examples include lengthening the term of protection for copyrights, an increase in criminal liability for IP infringement, and extending IP law to include protection against the cracking of proprietary content-protection technologies (that is, the Digital Millennium Copyright Act of 1998).[49] From the perspective of rights owners, it is perhaps understandable that widespread infringement that cannot be effectively policed would lead to a desire for stronger IP protection. Partly this is a sort of psychological response, a reaction to an increasing tide of noncommercial infringement. But it may make economic sense. Ceding more terrain to extensive noncommercial copying may provoke a commitment to holding a firmer line against commercial infringers operating on a larger scale. Where profit leakage from noncommercial copying is relatively minor, a nontrivial volume of commercial copying may be tolerated. But when noncommercial copying is seen making major inroads on revenue, the previously tolerable leakage from commercial copying may appear untenable. The shifting enforcement calculus may, in other words, benefit the individual consumer yet nevertheless lead to a call for IP rights that are stronger along various dimensions.

Taking Creators' Rights into Account: The Design of Digital Technologies

One flashpoint in recent years involves technologies for distributing digital works, in particular online file-sharing utilities. The Supreme Court's 2005 *Grokster* case placed the utility designers' knowledge and planning concerning the extent of potential infringement at the center of copyright liability when it comes to these sorts of technologies. This had the effect of shifting attention somewhat from the well-established standard, which permits the making and selling of potentially infringing technologies when they are shown to have a "substantial noninfringing use."[50]

The substantial noninfringing use standard has many supporters, who see in it a safe harbor for those who develop technologies useful for distributing copyrighted works. But it also has its detractors. One objection is that the safe harbor creates the wrong incentives for technology developers. So long as the technologies they work on meet the substantial noninfringing use test, they are in the clear. The criticism is this: there is no reason to design a technology so as to minimize the impact on copyright owners. So long as the threshold level of noninfrignement is met, the magnitude of the impact on copyright owners is irrelevant. The threshold test removes any need for balancing. A distribution technology can create massive, irreparable losses and still escape any copyright liability, as long as it is also capable of substantial noninfringing uses.

The critique of this standard begins from the proposition that designers of distribution technologies should be given incentives that better reflect the overall costs and benefits of what they design.[51] Incentives such as this are built into the general tort standard applied to the design of potentially dangerous products. The appeal of this alternative standard is that it more properly balances the total harm produced by a new technology against the total societal benefits. Removing the safe harbor may indeed add an extra layer of concern for the designers of these technologies, yet that is precisely what the standard contemplates. Even so, there is no evidence that the threat of liability in these cases does indeed suppress innovation to any significant extent. The "chilled innovation" hypothesis, which was common in the wake of the *Grokster* case, has been refuted by evidence that new digital distribution technologies are still being developed at a rapid clip.[52]

HARM TO CREATORS: RESPECTING IP AS A *RIGHT*

What I like about the more balanced approach is that it takes more seriously the harm to creators caused by innovative distribution technologies. This is precisely what it means to give full credit and appropriate due to the value of creative work—a theme I have emphasized throughout this book. The balanced approach requires that designers be fully cognizant of the harms that may or will spring from the technology being designed. The tort law origins of this cost-benefit approach fit the contours of IP theory quite well, because this way of handling problems from product design places real weight on the harms that are caused and, by implication, on avoiding those harms. The law of product design makes clear that, if an alternative, feasible design is available that will avoid or reduce a certain type of harm, that alternative should be chosen. Notice the difference in emphasis as compared to the "substantial noninfringing use" standard, where as long as a threshold test is satisfied there is no need to consider either the overall magnitude of harm or alternative designs that might reduce the total level of harm.

In the case of digital distribution technologies, the harm to be considered is the harm to creators. Applying the balancing standard to this issue would require a full weighing of the damage to markets for copyrighted works—a type of harm that falls largely on the shoulders of the creative community. Unlike the substantial noninfringing use test, which looks only to whether a minimum interest of users is implicated, the full cost-benefit standard takes into account the total level of harm to creators, as well as the possibility of alternative designs that would cause less harm. Any design that preserves most or all of the potential for noninfringing uses, while simultaneously reducing the harm to original content creators, is to be strongly preferred under this test.

Which is precisely as it should be. Only a test like this takes seriously the rights of creators—really treats them as *rights*. As I mentioned, there is reason to believe that such a balanced copyright infringement standard has not and will not seriously impede the development of digital technologies. But even if it did raise the cost of new technologies, this would not necessarily point to rejection of the test out of hand. As I said in the Introduction, "the hallmark of a right is that social utility alone is not reason enough to override it." If we are to take the idea of IP rights seriously—if we are to give life to the idea as opposed to using it as a hollow label—then a slight increase in net costs ought not be reason enough to permit dilution of IP through digital technologies that severely harm original creators.

IP AS PROTECTION FROM HARM

One final, theoretical, point about the tort standard for digital technologies is in order here. We saw in Chapter 3 that Kant's property theory envisions a seamless transition from a concern with protection from harm (a tort concept) to a universal right "good against the world." (Recall the example of the right of publicity, the development of which proceeded along similar lines.) Protection against the harm of interference becomes universalized through the vehicle of a general right in an object. The same interplay is at work in determining the proper liability standard for design of digital technologies. The protection against harm that should be built into the proper legal standard is very closely related to the interests promoted by property law. From a certain point of view, IP rights for the creator can be conceptualized as the culmination of a right not to be harmed by others, a right not to have creative works interfered with by others. The cases on digital technology begin with the fact of individual IP rights, and work from there toward protection (or not) against harm from new digital technologies. But IP protection in this area can also be conceptualized from the opposite direction. The right of a creator to be free from the harm of digital technologies can be placed front and center, and considered, conceptually, first; from this starting point, IP rights can be seen as the logical outgrowth of protection from this sort of harm. Either way, the total harm to creators from various acts of infringement is what drives the analysis—which is appropriate, given that what is at stake is the rights of these very creators.

Property in an Age of Ubiquitous Contracting

File sharing is not the only new practice made possible in the digital age. Ubiquitous contracting is also now a fact of life. By this I mean the ability to require user assent to terms and conditions prior to permitting access to a digital work. These online contracts are extremely common now, and many scholars have seen in them the end of IP as an important stand-alone institution. These scholars share a simple idea: because access to digital works can now be conditioned on assent to contractual terms, and because contracts can be used to in effect make for a sort of super IP right, contracts can and will eventually displace property. Because people can be made to agree to terms of use for all sorts of things, there will no longer be a need for the standardized terms of use provided by property rights. Individual agreements, shaped for specific purposes and adapted to the needs of the hour or the demands of the situation, will crowd out the old-fashioned, off-the-rack sets of rights we know as property. In a related vein, technological protection systems—technologies for wrapping content, which permit access only by those with permission codes—were thought to be the perfect adjunct to contractual restrictions. Contracts would set forth terms of use, and technological protection systems would see that those terms were enforced, or else deny access to the desired content.

Aside from whether contract is normatively preferable to property—and scholars such as Henry Smith and Thomas Merrill have surely sown grave doubts[53]—I do not think it is actually very likely that property will be displaced. Though contracts may come to occupy some of the territory formerly occupied by property alone, I doubt they will ever completely displace property. The basic logic of a right "good against the world," and carried on the face of an object, so to speak, is too powerful for even the amazingly flexible mechanism of bilateral contract to crowd it out entirely.

It is not that contracts are inadequate to the task. It is that contracting, the process of entering a contract, will always involve a more elaborate legal apparatus than a property right. Contracts require at least two parties to come together in some moment of agreement. That moment has been shrinking, actually and conceptually, in recent years as online licenses diffuse through the commercial and legal landscape. But despite the ease of contracting, its apparent seamlessness, it is still not quite as reliable a legal instrument as property. The reason is that contracts require some sort of privity: for A to bind B, and perhaps subsequently C, D, and E, all these people need to be connected in an unbroken chain of contracts. Any lapse in the complex apparatus, any break in the chain, and the connection between the parties may be severed. Thus even though the parties' respective rights can be carefully crafted via contract, the rights are not binding in the absence of contractual assent. Sophisticated participants in online exchange understand this well, so they go to great lengths to make sure that "the contract follows the content." Somewhat obscure doctrines of personal property law have even been dusted off and dressed up to try to address the issue. But despite the best efforts of some clever and well-intentioned people, it has so far proven impossible to come up with an ironclad, unbreakable chain of agreements that is identical to the force and effect of a property right.

In a way, these efforts have been quite enlightening. After all sorts of rambles and digressions, they lead us back to a central truth. There is great value in having rights that are granted by the state, and which specify off-the-rack duties and privileges binding on all comers, without more. Property assumes a kind of metaprivity: we are citizens of the same state, so property rights conferred by that state are binding on all of us. The legal relations (an older generation might have said, instructively, "juridical" relations) between citizens are established by shared citizenry, and no special bilateral arrangement is necessary for rights to come into being. The precondition for enforcement is being subject to the same state, rather than an act of specific agreement. Property, a right "good against the world," binds all citizens because they share that political, economic, and social "world"—that state. The power and necessity of this institution is no less compelling today than it ever was. The fact that it applies to digital objects in an online world is a trivial innovation. The essential continuity springs from the need for a set of "prefab" rights that can be granted by the state and become, by virtue solely of that grant, binding on all others.

Updating—Not Eliminating—Property

I have argued in this and the previous chapter for continued solicitude for creative professionals, in the form of a renewed commitment to robust IP rights in the digital era. I have tried to make the case that it matters to society that this group of people be able to continue to earn a solid living in the era of widespread digital distribution of their works. This all forms a counterargument to proposals to deemphasize, narrow, or eliminate property rights in the digital realm.

Many commentators purport not to want to go so far, however. Lawrence Lessig and Terry Fisher, for example, have separately argued that the real problem in the digital era is not the compensation aspect of property rights, but the fact that they confer so much *control*.[54] They propose to separate these two effects of property rights by legislating some sort of blanket payment scheme for all content creators. The details vary, but the schemes as proposed have a basic similarity: creators would be paid on some sort of per-use basis, but would have no say over who gets to use their works, or when. They are in that sense "take now and pay later" schemes—compulsory licenses, to use IP jargon.[55]

I have written a fair amount over the years in opposition to expansive compulsory licensing,[56] and digital technology has not changed my views much. I still think privately ordered clearinghouses, founded by and accountable to their members, existing in competition with other clearinghouses in many cases, are superior to a one-shot legislative solution. These clearinghouses start from individual property rights but wind up being collectives that draw together a large number of rightholders into a single, one-stop "blanket licensing" organization. For reasons I have described elsewhere, I think these organizations give creators the best chance to profit from their works; I therefore think they may have an important role to play in maintaining the economic infrastructure that permits creative professionals to thrive.

I have also come to see that there is a dimension to these groups that goes beyond the utilitarian case for profit maximization. It has been argued that in practice they operate much as a government bureaucracy, so that in essence there is little to separate voluntary licensing organizations from a legislated compulsory license. Even if it were true at the operational level, about which I have grave doubts, they would still be different in principle from a legislated, or coerced, organization. An individual creator *chooses* to join a voluntary clearinghouse; he or she is not forced. This is a very small point, maybe, from a practical perspective; but a very large one philosophically. It means no one agrees to license works except voluntarily. And it means a persnickety individual, someone who wants *real* control, may elect to go it alone, licensing works only in individual transactions.

Of course, it is this quality of property—you have to get permission to use it first—that causes so many problems. Lawrence Lessig, in his book *Free Culture,* laments the rise of the "permissions culture," a direct outgrowth of the fact that IP rights are real property rights:

> [In the pre-Internet era,] [t]he focus of the law was on commercial creativity. At first slightly, then quite extensively, the law protected the incentives of creators by granting them exclusive rights to their creative work, so that they could sell those exclusive rights in a commercial marketplace. This is also, of course, an important part of creativity and culture, and it has become an increasingly important part in America. But in no sense was it dominant within our tradition. It was instead just one part, a controlled part, balanced with the free.
>
> This rough divide between the free and the controlled has now been erased. The Internet has set the stage for this erasure and, pushed by big media, the law has now affected it. For the first time in our tradition, the ordinary ways in which individuals create and share culture fall within the reach and regulation of the law, which has expanded to draw within its control a vast amount of culture and creativity that it never reached before. The technology that preserved the balance of our history—between uses of our culture that were free and uses of our culture that were only upon permission—has been undone. The consequence is that we are less and less a free culture, more and more a permission culture.[57]

The basic idea here holds that IP rights over digital creations clash violently with individual freedom in the Internet era. Of course, this is true of all property rights regimes: individual property claims always impinge on the freedom of others (*all* others, in theory, by virtue of being "good against the world").[58] What is frustrating to critics of the permissions culture is that the burden of getting permission seems to be increasing, compared to historical standards. (Again, I would point out the frequency of voluntary waiver of rights, which is now becoming very common.) This is so for two reasons: tighter IP laws, and the Internet's (at least theoretical) capacity to demand permission in more situations.

So: individual property rights versus the freedom of third parties—this is the crux of the problem. For my part, I resolve the problem this way. I do not think mere use of a digital creation is the type of freedom that ought to trump a claim of individual property.[59] At the same time, I recognize the burdens that are *potentially* created by stricter permissions requirements in the digital era. So I therefore recognize a serious social interest in reducing transaction costs.

What does this insistence on property get us anymore; what is the pay-off from requiring all these permissions? Here is a thought: for some creators, it is more important to maintain the integrity of their work than to command a high price. Perhaps the primary reason they do the work in the first place is to express a certain aspect of themselves, or to communicate a certain feeling or idea. For these creators, control is not a distant concern that falls far down the list. It is central to their decision to create and distribute their works. It makes no sense to tell them, "don't worry, you will be paid no matter how your work is used." They might respond, "that makes it worse than if I had never created it. I want to shape how the work is presented—to control its presentation. That's why I did it and put it out there, it is a big part of what motivated me."

In this connection, remember Michelangelo approaching the marble in our discussion of Kant's theory of property. To fully realize his vision of a completed sculpture, the artist needs to know he can count on continued access that is free of unauthorized contributions from others. Creators of digital content are no less worthy of this sort of right. Though the medium they work in is inherently malleable, this is not reason enough to deprive them of equal treatment vis-à-vis the sculptor or painter. Of course, if malleability is at the core of the creator's vision, then she can invite others to remix at will—this is the value of waiver, once again. But the medium ought not dictate or constrain this result; it ought to be a matter of choice.

Some creators may really want to maintain control over their works. We might say that for them, control cannot effectively be separated from compensation,[60] because control *is* compensation, or part of it anyway. This is an expression of the Dignity Principle discussed in Chapter 5. It is part of the fabric of IP law, one of the basic principles enfolded into the structure of the field; as such, it should not be tossed aside because the nature of the new digital media makes this possible. As we saw earlier in discussing the DD (digital determinism) strain in IP scholarship, it would be a mistake to permit the technological features of digital media to dictate the fundamental outline of IP law as it applies to this field. Dignity is too important a part of IP to have it steamrollered out of existence just because digital technology lends itself too readily to this result.[61]

"Locke for the Masses": Exploring Group Rights

Here is a more radical idea.[62] One of the chief insights of the digital era is that collective efforts can lead to important creative works. Wikis and fan websites are examples; there are many others. I have rejected a number of critiques of the classic property rights story in the digital era, but in this area one such critique seems apt. Our system identifies individual authors, and is in fact designed to link individuals or small groups with the assets they create. But that system has difficulty recognizing affirmative rights in the fruits of group creativity. There are doctrines and rules that operate negatively, so to speak, preventing rightholders from reaping the fruits of group efforts. In a recent article, a coauthor and I describe just such a doctrine in cases where groups of technology adopters have adopted a standard technology on the assumption it is not covered by patents, or that any patents on it will not be enforced. We propose an estoppel doctrine in such cases, to prevent a patentee from reaping the rewards of group effort in cases such as this.[63]

A similar estoppel principle might make sense for such group efforts as fan sites that build upon "canonical works" (as they are described in Chapter 2).[64] If an IP rightholder allows fans to comment on, modify, and add to a canonical work or set of works, it would make sense to prevent a later change of heart requiring the removal of the material added by the fans.[65] This would create, in effect, a group-level implied license or waiver regime that has the effect of creating binding "reliance" rights on the part of fans who contribute material in the expectation that the copyright holder permits this activity. Perhaps this would increase the policing costs incumbent upon a copyright holder. If so, that is simply the cost to be paid for authoring a work that becomes canonical and attracts extensive commentary and fan contributions. A group-level right along these lines, grounded in estoppel principles, would do no more than implement the point I raised in Chapter 4 on Distributive Justice and IP: "Society helps to shape the works; social institutions are required to effectively protect the works; so by rights society retains a stake in every work. Seen this way, IP law encodes the deeply symbiotic relationship between an individual creator and the larger society he calls home." Group-level rights would simply ensure a balanced version of this legal codification.

What I am arguing for here is a stronger version of this—a more affirmative, and more general, way to recognize group rights. Models for such rights are starting to emerge, for example in the area of special IP rights for indigenous peoples who serve as the stewards of ancient cultural craft techniques, art styles, and the like. I think it is time to take ideas such as this and turn them more broadly on the digital era, to find a way to reward group-level effort with group-level rights. The precise scope of such a right will of course require some hard thought and no doubt some experimentation as well. But it will be integral to the process of adapting IP successfully to the digital world.

Conclusion

What am I really saying here? What does this add up to?

The central idea is fairly simple. If we award property rights, people or other entities that end up owning them can waive them if they see fit. If that is more profitable, or serves some other purpose, they can let them go. But if we make serious inroads on property rights, what then? Then we lose this flexibility. We mandate a "low protection" threshold for everyone. In the name of maximizing democratic creativity, we eliminate the possibility of choice on the part of the individual artist or assignee firm. One consequence of this, as I have suggested, is that we may also eliminate or (further) shrink the possible horizons of creative professionals.

The earlier discussion of digital resources was directed toward two main points. First, there is a strong element of digital determinism at work in much recent theorizing—what might almost be called a kind of digital defeatism. The trajectory and impetus of this major new technology is pushing us as a society away from property rights. Our best response, and maybe our only response, is to adapt ourselves to this new technology; to get used to it, to internalize it, to accept it as inevitable. The second major point is that the Internet and other digital technology has made possible a brave new world of collaborative, interactive creativity, whose logic and momentum are inconsistent with the strictures of property rights. To cling to the anachronistic idea that resources ought to be controlled in many cases by individuals thwarts the promise of this new technological paradigm.

The issue may come down to this: either you believe that this wondrous new technology has so fundamentally reshaped reality that all the old bets (including bets about human nature, the importance of the individual in our thinking) are off; or you believe that the Internet, and maybe no conceivable technology, can forever put an end to the age-old dialectic of individual and collective, self and society. Perhaps we are too early in the digital era to settle this. Perhaps I, a product of the old world, the analog era, am simply too bound to my formative *mentalité* to clearly grasp the emergent new reality. It's certainly possible.

I don't think so, though. For me, the first alternative above—the idea that digital technology will sweep away the importance of the individual on a tide of collective interaction and creativity—has little chance of panning out. The founder of Wikipedia, for example, was a wealthy individual who created the site in order to "give back" to society, which hardly seems like a viable economic model for the future of e-commerce. The second alternative therefore seems much more likely. While I think digital technology is fantastic in many ways, including its ability to foster some truly innovative collective enterprises such as open source software and Wikipedia, I do not think it marks a radical new direction in civilization, or the end of human nature as we know it. And I have also read enough history to know that similarly revolutionary rhetoric surrounded the birth of other, previous technologies: the telegraph, radio, television, atomic power, and space travel, to name just a few. No, if I have to bet whether the Internet changes us as a species, or if instead we end up putting our imperfect but distinctive imprint all over this technology (as with others before it), I place my money on the latter. To me, this means that property—as durable and flexible an economic institution as any we have known—is likely to have a long and promising future, into and through the digital era, and on to whatever era lies beyond.

CHAPTER NINE

Patents and Drugs for the Developing World

O NE OF THE GREATEST CHALLENGES facing the IP system today is what to do about patents on crucial pharmaceutical products needed in developing countries. For the most part, these patents are held by pharmaceutical companies in the developed world. Many argue that diseases in the developing world are ignored by "big pharma," that companies skew their research toward diseases or conditions of little relevance to the world's neediest populations. The same voices say that even when pharmaceutical companies have a drug that the developing world needs, the poor of the world seldom have access to it at a price they might be able to afford.

I believe the ideas I have developed can help us tackle this issue. It is in some ways a perfect test case, presenting a remarkably complex combination of economic and ethical considerations.

Before these issues can be clarified, I need to explain some facts about the developing world, the medicines needed there, and the complicated role patents play in regulating access to these medicines. After that, we return to John Locke for a review of the charity proviso that forms an integral part of his property theory (and that I discussed in Chapter 2). After reviewing how the charity concept applies to patented drugs in the developing world, I also discuss some limits on the idea—in particular, the difficult question of when drugs contribute to quality of life as opposed to strict survival.

Next we move from Locke to Rawls. Part of the Rawlsian understanding of distributive justice is the notion of the "fair savings" principle, one way of expressing the more general idea known as "intergenerational equity." This idea, which requires taking account of future generations when making decisions about resource use, turns out to be crucial to the problem of drug patents and the developing world. The reason is this: a wholesale policy of redistribution *today* carries the distinct risk of dismantling the research infrastructure needed to develop drugs for *tomorrow.* Only a sophisticated understanding of the charity proviso and intergenerational equity, infused with a detailed understanding of the practicalities of pharmaceutical research and the mechanics of drug distribution, can do full justice to the complex problem of fair access to medicines.

Some Background Facts

Overall health is much better in the developed world than in the developing world. Judging from mortality statistics, the single largest cause seems to be differences in nutrition.[1] But differential rates of disease are also very important, particularly infectious diseases such as malaria.[2] Because pharmaceutical products can effectively treat many of these diseases, and because patents are so important to the pharmaceutical industry, the patent/developing country controversy centers primarily on patents for infectious disease therapies. In particular, the following diseases have drawn most of the attention with respect to this debate: (1) malaria; (2) HIV/AIDS; and (3) tuberculosis.[3]

HIV/AIDS was perhaps the preeminent example of the problem of pharmaceutical patents and the developing world. In the 1990s, when the HIV epidemic was first fully understood, some of the early HIV drug therapies were developed, patented, and diffused rapidly throughout the developed world, despite the high cost. The same was not true, however, in the developing world. Although the issue of differential access was by no means novel at this time, the HIV epidemic brought a new urgency to the issue and was the object of a major policy discussion among health experts and academics.

A compounding factor was that at the same time the HIV epidemic was coming into focus, the global patent regime was changing rapidly. As part of a broader set of reforms, the General Agreement on Tariffs and Trade (GATT) had initiated a new round of negotiations on Trade-Related Aspects of Intellectual Property (TRIPs). The TRIPs accord was signed in 1995; under it, developing countries agreed to phase in minimum protection levels for a number of patentable items, including pharmaceuticals. However, almost as soon as the agreement was signed, it was surrounded by a great controversy. The confluence of stronger patent protection and the growing gap in access to patented medicines (most prominently HIV therapies) created enormous strains in global patent policy and world health.

These strains put pressure on certain provisions of the TRIPs accord that had been designed as a compromise between the interests of developing countries and those of the developed world, most importantly the large pharmaceutical companies of the United States, Europe, and Japan. These provisions were designed to serve as "safety valves" in the global IP system. One particularly important measure in the TRIPs treaty provided for nation-by-nation "compulsory licensing" of patents over products crucial to public health, in the event of a grave or serious threat to public health. Pro-access forces in the developing world, and the nongovernmental organizations (NGOs) sympathetic to them, argued that the HIV crisis was just the sort of emergency envisioned by these provisions. Trade negotiators from the developed world, informed and backed by large pharmaceutical companies, resisted these arguments at first. They argued that a lack of access to patented drugs was not the real cause of differential access rates; for them, weak health services and high-risk patient behaviors were the real culprits. Even so, partly in response to the pressure from NGOs and general bad publicity, many pharmaceutical companies ramped up or initiated voluntary pharmaceutical "gifting" programs around this time.[4] Next came a major development, in the form of a formal declaration that the compulsory licensing provisions could be invoked fairly widely to respond to drug access concerns. Even after this "Doha Declaration," named for the city in which the resolution was adopted, controversy over access to patented drugs continued.

The Right to Access—And Its Limits

Access to patent-protected pharmaceuticals represents a classic fairness-based challenge to property rights. The exclusionary right of property takes away the lives of disease victims who happen to live in places where the patented medicines are unavailable. Does this situation prove the point of all those who criticize property, especially property conceived of as a right? Or is there a way to reconcile the obvious appeal of fair access here with the overall idea of property, that is, individual control over discrete assets?

The answer is a resounding yes. And the raw material for it was laid out earlier, in Chapters 2 through 4. Each of the foundational normative theories we discussed—the property theories of Locke and Kant, and the distributive justice concerns of John Rawls—quite effectively accommodates the problem of access to patented pharmaceuticals. Although the details of any actual access policy would be difficult to discern from these foundational writings, the basic principles can all be found there with little room for doubt. A brief review of the relevant aspects of each theory will show what I mean.

Locke's Charity Proviso

As we saw in Chapter 2, John Locke provided both a powerful theory of original acquisition of property *and* a robust set of limitations on that right. In that chapter I described at length some of the controversies surrounding application of the appropriation theory to the case of IP rights. I also went into a good bit of detail in discussing the sufficiency and waste provisos, again with significant attention to how they apply in the case of IP rights. I also mentioned the third major limitation on property rights, the charity proviso. Because this is the aspect of Locke's theory that so closely relates to the problem of access to patented medicines, I saved for this chapter a detailed application of this part of Locke's theory.

Locke states the charity proviso in paragraph 42 of his *First Treatise of Government:*

> God the Lord and Father of all, has given no one of his Children such a Property, in his peculiar Portion of the things of this World, but that he has given his needy Brother a Right to the Surplusage of his Goods; so that it cannot be justly denied him, when his pressing Wants call for it. And therefore no Man could ever have a just Power over the life of another, by right of property in Land or Possessions; since 'twould always be a Sin in any Man of Estate, to let his Brother perish for want of affording him Relief out of his Plenty. As Justice gives every Man a Title to the product of his honest Industry, and the fair Acquisitions of his Ancestors descended to him; so Charity gives every Man a Title to so much out of another's Plenty, as will keep him from extreme want, where he has no means to subsist otherwise. . . . [5]

In this passage, Locke is saying two important things: (1) that property does not confer the right to deny relief to those in "pressing want"; and (2) that people in desperate need have an actual, binding *right* to the assets held by legitimate owners, and this right arises from the same source, and carries the same weight, as an initial appropriator's right. I take each of these points in order, and then relate them to the problem of pharmaceutical patents.

PRESSING WANT

Locke's first point can be stated simply: property is not absolute. It may be a right—as we saw in Chapter 2, for Locke it most certainly is—but it is not an *absolute* right. In that same chapter I explained why this is so. Locke says that property furthers the broader purpose of sustaining human survival and flourishing. It is a right that follows from the divine command to grow, multiply, and thrive. Individual ownership is necessary because it is too difficult and costly to coordinate resource use among all of the true initial titleholders of the resources we are given, that is, all humankind. Because survival requires removing some things that are commonly owned out of the original state of common ownership, we have property.

For Locke, it would be absurd to argue that property rights held by person A trump the basic right to survive held by person B. If the entire point of property is to further survival and human flourishing, how can this right be used to deny someone else's very survival? That would make no sense at all.

A little later in this chapter I consider some complexities of the charity proviso as applied to pharmaceutical patents in the developing world. But in a simple case of company A's patents standing clearly and directly in the way of person B's survival, the charity proviso is easy to apply. B wins.

TITLE FOR THE DESTITUTE

For Locke, the destitute have title to the goods they need to survive, even when those goods are otherwise legitimately held by others, either through valid original appropriation or a subsequent transfer from an original acquisition. This is a distinctive approach to charity for two primary reasons. First, it is a way of describing charity from the perspective of the recipient, the person in need. And second, it states a particularly strong, and in fact quite novel, version of the traditional view of the duty to show charity.

From very early times, charity was described in the Judeo-Christian tradition as an obligation whose primary function is to improve the spiritual well-being of the *giver*.[6] Indeed, well into the Middle Ages some theologians thought that poverty exists, in part at least, so that charity may be shown.[7] From this perspective, the recipients of charity are important only insofar as they provoke the occasion of generous charity; they are certainly not at the center of the picture. Charity is seen as a virtue that is applied by a righteous person to the whole of what he owns. And it is virtuous precisely because it is not required by positive law or the civil state. Charity dictates that, in the presence of great need, one does the right thing with some of what one owns.

Notice in this formulation that ownership is presumed. Charity is a virtue that operates "on top of" the unquestioned fact of ownership. It modifies ownership in the practical sense that a generous person will part with some of what he owns when the moral duty of charity applies. But that duty is separate from matters of ownership and title. Charitable gifts are a voluntary transfer, willingly made, of some portion of the goods one has unquestioned title over.

Locke intrudes here to shake things up. He places the needy themselves at the center of the picture: it is their need, and not the virtue of the giver, that commands our attention. And in Locke's formulation, charity is not a matter apart from issues of ownership and title. Charity is integral to title, because under this proviso the needy have an actual claim on the goods held and owned by the holder of property rights. Charity is not separate from issues of title; it is integral to them.

Recall Locke's forceful words: "As Justice gives every Man a Title to the product of his honest Industry, and the fair Acquisitions of his Ancestors descended to him; so Charity gives every Man a Title to so much out of another's Plenty, as will keep him from extreme want, where he has no means to subsist otherwise." This sentence presents a powerful set of parallels. Justice and Charity are matching origins of strong property claims, each of which culminates in formal title over assets. Likewise "honest Industry" is paired with the lack of "means to subsist otherwise" as equally valid justifications for the respective property claims. And finally, the "product" of industry is paired with "extreme want" as implied limits on the scope of property claims. Initial appropriation and the charity proviso form a matched pair, with equally valid and effective origins, justifications, and limits. The structure of the sentence discloses the structure of the rights: "As Justice gives, . . . so Charity gives. . . ."

With this formulation, Locke moves the recipient of charity out of the background and into the foreground. The giver's aspirational duty is transformed into the receiver's ineluctable right. In the process, the recipient is shown as deserving of the same dignity as an initial appropriator. The passage thus represents unassailable evidence for an egalitarian reading of Locke as described in Chapter 2. More to the point here, it serves as a solid foundation for the argument that the destitute have a firm claim to patented pharmaceuticals, at least when their very lives are at stake.

Kant's Universal Principle

Under Kant's Universal Principle of Right (UPR), "laws secure our right to external freedom of choice to the extent that this freedom is compatible with everyone else's freedom of choice under a universal law."[8] As I explained in Chapter 3, Kant's theory of property rights expresses a special instance of this general principle: property is widely available, yet denied when individual appropriation interferes with the freedom of others. Kant says that although the need for robust property drives the formation of civil society, property rights are nonetheless subject to this "universalizing" principle. Under the operation of the UPR, property rights are constrained: they must not be so broad that they interfere with the freedom of fellow citizens. In a Kantian state, individual property is both necessary—to promote autonomy and self-development; see Chapter 3—and necessarily restricted under the UPR.[9]

Death is the ultimate restraint on autonomy; there is no more "self" to guide after a person dies. So when a claim to property by person A leads to the death of person B, Kant's Universal Principle would seem to rebut that claim. As with other issues, however, Kant's views in this regard are not so simple. In particular, he expressed complex views on the legal defense of "necessity," which bears a close resemblance to the property-limiting principle I am attributing to him here.[10] Kant says, in effect, that in at least one important example of necessity—where A kills B, or at least puts B in immediate grave danger, to save A's own life—one who commits a necessary act is *culpable* but not *punishable*.[11] As with so much in the Kantian canon, there is a great deal of debate over just what Kant was trying to say about necessity. One view—at least as plausible as most others, and more plausible than some—holds that Kant thought of necessity as something like an excuse or defense: a wrong act is not made right by necessity, but it is insulated from formal legal liability.[12] This view, well described by among others the Kant scholar Arthur Ripstein, depends on the distinction between formal, positive law ("external," in Kant's terminology; see Chapter 3) and "internal" morality. Property for Kant is an absolute right, and taking it without permission is always objectively wrong. But at the same time, some takings are not punishable by the state because they fall outside the proper bounds of legitimate lawmaking.

Because Kant did not explicitly discuss the necessity defense as it pertains to property rights, we can only speculate about how to apply his thinking to the case of pharmaceutical patents. Even so, there is one point to make. As I explained in some detail in Chapter 3, there is generally a high degree of symmetry between Kant's thinking on law and his theory of property. The UPR is a good example; as I explained in Chapter 3, the idea that property can extend only up to the point that it interferes with the freedom of others is simply one specific application of the general Kantian take on law and freedom. Thus, the analysis of the pharmaceutical patents problem would turn on the issue of property's effect on the freedom of those suffering from treatable diseases. To put it simply, it is difficult to be sure of the exact conclusion Kant would reach with regard to the issue, but I *am* sure that the analysis would turn on the freedom-restricting qualities of pharmaceutical patents. It is hard to know the right answer, but not hard to pose the right question: should property extend so far as to cut off or restrain the freedom of those who might be treated?

In my view, the freedom of disease sufferers is so constrained that the property rights in pharmaceutical patents must give way. As I said, this is not the only plausible reading of Kant's Universal Principle with respect to the problem at hand. But I think it is the best reading, and it is certainly the best *I* can do, given Kant's text and the problem of pharmaceutical patents as I understand it.

Distributive Justice and Pharmaceutical Patents

Of the three major foundational thinkers whose ideas I explore in Part I of this book, the easiest to apply to the problem of this chapter is Rawls. Recall that in Chapter 4 I summarized Rawls's view that property is one among a number of secondary rights that occupy a lower level of priority in his philosophical thinking. It is not, in the Rawlsian lexicon, a "primary good." But food, shelter, and access to basic health care are such goods. For Rawls, then, there would be little doubt that property rights must give way in the face of a claim that they gravely threaten someone's very survival. The entire point of the Rawlsian hierarchy is to render straightforward these sorts of issues. Political systems are supposed to be designed (would be designed, if the veil of ignorance dropped and the concomitant deliberative procedures were implemented) such that primary goods are given priority. The pharmaceutical patent problem is precisely the sort of issue Rawls seems to have had in mind when he constructed his system as he did.

The only possible exception to this is the issue of intergenerational equity—what Rawls called the "fair savings" principle. I discuss this in the context of pharmaceutical patents in the next section.

Pharmaceutical Patents and the Midlevel Principles

So far I have couched the pharmaceutical patent issue in the language of the various foundational theories examined in Part I of this book: Locke, Kant, and Rawls, as well as utilitarian theory as described in the Introduction. If I am to stay true to the pluralism I espouse in Chapter 5, however, it would seem necessary also to discuss the issue in terms of the midlevel principles of IP law. As I argued there, we need not agree on the ultimate foundations of IP law to have a sensible policy discussion about the important details of patent law that affect access to patented pharmaceuticals. That's what the midlevel principles are for.

For the most part the question of destitute people and pharmaceutical patents implicates the principles of efficiency and, to a lesser extent, proportionality. The dignity interest of researchers who develop the drug is not directly at issue, nor is the nonremoval principle. So I will confine myself here to efficiency and proportionality.

How is it possible to talk about efficiency when access to pharmaceuticals seems like such a classic case of a right—a human right, in fact—that conflicts with economic interests (in this case, those of the pharmaceutical companies)? Shouldn't human lives trump mere efficiency? Shouldn't helping people to survive take precedence over the economic well-being of pharmaceutical innovators?

I do not think the issue is that simple. In fact, it is possible to restate the access questions in efficiency terms, and in the process identify the needs of the destitute as an important element of the discussion. Maybe the real question is this: given a large supply of human diseases, and a large population needing treatment for them, what is the best way to maximize the number of effective pharmaceutical products that are brought to bear on these diseases? How do we get the greatest mileage out of all the available resources—products of nature, human skill, scientific knowledge, and so forth—that need to come together to solve the problem of treating diseases worldwide?

When stated this way, the efficiency principle obviously has an important place in the conversation. It leads us to look into whether the total supply of medicine is greater, overall and in the long run, when developed countries devote substantial resources to drug innovation while temporarily putting off access by the poor to a later date. Are more people helped in the long run even though many are clearly excluded from the best treatments in the short run? Put another way, the efficiency principle would guide us to a discussion of whether an open-hearted policy of access to all drugs immediately, by anyone who could benefit from them, would amount to a one-time distributional bonanza at the expense of the long-term viability of the drug innovation infrastructure? I consider these issues in some detail below; at this point, I simply want to state that the efficiency principle provides a helpful and useful terminological frame for addressing this crucial question.

The second midlevel principle that bears discussing in this context is proportionality. Recall that the basic idea behind this principle is that the reward to a creator or innovator ought to be proportional to his contribution. This comes into play in an obvious way in the pharmaceutical patent debate, though the ultimate conclusion is by no means straightforward. If the structure of pharmaceutical patent law, together with the entire regulatory and competitive environment of the pharmaceutical industry, leads to excessive rewards in light of the benefits conferred, then the economic power of pharmaceutical patents can be trimmed back so as to restore a better sense of proportion. If even a small portion of the suffering of those who require access to patented drugs is a result of overreward to patentees, the proportionality principle dictates that the state cut back on the reward. Disproportionate reward coupled with grave suffering makes a powerful case for this.

There are, to be sure, grave difficulties in *applying* this principle in the pharmaceutical case. The skewed nature of success in pharmaceuticals— where a few drugs are wildly successful (and profitable) while most languish and do not even recoup the cost of developing them—ensures this. Determining whether a particular patented drug deserves to earn its creators massive rewards requires that we consider how many unsuccessful research projects are funded by each successful drug product. The "deserving" payoff from a well that is a gusher must take account of all the dry holes that came before, and will come after as well.

Nevertheless, at least in theory, we can be guided by the proportionality principle. If access to medicines is blocked by the exclusionary power of a disproportionately large reward, this principle informs what we should do: scale back the reward.

Limits

So far, then, I have tried to establish that Locke, Kant, and Rawls all support a relaxing of patent rights over life-saving pharmaceuticals. I have also referred back to the midlevel principles to show that they are consistent with this conclusion. The goal in this section is to describe a few limits to the general principle that patents must give way in this area. In particular, I want to emphasize (1) cutting off the "right to access" when the relationship between the pharmaceutical in question and actual survival is too remote or attenuated; and (2) the need to preserve the pharmaceutical industry's infrastructure so it can be deployed to find cures for as yet untreatable diseases. I take each in turn here.

WHEN DOES A PHARMACEUTICAL SAVE LIVES?

In some sense, the problem of pharmaceutical patents is not as difficult as it is conventionally stated. Rather, it seems fairly obvious that where access to a specific pharmaceutical at a specific time would clearly and unquestionably save a life, fairness requires that access be granted, notwithstanding the presence of a patent. The problem is that most real-world situations are not as clear-cut. The primary issue is this: access to medicines is part of a much broader array of health-related interventions that are required to lower mortality in many situations involving destitute populations, so much so that it can be difficult to identify the precise contribution to health that is made by the pharmaceutical in isolation. Because of this, it can be difficult to say for sure that access to a pharmaceutical in a given situation would clearly and definitely save a life.

The World Health Organization has studied particularly important health threats in the developing world, including malaria. It is true that (a) not enough resources are devoted to antimalarial treatments, an example of the lack of attention to diseases that disproportionately affect the destitute;[13] and (b) the antimalarials that do exist are often not available in an effective way to those who most need them. Yet despite the truth of these facts, the picture is considerably more complex.

Successful campaigns against infectious diseases such as malaria require a number of simultaneous interventions. The reservoirs in which mosquitoes or other "disease vectors" breed must be treated so that the specific disease factor (the bacterium or virus, for example) does not find its way into the vector. These treatments need to be repeated, and the reservoir conditions monitored, if success is to be achieved. It is true that once a person is infected, pharmaceuticals may save his life. But a program of treating only infected persons, without addressing the reservoirs and vectors, will ultimately make little difference. Individuals will be reinfected, infections will outpace treatments, and eventually a mutation in the disease factor—caused by overexposure to the pharmaceutical treatment—may result, wiping out all chances of long-term success.

To put it simply, a series of interventions are required to save lives in this sort of setting. Permitting infected people to override patent rights may not make that much difference—might not save that many lives. Of course, Locke, Kant, and Rawls may still say that where a single life is at stake, property rights ought not to stand in the way. And that seems true. It's just that the number of people who will actually be helped by application of this principle may be lower than many expect.

Things become yet more complex when we vary the facts just a bit. If a drug does not cure a disease, but instead extends life or treats a major symptom, what then? In such a case I do not believe Locke and Kant can be read to strictly dictate that access trumps property. In such a scenario, the destitute seem not to meet Locke's requirements for a claim to title over the patent; only matters of absolute life and death meet the test. Kant would seem to offer more support for a right to access in such cases, given that disease conditions may often limit the effective autonomy of the destitute. Yet even for Kant, things may not be quite so straightforward. The very universality of the UPR means that a just principle must take account of the autonomy interests of many people. Because some of these people are as yet unborn, and because major inroads on pharmaceutical patents may reduce the future efficacy of the drug research enterprise, we cannot be too quick to permit access under the UPR where imminent life and death are not at stake.

INTERGENERATIONAL CONSIDERATIONS

The paradigm case that concerned Locke and Kant poses a stark yet simple choice. A destitute person needs something to survive, but that need is blocked by the legal rights of another—a property right in the desperately needed thing. Both philosophers reach the same conclusion: the property right must yield.

This story is simple in part because it involves only two actors, the destitute person and the property owner. The situation becomes considerably more complex—and the conclusions less straightforward—when the story is expanded to include other actors as well. One example of this is to consider other citizens who may be affected by a rule relaxing property rights in cases of dire need. Will destitute people overuse the rule, or will the near-destitute try to expand it? Will expectations about stable ownership begin to break down, resulting in greater reliance on self-help (for example, armed defense of an owner's property), and perhaps a reduction in economic activity and ultimately wealth? These are examples of what might be called the dynamic effects of a broad application of Locke's charity proviso and Kant's universal principle.

This expanded range of considerations applies to all types of property. Indeed, it applies to all legal rules; the analysis of dynamic effects, of long-term systematic responses to legal rules, is the hallmark of the law and economics approach to law. Law and economics scholars have long taught that the most important impact of a particular case is not the resolution of a particular dispute involving two discrete actors, but is instead the systematic incentives and payoffs established by the rule in the case.[14] In this view, for every two disputants there are many untold *future* actors who will incorporate the rule established in one case into the payoff matrix they face. The normative thrust of this view is quite clear: the legal system ought not to be overly concerned with the apparent fairness of a particular rule in the case where the rule originates, but ought instead to pay close attention to the ex ante incentives the rule creates for future actors.

In the case of pharmaceutical patents, this admonition would mean that, before legal actors permit overriding of property rights, they must account for the effects on other people. Given the nature of pharmaceutical research, it would seem that the most important class of people to consider is the group of all those who will suffer from potentially treatable diseases in the future.[15]

So the question is this: how would overriding patent rights to help today's destitute people affect future generations of people suffering from diseases? The answer depends on three important factors:

1. How much pharmaceutical R&D would take place in the presence of weakened patent rights?
2. Would the resulting level of R&D result in fewer actual new pharmaceutical products for treating diseases?
3. If the level of R&D were reduced, and fewer new drugs were developed, would the reduction in future disease treatments offset the increase in access to currently available pharmaceuticals?

The problem, in other words, is to weigh the intergenerational effects against the immediate benefits of expanded access.

It would of course be incredibly difficult to answer these questions in detail. The key to gaining a foothold on them, however, is to understand how patents on pharmaceuticals affect incentives for drug research, as well as the overall structure of the pharmaceutical R&D infrastructure. So we begin with these topics.

Pharmaceuticals and Patent Protection. There are a lot of unknowns in the world of patent scholarship. As I said in the Introduction, the empirical data on the overall effectiveness of patents are surprisingly indeterminate. There is simply a lot we do not know. (That's what drove me to look for normative foundations outside the conventional utilitarian framework, as I explained in the Introduction and elaborated on in Chapters 2 through 4.)

But there is one consistent finding across all the empirical literature on patents, one canonical truth that has been repeatedly established and confirmed beyond a peradventure of doubt: the pharmaceutical industry needs patents to survive.[16] If there is one industry where the conventional "incentive theory" of patents is actually true, it is the pharmaceutical industry. As a result, it is equally well understood that eliminating or weakening patent protection in this industry would significantly reduce the volume of R&D and consequently the supply of new drugs. This is as close as we have to an established fact, or strict empirical regularity, in the economic literature on patents.

The tricky question of course is this: how *much* would R&D be reduced if patents were weakened; and how weak would patents have to be to reduce pharmaceutical innovation so far as to have serious public health consequences? Unfortunately, this we do not know. But the general consensus is that even a minor reduction in patent protection might—note that word—have a significant effect on ultimate measures of public health.

Estimating the Impact: The Pharmaceutical R&D Infrastructure. To understand what would happen if the rewards from R&D were reduced in the pharmaceutical industry, it is helpful to understand some basic information about the industry's research infrastructure.

The overriding fact to keep in mind is that pharmaceutical R&D is enormously expensive. One oft-cited study found that it costs on average $802 million to go from the initial discovery of a promising molecule to a marketable drug product.[17] These costs are spread over many years: it takes on average 12.8 years to develop a pharmaceutical product from the initial synthesis of a new chemical compound to government approval for a new drug product.[18] The overall expenditure for pharmaceutical R&D in the United States exceeds $65 billion per year, considerably higher than the expenditure of public funds on medically related scientific research.[19] By any measure, the U.S. pharmaceutical research enterprise is a large, complex, and expensive operation.

This complexity shows itself in a number of ways. For example, the organizational landscape in the industry reveals distinct but important roles for both large and small companies. Traditionally, as the pharmaceutical industry grew from its early origins, a number of large, vertically integrated companies developed in parallel.[20] Economies of scale (pure size) and scope (the range of a company's activities) rewarded large companies and weeded out smaller ones.[21] This dynamic held sway from the early twentieth century until well after World War II. However, the advent of new scientific techniques beginning in the 1970s changed this. The emergence of modern genetic engineering, and biotechnology generally, provided an opening for small, research-intensive start-up companies. Many such companies are based on university research and a good number were founded by individual university scientists from various life sciences departments.[22]

Many scholars have seen the modern biotechnology industry as a fine exemplar of the way small, research-intensive companies can carve out a viable role in industries dominated by large, vertically integrated companies.[23]

If we look at the pharmaceutical industry from this perspective, we can identify a role for patent protection that goes beyond providing incentives to create and produce saleable drugs. Patents, as I argued in Chapter 7, enable small companies to remain independent. Patent protection makes it possible for a small company to specialize in a technology-intensive field, yet still integrate its product into the overall operations of a much larger company.[24] A small biotechnology company can concentrate on what it does best—research in a highly specialized field—and transfer the results of its work to a large company without the threat that its work will be illicitly copied. Thus patents have a dual function in the industry: they protect overall R&D incentives, but they also influence the way the industry is organized, in particular making it more likely that a small, specialized company can set up shop and remain independent. Again, this theme was developed at length in Chapter 7 as a practical example of what it means to apply the abstract goal of autonomy described by Kant and other theorists.

Let us return to the idea of invading patent rights on pharmaceuticals to help the destitute. I am arguing that we need to gauge the effect of this policy on the long-term viability of the research infrastructure of the pharmaceutical industry. To do so, we need to take into account not only the macro-level or aggregate effects, but also the more subtle or second-order effects. These include reducing the viability of small, research-intensive companies. The paradoxical result of reducing patent protection on pharmaceuticals might well be to cause an *increase* in the average firm size in this industry; pharmaceutical research might become more concentrated. This in turn could have consequences worth considering, including perhaps an ultimate reduction in the innovative capacity of the industry. If small companies disproportionately rely on patent protection, and if small companies also contribute significantly to industry innovation, overriding patents may diminish the innovative capacity of the industry, to the detriment of those who suffer from potentially treatable diseases in the future.

The Risk of Arbitrage. This is the really hard question: would reduced pharmaceutical innovation tomorrow be worth it, when compared to the increased access to health care today? This reduces to two related questions: Would uncompensated access to patented drugs by the developing world appreciably reduce pharmaceutical company profits? And if so, would this reduction in profits at some point reduce the number of pharmaceutical innovations these companies would develop?

It might seem at first that market prices for standard pharmaceuticals are in most cases far beyond what citizens of the developing world can afford. This implies that opening access to drugs in these markets will have little effect on the fortunes of pharmaceutical companies. After all, if a buyer cannot pay the going rate for a seller's product, it may seem hard to argue that the seller loses a sale when the buyer gets hold of the product for free, or at a greatly reduced price. This is true, but misses an important point. The availability of an expensive product at greatly reduced prices invites arbitrage—buying the product at the reduced rate and reselling it to others. If arbitrage is permitted, or difficult to prevent, sales at reduced prices may indeed have an effect on the seller's overall profits.

There is a serious risk of arbitrage in the context of access to pharmaceuticals. Many patented pharmaceuticals come in the form of pills—small, easy to hide, and easy to smuggle. In addition, destitute populations are often found in corrupt or failed states, countries with underdeveloped institutions and sometimes a rapacious governing class. There is a real possibility in this setting that drugs intended for destitute citizens will be commandeered and resold to disease sufferers in more developed countries.[25]

From the standpoint of the theories espoused in this book, the problem with arbitrage is that it complicates the right to access by the destitute. In particular, arbitrage brings the potential for consequences from access that we must consider. From a Lockean perspective, the clear-cut case for the charity proviso is undermined when today's charity runs the risk of harming people in the future. Likewise with Kant's Universal Principal: the freedom of others is affected by limits on property rights today that could impact other people in the future. And Rawls's principle of just savings points in much the same direction. If arbitrage were to undermine pharmaceutical company profits enough, future generations might suffer. If restricting access today is necessary to preserve the research infrastructure that serves as the engine driving pharmaceutical innovation, fair savings would require that this be done.

Intergenerational Effects and Normative Theories. The difficult issues we have been exploring here may serve as an excellent reminder of why I threw up my hands over utilitarianism in IP in the first place. The problem seems insoluble when looked at from the perspective of weighing costs and benefits. Furthermore, I think the more deontological approach of Locke and Kant, and to some extent Rawls, does not really resolve the issues any more cleanly. In fact, if we look at Locke's theory of property as a whole, or recall carefully some nuances in Kant's Universal Principle, or take seriously Rawls's principle of fair savings, we arrive at much the same destination as we would if we scrupulously follow the utilitarian pathway through these issues. That is to say, even if we put fairness and justice at the forefront, we have to consider how it would affect future generations if we were to advocate the widescale overriding of pharmaceutical patent rights. If we accept the facts I presented earlier about the nature of pharmaceutical research, especially the perhaps irreplaceable nature of the private pharmaceutical R&D infrastructure, there is no escaping the fact that access to current patented medicines entails a trade-off between current and future well-being. With this seemingly inescapable fact in mind, I turn to a few modest thoughts about how we might navigate this trade-off.

Fairness in Practice: Policies for Access to Patented Pharmaceuticals

The preceding discussion has identified a theoretical, normative basis for a claim by the destitute to desperately needed pharmaceuticals covered by patents. It is quite instructive, in light of this background, to observe the actual policies and practices that have emerged in this area over the past ten or so years. These can be summarized as follows:

1. Most major pharmaceutical companies have undertaken voluntary free drug distribution programs. From the perspective of IP rights, they have selectively waived their rights in countries that have a desperate need.[26]
2. The developing world has pushed back against an international patent regime seen as too restrictive. In the process, the poorest countries have won back the right to declare health-related emergencies that justify overriding patent rights—compulsory licenses for patented drugs.[27]
3. International foundations have stepped onto the scene with innovative programs for developing and distributing drugs aimed specifically at the health problems of the poorest countries. The Gates Foundation has been at the forefront here.[28]

What is most interesting about these developments is that they seem to indicate a shared understanding by many interested parties that property claims in this area must necessarily give way in the face of the more pressing needs of the destitute. It is not too grandiose to put it this way: they show an instinct for charity. From this perspective, the normative theories of Locke, Kant, and Rawls seem not so much to create binding limits on property rights as to reflect shared understandings of what those limits ought to be. As I mentioned, first in Chapter 3 and later in Chapter 8, the ability to waive property rights is a crucial benefit. This charity instinct at work in the patented pharmaceutical area shows this once again. The choice to waive property rights is part and parcel of the property system, and owners often exercise this choice so as to reduce the worst potential effects of property rights. Although it would be going too far to say that waiver renders property somehow perfectly self-regulating, it is fair to say—as I have at several points in this book—that an awareness of voluntary waiver can significantly influence our understanding of how property works in practice.

CHAPTER TEN

Conclusion

The Future of Property

PROPERTY DOES HAVE A FUTURE. Especially if it reflects a proper respect both for individual owners and the needs of the community—that is, if it is based on what a philosopher would call a liberal theory of property—it can continue to serve a vital function in a well-designed sociopolitical system. As more and more of society's valuable assets come to be incorporeal and intangible, this function will more and more come to be served by the species of property we call IP. So in constructing a viable theory of property, it makes sense to start with IP, or at the very least to include it.

In this spirit, I want to set out as clearly as I can the basic elements of a workable theory of IP. They will all be familiar; they are the same ones I have been talking about since the first page of this book. In this final chapter, I just want to gather them together, restate them simply, and show some relationships between them.

The elements as I see them are these:

1. *Propertize creative labor.* Recognize and reward creative work with true legal rights, thereby converting that work from hourly wage labor into a freestanding *economic asset* wherever possible. Allow individuals to control the works they create, via the one-to-one mapping between owners and assets that is the essence of property. Replace the discredited "heroic author" with a more realistic construct: the "prosaic author," a creative professional trying to

make a decent living from his or her talent. Acknowledge that rewarding the prosaic creator means encouraging not only individual and small team ownership, but also large corporate entities, which form an important part of the ecosystem that nurtures and supports individual creative professionals.

2. *Grant real rights, but not absolute rights.* Recognize each creator's unique contribution by granting IP rights that are truly rights, but also recognize society's contribution to creative work. Envision a *deserving core* anchoring each property right, surrounded by a *social periphery.* Honor the former with a solid entitlement, a real desert claim, and the latter by permitting taxation of creative products. Conceptualize these taxes as compensation to society for the myriad social contributions to every creative work.

3. *Accommodate the needs of consumers and users by (a) facilitating and encouraging cheap and easy IP permission and licensing mechanisms, together with (b) simple waiver techniques that permit binding dedication of rights to the public.* In the long-standing debate over incentives versus access, creators/owners versus consumers/users, recognize that *there is a solution.* Rightholders can continue to receive rights, while consumers and users can gain access to the works they want to use, if resources are directed to creating efficient transactional mechanisms that allow IP rights to flow through commercial channels as smoothly, or almost as smoothly, as do the works covered by those rights. Recognize that, in a world with numerous IP rights, the market for creative *works* necessitates also a (separate, but related) market for the *rights covering those works.* Encourage market making in this secondary market! Encourage collective action and competition in this market. This will ensure the smallest dislocation from the desirable policy of awarding real IP rights, and thus the largest net reward. At the same time, create a simple and binding mechanism for *waiver*—allowing a rightholder to make a binding dedication of his works to the public, and thus implementing a *right to include* that is coextensive with the traditional right to exclude at the heart of IP and property generally.

In my discussion of these elements, I will touch on a number of themes that have permeated this book. These are not, strictly speaking, required components of a workable IP theory. They are more like intellectual motifs that, for me at least, tie together and animate the elements I just listed; they help me make a coherent whole out of the myriad details and countercurrents of IP law. These themes are as follows:

1. *There is room at the bottom.* IP law has many possible and plausible normative foundations. Acceptance of this basic fact can help usher in a constructive policy discussion (based I hope on the midlevel principles; see Chapter 5) without the need to argue about ultimate foundations.

2. *Locke and company have much to say about IP.* The basic insight that property makes sense at a deep ethical level is for me central to my understanding of IP—why we need this form of legal protection, why it has the shape it does (exclusive rights, and so on), and why it is worth defending from critiques that would render it irrelevant or ancillary under contemporary conditions. Because of the midlevel principles, you do not have to agree with me on this, or on the underlying premise that the utilitarian case for IP is as yet inadequate; but I hope you will.

3. *IP, properly conceived and constructed, makes sense on distributive justice grounds.* IP rights surely have an effect on distributive justice, but these rights are defensible nonetheless. Put simply, *IP is fair.* A just society awards exclusive property rights to creators, and also limits and structures those rights in a way consistent with overall distributive justice concerns. Time-limited rights, public-facing exceptions to rights, and permissible taxation of works covered by rights are examples of how IP rights fit into an overall scheme of distributive justice.

Finally, there is one conceptual thread that runs through the book that merits separate attention, and while it does not really qualify as an element of basic theory or an intellectual theme (it is more like a metatheme, though that is a term I use with some distaste), I thought I would list it here:

The contemporary literature on IP rights has many gems of wisdom but is wrong to advocate the shrinking or withering away of IP rights. I have learned much from IP academics, including (a) the limits of the heroic author idea (see Element 1 above); (b) the need to integrate IP into comprehensive theories of distributive justice (Element 2); and (c) the benefits of voluntary dedication to the public schemes (such as Creative Commons licensing), and thus the need for a robust "right to include." Notwithstanding all these positive contributions, I disagree with the general thesis that property rights over information are a bad idea or that IP has mutated into a gargantuan, monstrous parody of its traditional moderate form. In an economy where intangible assets are more valuable than ever, IP is more important than ever.

I will now consider each of the three elements listed above, working the three themes, as well as the one "metatheme," into the discussion when relevant.

Propertizing Labor

Property is a unique legal construct. Even the language we use—what scholars sometimes call "property talk"—is distinctive. We speak of the creation of property as a "grant," a word derived from the Latin term for "entrust." The state bestows property on an owner, who then carries a small piece, a tiny spark, of the state's power. It is this power that makes a property right "good against the world," which means two things at once: first, that the owner can invoke the power of the state to enforce the right; and second, that there need be no preexisting relationship between an owner and another person for the owner to bring that person to account for violating the property right. The only connection, in such a case, is that both the owner and the other person are subject to the law of the same state.

The state's delegation of power to an owner signifies something important. The owner is carrying out a function vital to the state. For Locke, mutual recognition of preexisting property claims and mutual commitment to the institution of ownership is the first cause, the big bang that sets in motion the forces of state formation. Kant said something similar. Without the state, there are no strong ownership claims extending over time and space and reaching beyond an individual's ability to physically grasp and work on an object.

To put these grand ideas into practice, an actual state, a recognized government, must grant property rights to individual owners. One classic rationale for private ownership appeals to efficiency: ownership concentrates incentives to develop, deploy, monitor, and maintain an asset in ways that a centralized bureaucracy can rarely match. Some think this same rationale is sufficient to explain the need for IP rights, and there is surely truth in this. It is obvious, though, that many contributions to culture, and much of the technology in a modern society, is not individually owned or controlled. Classical music, ancient texts, the design of the internal combustion engine, the Internet, and many more of our everyday artifacts are not individually owned. And if this is true of these products of human creativity, why have property over anything of the sort? Given the stark fact that property rights for person A restrict the freedom of action of everyone else in A's society, and that the ideas embodied in creative works can often be copied and borrowed by others, why have IP at all?

The reason is that creative labor is valuable and important. It is noble work, work that is worthy of recognition and reward. It is work that should be dignified with the grant of a small dollop of state power—a property right. This is right in itself, something a good society would and should do. And it is good policy: the behavior called forth when property is awarded in this way benefits and ennobles the rest of society. High-quality creative work is recognized and rewarded (through the market), and people with talent and the drive to put it to work have a chance to make for themselves a viable career doing what they are good at. IP rights make it possible for people to develop their talents and make a living practicing their skill and artistry—to become true *creative professionals*. We dignify this sort of labor when the state grants IP rights in recognition of it. The power to restrict the freedom of others, when that power is earned and appropriate, is the flip side of our token of respect, our societal reward. Not all labor results in works that qualify for state recognition via property rights. But in a system of IP law, some work may be "propertized," may be backed by a claim "good against the world," enforceable by invoking the power of the state against anyone who would violate it. A claim like this is potent recognition of the valuable work that underlies it. Not lightly does society permit a measure of effort to be converted into a long-standing, publicly enforceable legal claim, which may become a valuable economic asset.

Why IP Rights?

Why must IP be a right? There are other ways to recognize and reward activities useful to the state and society. We could give cash payments, award medals, or bestow recognition some other way. Assuming reward or recognition is merited, why must it be in the form of a right, a strong legal claim?

Because rights are associated with individuals, are held by individuals. And an individual reward-claim is precisely the right way to recognize the creation of IP-worthy items. Creativity is still, in most cases, an individual affair (or a small-team affair; see Chapter 7). An individual state-backed claim is the appropriate and fitting way to reward individual creative labor. Cash awards, public or professional recognition—these and other rewards have their place. But a creative professional ought also be able to obtain a state-backed grant that confers the right to individually shape and control the deployment of a creative work. The nature of the thing created justifies the award of a property right.

Speaking of IP *rights* also makes sense because of an implicit distinction suggested by this way of speaking. Users and consumers of creative works do have some rights, but for the most part when it comes to a work created by someone else they have what legal theorists would call *interests:* their activities and concerns touch on or bear on creative works, and creative works affect them and their activities. Readers have an interest in books and book publishing; users and adapters of technology have an interest in relevant technologies; and so on. But authors and inventors should have *rights:* strong, deep claims that take precedence over mere interests. I emphasize repeatedly in this book that these strong claims must be balanced in a number of ways: by limits on appropriation, as described by Locke, Kant, and Rawls, and as given expression by the midlevel nonremoval and proportionality principles; by the society's right to tax the proceeds of creative work; and by users' rights, in some cases. Nevertheless, I believe the position of creative persons should be a privileged one when it comes to the works they create. The most appropriate and most sensible way to embody this is to grant those persons a true legal right.

Individual Control over Individual Assets: The Once and Future Essence of Property

Especially in areas covered by IP, there seems to be a persistent resistance to the idea of individual control of assets. It looks to some like an excuse for "political" decisions, such as the allocation of power in a society. The "rights as a cover for politics" school sees collective contributions as the true essence of most valuable works, and argues that individual ownership is a fairly recent overlay on the "natural" situation of group effort and group control. The more recent manifestation of this school of thought centers mostly on digital works. It holds that individual contributions are being overshadowed by the power of dispersed, collective creativity. The future, it is understood, belongs to the amateurs, the wiki contributors, the open source software contributors. Discrete works, originating and belonging to an individual or a small creative team, are decidedly yesterday's news. These works, and the property rights associated with them, will for the most part just wither away in the future.

As I argued in Chapter 8, there is a lot to be said about the value of dispersed creativity. Wikipedia and fan websites, together with some open source projects, have indeed shown the value of dispersed teams of people each working on a bite-sized piece of a much larger whole, with no one person or company claiming ownership or exercising traditional incidents of control over the resulting work. And yet: there are still many works that are better shaped and controlled by a single individual. Those so made will often be superior to the decentralized, uncoordinated productions of far-flung amateur teams. For the very reasons that Locke first identified as the core case for property, people need a reason to work hard, to carry out a singular vision by dint of sometimes repetitive editing, shaping, and crafting. The persistent right to maintain control while such a vision is manifested and worked out—the central argument for property in Kant's view—is still necessary in many cases. Property still matters.

THE FLEXIBILITY OF EXCLUSIVITY

One reason people often take offense at the notion of property is that, since at least Blackstone's time, the definition of its essence invokes a concept that seems repugnant. Conventional wisdom, repeated ad nauseum, emphasizes that the essence of property is *the right to exclude*. To exclude means to shut out, to prevent access to—to slam the door in everyone's face, so to speak.[1] With this as its essence, it is not hard to see why property has a bad name among those who care about others.

In truth, though, it is not nearly so hard to defend property. The trick is to avoid getting hung up on the legal definition, the apparent power and effect that follows from the ominous-sounding "right to exclude." The moment of the initial grant, and the formal definition of the right being granted, draws attention away from what comes afterward. If we attend instead to what typically happens after property rights are assigned, a completely different picture comes into view. Attending to the crucial *postgrant* stage in the life of a typical property right (including especially most IP rights) reveals all sorts of ways that the supposedly exclusive right of property is actually bound up with various forms of *inclusion*.

The most obvious example is nonenforcement. As I have emphasized repeatedly, rights that are theoretically exclusive can be voluntarily left idle for all sorts of reasons—rendering them not very exclusive at all. Sometimes this is a simple matter of pragmatics: IP rights are not self-enforcing. The owner of an IP right is permitted to invoke the power of the state to exclude others, but of course he does not *have* to do so. The potential gain is often not worth the cost of engaging the expensive and slow-moving machinery of judicial enforcement. When it is not, rights that are putatively exclusive will in fact not wind up excluding anyone at all.

So too with waiver—a more voluntary, intentional form of nonenforcement. Often for strategic reasons, rightholders will take action that in effect says, yes, I have an exclusive right, but I hereby relinquish it. For my own ends, I choose not to assert it; I hereby allow it to lapse as against some or all of those I might otherwise exclude. These decisions, in my view, are an important part of the autonomy that property allows, and indeed promotes. Waiver reveals one of the great advantages of property as an institution: it is not an immovable obstacle—in fact, it's often easy to get around. All an owner need do is announce or otherwise signify the message "I have these rights but choose not to enforce them."

Waiver puts on display the flexibility of property. It can be instructive to compare this feature with the situation that would prevail under a regime where property is forbidden or strictly limited. It is very difficult for private actors operating under a regime of no-property to voluntarily opt out of that policy. Creating property by private initiative is very difficult. It requires a cumbersome series of contracts, or a shared understanding. The whole structure must be made to work without the support of a universal set of rights "good against the world." For this reason we might say the door into the regime of no-property is a one-way door; once through, there is no going back. A state that makes it difficult to acquire property rights also makes it difficult for private actors to work around that rule. Contrast that with the state that grants property rights. If enforcement costs something, or there are strategic gains to be had from waiver, there is a strong likelihood that at least some of the rights that are granted will not be enforced. Private actors who want to opt out of a property regime will be able to do so in at least some circumstances. True, the fear that others may assert their rights could keep people from waiving theirs; in this sense, it may not always be possible to act unilaterally. But sometimes it will. And sometimes people can join together, formally or informally, to create a shared zone of nonenforcement, and in so doing effectively opt out of the property regime at least in part, and at least with respect to others in the group. Property is in this sense a two-way door: we can enter the world of property, but private actors can choose to leave it if and when they wish. This is an enormous advantage over the world of no-property, it seems to me. And it is completely at odds with the superficial emphasis on property as a right to exclude. The ability to easily *include* is an important flip side to the grant of property rights—one that is obscured by an overemphasis on the muscular rights that accompany a grant of property.

The key in all this is to watch how rights are *deployed*—to pay attention to the postgrant environment in which property rights operate. When we do this, we are much less likely to get caught up in excessive claims about the power of property. We should pay at least as much attention to enforcement rates and the real-world impact of property rights as we do to the formal specification of rights. If we do we will get a much more realistic picture of the ground-level effect of property, including IP rights. And nine times out of ten, I will wager, the scary stories we tell ourselves about the potentially devastating scope of property will fade away in the cold light of day.

FLEXIBILITY IN ACTION: TWO EXAMPLES

So IP, as I conceive of it, is highly flexible. By way of example, consider two topics discussed in various parts of the book: online digital content and technological platforms. An understanding of the various business strategies enabled by IP rights, the experimentation this engenders, and the surrounding context of economic competition will go a long way toward illustrating how the flexible nature of IP rights operates in practice.

Musicians, authors, photographers, and artists have been struggling for some years, trying to hit on the right formula for making money in the era of digital copyright and transmission—the Internet era. Many observers of the digital scene have been advocating a brave new world free of IP rights, where content is given away or shared in the hope of voluntary payments. And in some cases the observers have been right: giving things away, it turns out, can sometimes help spread the word and thus seed a market. The Internet has made it possible to experiment with all sorts of free digital samples of creative work.

At the same time, the "just give it away" school of thought, standing alone, has not so far brought a decent living to too many people. As any business-person will attest, the free sample idea pays off only if it leads to an actual sale somewhere down the road. Digital seeding will only work where the seedlings grow up into cash-producing crops of one sort or another.

This is where IP rights reenter the story. At some point, a creative person who has generated some interest in her work needs to be able to charge for it. IP rights make this possible. If and when the market for a creative person has matured to the point where at least some consumers are willing to pay, IP enables a successful business model to take shape. So the musician may draw an audience by giving her music away, then later graduate to the sale of IP-protected music in a real market transaction.

But what is the ideal mix of free sample and for-pay, or premium, content? No one can say at this point. All sorts of combinations have been tried, and more are being tried every day. The point I want to emphasize is that the flexible structure of property, and IP law in particular, is what makes all this experimentation possible. The optimal mix of free and for-pay music is something that every musician can explore and experiment with on her own. There is no one-size-fits-all policy that dictates a uniform approach. Musicians can give away snippets of songs, whole songs, whole albums, or any combination of these. Likewise—and here is where IP really contributes—they can just as easily choose *not* to give away any or all of the above. They can make individual decisions based on their interests and values; property enables them all.

The experimentation spawned by property's flexibility gives consumers choices. Autonomy for creators means competition, which benefits consumers and users of IP-protected works. In the end, it is often the pressure of competing models of IP exploitation that protects consumers best from the potentially harmful effects of exclusivity. Put another way, IP guarantees exclusivity over *works*, but works compete in *markets*. An IP owner may have what Blackstone called "despotic dominion" over his works, but this very rarely translates into domination of a market. And market competition usually prevents IP owners from drastically overreaching. An IP owner who is seen as too restrictive, or who charges too much for protected works, will be disciplined. Not, in the usual case in our system, by a government agency, but by a better consumer watchdog: competition.

I have mentioned the powerful policing effect of competition at several points in this book. In Chapter 8 I talked about academics and observers of the IP scene who advocate a strong right for digital aficionados who want to remix the original content of others. I resisted this idea, on the ground that creators of original content should be privileged vis-à-vis re-mixers, that their work deserves a substantial legal right that is difficult to invade or override. But there are many people who enjoy remixing, and who therefore value public material, because they can remix it as much as they want with no legal repercussions. So, lo and behold, mechanisms have arisen to enable remixers to do their thing. Some private companies voluntarily waive their rights, wagering that the support of remixers will offset whatever is lost by not strictly enforcing their rights. (Fan websites of all sorts fit this description.) Other companies sell content specifically free of IP protection, which can be reproduced or reused in any way the purchaser desires. Other groups are composed of fellow amateurs and remixing fans who release their own original works into the cybersphere with no restrictions on remixing or reuse, via open-access licensing of one sort or another. Remixers can then contribute to and draw from large pools of such open-access material with no fear of IP-based legal liability.

Amongst all the blooming, buzzing diversity of digital content, one point stands out: competition among distribution models gives consumers many choices. The inherent flexibility of IP rights means that some content owners will protect them vigorously; others will give away some rights over some uses, while closely guarding some of their rights; and some people will generously donate pretty much everything they do for the use and pleasure of like-minded others.

This diversity of choice helps even those consumers who are willing to pay for premium content. Partially free and totally free content will naturally and inevitably put at least some downward pressure on the price that can be charged for the premium stuff. In this way, those who distribute content in copy- and remix-friendly forms do more than strike a blow for the freedom of their content. They also reduce the price of other content as well. From the perspective of creative professionals this may not always be a good thing. But for the consumer and user of digital material, it is a very good thing indeed.

The beneficial effects of competition are also on display in the matter of IP protection and technological platforms. Platforms such as Apple's iTunes/iPod system, various video game systems, and e-book readers such as Amazon's Kindle are often subject to controlled access regimes. Owners of these platforms use various measures—including IP protection—to prevent all comers from gaining free and open access to the platforms they control. Some academics, industry players, and regulators (particularly in Europe) fear that controlled access like this is a bad deal for consumers. Why shouldn't anyone who wants to sell or distribute compatible content be able to hook into these proprietary systems? Wouldn't it be great if legal and economic policy were designed so as to consistently favor interoperability?

The proconsumer consequences of robust interoperability would be a great boon, there is no doubt. But my point is that many of these consequences will follow even if the regulators use a much lighter touch on the interoperability issue. The reason is the same as we saw with respect to digital content: competition. It does not (always) take a government regulator to observe that consumers prefer a wide array of choices when it comes to content that can be played on a technological platform. Private companies can see that too. Which is why they will often be driven to line up a very wide assortment of content that works with a proprietary platform. And—more important—they will respond to consumers who are displeased with excessive restrictions on how content can be used. A platform seller who tightly restricts the number of copies that can be made, or the length of time a copy can be used, or any of a number of things consumers want to do, can expect competition from a rival platform owner. Maybe not right away (such is the power of short-term lock-in effects, as described in Chapter 8). But eventually; before too long, usually.

What we have seen in the marketplace is that, once consumers understand that restrictions on content are one of the dimensions or parameters that are relevant in platform markets, rival platform sellers start to emphasize the advantages they offer with respect to use restrictions. A digital music subscription service that cuts off access to its library when the consumer stops paying may be met with advertising from another platform where consumers pay once and can use the music any way they want. A system that allows a limited number of copies of content will be met by competition from a platform with a higher limit. And so on. Over time, consumers begin to catch on: when they buy content for a platform, they are actually buying a product that has two distinct attributes, the content itself and a *set of rights* that goes along with it. Consumers begin to disaggregate the bundle they buy into its component parts. Competition heats up over the number and scope of rights that are sold along with the content. All of this competition depends on the fact that the content owners have a set of rights to begin with, and that they are free to carve up and sell these rights in any way they see fit. Flexibility, experimentation, competition—again, these are the features of the IP system that best protect consumers. Regulatory intervention may be necessary in extreme cases of persistent market power and very high switching costs; but overall, the basic structure of the IP system and the economic competition that surrounds it are the best protectors of consumer interests.

WHY RIGHTS "GOOD AGAINST THE WORLD"?

One variant on the ideas about IP reviewed in Chapter 8 holds that, in the online world, contracts will eventually displace property. Because it is easy to require people to agree to a contract to access content, there will no longer be a need for property rights. As I argued in Chapter 8, there is reason to doubt the accuracy of the property-displacement theory, because of the logistical problems of attaching an unbroken chain of contracts to every piece of digital content. To this largely descriptive point I add here a more normative one. Property does more than bind unknown individuals to one another. It also unites all individuals in a larger set of relations. Because of this, it can serve as more than a floor upon which individuals base bilateral relations, such as by a contract that builds on a preexisting property right. It can also act as a ceiling or limit on permissible bilateral deals. So, for example, through various doctrines the law can prohibit private parties from contracting away certain core rights, such as moral rights (in the case of creatives) or fair use rights (in the case of users or consumers). In this way, property can be seen not only to precede contract, but also to transcend or in some cases supersede contract. It is a right not only good against the world, but a set of duties that is good for the world as well.

Recognizing Dynamics and Rejecting the Environmental Analogy

The traditional justification for IP rights is that they create incentives. They hold out rewards designed to elicit desirable behavior from people, in the form of extra effort and creativity which, it is believed, will redound to the benefit of society. I have mixed this traditional idea into my treatment of IP while rarely featuring it. Partly this is because the theorists I admire build their theories primarily on illustrations of older types of assets, usually land and other tangible items. Partly it is because the language of incentives is closely tied to utilitarian modes of thought, which I have sought to avoid for the most part. And partly it is because the "incentive story" of IP protection, while it surely has more than a grain of truth, is notoriously difficult to prove persuasively.

Nevertheless, before I leave the topic of why IP rights make basic sense, I do want to say a few words about the incentive story. Or, to be more accurate, I want to say something about why the *dynamic perspective* out of which this story comes is so right when it comes to IP.

As Jeremy Waldron points out, from one point of view Locke's emphasis on original appropriation makes the Lockean theory singularly irrelevant in the modern world, where many of the important assets (land, buildings, natural resources, and so forth) were long ago appropriated and where we are dealing in many instances now with the subsequent or downstream transfer of things that have been owned for a long time.[2] But as I noted in Chapter 2, when describing why Locke in some ways works better for IP than for traditional assets, this is not at all true in the world of IP. While the existing stock of creative works is no doubt very large, new works come into existence all the time. In this world, initial appropriation is not a historical curiosity; it happens every minute of every day.

My complaint about "the environmental analogy" in IP law is that it omits this crucial point. The world of created works is not a fixed corpus, like the natural world. While conservation is important, it is not and should not be the only focal point for the setting of IP policy. The stock of works relevant to IP grows every day, all the time. Conserving what is publicly available is important—that is why the nonremoval principle is included in Chapter 5. But preserving open access to the maximum number of created works is not and should not be the single goal of IP law. In a world where new material is constantly being created, there is less need to concentrate exclusively on preserving what came before. This is important, but not paramount, in a dynamic field such as IP. Conservation alone loses sight of a simple fact. Creative works do not come to us out of nowhere; the landscape is created, piece by piece, work by work, with great care, skill, and effort on the part of individual people. In a dynamic context where new material is constantly being added, maintaining access to the largest possible set of works (via an expansive legal public domain) is only one aspect of policy. Encouraging the next round of new additions is even more important.

Balanced Rights: Pregrant and Postgrant Considerations

It is easy to advocate "balanced" property rights. Hardly anyone opposes it. Many judicial opinions and academic articles argue that the results they contend for will produce a more balanced IP system. Usually, however, the call for balance is just so much ballast thrown into an argument to recognize that (1) it should not be taken too far, or (2) it should be seen as but one part of a complex whole, offset and softened in some way by other results and doctrines in IP law.

I have tried my best in this book to go beyond this conventional appeal to the often vacuous notion of balance. I have tried not to even talk about balance, but instead to *show what it looks like,* in detail.

The normative theories of appropriation I examined in Part I are all aimed explicitly at constructing a balanced understanding of property rights. Locke's labor-based justification for original appropriation is expansive, to be sure; but this aspect of his thought is offset with the equally expansive provisos, sufficiency, spoliation, and charity. The same with Kant: the fundamental need for individual property finds a counterweight in the Universal Principle, which bounds and restricts property at just as fundamental a level. And for Rawls, property plays only a small part in a comprehensive institutional setup whose primary purpose is to achieve distributive justice. For each of these theorists, property is an inherently balanced institution. And for good measure, I have tried in this book to integrate the three theories into a cohesive whole whose overall structure is even more balanced than each of them standing alone.

Granting Balanced Rights

Balance begins when rights do. In IP law, this means that limitations on rights, and counterbalancing rights for users and consumers, are built in from the outset. Locke's provisos, the Kantian Principle, and of course Rawls's whole approach to property ensure as much. In addition, much of the operational punch of the midlevel principles is aimed at maintaining balance. Nonremoval means that the public domain must never be depleted to provide a source of rights for creators. Efficiency compares the benefits of rights against their costs, and thus often points toward restrictions on rights that would be too costly for society. And most important, the proportionality principle has balance as its single-minded purpose. Granting rights that are commensurate with the achievement of valuable ends, but extend no further, is a shining exemplar of the idea of balance in action. Of the four midlevel principles described in Chapter 5, only the dignity principle can be said to favor one side of the IP equation, that of the creator. Yet even this one-sidedness is rooted in the benefits that creative people bestow on society, and so can be justified in a sense as a way to balance the debt society owes to those who labor to create things.

Postgrant Balancing

Compared to the initial grant of rights, where questions of balance are often extensively investigated, the postgrant stage is examined relatively little. But because of the many variables that affect how rights are actually deployed, many of the most important occasions for bringing balance occur after rights are granted. The dynamic nature of IP in practice makes the postgrant stage the crucial time for bringing balance to the IP system. Also, because it is difficult to assess the true impact of IP rights before they are granted and deployed, there are significant advantages to deferring questions of balance until this postgrant stage. Doing so prevents the pruning of IP rights based on speculative worries at the pregrant stage, and defers consideration until more information about the real impact of the rights has come to light.

What do I mean by postgrant balancing? Examples abound. Doctrines of estoppel, implied license, IP misuse, and infringement remedies are all applied in the postgrant phase of the life of an IP right. They are all capable, in one way or another, of achieving or restoring a measure of balance since they are all *responsive* to the way IP rights are being deployed in practice.

Take two specific instances as illustrations. In copyright law, it has become the rule that people who post copyrighted content on the Web are assumed to permit that content to be found, cataloged, indexed, and searched by systematic web-crawling and searching software. There are software settings a person may use to prevent crawling and indexing; but the burden is on the individual copyright holder to make these settings before posting his works. Neither copyright notice nor any other indirect objection to crawling and searching is enough to offset the default assumption that posted material can be crawled and indexed for search. This is a major adjustment in traditional notions of IP law, which presume that explicit legal permission is required prior to any copying or other infringing use of a work. But the new default makes sense in this setting. Courts have consistently held that the owner of a copyrighted work gives an implied license to the crawlers and indexers when he posts his work without indicating in software settings that he does not want it crawled. This might be described as an "opt-out" system, in which an owner of copyrighted works must now indicate explicit nonassent to what have become conventional online practices that technically implicate traditional copyright (that is, the right to prevent a copy from being made). But two things may be said briefly in defense of the new default. First, it makes sense given the enormous benefit derived from online crawling and indexing activities. Second, it is a far better alternative than trying to specify a new limitation in the initial grant of copyrights. The implied license concept emerged after the Internet had time to develop and crawling and indexing activities became established. It might well have been much more difficult to legislate an ex ante restriction or limitation in rights. Letting the practice emerge, then recognizing a reasonable and sensible scope for it via the implied license doctrine, seems to me a far superior approach to copyright policy in this and many other cases.

We can also consider another instance, this one from patent law. A high degree of anxiety has attended the issue of patents that cover all or part of a widely shared technological standard. Patented formats, interfaces, and other standardized technological components raise difficult questions about the need to balance incentives to innovate against the benefits of shared access or interoperability. The exclusive force inherent in patents makes some observers nervous; they worry that patents on standards may give their owners excessive leverage over those needing or wanting access to a widely used standard technology. One solution, as always, is to restrict patents with special potential to disrupt interoperability. But a superior solution, I think, is to put in place doctrines that prevent strategic misuse of standards-related patents. The advantage, as with the implied copyright licenses described above, is that this solution does not overreach. It saves the cost and controversy of defining at the outset which patents might influence interoperability. Instead, by its terms it applies only when patents are actually being used to thwart reasonable consumers' expectations—such as when a patent holder reneges on an earlier pledge not to enforce her patents, or when patents are hidden from sight during group standard-setting exercises, and later sprung like a trap on the unwary adopters of a standard.

My Favorite Normative Theories, and Why They Matter

In the Introduction I explained how I moved from a conventional utilitarian understanding of IP rights to something else, something based on the nonutilitarian philosophical ideas of Locke, Kant, and Rawls. Though, as I said in the Introduction and tried to illustrate in Chapter 5, you need not share my views about the correct ultimate normative foundations of IP law, I have tried to show why I came to reject the conventional view in favor of the foundational ideas of the three philosophers just mentioned. I hope that in the process I may have convinced you that there is something valuable in these alternative views as well.

What do I find so appealing in the theories of Locke, Kant, and Rawls? Let me take each in turn. Locke has a simple but convincing story about initial appropriation, the conditions under which property rights originally arise. Kant understands ownership to be crucial to the development of a person's full potential, which involves both extensive interaction with objects in the environment and also persistent rights over those objects, so that the individual can place his unique stamp on them. And for Rawls, property fits into the overall scheme of a fair and just society, taking its place alongside other institutions and rights that guarantee an equal chance at self-fulfillment to all citizens.

Property for Locke and Kant shares a critical feature that for me makes these theorists refreshing and indispensable when thinking about IP rights. They both connect property rights with the formation of government, the founding of civil society. This is about as far from much contemporary IP theory as it gets. For many today, IP retains at best a precarious toehold in the edifice of government policies. It is thought to be archaic, partly to mostly irrelevant, perhaps even a retrograde institution. What a difference in perspective to start instead from a theory that property—including, naturally, IP—is at the very center of state formation, and thus of the state itself. Locke emphasizes the priority and fundamental nature of initial claims, and the voluntary formation of governments to protect and enforce them. Kant says that the need for rights over objects that extend in time and space is the basic, primitive impetus behind state formation. I argued at length in Chapters 2 and 3 that these ideas, formed in an era when property applied mostly to tangible items, lose nothing in transit when applied to modern economic conditions, where IP rights are of paramount importance. The same need for equilibrium between individual autonomy and the rights of others that prevailed when Locke and Kant were writing still prevails today. Property is still a large piece of the puzzle. Theories that understand the centrality of property, and the ways it can be structured so as to advance and maintain a social equipoise, are therefore just as useful today.

Despite the basic similarities, however, there are of course also major differences between the eighteenth- and nineteenth-century scene and present conditions. One of the most important is the far bigger role that large private corporations play now as compared to earlier times. All the talk of individual autonomy in the works of Locke and Kant, and how the rights and duties of others counterbalance restrain autonomy, might appear tangential or even hollow in light of the rise of large corporate power. As I argued in Chapter 7, there is surely something to this; where, as is often the case today, large corporate entities acquire, hold, and deploy many of the works covered by IP rights, property surely has a different impact and a different set of meanings than it did historically. The tight connection between robust property rights and wide-ranging individual autonomy is obviously moderated, to at least some degree, when large corporations mediate between individuals and the direct ownership of property rights over their works. Yet as I explained in Chapter 7, the fact that there is no longer quite a short, tight line between creative professionals and the unfettered right to control their works does not mean that IP is irrelevant to the professional prospects or career discretion of the creative professional. Not at all. Large corporate entities now loom large in the industrial ecosystem surrounding many people who create things for a living. But these entities do not always work at cross-purposes with individual creators and small creative teams. In fact, large companies not only employ many creatives, they also constitute a vital outlet for the work product of many individuals and small teams. Corporate ownership, and the presence of large corporate entities generally, does not always replace opportunities for individual ownership and autonomy; it often supports or creates those opportunities as well. Thus the pro-autonomy effect of granting property rights may at times be more muted in tone than if all rights were held directly by individuals and small entities. But large entities are a long way from completely extinguishing the light of individual creativity and professional freedom. They also contribute to it as well.

Autonomy in Action

The foundational normative theories of Chapters 2 and 3 can be of great help in sorting through complex issues of contemporary IP law. For example, as I emphasized in Chapter 8, it is right to privilege original creators at the expense of those who would reuse or remix original creative works. The point is not that remixers are not original and creative; many surely are. It is just that IP law is designed to honor and reward individual creators. Remixers, at least sometimes, take as their starting point original works first created by someone else. This, and not a lack of creativity, is what earns them the second-tier status I have assigned to them. As I mentioned in Chapter 2, a primitive understanding of Locke's theory of appropriation might seem to imply that the labor of remixers earns them a property right. But this is not so. Locke says that a worker can contract away the right to own his work product, for example, when the worker agrees to labor on materials or assets already claimed and owned by someone else. In this way Locke signals his understanding that preexisting property claims sometimes take precedence over the labor-based claim of another. His rationale is quite clear: he says that allowing appropriation by the later laborer in this case would in effect work an injustice on the original property holder. And this his theory does not permit. Again, the point is not that the later laborer works less hard, or that his labor is necessarily less valuable in and of itself. It is just that labor cannot be used as a lever to pry away the rights of an owner. To allow it to do so would be to blur the line between appropriation and misappropriation, and this Locke says we must not do.

Kant's theory is in accord. For Kant, property is all about respect for autonomy. So he would almost surely reject the argument of the remixer that interference with the autonomy interest of the original creator is warranted by the rights of the remixer. Though he would no doubt credit the argument that the remixer wants to work his will on a found object, he would likely reject a property claim. To recognize such a strong claim by a remixer requires utter vitiation of the claims of the original content creator, and this Kant would surely disfavor.

In this case, as with other case studies in this book, I have tried to convince you that even though normative theory à la Locke, Kant, and Rawls is not essential to making policy and resolving controversies in IP law, it is very useful, and indeed superior to the alternatives. For my money, until utilitarian foundations become much more solid, these theorists provide the best account we have of why we have IP and what its basic structure ought to look like.

IP Is a Fair Institution

Like Locke and Kant, John Rawls believed that pure utilitarianism makes a poor theoretical foundation for a state. I wholeheartedly agree. The empty promise and ethical holes in the utilitarian theory of IP are just too glaring for my taste. Not that I did not give it a good try. I just came to see that as applied to IP law, utilitarian theory could not bear the load that has been assigned to it. At some point it became for me "the god that failed."

Rawls is brilliant at plucking the ideas of thinkers like Kant and placing them in a sweeping, society-wide panorama. Rawls thinks systematically, at the broad societal level, just as the utilitarians do; but he avoids the conceptual snares and ethical vacuum of utilitarian thinking. Rawls gives us a philosophy that systematically and broadly shows how to value each individual.

Despite its brilliance, undiluted Rawlsian theory has its problems too. Rawls is too skeptical of property, of strong private claims, to give it pride of place at the foundation of a fair state as he envisions it. In this, he is at odds with Locke, Kant, and others, who see property as a central rather than secondary institution. For my part, I sought to combine this traditional emphasis on the importance of property with Rawls's solicitude for social justice, particularly the plight of the most destitute.

The result, as I described in Chapter 4, is to reject both the "property first" and "property last" approaches. Instead I advocate something closer to "property, but." Yes, property: place strong individual claims over valuable assets at the center of the socioeconomic system. However: build in limits on these claims, and allow society its own claim to some of the proceeds from property, in the form of taxation. In IP as elsewhere, take the best of Locke and Kant and add in Rawls's concern with fairness. The result: a property-centric state that is also fair.

This may sound fine, as far as it goes. But clashes between people, want against want and need against need, are difficult to resolve at such a high level of abstraction. Put another way, Locke and Kant may be terrific, but how do they help us decide who should win a lawsuit under statute X brought by person A against person B? The answer of course is that theory at this level can only point us to general considerations, can only help restructure the issues in a way that gives us some insight into the deeper principles at stake in a specific dispute. At the end of the day, the ideas of Locke and Kant, tempered by Rawls's emphasis on social fairness, lead only to a high-level prescription: IP, and property in general, should be granted so as to promote autonomy, except where doing so would trample heavily on matters affecting other individuals or society as a whole.

It is wrong to say that application of this prescription is self-evident. A number of more granular principles (such as the midlevel principles of Chapter 5), and ultimately detailed statutes and doctrines, are required to carry it out. But it is also wrong to say that a general prescription for strong but fair IP rights is worthless. It can help organize and structure the more detailed, operational principles. And it can also remind us, amidst the clutter and welter of nits and specifics that make up the IP field, of the overall purpose and sustaining value of the IP system as a whole.

The Transactional Burden of IP Rights:
There Is a Solution

The best way to encourage and reward creative activity is to permit individuals to control the assets they create. And the best way to do that is to grant property rights. With so much decentralized control, however, come problems of coordination and interaction. Many activities require that disparate assets be identified and brought together. If each asset—or worse, each of many components of each asset—is owned by a separate entity, the cost of assembling the needed components and assets may become exorbitant. All those private rights, all that individual autonomy, comes at a steep cost.

How do we bring harmony amidst so much autonomy? That is a central question in IP policy, and in the law of property generally. Is there a solution to the high transaction costs imposed when individual IP rights wind up in widely dispersed hands?

I contend there are multiple solutions to the problems created by IP rights. There are all sorts of ways to square the grant of individual property rights and the need to buy and assemble numerous assets and rights. Many were discussed in Chapter 7: integration, rights pooling, clearinghouses, pre-assignment norms and agreements. Diverse and very different operational features characterize these many forms. But beneath the diversity of form there is a consistency in design. They are all designed to ameliorate the transactional burden that follows from the granting of many discrete IP rights.

Transactions: Flow and Movement across the
IP Landscape

In the Introduction to this book I compared the sprawl and chaos of the modern IP landscape to the configuration of a rapidly growing city. We can extend the metaphor to embrace the transactional burden of multiple, dispersed IP rights, by analogizing the transactional mechanisms of Chapter 7 to the transportation and communication grid of a city. Just as a city's infrastructure ties together and makes coherent the city's various neighborhoods and locales, so too transaction-facilitating mechanisms speed the movement of IP rights from those who hold them to those who need them. The more conduits there are to channel transactions, and the lower the cost of navigating and engaging them, the greater will be the volume of transactions and the smaller the burden of many and widespread rights.

Of course, in a city, too much sprawl is considered a bad thing. Rational planning requires that some building locations be ruled out, and that policies such as "in-fill" will produce the desired level of population and structural density. So too with IP: requirements for awarding rights must be enforced, and it does not makes sense to push out on every frontier just because there is a clamor for expansion.

Reducing the Transactional Burden

Nevertheless, the case for IP rights is a strong one. So we will often find ourselves in a situation where the transactional burden of awarding IP rights is worth it. The trick here, as I emphasized in Chapter 7, is to reduce this burden as far as possible. Creativity should be honored; property rights are the best way to do so. But the effect of implementing these rights, the cost to others of awarding and enforcing them—these we should strive to minimize, and even eliminate if possible. Indeed, the more a creator receives from the total cost burden of an IP right, the closer that right is to serving its basic social purpose. Wringing transaction costs out of the IP system is something that everyone—creators and consumers alike—can agree on completely.

The sprawling city of IP makes the best sense when IP rights are numerous, widely dispersed, and easily moved around. A healthy IP landscape will feature large, high-volume transactional mechanisms well populated by the flow of rights from owners to users. These IP aqueducts will ensure that the autonomy and independence of IP owners does not interfere unnecessarily with the needs of consumers and users. As explained in Chapter 7, the legal system ought to encourage private investment in these aqueducts as much as possible, and even kick in public resources when that will help. The result will be a well-functioning and well-balanced IP system, one that recognizes both the rights of creators and the needs of users.

If I had to reduce all this to a simple formula, it would look like this:

$$Rights + Transactions = The\ Solution$$

If we keep this basic guiding principle in mind, we can have a balanced and effective set of IP policies.

Some Final Thoughts

It takes courage to try to create something new, and even more courage to send it out into the world in hopes of a good reception. Any author, musician, songwriter, inventor, or designer can vouch for that. To me, IP rights represent an important token of respect and recognition for those souls brave enough to launch their creations out into the roiling sea in search of an audience or a market. These rights have a practical side too, of course; without them, these acts of bravery would often not add up financially. The prospect, or more often hope, of maybe making a living helps keep the creative class going. IP gives them a reason to believe that some day, for some of them anyway, a real career could be made by doing what they are best at.

There is no question that awarding IP rights costs something. Thomas Macauley's quote, no less accurate for being worn thin from overuse, says it all: copyright is a tax on readers for the benefit of writers. A commitment to IP reminds us to remember what we get in exchange for this tax. To paraphrase another quote, this one from Oliver Wendell Holmes, IP taxes are the price we pay for a creative civilization. To me, the cost is very much worth it.

In paying the IP tax, we recognize our interdependence. Creative people need to make a decent living. Consumers and users of creative works need dedicated professionals to keep doing what they do. Big anonymous companies may take in our money, but it does not stay there, at least not all of it. Some of it—enough to make a difference, we hope—finds its way into the hands of those whose works we use and enjoy. This all happens because IP rights are awarded by the government. The state mediates between creators and consumers. State-backed IP rights link creative people with those who enjoy their works. In this way, private ownership—which appears at times the opposite of a public-spirited institution, and seems even in some ways selfish—turns out to be just one part of a larger, interdependent structure. IP rights do not cut us off from one another; they are an instrument by which we meet each others' needs. It is this ability to unify, to knit together, that ultimately pushes to the forefront when we set ourselves the difficult but rewarding task of justifying intellectual property.

Notes

1. Introduction

1. In this, it appears I am not alone. See Peter Yu, "Anticircumvention and Anti-Anticircumvention," 84 *Denv. U. L. Rev.* 13, 14–15 (2006): "In the current DRM [digital rights management] debate, just like in most other intellectual property-related debates, there is a considerable divide between the rights holders, their investors and representatives on the one hand and academics, consumer advocates, and civil libertarians on the other side. . . . Unfortunately, neither side has sufficient empirical evidence to either support its position nor disprove its rivals'. Instead, as [scholar] David McGowan noted, both sides tactically push the burden of proof back and forth, knowing full well that '[w] hoever has to prove the unprovable facts is likely to lose.'" Citations omitted, citing David McGowan, "Copyright Nonconsequentialism," 69 *Mo. L. Rev.* 1, 1 (2004).

2. This is meant as a general description of what property is all about. In actuality, of course, multiple legal entities (people, corporations, etc.) can share ownership of a single asset; a single owner can own many assets; ownership claims can be broken down and parceled out in complex combinations; and so on.

3. Jules Coleman, *The Practice of Principle* (Oxford: Oxford Univ. Press, 2001).

4. See infra, Chapter 6, for more detail.

5. John Rawls, *Political Liberalism* (New York: Columbia Univ. Press, expanded ed. 2005).

6. Id., at 135: "[T]here are many conflicting reasonable comprehensive doctrines with their conceptions of the good, each compatible with the full rationality of

human persons, so far as that can be ascertained with the resources of a political conception of justice. . . . [T]his reasonable plurality of conflicting and incommensurable doctrines is seen as the characteristic work of practical reason over time under enduring free institutions" (footnotes omitted).

7. Cass Sunstein has a similar theory, the idea of "incompletely theorized agreement" (ITA). See Cass Sunstein, *Legal Reasoning and Political Conflict* (Oxford: Oxford Univ. Press, 1996). Sunstein's notion of an ITA applies primarily to judicial opinions and legal reasoning. The idea is that judges customarily avoid deep foundational theorizing in their opinions as a way of safeguarding pluralism: one may lose a case, based on conventional doctrine, precedent, and legal reasoning, without having one's deepest convictions rejected. Rawls's theory is aimed at a much different issue, the question whether individual citizens need to share a comprehensive moral/theological/foundational worldview to join together in civil society. For various reasons, Rawls says that individuals should have deep foundational beliefs; that society should be organized so that people with reasonable but conflicting basic beliefs can live and function together effectively; and that the overlapping consensus that fosters this effective coexistence should go beyond a mere operational détente, to embrace certain shared or "public" moral values. For a helpful comparison of Rawls's overlapping consensus and Sunstein's ITA, see Scott J. Shapiro, "Fear of Theory," 64 *U. Chi. L. Rev.* 389 (1997)(book review of Cass Sunstein, *Legal Reasoning and Political Conflict*).

8. Rawls, *Political Liberalism*, supra, at 213 ("Public reason is characteristic of a democratic people: it is the reason of its citizens, of those sharing the status of equal citizenship. The subject of their reason is the good of the public: what the political conception of justice requires of society's basic structure of institutions, and of the purposes and ends they are to serve.").

9. Rawls contrasts an overlapping consensus with a purely instrumental, negotiated "truce" among society's factions, which he terms a "modus vivendi." According to Thomas Pogge, "A modus vivendi among groups within [a] society generates [various] . . . dangers and problems. A rule-governed power struggle that is always also a struggle over those rules themselves, such a modus vivendi can provide neither lasting security nor justice on any group's conception of it. All groups invested in their long-term security therefore have reason to prefer, over the modus vivendi model, Rawls' idea of an overlapping consensus. This ideal envisions an institutional order that the various groups endorse as just and are willing to support, even through changes in their respective interests and relative power. Such an institutional order is not a fortuitous and transitory product of negotiation and compromise but an enduring structure based on substantive moral consensus among, and genuine moral allegiance by, its participants." Thomas Pogge, *John Rawls: His Life and Theory of Justice* 36–37 (Michelle Kosch, trans.) (Oxford: Oxford Univ. Press, 2007).

10. This is one aspect of what I refer to throughout this book as my "liberal" theory of property. In coarse terms, this means an idea of property somewhere between a pure libertarian ideal (where property is a coequal right with other basic rights and is administered by a minimalist government whose job largely ends with the granting and enforcing of individual property rights) and a

super-redistributive ideal, à la John Rawls circa 1974, wherein property is a distinctly secondary type of entitlement over which the government has broad and extensive claims in the interests of all citizens. I realize this is a broad middle ground, but at least I am not alone in thinking it is important to stake out and defend this terrain. See, e.g., Carol Rose, *Property and Persuasion* 1–7 (Boulder, CO: Westview Press, 1994) (contrasting economic-based with communitarian understandings of property, and forging a broad middle ground).

11. Jeremy Waldron, *The Right to Private Property* (Oxford: Clarendon Press, 1988).

12. Stephen Munzer, *A Theory of Property* (Cambridge: Cambridge Univ. Press, 1990).

13. See *Oxford English Dictionary* (Oxford: Oxford University Press, 2d ed. 1989), definition of *liberal*: "free from narrow prejudice, open-minded . . . esp. Free from . . . unreasonable prejudice in favor of traditional positions or established institutions; open to the reception of new ideas or proposals for reform." See generally Ruth W. Grant, *John Locke's Liberalism* 190 (Chicago: Univ. of Chicago Press, 1987): "[Locke's liberalism] is also far from a laissez-faire conception of the role of the state in liberal government. . . . [T]he state serves positive public purposes by establishing authoritative conventions and formal procedures that are necessary for the conduct of daily common life, by protecting private rights, and also by making legislative judgments about what actions will best promote the interests of the public."

14. This is also true of a famous example from Jeremy Waldron, where someone drops a diamond ring into a vat of cement as it hardens. This is discussed along with Nozick's tomato juice in Chapter 2.

15. In this, I was reminded of a wonderful quote from the pioneering social psychologist Kurt Lewin: "There is nothing quite so practical as a good theory." Kurt Lewin, *Field Theory in Social Science: Selected Theoretical Papers* 169 (New York: Harper & Row, 1951). For more on Kurt Lewin, see http://en.wikipedia.org/wiki/Kurt_Lewin.

16. Immanuel Kant, *Metaphysical Elements of Justice,* Intro. § C (Ladd, trans.) at 30.

17. See Chapter 3, infra, at 77–78.

18. Robert P. Merges, "The Law and Economics of Employee Inventions," 13 *Harv. J.L. & Tech.* 1 (1999).

19. Lawrence Lessig, *Code Version 2.0* (New York: Basic Books, 2006).

20. Jessica Litman, *Digital Copyright* (New York: Prometheus Books, 2006).

21. See, e.g., Jessica Litman, "The Exclusive Right to Read," 13 *Cardozo Arts & Ent. L.J.* 29 (1994).

2. Locke

1. For libertarian defenses of strong IP rights, see Ayn Rand et al., *Capitalism: The Unknown Ideal* 130–133 (New York: Signet Press, 1986); Tibor R. Machan, "Intellectual Products and the Right to Private Property," avail. at http://rebirthofreason.com/Articles/Machan/Intellectual_Products_and_the_Right_to_Private_Property.shtml (defense of strong IP rights by author of *Libertarianism*

Defended [Hampshire, England: Ashgate Publishing Co., 2006], and *The Right to Private Property* [Stanford, CA: Hoover Institution Press, 2002]). Some libertarians oppose IP protection as an illegitimate extension of government power. See, e.g., Tom G. Palmer, "Are Patents and Copyrights Morally Justified? The Philosophy of Property Rights and Ideal Objects," in "Symposium: Intellectual Property," 13 *Harv. J. L. & Pub. Pol'y* 818 (No. 3, Summer 1990); Stephan Kinsella, *Against Intellectual Property*, Ludwig von Mises Institute, 2008, avail. at http://mises.org/books/against.pdf. For a defense of IP rights against some of these charges, written from the perspective of a strenuous supporter of property rights, see Richard A. Epstein, "Why Libertarians Shouldn't Be (Too) Skeptical about Intellectual Property," Progress & Freedom Foundation, Progress on Point Paper No. 13.4 (February 13, 2006). Epstein argues that "the defenders of intellectual property only have to show that it meets the same kind of standards that are appropriate for physical property." This puts intellectual property on the same footing as real property.

2. There is in fact another relevant academic debate that is logically prior to goodness of fit. A fair amount of controversy surrounds the question whether IP rights are really property rights at all, or whether they should be grouped and discussed under a separate heading altogether. See, e.g., Neil Weinstock Netanel, "Impose a Noncommercial Use Levy to Allow Free Peer-to-Peer File Sharing," 17 *Harv. J.L. & Tech.* 1, 23 (2003) (Congress's first copyright statute [in 1790] established only a few rights for a few categories of works, and therefore the Founding Fathers' vision of copyright was a "decidedly limited grant [that] hardly exemplifies the copyright industries' current private property rhetoric."); Mark A. Lemley, "Romantic Authorship and the Rhetoric of Property," 75 *Tex. L. Rev.* 873, 896 n.123 (1997) ("Patent and copyright law have been around in the United States since its origin, but only recently has the term 'intellectual property' come into vogue."). See generally, Justin Hughes, "Copyright and Incomplete Historiographies: Of Piracy, Propertization, and Thomas Jefferson," 79 *S. Cal. L. Rev.* 993, 1002 (2006) (citing examples of more popular press items asserting that "intellectual property" came into vogue only after 1967, when a United Nations agency, the World Intellectual Property Organization, included the phrase in its official name). But Justin Hughes, in several articles that serve as well-crafted examples of the scholar's art, has disproven these assertions. Hughes shows, for example, that as far back as 1694, John Locke himself was referring to copyright as a form of property, and that phrases such as "literary property" were commonly and continuously used from the seventeenth century on. See Hughes, "Incomplete Historiographies," supra; Justin Hughes, "Locke's 1694 Memorandum (and More Incomplete Copyright Historiographies)," Cardozo Legal Studies Research Paper No. 167 (October, 2006), at 4, avail. at http://papers.ssrn.com/sol3/papers.cfm?abstract_id= 936353 (describing and reprinting a memorandum from John Locke to a member of Parliament, recommending reenactment of the Licensing Act, an early form of copyright, and proposing that when a publisher purchases rights "from authors that now live and write, it may be reasonable to limit their property to a certain number of years after the death of the author, or the first printing of

the book, as, suppose, fifty or seventy years.") (quoting from the memo as reprinted in 1 Lord Peter King, *The Life of John Locke* 375, 387 [London: Henry Colburn, 1830]). On the related scholarly debate about whether Locke's views on the Licensing Act are consistent with his overall property theory, or are instead an indication that Locke thought of intellectual creations as distinct from the subject matter of his property theory, see Simon Stern, "Copyright, Originality, and the Public Domain in Eighteenth-Century England," in *Originality and Intellectual Property in the French and English Enlightenment* 69–101 (Reginald McGinnis, ed.) (London: Routledge, 2008) (arguing that Locke's writings on the Licensing Act provide a glimpse of the fuller Lockean approach to property rights). But see Ruth W. Grant, *John Locke's Liberalism* 113 (Chicago: Univ. of Chicago Press, 1987) (arguing from fragments of Locke's text that he intended that intellectual creations remain in the commons). For a defense of the idea that IP is property, from a different perspective altogether, see Henry Smith, "Intellectual Property as Property: Delineating Entitlements in Information," 117 *Yale L. J.* Pocket Part 87 (2007) (arguing that the right to exclude at the heart of IP law permits a wide range of activities on the part of the owner, most of which need not be specified in detail by legal regulation; and hence that in this respect, the "exclusion strategy" of IP law mirrors that of other forms of property).

3. Lee J. Alston, Gary D. Libecap, & Bernardo Mueller, *Titles, Conflict, and Land Use: The Development of Property Rights and Land Reform on the Brazilian Amazon Frontier* (Ann Arbor: Univ. of Michigan Press, 1999); Lee J. Alston, Gary D. Libecap, & Robert Schneider, "The Determinants and Impact of Property Rights: Land Titles on the Brazilian Frontier," 12 *J.L. Econ. & Org.* 25, 32–33 (1996).

4. See, e.g., James Boyle, *The Public Domain: Enclosing the Commons of the Mind* (New Haven, CT: Yale Univ. Press, 2010); James Boyle, "The Second Enclosure Movement and the Construction of the Public Domain," 66 *L. & Contemp. Probs.* 33 (2003).

5. Vannevar Bush, *Science—The Endless Frontier* (Report to the President of the United States, by Vannevar Bush, Director of the Office of Scientific Research and Development, July 1945), avail. at http://www.nsf.gov/about/history/vbush1945.htm. See also G. Pascal Zachary, *Endless Frontier: Vannevar Bush, Engineer of the American Century* (New York: Free Press, 1997).

6. My view here runs counter to one interpretation of Locke: that Locke speaks only of mixing one's labor with what is already in existence, and therefore necessarily forecloses the idea of original creation. Because a creative person merely mixes his labor with what is already in the commons, the argument goes, he cannot create a truly original idea or work. See Lior Zemer, "The Making of a New Copyright Lockean," 29 *Harv. J.L. & Pub. Pol'y* 891 (2006). This perspective concentrates only on that which the labor is mixed with, items found in the common. It therefore obviously overlooks half of the Lockean equation, the labor contribution of an individual appropriator.

7. John Locke, *An Essay Concerning Human Understanding*, Epistle (Peter H. Nidditch, ed.) (Oxford: Oxford Univ. Press, 1979), at 10.

8. John Locke, *Two Treatises of Government, Second Treatise,* § 32 (Cambridge, Cambridge Univ. Press, 3rd ed., 1988) (Peter Laslett, ed.) (hereafter "Laslett"), at 290 ("As much Land as a Man Tills, Plants, Improves, Cultivates, and can use the Product of, so much is his Property.").

9. Locke, *Second Treatise* § 25, Laslett at 286.

10. Locke, *Second Treatise* § 26, Laslett at 286. It should be noted here that, despite his theological tone and imagery, Locke was by no means writing from within contemporary religious orthodoxy. There are in his writings significant departures from the traditional Christian natural law viewpoint. See Peter C. Myers, "Between Divine and Human Sovereignty: The State of Nature and the Basis of Locke's Political Thought," 27 *Polity* 629–649 (No. 4, Summer 1995).

11. Locke's underlying purpose in the *Second Treatise* is to counter the view that the British monarch is anointed by God and hence cannot be replaced by the people. One argument for the divine right theory Locke opposed was that the sovereign held title to all the land in the state by virtue of direct descent from Adam and Eve, as described in the biblical Book of Genesis. This divine descent concept relied on a parallel between land title and political sovereignty. To attack the latter, Locke had to address the former. Locke advocated an alternative: that the earth had been given to all people in common, rather than to the first people as described in the Bible. Locke's theory raised a challenge: how to explain individual ownership against the backdrop of original common ownership. This is where individual appropriation enters the story: "[I]f it be difficult to make out Property, upon a supposition, that God gave the World to Adam and his Posterity in common; it is impossible that any Man, but one universal Monarch, should have any Property, upon a supposition, that God gave the World to Adam, and his Heirs in Succession, exclusive of all the rest of his Posterity. But I shall endeavour to shew, how Men might come to have a Property in several parts of that which God gave to Mankind in common, . . . without any express Compact of all the Commoners." Locke, *Second Treatise* § 25, Laslett, at 286.

12. Locke, *Second Treatise* § 26, Laslett at 286.

13. Locke, *Second Treatise* § 26, Laslett at 286 (emphasis in original).

14. A. John Simmons, *The Lockean Theory of Rights* 222 (Princeton, NJ: Princeton Univ. Press, 2002) (Locke "relies exclusively on neither purely theological nor purely secular arguments, but a liberal mix of the two. . . . [and is] pluralistic and moderate.").

15. On this point, see David Post, "Jeffersonian Revisions of Locke: Education, Property Rights, and Liberty," 47 *J. Hist. Ideas* 147 (1986) (reading Locke as saying that individuals who have used their labor to appropriate—to acquire property—are those who have most effectively followed the divine directive).

16. The idea of a one-to-one mapping, which I will refer to often, is derived from Jeremy Waldron's description of private property as a system based on "name/ object correlation." Waldron says: "In a private property system, a rule is laid down that, in the case of each object, the individual person whose name is attached to that object is to determine how the object shall be used and by whom." Jeremy Waldron, *The Right to Private Property* 39 (Oxford: Oxford Univ. Press, 1988).

17. Locke, *Second Treatise* § 27, Laslett at 287–288.

18. It is this feature that leads Locke scholars to emphasize the egalitarian foundation of Locke's thought. See, e.g., Jeremy Waldron, *God, Locke and Equality: Christian Foundations in Locke's Political Thought* (Cambridge: Cambridge Univ. Press, 2002); Simmons, *The Lockean Theory of Rights* 79–87. For commentary on the larger sense in which Locke's thought supports a liberal egalitarianism, see Samuel Fleischacker, *A Short History of Distributive Justice* 36–37 (Cambridge, MA: Harvard Univ. Press 2004).

19. Locke, *Second Treatise* § 28, Laslett at 288: "And will anyone say that he had no right to those Acorns or Apples he thus appropriated, because he had not the consent of all Mankind to make them his? Was it a Robbery thus to assume to himself what belonged to all in Common? If such a consent as that was necessary, Man had starved, notwithstanding the Plenty God had given to him." See also Locke, *Second Treatise* § 25, Laslett at 286 ("I will endeavor to shew, how Men might come to have a property in several parts of that which God gave to mankind in common, and without any express Compact of all the Commoners.").

20. In this sense, Locke's theory of appropriation has at its core a concept that is well known in economics today: transaction costs. In the passage cited, Locke is not terribly clear on what kind of consent might be required for appropriation, but whatever its form, express consent in this situation would involve massive transaction costs and thus be impossible in a practical sense. Cf. Paul Russell, "Locke on Express and Tacit Consent: Misinterpretations and Inconsistencies," 14 *Pol. Theory* 291, 291–306 (No. 2, May 1986). Scholars have argued that Locke's concern with what we now call transaction costs is what sets his theory apart from those of his predecessors, particularly Hugo Grotius and Samuel Pufendorf. See Adam Mossof, "What Is Property? Putting the Pieces Back Together Again," 45 *Ariz. L. Rev.* 371, 385–390 (2003). I have drawn on these themes of owner's consent and transaction costs when discussing an extension of Locke's thinking about property rights, the case of group labor, or collective rights. See Robert P. Merges, "Locke for the Masses," 36 *Hofstra L. Rev.* 1179 (2008). Similar ideas figure prominently in Chapter 7, *infra*, which deals extensively with the relationship between individual IP rights and the transaction costs of administering them in a complex economy.

21. Cf. Timothy Sandefur, "A Critique of Ayn Rand's Theory of Intellectual Property Rights," 9 *J. Ayn Rand Stud.* 139–161 (No. 1, Fall 2007) (the nonrivalrous nature of information "deflates any hasty analogy between intellectual property and tangible property.").

22. See "Locke's Provisos," [Manuscript at p. 90] below. Briefly, I argue there for an IP system that (1) permits widespread initial appropriation, in the interest of creating new and original works, while (2) safeguarding the principle of equality of opportunity for other appropriators, and users/consumers of intellectual assets, through limits on what and how much may be appropriated in any particular case.

23. Richard Ashcraft, "Locke's Political Philosophy," in *The Cambridge Companion to Locke* (Vere Chappell, ed.) (Cambridge: Cambridge Univ. Press, 1994), 226, 246–247.

24. It is important to distinguish this point from the idea that Locke's theory states a utilitarian justification of property rights. The Lockean theory presupposes an individual right to thrive. Utilitarianism fits uncomfortably with the notion of rights. For utilitarians, there are in the first instance only preferences, which must be aggregated to produce the highest net social welfare. Rights will often get in the way of this, since they cannot by definition be overridden by countervaluing preferences. See generally H. L. A. Hart, "Between Utility and Rights," in *Essays in Jurisprudence and Philosophy* (Oxford: Clarendon Press, 1983), and Waldron, *Right to Private Property* 5–25. Thus for utilitarians, the only goal that matters is maximizing total utility. Now it happens that Locke believes full recognition of property rights will call forth productive labor and thus in general lead to a more abundant society. See, e.g., Locke, *Second Treatise* § 37, Laslett at 294 ("[H]e who appropriates land to himself by his labor does not lessen but increase the stock of mankind", because labor supplies the lion's share of value for items that are taken from the state of nature); Waldron, *Right to Private Property* 215 ("[A]llowing appropriation by a few might (as Locke believed) increase the net social product [citing *Second Treatise* §§ 36–37].*"). In this sense there is significant overlap between Lockean theory and utilitarianism. Nevertheless, while Locke's theory reflects a deep concern for incentives and consequences, it (1) points to an individual right to property and (2) completely avoids adherence to a calculus of preferences—and therefore is quite distinct from utilitarian justifications of IP. For an entirely unpersuasive argument that Locke is in fact a utilitarian, see Viktor Mayer-Schönberger, "In Search of the Story: Narratives of Intellectual Property," 10 *Va. J.L. & Tech.* 11, par. 9 (2005) ("Expanding on Lockean influence, copyright was seen not just as an extension of his labor theory of property, but also as one of his more general ideas of utilitarianism.").

25. The irrelevance of Locke to IP rights is argued in Seana Valentine Shiffrin, "Lockean Arguments for Intellectual Property Rights," in *New Essays in the Legal and Political Theory of Property* (Stephen R. Munzer, ed.) (Cambridge: Cambridge Univ. Press 2002), at 139–167; see especially page 143, where Professor Shiffrin introduces her idea that Locke's theory is closely connected to initial common ownership, and that therefore, because of the nature of intellectual property, "Locke's view does not endorse Lockean appropriation of most intellectual products."

26. Seana Valentine Shiffrin, for one, believes that for just this reason no amount of adjustment can make Locke fit the realities of intellectual property. One important aspect of her argument is precisely the nonrivalrous nature of intellectual creations: "The fully effective use of an idea, proposition, concept, method, invention, melody, picture or sculpture generally does not require, by its nature, prolonged exclusive use or control. Generally, one's use or consumption of an idea . . . and so forth, is fully compatible with others' use, even their simultaneous use. Moreover, intellectual products often require at least some fairly concurrent, shared (though not necessarily coordinated) use for their full value to be achieved and appreciated. Ideas and their expressions are usually most effective when contemplated by many—when their truths are

commonly appreciated and implemented, and their flaws discovered and shared. Indeed, there is a social presumption and expressions are the object of open dialogue, exchange, and discussion. Attempts to control, suppress, manipulate, or monopolize ideas and information run counter to the intellectual spirit of open discussions that promote learning and appreciation for the truth." Shiffrin, *Lockean Arguments*, supra, at 156. In the text accompanying this note I address the statement that an intellectual creation "by its nature" need not be individually appropriated to be useful, as well as the broader idea that Locke's paramount concern is with the "nature" of objects people might find and potentially appropriate. Other aspects of Shiffrin's position are addressed throughout this book: (1) in this chapter, as well as Chapter 8 on digital technology, I defend the idea that exclusive rights in creative works are necessary to permit creative professionals to thrive; and (2) just below, in my comments on removal, and in Chapter 5 on midlevel principles, the section on the nonremoval principle, I refute the argument, implicit in what Shiffrin says, that exclusive IP rights completely preclude others' use of ideas and concepts. Shiffrin says that in Locke's theory labor grounds property claims under two important conditions: (1) a backdrop of common ownership—what she calls "the presumption for common ownership" (at page 148), and (2) the notion that labor is justified as a ground for property only when it is labor that adds the greatest increment of value to a labor-plus-found-thing combination (page 152, rejecting interpretations of Locke that do not emphasize the centrality of "the nature of the thing to be used and the natural requirements of its use"). I of course recognize that common ownership is a starting point for Locke, but implicitly reject a reading of Locke under which common ownership remains always the preferred policy; I address this issue in my treatment of the proportionality principle in Chapter 6.

27. One complication arises from the fact that IP law is traditionally applied on a country-by-country basis, so that technically, something may be protected by an IP right in one country yet not protected in another country. The precise makeup of the public domain may differ from one country to the next, in other words. See Andrew R. Sommer, "Trouble on the Commons: A Lockean Justification for Patent Law," 87 *J. Pat. & Trademark Off. Soc'y* 141 (2005). If the basic principles of IP protection are applied uniformly, however, there should be roughly equal conformity in the IP protection granted across countries, and hence a fairly even and predictable worldwide public domain.

28. Another way to say this is that autonomy, an important Lockean value, is not the same as primitive self-interest. It is worthwhile to consider that autonomy means, literally, self-rule or the law (nomos) within oneself. Many believe that internally residing norms come ultimately from a collective source, and that they have an other-regarding dimension as well. Thus respect for IP rights may flow from a source of norms that precedes the formation of a formal state, even though these rights are relevant only to economic conditions that are far from the Lockean state of nature. The normative source of IP rights may precede (conceptually) the formation of a polity or civil society, even though the subject of these rights, information goods, is a far more common occurrence in

the type of advanced economy that depends on a well-established and functioning polity.

29. Stated somewhat differently, people can share an understanding of effective rights, or social facts, such as the rightness of surviving and thriving on the basis of information goods and legal rights over them.

30. Locke, *Second Treatise* § 27, Laslett at 288.

31. I want to emphasize here that I aim my comments at the "early Waldron" of "Two Worries about Mixing" (1983); the "later Waldron" of *God, Locke and Equality* (2002) takes a very different tack on the mixing issue, emphasizing in particular two points about the specialness of labor: the "teleological" nature of Locke's theory, where labor is the means by which humans carry out the divine order to survive and thrive on earth; and the (concomitant) unique quality of labor, as something different in kind from other "substances," which confers special qualities on any substance or resource with which it comes to be mixed. See Jeremy Waldron, "Two Worries about Mixing One's Labor," 33 *Phil. Q.* 37–44 (1983); Waldron, *God, Locke and Equality* (2002).

32. While it is true that Locke's state of nature is itself a thought experiment, it has the purpose or function of grounding claims to very practical resources, viz., those needed for immediate survival. So the state of nature is in service of very pragmatic ends. The tomato juice and ring examples are a far cry from this; what pragmatic goal is served by claims to the entire ocean, or to a vat of cured cement?

33. Of course, there is a small degree of pure labor involved in the Nozick and Waldron examples. The tomato juice must be poured and the ring must be thrown. But neither author dwells at any length on the special status of the labor involved, or (most important), the amount of labor involved, which is of course trivial when compared to the other assets in the stories (the ocean, the vat of cement). All the attention is given to an isolated item of tangible property, viz., the tomato juice and the ring.

34. For a detailed account of this "workmanship model" of labor and ownership, see James Tully, *A Discourse on Property: John Locke and His Adversaries* 35–42, 109–110 (Cambridge: Cambridge Univ. Press, 1980). Tully argues that the workmanship model is based on an analogy: as God is related to, or "owns," that which He makes, so humans are related to, or own, that which they make. Jeremy Waldron, in a typically insightful passage on these matters, says that "the importance of this analogy in Locke's thought has been exaggerated." Jeremy Waldron, *God, Locke and Equality*, supra, 163. Waldron lays significant stress on passages in which Locke describes labor less as a Godlike act of creation and more of a responsibility humans must discharge to fulfill the divine command to survive and thrive. To be fair, however, it should be noted that Tully employs the God-man workmanship concept primarily in service of his argument that labor for Locke is a highly purposeful concept that combines intent and actions. Just as God created humans with and for a purpose, so real labor involves action directed at an intended aim. Stated this way, there is far less disagreement on this point between Tully and Waldron (or at least the later Waldron—his original critique of the whole labor and mixing idea is

from 1983) than may at first appear, since Waldron too emphasizes that underlying humans' right to appropriate things is an underlying (divine) purpose—to survive and thrive: "[Locke] talks of our right to make use of things that are useful or necessary to our being. But the right is also one of those Lockean rights that is also a duty. Each person is directed 'to the use of those things, which [are] serviceable for his Subsistence' [Locke's *First Treatise* § 86]. Each is required to help himself. And so his having the right to help himself to natural resources is intelligible not just in the light of his own purposes for himself, but in the light of God's purposes for him. . . . [T]his also provides a theological context for the particular mode of helping oneself—labor—that Locke thinks God has commanded. Laboring is not just something we happen to do to resources . . . : it is the appropriate mode of helping ourselves to resources given what resources are *for*." Waldron, *God, Locke and Equality*, supra, at 160 (footnote omitted; emphasis in original). Cf. Waldron, "Two Worries about Mixing," supra (technical critique of Locke, including the "diamond ring in the vat of cement" hypothetical that I discuss infra).

35. See Thom Brooks, *Hegel's Political Philosophy* (Edinburgh: Edinburgh Univ. Press, 2007), Chapter 2, Property, at 29–38, 32 (stating Hegel's views: "When I shape the world insofar as I claim something as mine, this activity is the most fundamental way that my free will becomes external and actualized."); Waldron, *Right to Private Property*, at Chapter 10, "Hegel's Discussion of Property," 343–389 (emphasizing distributional implications of Hegel's approach to property). Note that Brooks treats Hegel's statements on property as illustrative more of his approach to the development of the free will than to issues of value, distribution, etc., usually associated with property theory; Brooks believes that Hegel's fuller treatment of civil society incorporates these aspects of property theory. See Brooks, *Hegel's Political Philosophy*, at Chapter 6, "Law," 82–95.

36. Others have noticed this too. See Steven J. Horowitz, "Competing Lockean Claims to Virtual Property," 20 *Harv. J.L. & Tech.* 43 (2007) (In online "virtual" worlds, Lockean notions of labor and property are being used to examine and define the respective rights of virtual world players and game operators.)

37. Compare the following uses in context, all roughly contemporaneous to Locke: "Some ware all small ribban, others brode ribbans, others broad and small mixed." Lady M. Bertie, 12th Report of the Historical Manuscripts Committee Appendix to vol. 22 (1670), quoted in "Mix," the Oxford English Dictionary (version 3.1 [electronic] ed., 2004); "There was a mixture of company." Jonathan Swift, 1712–13, Journal to Stella, quoted in "Mixture," id.; "That mixtures in garments, seedes, and the like, were forbidden by the Law of Moses." Purchas, *Pilgrimage* (1613), at 62, quoted in "Mixture," id.

38. John Locke, *Two Treatises of Government*, *Second Treatise* ("2T") § 28, Laslett at 228 (emphasis added).

39. It is interesting in this connection that long-standing common law property doctrines follow the contours of a principle that is very closely related to annexation. I speak here of the ancient principle of accession, under which the owner of an animal normally owns its offspring; the owner of a plant owns its

fruits; the owner of monetary principal owns the interest that accrues on it; etc. See Thomas W. Merrill, "Accession and Original Ownership," 1 *J. Legal Analysis* 459 (2009). A related idea, quite relevant here, is that of *specificatio* in Roman law, which means the analysis of ownership when party A contributes starting materials and party B uses them to make something novel. See Barry Nicholas, *An Introduction to Roman Law* 136–138 (Oxford: Clarendon Press, 1962); Thomas W. Merrill, "Accession," supra. For applications of *specificatio* to IP law, see Russ VerSteeg, "The Roman Law Roots of Copyright," 59 *Md. L. Rev.* 522 (2000); Aaron Keyt, Comment, "An Improved Framework for Music Plagiarism Litigation," 76 *Cal. L. Rev.* 421 (1988).

40. Jeremy Waldron shows convincingly that Locke's account of appropriation is rooted in the biblical admonition to man to "be fruitful and multiply." Waldron, *God, Locke and Equality* at 24. Ruth W. Grant also highlights the purposive quality of Locke's writing. Sir Robert Filmer had argued that God bestowed political authority on a given monarch initially, and it thereafter passes to the monarch's offspring in an unbroken chain. In one of many passages refuting an aspect of Filmer's monarchical theory, Locke disagrees that political authority works this way. He also states that even with respect to property, ownership has an unselfish "trust-like" aspect, in which parents hold property partly to pass it to their children by inheritance. This comes in the context of one of Locke's refutations of the divine right of the monarch, his argument distinguishing property, which was intended to be passed to our offspring, from political power, which was not. According to Ruth Grant, "In developing the distinction between property and political power with respect to inheritance, Locke refers to a reason for a right . . . ; the end or purpose of the right, rather than its origin. Government is for the preservation of right and property from the injury of others and is for the benefit of the governed. Property, originating from man's right to use inferior creatures for his subsistence and destroy them if need be, is for the benefit of the proprietor. Rule or dominion has 'another original and a different end' from property in the creatures of the earth. A child's dependence on his parents for subsistence gives him a right to inherit their property for his own benefit. But if his father had any political power, it 'was vested in him, for the good and behoof of others, and therefore the Son cannot Claim or Inherit it by a Title, which is founded only on his own private good and advantage' . . . [*First Treatise* § 93]. A claim to property or rule must accord with the purpose, end or reason for property or rule." Ruth W. Grant, *John Locke's Liberalism* 61 (Chicago: Univ. of Chicago Press, 1987).

41. See generally Tully, *Discourse on Property,* supra, at 61: "Locke's property has a specified end," that is, a goal, a purpose: sustenance and maintenance, as opposed to pure despotic dominion (as was posited by Locke's great rival Robert Filmer). Tully, like many others, describes Locke's view of individual ownership as a stewardship relationship (holding property to serve a higher directive or goal)—i.e., stewardship for a purpose. While Tully makes some instructive points about the purposiveness of appropriation in Locke, he clearly carries the argument too far when he argues that Locke's theory supports only

"use rights," as opposed to true, exclusive, individual property rights. For critiques of Tully on this point, see Simmons, *Lockean Theory of Rights* 234; Waldron, *Right to Private Property* 156–157.

42. In another passage, Jeremy Waldron states this idea quite clearly: "[I]n performing [an action] A, x [the owner] intends to affect r [the resource] in some way. This is characteristic of Labour Theories of acquisition, such as Locke's theory. The acquisitive action, A, on the Lockean view, is the action of laboring on the resource: one removes something out of its natural state by hunting and killing it, or by gathering it, or, in the case of a piece of land, by tilling, planting, cultivating, or otherwise improving it. In all these instances, some physical change is wrought on the object. (Locke's example of the hare, which is to be the property of its pursuer even before he catches it, is an exception to the general character of his theory in this respect.)" Waldron, *Right to Private Property* 263–264 (emphasis in original, footnotes omitted). The final sentence refers to Locke's recognition of a (perhaps inchoate) property right for one in "hot pursuit" of wild game—the scenario of the famous property case of *Pierson v. Post, 3 Cai. R. 175, 2 Am. Dec. 264 (N.Y. 1805)*. Whether the "hare example" is an exception to the general character of Locke's theory, it is interesting for two reasons: (1) it is further evidence of a point I made earlier, that Locke's theory requires not "blending" but "joining" or "annexing" of labor to unowned resources (there being no "mixing" of the pursuer's efforts and the hare itself, at least not until it is caught); and (2) Locke's theory does not require physical alteration as a result of the joining of labor, which makes it easy to apply that theory in the IP context, as I do implicitly throughout this chapter.

43. One obvious objection is that survival and physical flourishing are immediate and direct benefits, and thus far removed from the financial rewards delivered by IP protection in a modern economy. In Chapter 7 I show how the extra income that comes with IP protection helps creative professionals make a decent living, which I argue is the contemporary version of human thriving championed by Locke. At the same time, in Chapter 9 I argue that where IP rights are an immediate threat to the survival of others—as with some patents on life-saving pharmaceutical products in developing countries—those rights must give way to the claims of the destitute under Locke's charity proviso.

44. A. John Simmons says that for Locke, labor should not be thought of as a "thing" at all: "Let us try to think of labor in Locke's texts, then, not as a kind of substance, to be literally mixed or blended with an object, but as a kind of purposive activity aimed at satisfying needs or supplying the conveniences of life. Labor in this sense can include (be mixed with) external things in a fairly straightforward way. As we think about, choose, or carry out various aspects of our life plans (our projects and pursuits), external things are often central to them. . . . We bring things within our purposive activities ('mixing our labor' with them) when we gather them, enclose them, and use them in other productive ways." Simmons, *Lockean Theory of Rights* 273. See also Roberta Kwall, "The Author as Steward 'For Limited Times': A Review of the Idea of Authorship in Copyright," 88 *B.U. L. Rev.* 685, 692 (2008) (book review of Lior Zemer, *The Idea of Authorship in Copyright* [Hampshire, England: Ashgate Publishing Co.,

2007]) ("[A]ccording to a Lockean theory of copyright law, an author's expression, having been created through his mental labor, is an ideal object for commodification. A Lockean theory of copyright law, therefore, defines labor, and the external product in which it results, in terms of potential commodification. Moreover, once something becomes externalized, the object loses the aspect of it characterized by personal autonomy as an inalienable gift from God because the object itself is capable of commodification." (footnotes omitted).

45. In Chapter 7, I explain specifically how IP rights help professional creators maintain their independence and make a decent living. So IP rights, in these cases, help laboring people to thrive in a modern economy—consistent, I would claim, with the purpose Locke identified for property. In Chapter 6, I explore further the idea of "proportionality" between labor expended and the scope of resulting property rights, one example of the midlevel principles described in Chapter 1 and laid out in more detail in Chapter 5.

46. Locke, *Second Treatise* § 27, Laslett at 288.

47. Locke, *Second Treatise* § 31, Laslett at 290. The language of limitation could hardly be more forceful: "The same Law of Nature that . . . give[s] us Property, does also bound that Property too."

48. Emphasis in the original.

49. Locke, *Second Treatise* § 34, Laslett at 291.

50. In an oft-cited article from 1979, Waldron argued that the language of § 27—"no Man but he can have a claim to what [his labor] is once joyned to, at least where there is enough, and as good left in common for others"— means that property is justified when the sufficiency condition is met, but that compliance with the sufficiency proviso is not necessary for a valid property claim. Jeremy Waldron, "Enough and As Good Left for Others," 29 Phil. Q. 319–328 (1979) (arguing, among other things, that "at least where" X means "certainly in those cases where X is true," but not that X is a requirement in all cases. See also Jeremy Waldron, *The Right to Private Property* 209–215 (1988) (expanding on the earlier article, and emphasizing that eschewing appropriation in a situation of scarcity would condemn a would-be appropriator to death, which is at odds with the fundamental reason why resources were provided to mankind in the first place, to permit survival). For a similar perspective, see Judith Jarvis Thomson, "Property Acquisition," 73 *J. Phil.* (Ann. Mtg. Vol.) 664A–666A (October, 1976) (because there is no way that land appropriation can take place and yet comply with the sufficiency proviso, this proviso must therefore be, in logical terms, a sufficient condition, and not a necessary one).

51. There are also other indications in Locke's text that sufficiency was not intended to supplement spoliation as a full-fledged proviso. See Jeremy Waldron, "Enough and as Good Left for Others," 29 *Phil.* Q. 319–328, 320–324 (1979).

52. Simmons, *Lockean Theory of Rights* 286 (citing 2 H. R. Fox Bourne, *The Life of John Locke* 536 [London: Henry S. King 1876]).

53. Other passages in the property chapter say the same thing. When we read that "Nothing was made by God for Man to spoil or destroy," and recall Locke's consistent emphasis on the purpose of appropriation as furthering human

thriving, it is very difficult to justify appropriations that lead to waste or spoilage.

54. Locke says at one point that "he that leaves as much as another can make use of, does as good as take nothing at all" (paragraph 33). And if I effectively take nothing, what harm can follow from my use (or nonuse) of what I do in fact take? So long as others are not harmed, it is irrelevant what happens to what I do in fact take, whether I choose to employ it fully or let it spoil. Though perhaps plausible, it is very difficult to reconcile this view with Locke's repeatedly expressed distaste for waste. The best one can say, perhaps, is that Locke can sometimes be maddeningly inconsistent.

55. Lockean scholar A. John Simmons, who is in general quite good on the importance of this proviso, states the spoilage rationale in terms of preventing harm to third parties. Simmons, *Lockean Theory,* supra, at 286 ("If I waste what others would otherwise use, I deny them the opportunity of productive use (and show that I do not respect them or their projects). Since their right is to make property by their labor in whatever fair share of the common they choose, I infringe their right by precluding their choice of the goods I waste." [footnote omitted]). Briefly, Simmons implies that spoilage furthers a more general other-regarding policy, as compared to the sufficiency proviso. Forbidding waste protects rights that sufficiency does not. One can satisfy the sufficiency proviso—leaving as much and as good for others—yet still deprive those others of some resources they would like to take. Implicit in this view is the notion that while resources may be objectively interchangeable to some degree, individuals may subjectively prefer some resources over others. If person B would prefer a certain resource, and that resource is taken and wasted by A, B is harmed, even though B had available "enough and as good" (viewed objectively) as A. Although Simmons does not say so, perhaps the spoilage proviso could also be seen as protecting a wider range of third parties than the sufficiency proviso. "As much, and as good for others" might include a narrower class of "others"—for example, perhaps only people known by the initial appropriator, or alive when the initial appropriation occurs. Prohibiting spoilage might protect people far removed in time and space, those far away or far in the future. (This works only for resources that do not naturally spoil on their own; think of iron ore, removed from the ground and smelted, which then sits and rusts.) Because I find this "other-regarding" explanation less than airtight, I am open to the view that for Locke the spoilage proviso is a different kind of duty altogether—a duty to God, so to speak, and not directly to others. Even this absolutist view (which has a Kantian flavor) might be seen ultimately as other-regarding; perhaps the duty is absolute to prevent short-sighted appropriators from fooling themselves into believing they have accounted for everyone else when in fact they have not.

56. Gordon's overall thesis is as follows: "The proviso that 'enough and as good [be] left' lies at the center of this Article's thesis: that creators should have property in their original works, only provided that such grant of property does no harm to other persons' equal abilities to create or to draw upon the preexisting cultural matrix and scientific heritage. All persons are equal and

have an equal right to the common." Wendy J. Gordon, "A Property Right in Self-Expression: Equality and Individualism in the Natural Law of Intellectual Property," 102 *Yale L.J.* 1533, 1563–1564 (1993) (footnotes omitted).

57. Gordon, "Natural Law of IP," supra, at 1567. Gordon continues: "Giving A ownership of the enzyme or a patent over its method of manufacture would leave the proviso unsatisfied, for even if A's appropriation leaves 'as much' for others, it does not leave "enough, and as good." Mere quantitative identity is not enough. This is essentially a reliance argument: having changed people's position, the inventor cannot then refuse them the tools they need for surviving under their new condition. . . . Intellectual products, once they are made public in an interdependent world, change that world. To deal with those changes, users may have need of a freedom inconsistent with first creators' property rights. If they are forbidden to use the creation that was the agent of the change, all they will have to work from will be the now devalued common. The proviso eliminates this danger. It guarantees an equality between earlier and later creators. The proviso would thus ensure later comers a right to the broad freedom of expression, interpretation, and reaction which earlier creators had, a right which cannot be outweighed by other sorts of benefits." Gordon, "Natural Law of IP," supra, at 1533, 1567–1568; 1570.

58. See Steven N. S. Cheung, "Property Rights and Invention," in 8 *Research in Law and Economics: The Economics of Patents and Copyrights* 5, 6 (John Palmer and Richard O. Zerbe Jr., eds., 1986). Wendy Gordon refers to this as the "something-for-nothing thesis." See Gordon, "Natural Law of IP," supra, at 1533, 1566. A representative statement of the idea may be found in John Stuart Mill's *Principles of Political Economy:* "The institution of property, when limited to its essential elements, consists in the recognition, in each person, of a right to the exclusive disposal of what he or she have produced by their own exertions, or received either by gift or by fair agreement, without force or fraud, from those who produced it. The foundation of the whole is the right of producers to what they themselves have produced. . . ." John Stuart Mill, *Principles of Political Economy with some of their Applications to Social Philosophy*, Bk. 2, Ch. 2, par. 2 (1842), avail. at http://www.econlib.org/library/Mill/mlP15.html#II.2.2. Mill continues: "It is no hardship to any one to be excluded from what others have produced: they were not bound to produce it for his use, and he loses nothing by not sharing in what otherwise would not have existed at all. But it is some hardship to be born into the world and to find all nature's gifts previously engrossed, and no place left for the newcomer." Mill, *Principles of Political Economy*, Bk. 2, Ch. 2, pars. 25–26 (1842), http://www.econlib.org/library/Mill/mlP15.html#II.2.26.

59. See, e.g., Motion Picture Patents Co. v. Universal Film Mfg. Co., 243 U.S. 502, 510 (1917) (Holmes, J., dissenting) (arguing that, since patentee has right to withhold invention from the public entirely, it necessarily has the right to license a patent under restrictive conditions).

60. See Jeffrey Kuhn & Robert P. Merges, "An Estoppel Doctrine for Patented Standards," 97 *Cal. L. Rev.* 1 (2009) (patentee-induced reliance by standard users should give rise to continuing use rights despite patentee's decision to

enforce patent); Robert P. Merges, "Who Owns the Charles River Bridge? Intellectual Property and Competition in the Software Industry," avail. at http://papers.ssrn.com/sol3/papers.cfm?abstract_id=208089 (discussing the concept of "technological genericide," whereby the IP rights in a wildly successful technological standard might be reduced over time because of the reliance of users and the need for competitive alternative technologies).

61. See Robert P. Merges, "Locke for the Masses," 36 *Hofstra L. Rev.* 1179 (2008).

62. See, e.g., Rosemary J. Coombe, *The Cultural Life of Intellectual Properties: Authorship, Appropriation and the Law* 124–127 (Durham, NC: Duke University Press, 1998) (describing early fan magazine participants and their desire to recast canonical material such as *Star Trek* characters to express important values and alternative, often "transgressive," visions of the characters). The reliance concept finds its way into many other critiques as well, though not always framed in Lockean terms and not always tied to Gordon's terms of debate. See, e.g., Jack M. Balkin, "Digital Speech and Democratic Culture: A Theory of Freedom of Expression for the Information Society," 79 *N.Y.U. L. Rev.* 1, 12 (2004): "Precisely because of the astounding success of mass media in capturing the public imagination during the twentieth century, the products of mass media, now everywhere present, are central features of everyday life and thought. Mass media products—popular movies, popular music, trademarks, commercial slogans, and commercial iconography—have become the common reference points of popular culture. Hence, it is not surprising that they have become the raw materials of the bricolage that characterizes the Internet."

63. I also think it is more possible to avoid the onslaught of culture than many seem to believe. See Robert P. Merges, "Locke Remixed ;-)," 40 *U.C. Davis L. Rev.* 1259 (2007). See also Kenneth Einar Himma, "The Legitimacy of Intellectual Property Rights: The Irrelevance of Two Conceptions of an Information Commons" (May 1, 2007), avail. at http://ssrn.com/abstract=983961. Himma argues that Locke's sufficiency proviso does not apply to appropriations of intellectual assets, because such appropriation does not interfere with human survival. Himma acknowledges that a life without information would not be "meaningful or flourishing" but insists that such concerns are beyond Locke. I agree that the sufficiency proviso is often over-used by critics of IP. But in my understanding Locke was concerned not merely with human survival, but also with human flourishing, which requires some way to appropriate items out of the information commons by expending labor. Thus for me, the sufficiency proviso is a necessary adjunct to initial appropriation, in the case of IP as with property generally; but, with Himma, I disagree with many who believe that application of this proviso in the case of IP leads to a restrictive and minimalist regime of IP protection.

64. A common motif in this literature is the repeated anecdote about a threatened enforcement action that never came to fruition, or the "chilling effect" of potential enforcement actions. For a pragmatic discussion of the de facto expansion of user rights in an era of difficult enforcement economics, see Chapter 8, "Property in the Digital Era."

65. See, e.g., Eldred v. Ashcroft, 587 U.S. 186, 221 (2003): "The First Amendment securely protects the freedom to make—or decline to make—one's own speech; it bears less heavily when speakers assert the right to make other people's speeches. To the extent such assertions raise First Amendment concerns, copyright's built-in free speech safeguards are generally adequate to address them." See also Chapter 8 on digital technology (discussing how high enforcement costs have created broader de facto rights for users of digital works).

66. Gordon Hull, "Clearing the Rubbish: Locke, the Waste Proviso, and the Moral Justification of Intellectual Property," 23 *Pub. Aff. Q.* 67 (2009), unpub. version avail. at http://ssrn.com/abstract=1082597, at 23 ("intellectual labor is presupposed in all other forms of labor.").

67. Hull, "Clearing the Rubbish," supra. By contrast, the philosopher Kenneth Eimar Himma has argued that the sufficiency proviso does not fit the case of IP at all. Himma, Property Rights, supra. Despite my respect for Himma's philosophical work on IP, I take a more expansive and figurative approach to the application of Locke's writings on property.

68. "Locke's provisos—specifically the widely neglected spoilage proviso—would sharply limit the scope of any entitlements." Hull, "Clearing the Rubbish," supra at 2.

69. Id. at 26. Hull then articulates a fuller version of the Lockean principle: "[S]poilage occurs when (a) there is irrevocably unmet demand, (b) the goods to satisfy that demand already exist, and (c) property claims prevent satisfaction of those demands." Hull, "Clearing the Rubbish," at 29.

70. See, e.g., Benjamin G. Damstedt, "Limiting Locke: A Natural Law Justification for the Fair Use Doctrine," 112 *Yale L.J.* 1179 (2003).

71. On which, see earlier this chapter, the section on "Locke's Common and the Public Domain."

72. Damstedt, "Limiting Locke," supra, at 1182–1183: "The waste prohibition is of negligible importance for tangible goods, but is immensely important when constructing a Lockean theory of intangible goods. . . . The nonrivalrous nature of intangible goods can be characterized as the production of an unlimited number of 'intangible units' at the initial creation of any intangible good. Although the limited number of units of a tangible good can usually be converted into nonwasting money, the unlimited number of intangible units suggests that the laborer will not be able or willing to convert all of the intangible units into money whenever any intangible good is produced. The combination of nonconversion and nonuse constitutes a violation of the waste prohibition."

73. I am assuming away price discrimination here.

74. This may seem harsh. One might reasonably ask, does Locke's theory really dictate that many people, willing to pay a "reasonable" price for something, can be deprived of it simply because it is owned by someone whose expenditure of labor justifies a property right over it? At the outset, it is important to remember that the choice between total dominion and reasonable access by all comers may not be as stark as it at first appears. The sufficiency, spoliation, and charity provisos, especially the latter, may soften the impact of property

rights in such cases. Even so, it is probably unavoidable that property rights may clash with one's sense of fairness in some cases. For example, there may be a legitimate argument that even though a patent on a cancer therapy is well deserved given the work involved; even though the patent owner is making it available to some population (those willing to pay the asking price); and even though the patent owner is a good citizen and donates the therapy to people who are destitute, the market price of the therapy makes it effectively unavailable to people who would benefit greatly from it. Unless sheer survival is at stake (in which case the needy patients might make out a legitimate case under the charity proviso), Lockean theory does authorize this seemingly harsh result. This is simply one consequence—a not altogether happy one, at times—of privileging claims based on work and labor over some other types of claims. I should quickly add that, despite a long history of libertarian rhetoric, this view is in no way inconsistent with a tax regime that redistributes some of the gains of property owners to those who are in need—an issue I take up in detail in Chapter 4. Indeed, given Locke's emphasis on human survival and thriving, it is arguably imperative to link strong property rights to a fair degree of redistribution. In the end, then, I offer solace to the suffering cancer patient not through the device of limiting property rights in cancer drugs, but instead through the device of redistributive payments that offset the high cost of these property-protected drugs.

75. See Hull, "Clearing the Rubbish," supra. Notice that there is a good deal of overlap between this reading of the spoilage proviso and what I call the proportionality principle—the idea that IP rights ought to be trimmed to reflect the magnitude of each creator's contribution. See Chapter 6, The Proportionality Principle.

76. Why only "might"? Because under some circumstances Maserati might justify a property right over more than the one or two variant designs it actually plans to use. For example, if some of the variants are close enough to the actual design Maserati implements, then allowing other companies to use those variant designs might undermine Maserati's ability to effectively exploit its chosen design. This possibility is discussed in the next section, under the rubric of IP "fences."

77. Another apparently complicating factor is the time frame used to assess the waste issue. Intangibles, as such, never literally waste away. The idea of an extended poem of longing and cherishing, such as the Song of Solomon, never decays, never rots away. The medium on which it is written may fade and crumble, but the idea by itself never does. By extension, if we were to imagine a property right over this idea, and were to apply Locke's spoliation proviso to it, we might argue that the right would never lapse, because the idea never spoils. It would never become unusable, as is the case with apples and acorns. There is a ready retort: Locke also spoke of land as a resource that might go to waste. Land does not spoil or rot in the literal sense, and so is unlike apples and acorns. Thus we might say that for Locke, a resource that is completely unused over a long period of time can be said to spoil, even if that resource never literally rots away. If land can go to waste, so can an idea. Also, we need

to recall that although Locke advocated a long term for copyright—life of the author plus seventy years—it was not an infinite term.

78. A patent case from a few years ago illustrates the issue nicely. In Rite-Hite v. Kelley, 56 F.3d 1538 (Fed. Cir. 1995), a business owner held a patent on "first-generation" technology but was selling a product incorporating "second-generation" technology. An infringer came along and copied the first-generation design. The court allowed the patent owner to recover damages, measuring the patent owner's lost sales in second-generation technology. The infringer had argued for reduced damages, on the theory that the patent owner was not actually selling first-generation technology anymore. The court rejected this argument, reasoning that the infringer had harmed the patent owner; and even though that harm did not take the form of lost sales of the patented first-generation technology, the patent owner could recover for it anyway. In effect, the court allowed the patent owner to use its patent on first-generation technology to protect its market in second-generation technology. A dissent in the case argued that this was not what Congress had in mind when it enacted the patent law, but the majority in the case disagreed and found this a perfectly appropriate use of a patent. The indirect protection of the market for second-generation technology was enough for the majority, in other words.

79. The definitive theoretical treatment of these issues is to be found in Suzanne Scotchmer, *Innovation and Incentives* (Cambridge, MA: MIT Press, 2004), at 103–107 (discussing patent breadth as a "policy lever" in patent law).

80. See generally, Henry E. Smith, "Institutions and Indirectness in Intellectual Property," 157 *U. Pa. L. Rev.* 2083, 2101–2114 (2009) (explaining application of real options theory to IP law); Dan L. Burk, "Critical Analysis: Property Rule, Liability Rules, and Molecular Futures: Bargaining in the Shadow of the Cathedral," in *Gene Patents and Collaborative Licensing Models: Patent Pools, Clearinghouses, Open Source Models and Liability Regimes* (Geertrui Van Overwalle, ed.) (Cambridge: Cambridge Univ. Press, 2009) at 294, 298–305 (describing application of "real options theory" to specific problems and institutional arrangements in IP law).

81. Differences between patents, on the one hand, and copyrights and trademarks, on the other, are relevant to this discussion. Many patents will expire without Lockean spoliation coming into play; unbuilt variants may well remain viable and conceivable over the entire fifteen- to twenty-year life of many inventions claimed under patent law. But the other IP rights mentioned can in many cases last much longer. So even though the "scope" of copyrights and trademarks is in most senses much narrower than patents, they may reach very far in time. In trademark law, the doctrine of abandonment serves in some ways to protect against the continuation of legal rights after the point where the trademark is being actively used by a seller of goods to identify its products. And in copyright, in addition to various renewal requirements, some scholars have argued that the scope of a given copyright ought in effect to narrow over time, through the mechanism of an expansion of the public's fair use rights. See Joseph P. Liu, "Copyright and Time: A Proposal," 101 *Mich. L. Rev.* 409 (2002); Justin Hughes, "Fair Use Across Time," 50 *UCLA L. Rev.* 775 (2003). In addition to

all these rules, the equitable doctrine of laches sometimes prevents an IP owner from reviving a right that he or she has neglected to enforce in the face of ongoing use by a third party. There is a complex interplay between IP doctrines at work in these cases, a situation matched in the context of real property, where doctrines such as adverse possession work to cut back against overbroad and unused property rights. See Michael Carrier, "Cabining Intellectual Property Through a Property Paradigm," 54 *Duke L.J.* 1 (2004).

82. I thus implicitly reject the view that the waste proviso is the key to applying Locke to IP, that IP rules systematically promote waste, and that therefore Lockean IP rights ought to be quite limited. For an explication of this view, see Hull, "Clearing the Rubbish," supra; Damstedt, "Limiting Locke," supra.

83. John Locke, *Two Treatises of Government, First Treatise*, Chap. IV, § 42 (Peter Laslett, ed.) at 170.

84. Genesis 1:28 reads: "God blessed them, and God said to them, 'Be fruitful and multiply, and fill the earth and subdue it; and have dominion over the fish of the sea and over the birds of the air and over every living thing that moves upon the earth.'" The Holy Bible (New Revised Standard Version), Genesis 1:28.

85. Charity serves in some ways as an early prototype of other inherent or implied restrictions on the purportedly absolute power of property rights. For some background, see Carol Rose, "Canons of Property Talk, or Blackstone's Anxiety," 108 *Yale L.J.* 601, 631 (1998) (describing the notion of "property as exclusive dominion" as "at most a cartoon or trope").

86. This is discussed in depth in Chapter 9, "Patents and Drugs for the Developing World."

87. Though here, complications of corruption, transborder trafficking in drugs, and intergenerational equity must also be considered, in my opinion.

88. See, e.g., James Thuo Gathii, "The Structural Power of Strong Pharmaceutical Patent Protection in U.S. Foreign Policy," 7 *J. Gender, Race & Justice* 267 (2003) (claiming that government-sponsored programs to encourage donation of patented medicines merely disguise the fact that strong pro-patent policies block access to medicines by many who need them).

89. See Amartya Sen, *Development and Freedom* (Oxford: Oxford Univ. Press, 1999).

90. Examples of this would include arbitrage from a country with weak or nonexistent IP enforcement, and incentives to produce goods that contribute to cultural development, respectively.

91. I am well aware of the lack of symmetry between this argument regarding cultural development and my earlier advocacy for a broad reading of the Lockean notion of human survival and thriving. Earlier in this chapter I pushed the view that human thriving or flourishing includes a concern for the financial well-being of creative professionals. When discussing the purposive role of labor in appropriation, I was willing to extrapolate from acorn and apple gathering to enhanced income levels in highly developed economies. But I resist this same type of extrapolation when it comes to the charity proviso. Here I argue for a limited reading of charity as extending only to cases of immediate physical survival or actual destitution. The reason for the difference is

that I see IP as a right, and hence a strong set of claims, whereas charity, while a real limit on that right, represents a subservient claim that is carved out of the larger, dominant claim. I recognize that there are many who would disagree, who would argue that this is precisely the sort of view that permits "liberal" political theory to paper over vast and gross inequality and injustice. Though sympathetic, I must say in the end that this is simply what it means for a political system to favor individual appropriation, and what it means for property to be a real right. I would also add that the various historical experiments that seek to go further, and to establish the charity principle as a coequal or dominant principle in political life, have tended to end in chaos and stagnation at best, and concentration camps at worst. From that perspective, property rights don't look so bad.

92. This assumes that arbitrage can be kept to reasonable levels. No one likes to be played for a fool—to have their works copied on a wide scale in a poor country, only to have them turn up as pirate copies in a country where most people are perfectly capable of paying the market price.

93. The development of IP rights covering products that bring profits to the developing world can help buttress the view that intellectual property should be thought of as a real right. The literature on human rights has sought to establish what it means to elevate the interests of the very poor to the status of rights. So it might make sense, if IP comes to be associated with the interests of the developing world, to more naturally think of IP as real rights. See, e.g., Lawrence Helfer, "Human Rights and Intellectual Property: Conflict or Coexistence?" Princeton Law and Public Affairs Working Paper No. 04-003 (May 25, 2007), avail. at http://papers.ssrn.com/sol3/papers.cfm?abstract_id=459120; Susan Corbett, "A Human Rights Perspective on the Database Debate," 28 *Euro. Intell. Prop. Rev.* 83 (2006). See also Laurence Helfer & Graeme W. Austin, *Human Rights and Intellectual Property: Analysis and Sources* (Cambridge: Cambridge University Press, forthcoming 2011).

3. Kant

1. Kant's contributions to property theory have only recently been recognized among legal scholars. His stature in other areas, however, is of course virtually unparalleled. The great milestones of Kant's writing career were the three famous Critiques: *The Critique of Pure Reason* (1781), *The Critique of Practical Reason* (1788), and *The Critique of Judgment* (1790). Together with *The Groundwork of the Metaphysics of Morals* (1785), they are considered the most important works in Kant's rather extensive oeuvre. Kant covers property in *The Doctrine of Right* (DOR), or Rechtslehre, reprinted in *The Cambridge Edition of the Works of Immanuel Kant: Practical Philosophy* (Mary J. Gregor, trans. and ed.) (New York: Cambridge University Press 1996) (hereafter "Gregor"). The DOR was originally published under the title *Anfangsgrunde der Rechtslehre* (Preussische Akademie der Wissenschaften [Prussian Academy] 2d ed. 1798). This book came very near the end of Kant's writing career. It forms Part I of a larger work whose title is *The Metaphysics of Morals*, which

was completed in 1797. Part II is called the Doctrine of Virtue or *Tuglundehre*. Since there are so many different translations and editions of these works, all with differing pagination, all references to these works will cite the Prussian Academy pagination as well as that of the Gregor translation. The DOR has also been called *The Metaphysical Elements of Justice* (reprinted 1999, John Ladd, trans.) (Indianapolis: Hackett Pub., 1999). This is a somewhat idiosyncratic translation, but it has a few useful features; I cite it occasionally and refer to it as "DOR (MEJ version)," "Ladd").

2. For background on Kant's conceptual approach, see Brian Tierney, "Permissive Natural Law and Property: Gratian to Kant," 62 *J. Hist. Ideas* 301 (2001) (describing Kant's conceptual, as opposed to historical-empirical, approach to property and law generally, in the context of a general account of the "permissive" natural law tradition). For more background on medieval champions of this natural law tradition, see A. Brundage, *The Medieval Origins of the Legal Profession: Canonists, Civilians, and Courts* (Chicago: Univ. of Chicago Press, 2008), at 560 et seq.

3. While Hume's approach to property was in some ways influenced by Locke (whose two treatises Hume cited extensively in his own work), it is tightly connected to Hume's comprehensive theory of knowledge, ethics, and society, and therefore differs in emphasis substantially from Locke's.

4. David Hume, *A Treatise of Human Nature*, reprinted from the Original Edition of 1739 in three volumes and edited, with an analytical index, by L. A. Selby-Bigge, M.A. (Oxford: Clarendon Press, 1896), at Book II, Part 3, section 2, pars. 3 and 9, avail. at http://oll.libertyfund.org/title/342/55219, accessed on November 16, 2010.

5. "Two men, who pull the oars of a boat, do it by an agreement or convention, tho' they have never given promises to each other." Hume, *Treatise*, Book III, part 2, section 2, par. 10.

6. See Samuel Fleischacker, *On Adam Smith's Wealth of Nations* 179 (Princeton, NJ: Princeton Univ. Press, 2004) (describing Hume's approach to property, which informed that of Adam Smith).

7. For Bentham's view on property, see Jeremy Bentham, *Traités de legislation civile et pénale*, 3 volumes, translated by Etienne Dumont (Paris: Boussange, Masson & Besson, 1802); first published in English as *Theory of Legislation*, 1 volume, translated by Richard Hildreth (London: Kegan Paul, Trench, Trübner, 1864). Bentham agreed with Hume that property was not derived from a natural, God-given set of rights, but was instead a purely human institution, developed to meet human needs. Hume saw a greater role for custom, however, whereas Bentham saw property as basically whatever the lawfully created state said it was. Both contributed to the modern, positivist conception of property.

8. See generally Henry E. Smith, "Community and Custom in Property," 10 *Theoretical Inquiries L.* 5 (2009); Michael A. Heller, "The Boundaries of Private Property," 108 *Yale L.J.* 1163, 1193 (1999) ("While the modern bundle-of-legal relations metaphor reflects well the possibility of complex relational fragmentation, it gives a weak sense of the 'thingness' of private property."). The realist-based view of property has been criticized in the context of IP rights by legal

scholar Adam Mossoff, who also argues that the early realists inappropriately borrowed examples from IP law to illustrate their view of property. See Adam Mossoff, "The Use and Abuse of IP at the Birth of the Administrative State," 157 *U. Pa. L. Rev.* 2001, 2010–2011 (2009).

9. For an account that traces the development of property concepts from Locke to Hume to Bentham and beyond, see Nestor M. Davidson, "Standardization and Pluralism in Property Law," 61 *Vand. L. Rev.* 1597, 1645–1646 (2008).

10. See generally John Henry Schlegel, *American Legal Realism and Empirical Social Science* (Chapel Hill: Univ. of North Carolina Press, 1995); Laura Kalman, *Legal Realism at Yale, 1927–1960* (Chapel Hill: Univ. of North Carolina Press, 1986).

11. See Thomas W. Merrill & Henry E. Smith, "What Happened to Property in Law and Economics?" 111 *Yale L. J.* 357 (2001). See generally, John P. Dwyer and Peter S. Menell, *Property Law and Policy: A Comparative Institutional Perspective* (Eagan , MN: Foundation Press, 1997). I should note here that I am speaking of the situation in the U.S. Elsewhere, things are considerably different. In Europe, in particular, there remains a stronger Kantian tradition in private law (including property) theory, and this is as true in IP as in other branches of the field. See, e.g., James Gordley, *Foundations of Private Law: Property, Tort, Contract, Unjust Enrichment* 15 (Oxford: Oxford Univ. Press, 2006). A classic statement of Kantian themes, in particular the "personality theory" of IP rights still commonly found in Europe, is found in Otto Friederich von Gierke, *Deutsches Privatrecht*, ed. K. Binding, 2 vols., Systematisches Handbuch der deutschen Rechtwissenschaft (Leipzig: Duncker & Humblot, 1895–1905). See also Neil Netanel, "Copyright Alienability Restrictions and the Enhancement of Author Autonomy: A Normative Evaluation," 24 *Rutgers L.J.* 347, 378 (1993) (discussion of impact of Kant on continental copyright law); Kim Treiger-Bar-Am, "Kant on Copyright: Rights of Transformative Authorship," 25 *Cardozo L. Rev.* 1059 (2008) (drawing on Kant for non-traditional arguments about copyright policy).

12. Immanuel Kant, *The Critique of Practical Reason* 12 (Mary Gregor, ed.) (Cambridge: Cambridge Univ. Press, 1997) (Prussian Academy Edition page 15): "[R]eason is concerned with the determining grounds of will, which is a faculty either of producing objects corresponding to representations or of determining itself to effect such objects (whether the physical power is sufficient or not), that is, of determining its causality. For, in that, reason can at least suffice to determine the will and always has objective reality insofar as volition alone is at issue." Note that when Kant writes of "objects" in this passage, he is talking about all ends or goals, and not just physical things. See Andrews Reath, "Introduction to Kant," *Critique of Practical Reason* (Mary Gregor, ed.), supra, at xvi.

13. See Arthur Ripstein, *Force and Freedom: Kant's Legal and Political Philosophy* 67 (Cambridge, MA: Harvard Univ. Press, 2009): "For Kant, property in an external thing—something other than your own person—is simply the right to have that thing at your disposal [so as] to set and pursue your own ends. Secure title in things is prerequisite to the capacity to use an object to set

and pursue ends. . . . You have the right to use a thing if you are free to exploit it to pursue such ends as you might set, and do not require the consent of anyone else in order to do so."

14. As the philosopher Allen Wood puts it, "Kantian morality, however—though the content of its duties may be socially oriented—is never about the social regulation of individual conduct. It is entirely about enlightened individuals autonomously directing their own lives." Allen Wood, "The Final Form of Kant's Practical Philosophy," in *Kant's Metaphysics of Morals: Interpretive Essays* (Mark Timmons, ed.) (Oxford: Oxford Univ. Press, 2002).

15. Kant, DOR 6:245, Gregor at 401 (emphasis in original).

16. See generally Paul Guyer, "The Value of Reason and the Value of Freedom," 109 *Ethics* 22 (1998) (describing some of the complex questions regarding reason and the will raised by Kant's writings on freedom).

17. Paul Guyer, "Kantian Foundations for Liberalism," in *Kant on Freedom, Law, and Happiness* 235, 243 (New York: Cambridge Univ. Press, 2000).

18. On the sometimes complex relationship between ownership and possession, see Joshua C. Tate, "Ownership and Possession in the Early Common Law," 48 *Am. J. Leg. Hist.* 280 (2006). See also Richard A. Epstein, "Possession as the Root of Title," 13 *Ga. L. Rev.* 1221 (1979).

19. In this he obviously differs from Locke, whose examples serve almost as parables, sprinkled with details and ripe for extension and analogy. On Kant's highly abstract conception of property, see Ripstein, *Force and Freedom*, supra, at 86: "For purposive beings, for whom having means is prior to setting ends, the entitlement to have something subject to their choice must be abstract, because it must not depend on the content of their particular choices. Your freedom to decide just is your freedom to use what is yours for your own purposes."

20. He comes at the same issue from the opposite direction in the *Groundwork of the Metaphysics of Morals*, where he defines the autonomy of the will as "the property of the will through which it is a law to itself (independently of any property of the objects of volition)." *Groundwork* at 431.

21. Kant voices similar ideas in his discussion of why people should not be able to sell parts of their bodies: "The principle of all duties is that the use of freedom must be in keeping with the essential ends of humanity. Thus, for instance, a human being is not entitled to sell his limbs for money, even if he were offered ten thousand thalers [i.e., a huge payment] for a single finger. If he were so entitled, he could sell all his limbs. We can dispose of things which have no freedom but not of a being which has free will. A man who sells himself makes himself a thing and, as he has jettisoned his person, it is open to anyone to deal with him as he pleases." Kant, *Lectures on Ethics (1755–1780)* (trans. L. Infield) (Indianapolis: Hackett Publishing, 1963), at 124. For expansion, see the excellent article by Steven R. Munzer, "Kant and Property Rights in Body Parts," 6 *Can. J. L. & Juris.* 319 (1993).

22. See Michael A. Heller, "The Boundaries of Private Property," 108 *Yale L.J.* 1163, 1193 (1999) ("While the modern bundle-of-legal relations metaphor reflects well the possibility of complex relational fragmentation, it gives a

weak sense of the 'thingness' of private property."). For applications to IP rights, see Michael J. Madison, "Law as Design: Objects, Concepts, and Digital Things," 56 *Case W. Res. L. Rev.* 381 (2005); Clarisa Long, "Information Costs in Patent and Copyright," 90 *U. Va. L. Rev.* 465, 471–474 (2004).

23. Merrill & Smith, "What Happened to Property," supra; Thomas W. Merrill & Henry E. Smith, "Optimal Standardization in the Law of Property: The *Numerus Clausus* Principle," 110 *Yale L.J.* 1, 3–9 (2000) (explaining that standardized forms of property reduce transaction costs).

24. To speak accurately, I am discussing here primarily one aspect of what Kant calls will, the "personal will." The other aspect, universal, rationalizing will, is a sort of "internal lawgiver" that draws on a universal, collective sense of reason. The Kant commentator Lewis White Beck describes the difference between personal will (the German for which is *Willkur*) and universal, rational will (German: *Wille*) this way: "We cannot say that the actions of Wille are free, because Wille does not act. It gives only a law for the submission of Willkur, which does act. Yet it is free in that its decree follows from its own nature. It does not mediate laws of nature to Willkur bent upon the satisfaction of some arbitrary purpose; . . . It . . . commands, and it commands as a principal, not as an agent. Through submission to it, Willkur supplements its negative freedom [e.g., freedom from physical constraints] with a positive freedom which comes from [voluntary] submission to . . . [the] purely rational will. Using a political metaphor, as he so often did in speaking of the realms and territories of the legislation of reason, Kant says [Wille, the universal, rationalizing will] is autonomous, free in itself, i.e., free in the positive sense. Willkur participates in this autonomy to the degree that its negative freedom vis-à-vis nature [i.e., "freedom from" natural constraints] is exercised in adherence to the law of pure practical reason [supplied by Wille]. Pure practical reason [operating through the Wille] spontaneously creates an Idea of a natura archetypa, and Willkur, taking this as its object, can become an efficient cause of giving to the world of nature the form of such an intelligible world." Lewis White Beck, *A Commentary on Kant's Critique of Practical Reason* 180 (Chicago: Univ. of Chicago Press, 1960). The internal "legislative process" involves imposition of law upon the individual, by the individual. This system of self-legislation preserves autonomy and freedom, the paramount values in Kant's thinking. Andrews Reath, "Legislating the Moral Law," 28 *Noûs* 435 (1994).

25. Beck, trying to be helpful, puts is this way: "It [*Willkur*] has, therefore, an incentive (Triebfeder) for action in addition to the law [or principle of action], while Wille has no Triebfeder [incentive]. . . ." Beck, *Commentary on Kant's Critique of Practical Reason*, supra, at 180.

26. One aspect of this is the first idea of will, *Wille*.

27. Beck cautions against an overly rigid dichotomy between the two senses of will, and roots their ultimate unity in Kant's complex notions of freedom. Beck, *Commentary on Kant's Critique of Practical Reason*, supra, at 180.

28. See, e.g., William Cronon, *Changes in the Land* (New York: Hill & Wang, 1983) (detailing the aggregate impact of colonists and Indians on the landscape of New England).

29. Later in this chapter, when talking about the right of publicity in IP law, I even argue that a budding performer who consciously shapes a public persona out of native talent and physical attributes (appearance, voice, etc.) acts in a sense on a found object.

30. See my comments in Chapter 2, supra, at "Locke's Common and the Public Domain," for critiques of the idea that the "nonrivalrous" nature of intangibles renders property rights less necessary in this context. For a related argument, see Richard A. Epstein, "The Disintegration of Intellectual Property? A Classical Liberal Response to a Premature Obituary," 62 *Stan. L. Rev.* 455, 458 (2010) ("[T]he inability of an owner to take physical possession of what he owns does not make it impossible for one person to have rights of exclusive use and disposition of the property in question. It only means that a legal system has to become more mature before it can handle the greater administrative burdens. In my view, the general heritage of tangible property cannot be disregarded because of the evident differences in the two systems of property rights.").

31. Ownership in the information age is discussed at length in Chapter 8, "Property in the Digital Era."

32. One scholar argues that what Kant is talking about in the *DOR* is not even property, but merely a "right to use." See Kenneth R. Westphal, "A Kantian Justification of Possession," in *Kant's Metaphysics of Morals* 89–109 (Mark Timmons, ed.) (Oxford: Oxford Univ. Press, 2002). Despite the fact that Westphal makes some very cogent observations about Kant's writings in this area—particularly with respect to reciprocity (see just above)—I think he is wrong in arguing that Kant's discussion is limited to "use rights." See id., at 91. First, because Kant consistently uses the Latin phraseology pertaining to full-on property rights. See DOR, 6:261, Gregor at 413 ("Kant introduces the term "property" (Eigentum, dominium), a full right to a thing, in his concluding remarks to this section, 6:270"). See also Barry Nicholas, *An Introduction to Roman Law* 157 (Oxford: Oxford Univ. Press 1962) (discussing *dominus* in section describing "the absoluteness of Roman ownership"). Second, because Kant mentions in passing many of the "incidents of ownership" other than mere use rights at various points in the DOR. See, e.g., Kant, DOR, 6:271, Gregor at 422 ("Transfer of the *property* of one to another is *alienation*." (emphasis in original)). And third, because the whole structure of Kant's argument about the need for civil society to guarantee property rights makes far less sense if he is only arguing for a very limited set of rights over objects. While it is perhaps minimally plausible to argue that civil society is necessary to guarantee "use rights" that extend beyond mere possession, it is much more logical to say that the driving force behind the state is the need to protect and administer the full panoply of rights over objects—i.e., property rights in the full sense.

33. Kant, DOR, MEJ Version, Ladd at 44, Comment (b); see also DOR 6: 248, Gregory at 402.

34. He goes on to say, "I must be able to think of myself as having possession of this object quite independently of temporal limitations and empirical possession." Id. at 45.

35. Kant also refers to another sort of possession: authority relations in the family setting, as a legitimate object of legal interest. It is plain that by including authority relations as something that can be possessed, Kant is showing us a quite liberal conception of possession. It is not necessary to get into the details (or controversies!) of Kant's conception of family authority to grasp a simple point: that Kant's understanding of possession was quite inclusive, easily broad enough to encompass the category of intellectual property.

36. Immanuel Kant, "On the Wrongfulness of the Unauthorized Publication of Books (1785)," originally published 1785, reprinted as "On the Wrongfulness of Unauthorized Publication of Books (1785)," in *Cambridge Edition of the Works of Immanuel Kant: Practical Philosophy* (Mary J. Gregor, trans. and ed.) (New York: Cambridge Univ. Press, 1996) (cited hereafter by both standard pagination from the Prussian Academy edition, see supra note 2, and the Gregor transation). An "adapted" copy and commentary of this essay can also be found at *Primary Sources on Copyright (1450–1900)*, ed. L. Bently & M. Kretschmer, www.copyrighthistory.org (under title "On the Unlawfulness of Reprinting") (hereinafter "Copyrighthistory.org version"), with commentary written by Friedemann Kawohl, "Commentary on Kant's Essay On the Injustice of Reprinting Books (1785)," in *Primary Sources on Copyright (1450–1900)*, supra. Note that the text of the essay is also almost identical to a portion of the Doctrine of Right, and so it appears that Kant simply adapted this essay and inserted it into the relevant portion of the DOR. See Kant, DOR, II. What is a Book?, 6:289–291, Gregor at 437–439.

37. On the Wrongulness of Unauthorized Publication, 8:79, Gregor at 29.

38. Kant's writings in this area significantly affected the development of a "personality approach" to IP rights that has long thrived in Europe. See, e.g., Francis J. Kase, *Copyright Thought in Continental Europe: Its Development, Legal Theories and Philosophy, A Selected and Annotated Bibliography* (South Hackensack, NJ: Fred B. Rothman, 1967); Neil Netanel, "Alienability Restrictions and the Enhancement of Author Autonomy in United States and Continental Copyright Law," 12 *Cardozo Arts & Ent. L.J.* 1, 17, 19 (1994). For a further exploration of the personality theory in the United States, with a special emphasis on the property theory of Hegel, see the pathbreaking article by Margaret Jane Radin, in "Property and Personhood," 34 *Stan. L. Rev.* 957 (1982). See also in this regard Paul Edward Geller, "Must Copyright be Forever Caught between Marketplace and Authorship Norms?" in *Of Authors and Origins* (Brad Sherman & Alain Strowel eds., New York: Oxford Univ. Press 1994).

39. See, e.g., Copyrighthistory.org translation. This interpretation seems at odds with the translator's own rendition of the introductory passage I cited in note 37; see id., at 2 (translating the same passage as follows: "For the author's ownership to his thoughts (assuming in the first place that such ownership applies according to external rights) remains his in spite of any reprinting. . . ."). Clearly the commentator sees a difference between "ownership" and true property rights; or interprets the parenthetical to indicate disapproval of positive laws that grant copyrights; or perhaps both. See also Maria Chiara Pieva-

tolo, "Freedom, Ownership and Copyright: Why Does Kant Reject the Concept of Intellectual Property?" working paper (July 2, 2010), avail. at http://ssrn.com/abstract=1540095.

40. There is a counterargument to the view that Kant in this essay endorses a broad and open-ended IP right for authors. To begin, he distinguishes ownership of a tangible copy of a book from the author's right over his expression, as embodied in those copies. According to Kant only the former type of ownership confers true *in rem* rights, while the author's continuing rights over his expression are in the nature of *in personam* rights, such as those conferred by contract. DOR, 8:79, Gregor at 29. Second, he argues for what seem by today's standards to be broad exceptions to an author's rights, stating that an abridgement or translation prepared by another person would not infringe the rights of the original author. 8:86–87, Gregor at 34–35. Much is made of these statements by copyright scholar Kim Treiger-Bar-Am, "Kant on Copyright: Rights of Transformative Authorship," 25 *Cardozo L. Rev. 1059* (2008). In response, I would first emphasize the context and purpose of this essay. Some of Kant's works had been copied and published in unauthorized editions, and, because of the undeveloped state of copyright law in the late eighteenth century, is was an open question whether Kant had any legal redress under existing law. ("If the idea of publication of a book, on which this [essay] is based, were firmly grasped and (as I flatter myself it could be) elaborated with the requisite elegance of Roman legal scholarship, complaints against unauthorized publishers could indeed be taken to court without it being necessary first to wait for a new law." DOR 8:87, Gregor at 35.) While he purported to write his essay strictly from first philosophical principles, it has many of the earmarks of a work of advocacy. It is, in truth, equal parts legal brief and philosophical argument. Thus we should not be surprised to see Kant conceding points that were not relevant to the case he most cared about—the direct copying of entire texts, i.e., preparation of unauthorized editions. Second, his somewhat awkward attempt to distinguish ownership of a tangible copy from ownership of the underlying expression does not work very well on its own terms. He begins his analysis by focusing on the contract between an author and his publisher; this contract becomes in Kant's analysis the locus of the authorial interest in his work. Because contracts are rights *in personam*, and because Kant cannot imagine the idea that the buyer of a book can have a personal property interest in the book yet still leave some reserved property rights in the hands of the author (DOR 8:80 n*, Gregor at 29), his entire analysis turns on the distinction between the "true" property interest of a book owner and the personal (or vaguely non-property) interest of the book's author. See DOR, 8:79, Gregor at 29; 8:83, Gregor at 32. This leads him to stress the reputational interest of the author, an interest which is violated when unauthorized editions are published. But this right, which in truth sounds more in what today would be classified as trademark law, is hardly *in personam* in the classical sense. For while the author may contract with a publisher, the publisher typically does not, and in Kant's time never did, enter into a contract with the buyer of each copy of a book. The focus on the author-publisher contract, in other words, elides the

difficult problem of the author's cause of action versus parties other than the authorized publisher, or the cause of action by an authorized versus an unauthorized publisher. Perhaps in Kant's world the world of authors and publishers was small enough that everyone involved knew which publisher was authorized and which ones therefore were not, so that an unauthorized publisher could be seen as interfering with the contractual advantage of the author, and thus be subject to a suit under what would now be called a business tort theory. This would be consistent with the quasi-contractual nature of author's rights that Kant seems to emphasize. But even if this were true then, it is no longer so now, which only points up the contingent and conceptually limited nature of Kant's argument *qua* legal analysis. The simple fact is that a general legal right, good "against the world," is necessary to give full force and effect to the interests of authors that Kant describes. Only a true property right will do. Thus I would argue that when Kant speaks of "the author's property in his thought" he says all that needs to be said about the nature of the author's legal rights.

41. Freedom typically has a number of dimensions in Kantian philosophy. In opposition to empiricists such as Hume, Kant says our actions are not dictated or determined by empirical events; one might say we are free from these constraints. But Kant also talks about a self-regulative aspect of freedom, based on universal, shared, rational principles. We are free to elect to follow these principles—which is important, because in this way Kant distances himself from a capricious or selfish concept of freedom. This same dual impulse—wide autonomy, informed by an innate knowledge of and attraction to universal rational principles—governs internal thinking and choice, as well as action at the legal-social level.

42. Kant, *Critique of Judgment*, § 43 (Werner S. Pluhar, trans.) (Indianapolis: Hackett Pub., 1987), at 170 (Prussian Academy ed. at 303) (hereinafter COJ). Kant goes on in this passage to distinguish natural creation—perhaps the purest form of true inspiration (through instinct)—from production through freedom by an act of will: "For though we like to call the product that bees make (the regularly constructed honeycombs) a work of art, we do so only by virtue of an analogy with art; for as soon as we recall that their labor is not based on any rational deliberation on their part, we say at once that the product is a product of their nature (namely, of instinct), and it is only to their creator that we ascribe it as art." Id.

43. See, e.g., COJ § 49 (Pluhar trans.) at 183 (Prussian Academy ed. at 314–315) where Kant writes: "Now if a concept is provided with [unterlegen] a presentation of the imagination such that, even though this presentation belongs to the exhibition of the concept, yet it prompts, even by itself, so much thought as can never be comprehended within a determinate concept and thereby the presentation aesthetically expands the concept itself in an unlimited way, then the imagination is creative in [all of] this and sets the power of intellectual ideas (i.e., reason) in motion: it makes reason think more, when prompted by a certain presentation, than what can be apprehended and made distinct in the presentation (though the thought does pertain to the object [presented])."

44. "Art is . . . doing . . . ; and the product or result of art is . . . a work (opus). . . ." COJ § 43 (Pluhar trans.), at 170 (Prussian Academy ed. at 303).

45. Kant, DOR, 6:258, Gregor at 411.
46. MEJ, § 10, Ladd at 56. This same passage is translated by Gregor somewhat differently: "It is possible for me to have any external object of my choice as mine, that is, a maxim by which, if it were to become a law, an object of choice would *in itself* (objectively) have to *belong to no one (res nullius)* is contrary to rights. For an object of my choice is something that I have the *physical* power to use. If it were nevertheless absolutely not within my *rightful* power to make use of it, that is, if the use of it could not coexist with the freedom of everyone in accordance with a universal law (would be wrong), then freedom would be depriving itself of the use of its choice, by putting *usable* objects beyond any possibility of being *used*; in other words, it would annihilate them in a practical respect and make them into *res nullius*, even though in the use of things choice was formally consistent with everyone's outer freedom in accordance with universal laws. Kant, DOR, 6:250, Gregor at 404–405. It might be argued in response that *res nullius* is a category of property that precedes the state, and that things in this category are by their nature, not simply by decree, unownable. Kant would object to this on the grounds that formal property categories can never precede the state, since property presupposes (indeed, calls into being) the apparatus of civil society. For this reason, it might be supposed that Kant would subsume the *res nullius* category into the related category of *res communis*, things held in common ownership under the stewardship of the state. See, e.g., Kant, DOR § 10 6:258, Gregor at 411 (where Kant states that at the origins of civil society all objects are in a sense held in common, in that a common purpose must unite the citizens of the newly founded state, and no individual in the state of nature (or primitive condition) can truly be said to possess an object in the full legal sense). See also Ripstein, *Force and Freedom*, at Chapter 6, p. 145 et seq., "Three Defects in the State of Nature." The distinction between *res nullius* and *res communis* is at any rate a very fine one. See Carol M. Rose, "Romans, Roads and Romantic Creators: Traditions of Public Property in the Information Age," 66 *Law. & Contemp. Prob.* 89 (2003).
47. In addition, Kant's quite favorable views on the appropriateness of redistribution of property are distinctly at odds with an absolutist property theory. On this topic, see Chapter 4, infra; see also Samuel Fleischacker, *A Short History of Distributive Justice* (Cambridge, MA: Harvard Univ. Press, 2004), at 70–71 (contrasting Kant's emphatic and expansive notions of property, which might in themselves have appeal to modern libertarians, with his equally expansive embrace of redistributive state policies). The key to resolving the seeming contradiction between strong property rights and support for redistribution is to remember that property depends on the existence of a state, which is the product of a united, general will, and that a minimal level of public support is necessary for some to develop and express their will. See Ripstein, *Force and Freedom*, supra, at 25–26 ("The requirement that the state support those who are unable to support themselves follows from the need for the people to be able to share a united will, as a precondition of their giving themselves laws together. . . . The only way in which the right to exclude [i.e., strong property

rights] can be made the object of the general will is to guarantee public support for those unable to support themselves.").

48. Oliver Williamson, *Mechanisms of Governance* (Oxford: Oxford Univ. Press, 1996), at 43.

49. For a summary of this literature, see Robert P. Merges, "A Transactional View of Property Rights," 20 *Berkeley Tech. L.J.* 1477 (2005).

50. See, e.g., Boosey & Hawkes Music Publishers Ltd. v. Walt Disney Co., 145 F.3d 481, 487 (2d Cir. 1998) (in case involving license of "film rights," where Boosey, owner of movie copyright, argued it should be able to sign new contract with another company for videocassette version of the movie, court held for Disney, to whom Boosey originally licensed film rights; "[t]he words of Disney's license are more reasonably read to include than to exclude a motion picture distributed in video format"). See also Cohen v. Paramount Pictures Corp., 845 F.2d 851 (9th Cir. 1988) (interpreting "television" rights); Paramount Publix Corp. v. Am. TriErgon Corp., 294 U.S. 464 (1935) (rights to "sound recordings"). For a summary of the approaches courts have taken to these cases, see 3 Melville Nimmer & David Nimmer, *Nimmer on Copyright* § 10.10[B] (Albany, NY: Matthew Bender Publishing, 2010) (contrasting narrow, prolicensor (creator) view in the cases, that licenses cover only media within the unambiguous core of the license grant, with broad, prolicensee view, that licenses cover any use reasonably related to the use contemplated by the original grant). To the extent that *Nimmer* expresses a preference for the latter, broad view—which favors licensees—I disagree, for the reasons set forth in the text.

51. See Ashish Arora & Robert P. Merges, "Specialized Supply Firms, Property Rights, and Firm Boundaries," 13 *Indus. & Corp. Change* 451–475 (2004); Merges, "A Transactional View of Property Rights," supra.

52. This situation is viewed in economics largely from the perspective of the buyers of inputs; indeed, it is known as the "make or buy" problem. The issue is whether to employ the input makers or to allow them to set up independently. In the economics literature, this is modeled as a strict trade-off: increases in the quality of inputs made by independent firms are traded off against greater managerial control over employees. I have argued that a normative element might usefully be introduced into the conversation; that encouraging more small companies might be a good idea in and of itself, even when this is not strictly speaking the most optimal mode of production. See Robert P. Merges, "Autonomy and Independence: The Normative Face of Transaction Costs," forthcoming, *Ariz. L. Rev.* (2011). Of course, exactly how far to permit this normative consideration to override efficiency concerns is a difficult question; I do not think the separate normative value of encouraging autonomy justifies eating away huge chunks of efficiency. I see it more as a "plus factor" in the equation.

53. See Lawrence Lessig, *Free Culture* 8 (New York: Penguin Press, 2004) (noting that the "rough divide between the free and the controlled has now been erased" such that less free culture exists and, in its place, more of our culture can only be used "upon permission"). See generally Chapter 8, "Property in the Digital Era."

54. An extended defense of a higher permissions burden, in service of greater authorial rights, is presented in Chapter 8, Property in the Digital Era. Note that the expansive Kantian embrace of waiver, described just below, reduces the effective burden somewhat.

55. See Gottlied Hufeland, Wikipedia, avail. at http://en.wikipedia.org/wiki/Gottlieb_Hufeland.

56. The book review is reprinted in the Prussian Academy version of Kant's collected works, 8 Royal Prussian Academy of Sciences, *Kant's Gesammelte Schriften* 128–129 (Berlin: Georg Reimer, later Walter de Gruyter & Co., 1990).

57. Wood, "The Final Form of Kant's Practical Philosophy," supra, at 1–21, 7.

58. See, e.g., James Boyle, *The Public Domain: Enclosing the Commons of the Mind* 42–53 (New Haven, CT: Yale Univ. Press, 2008); James Boyle, "The Second Enclosure Movement and the Construction of the Public Domain," 66 *L. & Contemp. Probs.* 33 (Spring 2003). In a related vein, Jonathan Barnett has described what might be called the political economy of propertization, the mechanisms by which competitive dynamics in certain circumstances cause firms to pursue stronger-than-optimal IP rights. See Jonathan M. Barnett, "Property as Process: How Innovation Markets Select Innovation Regimes," 119 *Yale L.J.* 384, 414–443 (2009) (explaining the property trap thesis in detail).

59. See Robert P. Merges, "Locke Remixed ;-)," 40 *U.C. Davis L. Rev.* 1259, 1262 (2007) ("[H]uge truckloads of IP rights are voluntarily waived every day by those who hold them."). Those who do mention waiver assert in a vague way that it is not sufficient to protect the interests of amateur creators and others who want to rely on nonenforcement of IP rights; yet these accounts fail to explain why a vibrant amateur creative movement has sprung up coincidentally with the overpropertization of creative work. See, e.g., John Quiggin & Dan Hunter, "Money Ruins Everything," 30 *Hastings Comm. & Ent. L.J.* 203, 246–247 (2008) ("It is not an answer to say that copyright owners do not usually bother to sue. . . . It would be better to establish a principle that, for example, non-commercial use of copyright material (as on a blog or in other amateur content forms) is not copyright infringement. . . .").

60. See, e.g., Remix Theory Home Page, http://remixtheory.net/ (accessed November 16, 2010) (online resource designed to "host, archive, and promote projects which explore the current possibilities of Remix").

61. See generally, Hal Varian & Carl Shapiro, *Information Rules* (Boston: Harvard Bus. School Press, 1998).

62. See http://creativecommons.org/; http://www.plos.org/. See generally Wikipedia, "Open Access (Publishing)", at http://en.wikipedia.org/wiki/Open_access_(publishing).

63. See generally Michael J. Madison, Brett Frischmann, & Katherine J. Strandburg, "Constructing Commons in the Cultural Environment," 95 *Cornell L. Rev.* 657 (2010) (analyzing process by which norms contribute to a cultural "commons" of bartered, sold, and shared information).

64. Similar points can be found in a book by Lawrence Lessig, which talks about the emergence of "hybrid economies," those that involve a mixture of commercial exploitation and sharing. In this, his position and mine are fairly close, though

we begin perhaps at divergent starting points. Lawrence Lessig, *Remix: Making Art and Commerce Thrive in the Hybrid Economy* (New York: Penguin Press, 2008).

65. See Robert P. Merges, "A New Dynamism in the Public Domain," 71 *U. Chi. L. Rev.* 183 (2004).

66. Where certain works are so canonical that there are no effective substitutes with fewer use-restrictions attached, IP law still allows criticism (e.g., an essay or entire website devoted to "Barbie as Ideology"), commentary (an essay on "Countering the Limiting Vision of 'The Little Mermaid' "), and even parody (a play lampooning Hogwarts Academy and the Harry Potter stories). But commercial remixes of canonical works can be prevented by IP law. Does this restrict freedom? Yes, but for a good reason (to support canonical works) and in a limited way (one may always appropriate ideas from these works, and incorporate those basic ideas into one's own original work; criticize and comment on them; and parody them).

67. I am thinking of course of Robert Nozick, *Anarchy, State and Utopia* (New York: Basic Books, 1974).

68. On the natural law antecedents of this aspect of Kant's thought, you might want to read Brian Tierney, "Permissive Natural Law and Property: Gratian to Kant," 62 *J. Hist. Ideas* 381 (2001), especially at 395 (quoting from MEJ, Ladd at 36).

69. Kevin E. Dodson, "Autonomy and Authority in Kant's Rechtslehre," 25 *Pol. Theory* 93, 99 (1997) (quoting Kant's DOR).

70. Westphal, "A Kantian Justification of Possession," supra, at 103.

71. I address the treatment of those who own nothing in Chapter 4.

72. See Andrew Botterell, "Property, Corrective Justice, and the Nature of the Cause of Action in Unjust Enrichment," 20 *Can. J. L. & Juris.* 275 (July 2007) (applying Kantian theory to unjust enrichment cause of action). I return in Chapter 5 to a discussion of Gordon's use of the language of restitution—a traditional legal/policy instrument—as an example of the use of a "mid-level principle," a shared or common conceptual vocabulary that sidesteps the need for agreement about deep normative issues. Thus for me, what Gordon says is perfectly consistent with Kant's views on property; yet a dyed-in-the wool utilitarian, or anyone who rejects the Kantian approach, can nevertheless engage with Gordon's discussion of restitution. This is an example of what I meant in Chapter 1 when I said there is "room at the bottom," i.e., space for pluralism about normative foundations, in the IP field.

73. DOR, Intro. § C, 6:230, Gregor at 387.

74. For Kant, a "maxim" is a rule of action. See Robert Paul Wolff, "The Completion of Kant's Moral Theory in the Tenets of the Rechtslehre," in *Autonomy and Community: Readings in Contemporary Kantian Social Philosophy* 39, 41 (Jane Kneller & Sidney Axinn, eds.) (Albany, NY: SUNY Press, 1998).

75. Wolff, "The Completion of Kant's Moral Theory," supra, 39–61, at 41.

76. The connection with the Categorical Imperative is apparent in Kant's introductory comments to the DOR. See, e.g., § III, 6: 225, Gregor at 379 ("The categorical imperative, which as such only affirms what obligation is is: act

upon a maxim that can also hold as a universal law. You must therefore first consider your actions in terms of their subjective principles; but you can know whether this principle also holds objectively only in this way: that when your reason subjects it to the test of conceiving yourself as also giving universal law through it, it qualifies for such a giving of universal law." The technical differences between the categorical imperative and the UPR in Kant's highly systematic philosophy include these: (1) the categorical imperative is an ethical rule that is concerned with one's internal, self-regulative moral process, and also constrains the individual free will; and (2) the UPR is concerned with external, legislatively imposed duties, which are a product of the "general will," i.e., the idealized rational legislative will or power. The relationship between the two is complex and somewhat controversial, making it problematical to fit Kant into the conventional debate in legal philosophy about whether unjust laws are "really" laws, i.e., the positivism versus natural law question. For a sense of Kant's confusing treatment of these issues, consider this: "Duties in according with rightful lawgiving can be only external duties, since this lawgiving does not require that the idea of this duty, which is internal, itself be the determining ground of the agent's choice; and since it still needs an incentive suited to the law, it can connect only eternal incentives with it. On the other hand, ethical lawgiving, while it also makes internal actions duties, does not exclude external actions but applies to everything that is a duty in general. But just because ethical lawgiving includes within its law the internal incentive to action (the idea of duty), and this feature must not be present in external lawgiving, ethical lawgiving cannot be external (not even the external lawgiving of a divine will), although it does take up duties which rest on another, namely an external, lawgiving by making them, *as duties*, incentives in its lawgiving." DOR, 6:219, Gregor at 383–384. Got that? See generally George P. Fletcher, "Law and Morality: A Kantian Perspective," 87 *Colum. L. Rev.* 533, 537 (1987); Jeremy Waldron, "Kant's Legal Positivism," 109 *Harv. L. Rev.* 1535 (1996). Professor Fletcher's work on this subject is reviewed and critiqued in Peter Benson, "External Freedom According to Kant," 97 *Colum. L. Rev.* 559 (1987). For an examination of the complexities within the categorical imperative itself, and of Kant's different formulations of it, see Paul Guyer, "The Possibility of the Categorical Imperative," 104 *Phil. Rev.* 353–385 (1995). For a taste of the vastness of the categorical imperative's reach in the hands of an accomplished Kant scholar, see Onora O'Neill, *Constructions of Reason: Explorations of Kant's Practical Philosophy* (Cambridge: Cambridge Univ. Press 1989) (arguing that even Kant's epistemology is subservient to the categorical imperative, in the sense that communal vindication—of knowledge as well as the rightness of actions—is the keystone of Kant's philosophy).

77. B. Sharon Byrd & Joachim Hruschka, "The Natural Law Duty to Recognize Private Law Ownership: Kant's Theory of Property in His Doctrine of Right," 56 *U. Tor. L.J.* 217, 219–221 (2006).

78. See generally Robert B. Louden, "Kant's Virtue Ethics," 61 *Phil.* 473 (1986).

79. See Byrd & Hruschka, "The Natural Law Duty to Recognize Private Law Ownership," supra, at 221: "In the original community of the land and the

things upon it, we legislate . . . with respect to our freedom to use external objects of choice as we like, for as long as we like, and for whatever purpose we choose. Our legislation in this community also proceeds from the a priori necessarily united will of all. This will obligates each person not to interfere with objects of choice others have acquired and declared to be their own. The a priori necessarily united will of all recognizes and secures individual property ownership rights to avoid conflict in the use of external objects of choice."

80. Jeremy Waldron, *God, Locke and Equality: Christian Foundations in Locke's Political Thought* (Cambridge: Cambridge Univ. Press, 2002).

81. See, e.g., Yochai Benkler, *The Wealth of Networks: How Social Production Transforms Markets and Freedom* 60 (New Haven, CT: Yale Univ. Press, 2007) (extolling the virtues of "commons-based peer production" as more than a fad, and as capable of fundamentally reshaping the ecology of digital production). See generally Chapter 8, Property in the Digital Era.

82. COJ § 49. On the relationship between genius and "rules," see Orrin N. C. Wang, "Kant's Strange Light: Romanticism, Periodicity, and the Catachresis of Genius," 30 *Diacritics* 13–37 (2000), at 24 (footnote omitted): "Through genius, something like a rule or concept, but not a rule or concept, is given, thereby realizing the artistic creation of beauty. . . . Kant's genius thus gives rule to art in two ways: first, as the originary nonrule that allows beautiful art to resolve the contradiction between its conceptual and nonconceptual character and, second, as the nonrule that becomes an ordinary rule for artistic schools of imitation." See also Paul Guyer, "Kant's Ambitions in the Third Critique," in *The Cambridge Companion to Kant and Modern Philosophy* 538, 538 (Paul Guyer, ed.) (Cambridge: Cambridge Univ. Press, 2006) (for Kant, "[o]ur aesthetic judgments and practices have a rational foundation even though they cannot be grounded on determinate principles.").

83. Milton C. Nahm, "Creativity in Art," in 1 *The Dictionary of the History of Ideas: Studies of Selected Pivotal Ideas* 577, 588 (Philip P. Wiener, ed.) (New York: Charles Scribner's Sons, 1973–1974), avail. at http://virgobeta.lib.virginia.edu/catalog/uva-lib:497916. See also Milton C. Nahm, *The Artist as Creator: An Essay of Human Freedom* 54–55 (Baltimore: Johns Hopkins Univ. Press, 1956) (elaborating on the distinction between inspiration and the expression of imagination in Kant's Critique of Judgment).

84. Indeed, according to Kant scholar Paul Guyer, this passage not only introduced a new understanding of genius, transcending the received tradition of genius as an isolated instance of unusual felicity; it also opened the way for a sort of permanent avant garde in the world of the arts. Guyer wrote: "Immanuel Kant was the first to recognize that genius, as exemplary originality, would be a stimulus and provocation to continuing revolution in the history of art. . . ." Paul Guyer, *Values of Beauty: Historical Essays on Aesthetics* (Cambridge: Cambridge Univ. Press, 2005), Chapter 10: "Exemplary Originality: Genius, Universality and Individuality," at 242. Guyer points out the relevance of Kant's conception for our times, "an age of perpetual revolution in the arts," Id. Guyer considers Kant among other "apostles of genius" in the

eighteenth century (including, surprisingly, John Stuart Mill). With these others, Kant pioneered an understanding of both the costs and benefits of "genuine artistic innovation and individuality," and thus opened the way for a new understanding of change and continuity in the arts.

85. Paul Guyer, *Kant and the Claims of Taste* (Cambridge: Cambridge University Press, 2d ed. 1997), at 2.

86. Richard Eldridge, *The Persistence of Romanticism: Essays in Philosophy and Literature* (Cambridge: Cambridge Univ. Press, 2001), at 75.

87. Nahm puts it this way: "Kant insists that productivity is not capricious. Genius cannot throw off the constraint of all rules. Imagination itself must be brought under the laws of the Understanding (the source of the categories, such as causality, relation, necessity, etc.)." Milton C. Nahm, "Creativity in Art," supra, 577, 588 (New York: Charles Scribner's Sons, 1973–1974), avail. at http://virgobeta.lib.virginia.edu/catalog/uva-lib:497916.

88. Richard Eldridge, *The Persistence of Romanticism*, supra, at 75. Eldridge says that this aspect of Kant was the source of T. S. Eliot's views in his essay, "Tradition and the Individual Talent." Id., at 76. Eldridge also speaks of a "second order" capacity for freedom, akin to our capacity to absorb language; and implicitly, I see this as a helpful way to frame what I am trying to say about originality and intellectual property. What our law ought to be about—and what I think the deep logic of intellectual property is about, in many ways—is stimulating this second-order capacity to be creative, through protection of "first-order" works of expression.

89. This of course makes perfect sense given the context of Locke's writings: he was defending the right of a sovereign people to reconstitute its basic form of government (viz.: the Glorious Revolution of 1688), over objections that the traditional monarchy was the only legitimate political system for Britain.

90. Ripstein, *Force and Freedom*, supra at 24: "By passing a law, a legislature purports to place citizens under an obligation that they would not be under had the law not been passed. The acquisition of unowned property shows that private right presupposes such public authority relations. One person, acting on his or her own initiative, unilaterally places others under a new obligation to stay off the property. Such a unilateral act could only be consistent with the freedom of others provided that it has a more general, omnilateral authorization. The omnilateral authorization is only possible in a rightful condition [i.e., within an established civil society]. Any other legal act, including that of resolving a private dispute or enforcing a binding resolution, requires legal authorization for just the same reasons." See also Byrd & Hruschka, *The Natural Law Duty to Recognize Private Law Ownership*, supra, at 221.

91. See, e.g., John Umbeck, *A Theory of Property Rights: With Application to the California Gold Rush* (Ames: Iowa St. Univ. Press, 1981). See also Robert C. Ellickson, *Order without Law: How Neighbors Settle Disputes* (Cambridge, MA: Harvard Univ. Press, 1994).

92. See, e.g., Dotan Oliar & Christopher Sprigman, "There's No Free Laugh (Anymore): The Emergence of Intellectual Property Norms and the Transformation

of Stand-up Comedy," 94 *Va. L. Rev.* 1787 (2008); Robert P. Merges, "Contracting into Liability Rules: Intellectual Property Rights and Collective Rights Organizations," 84 *Cal. L. Rev.* 1293 (1996) (describing emergence of "private IP systems" in some limited circumstances); Robert P. Merges, "Property Rights Theory and the Commons: The Case of Scientific Research," 13 *Soc. Phil. & Pol'y* 145–167 (1996) (social norms modify formal legal rights in dealings between research scientists); Robert P. Merges, "From Medieval Guilds to Open Source Software: Informal Norms, Appropriability Institutions, and Innovation," Conf. on the Legal Hist. of Intell. Prop., Working Paper (2004), avail. at http://ssrn.com/abstract=661543 (guilds as premodern IP enforcement mechanism; but ineffective when technology is too "public" to effectively maintain group secrecy); Robert C. Allen, "Collective Invention," 4 *J. Econ. Behavior and Org.* 1 (1983) (reciprocal information sharing during industrial revolution). See generally Michael J. Madison, Brett Frischmann, & Katherine J. Strandburg, "Constructing Commons in the Cultural Environment," 95 *Cornell L. Rev.* 657 (2010) (analyzing process by which norms contribute to a cultural "commons" of bartered, sold, and shared information). Some have disputed the effectiveness of certain norms that displace formal IP rights. Compare Kal Raustiala & Christopher Sprigman, "The Piracy Paradox: Innovation and Intellectual Property in Fashion Design," 92 *Va. L. Rev.* 1687 (2006) (arguing that a shared norm of nonprotection for IP actually leads to more innovation in the fashion industry, a dynamic that might work for other industries as well) with C. Scott Hemphill & Jeannie Suk, "The Law, Culture, and Economics of Fashion," 61 *Stan. L. Rev.* 1147 (2009) (arguing persuasively that rapid copying of successful fashion designs harms innovation in fashion, and therefore the IP system ought to enact a limited form of IP protection for fashions).

93. The cases are Millar v. Taylor, 4 Burr. 2303, 98 Eng. Rep. 201 (K.B. 1769) and Donaldson v. Beckett, 2 Brown's Parl. Cases 129, 1 Eng. Rep. 837; 4 Burr. 2408, 98 Eng. Rep. 257 (1774). For the United States, see Wheaton v. Peters, 33 U.S. (Pet. 8) 591 (1834).

94. See Benjamin Kaplan, *An Unhurried View of Copyright* (New York: Columbia Univ. Press, 1967), at 15; Mark Rose, "The Author as Proprietor: *Donaldson v. Becket* and the Genealogy of Modern Authorship," 23 *Representations* 51 (1988). See generally Lyman Roy Patterson, *Copyright in Historical Perspective* 175 (Nashville, TN: Vanderbilt Univ. Press, 1968).

95. Jane Ginsburg, "A Tale of Two Copyrights: Literary Property Rights in Revolutionary France and America," 64 *Tul. L. Rev.* 991 (1990). See also Adam Mossoff, "Rethinking the Development of Patents: An Intellectual History, 1550–1800," 52 *Hastings L.J.* 1255 (2001) (emphasizing natural law aspects of development of U.S. patent law).

96. Put briefly, Kant rejects the state of nature as an effective foundation for civil society because (1) a properly founded state has powers that no individual has, and therefore individual members cannot form a state by a simple agreement to pool their individual powers; and (2) a voluntary association formed by members of one generation cannot effectively bind autonomus individuals

born into later generations. As Ripstein puts it, "by what authority does the conventional practice [described e.g., by Locke] bind people who were not party to it?" Ripstein, *Force and Freedom*, supra, at 148. In the same vein, Kant argues the ineffectiveness of basing property rights on one's rights over one's own body. The key to property is not only that it represents an extension of a person, but also that it binds others—third parties—in ways that restrict their autonomy. No unilateral act of appropriation can so bind others, Kant said, if it is based only on unilateral preference or will. The act must be based in a legitimate political system, i.e., it must carry with it the authorization of the omnilateral will of the properly constituted state, to legitimately restrict the freedom of others. See Ripstein, *Force and Freedom*, supra, at 149–150.

97. Guyer, "Kantian Foundations for Liberalism," supra, at 235. Guyer contrasts property with other rights, such as freedom of expression. Unlike regulation of property, he argues, the state should not be permitted to place restrictions on expression, because individual beliefs are not dependent on mutual agreement. Id., at 237–38. See Andrews Reath, "Review Essay: Value and Law in Kant's Moral Theory," 114 *Ethics* 127, 129 (2003) (reviewing and expanding on Guyer's book). See also Ripstein, *Force and Freedom*, supra, at 155 (arguing that a properly constituted state could not prohibit all acquisition of property, but could "restrict initial acquisition in various ways—for example, setting aside areas as nature preserves for future generations." Time limits on IP rights are quite consistent with this example.

98. See, e.g., Adam Mossoff, "Patents as Constitutional Private Property: The Historical Protection of Patents under the Takings Clause," 87 *B.U. L. Rev.* 689 (2007).

99. "But just as there must be principles in a metaphysics of nature for applying those highest universal principles of a nature in general to objects of experience, a metaphysics of morals cannot dispense with principles of application, and we shall often have to take as our object the particular *nature* of human beings, which is cognized only by experience, in order to *show* in it what can be inferred from universal moral principles. But this will in no way detract from the purity of these principles or cast doubt on their a priori source. This is to say, in effect, that a metaphysics of morals cannot be based upon anthropology but can still be applied to it." DOR, Introduction § I, 6:216–217, Gregor at 372 (emphasis in original). Indeed, there is a sense in which empirical facts inform the formulation of the basic principles of justice Kant describes: "Because . . . the concept of justice is a pure concept which at the same time also takes practice (i.e., the application of the concept to particular cases presented in experience) into consideration, it follows that, in making a subdivision [of its concepts], a metaphysical system of justice would have to take into account the empirical diversity and manifoldness of those cases in order to be complete in its subdivision (and completeness in its subdivision is an indispensable requirement of a system of reason.)" DOR (MEJ version), Preface, Ladd at 1. For more on the nuances here, see Jeremy Waldron, "Kant's Legal Positivism," 109 *Harv. L. Rev.* 1535 (1996). On how this relates to traditional debates in legal philosophy between natural law and positivisim, see George

P. Fletcher, "Law and Morality: A Kantian Perspective," 87 *Colum. L. Rev.* 533, 537 (1987).

100. Cf. DOR Introduction, § I, 6:216, Gregor at 371: "[R]eason commands how we are to act even though no example of this could be found, and it takes no account of the advantages we can thereby gain, which only experience could teach us. For although reason allows us to seek our advantage in every way possible to us and can even promise us, on the testimony of experience, that it will probably be more to our advantage on the whole to obey its commands than to transgress them, especially if obedience is accompanied with prudence, still the authority of its precepts *as commands* is not based on these considerations." See also Ripstein, *Force and Freedom*, supra, at 148–149 (pointing out the difference between conventional and efficient arrangements and those that are based in a legitimate Kantian state).

101. See Robert P. Merges, Peter S, Menell, & Mark A. Lemley, *Intellectual Property in the New Technological Age* (New York: Aspen Publishers, 5th ed., 2010), at 1020–1051.

102. What would an interference with this possession look like? Perhaps a directive from the state Department of Job Assignments, directing an aspiring clarinetist to go to work in a flower shop or on a road paving crew. Perhaps a mandatory requirement that all aspiring actors appear in manadatory state-sponsored patriotic reenactments. Perhaps a requirement that an aspiring athlete work as a gym instructor in state-sponsored prisons or schools. These are extreme examples, but they all demonstrate what it would mean for an outside authority to interfere with people's *possession* of a thing, i.e., their developing talents and persona. This is of course a broad understanding of an object, and of possession, which is fully consistent with Kant's approach to property.

103. Some have seen a reflection of Kantian ideas in moral rights, which have some property-like features and which also protect unique personal features of creative people. See Leslie Kim Treiger-Bar-Am and Michael J. Spence, "Private Control/Public Speech" (working paper, 2010), avail. at http://ssrn.com/abstract=1020882. Indeed, the shared doctrinal foundation of both publicity and moral rights is the concept of autonomy, a thoroughly Kantian idea. For an excellent recent account of moral rights, see Roberta Rosenthal Kwall, *The Soul of Creativity: Forging a Moral Rights Law for the United States* (Stanford, CA: Stanford Univ. Press, 2009).

104. Treating a person's natural talents as a kind of "found object" is related to the topic of whether one deserves one's innate abilities, a problem of great concern for the philosopher John Rawls, and one I take up when discussing Rawls's work in Chapter 4.

105. For an excellent account of this, see Alice Haemmerli, "Whose Who? The Case for a Kantian Right of Publicity," 49 *Duke L.J.* 383 (1999).

106. See generally William Prosser, "Privacy," 48 *Cal. L. Rev.* 383 (1960).

107. See Haelen Laboratories, Inc. v. Topps Chewing Gum, Inc., 202 F.2d 866 (2d Cir. 1953). See generally William Prosser, "Privacy," supra.

108. 202 F.2d 866 (2d Cir. 1953).
109. 202 F.2d 866, at 868.
110. Technically, the court seems to overstate its case a bit; it implies that a release from liability under the players' right "not to have their feelings hurt," i.e., from liability under the personal, limited right to privacy, would be worthless. This may not be correct in every case, as it implies that tort suit settlements are generally worthless. But the court's overall point—that what logic demands in this situation is a full-blown property right—is surely correct.

4. Distributive Justice and IP Rights

1. John Rawls, *A Theory of Justice* (Cambridge, MA: Harvard Univ. Press, 1971) (hereinafter "TJ"), § 46, at 302.
2. This first principle obviously sounds similar to Kant's universal principle of justice, which we saw in Chapter 3. See, e.g., Thomas Pogge, *John Rawls: His Life and Thought* 188–195 (Oxford: Oxford Univ. Press, 2007) (describing Rawls's overall connections to Kantian thought). Note that the first principle has "lexical priority" over the second, meaning that it must be satisfied first, before the distributional considerations of the second principle kick in. TJ, § 46, at 302.
3. The "just savings" principle is Rawls's version of what is generally called "intergenerational equity": the idea that today's choice of policies must take into account, and be fair to, later generations as well as the current one. See generally Roger Paden, "Rawls' Just Savings Principle and the Sense of Justice," 23 *Soc. Theory & Pract.* 27–51 (1997). I address this important issue in depth in Chapter 9, through the case study of pharmaceutical patents and developing countries, an issue that also implicates the closely related topic of international distributional concerns in the design of the worldwide IP system.
4. Rawls, TJ, § 11, at 60; § 13, at 78–79.
5. John Rawls, *Justice as Fairness: A Restatement* 43 (Cambridge, MA: Harvard University Press, 2001) (hereinafter "JF") (explaining why, as against alternatives, "difference principle" best describes this concept).
6. Rawls, TJ, § 26, at 152–158.
7. Rawls, TJ, § 11, at 61.
8. See TJ, § 11, at 61, 66 (contrasting "freedom of the person along with the right to hold (personal) property" with an initial assumption that in the just society "the economy is roughly a free market system, although the means of production may or may not be privately owned"); see also JF at 138 ("private personal property" versus "right of private property in productive assets").
9. John Rawls, *Political Liberalism* 298 (New York: Columbia Univ. Press, 1993).
10. See TJ, § 42, at 270–274, where Rawls is agnostic about the choice between socialist and capitalist production.

11. See TJ, § 42, at 271, where Rawls distinguishes between the use of markets—which he broadly endorses—and expansive notions of private property, on which he is agnostic: "It is evident, then, that there is no essential tie between the use of free markets and private ownership of the instruments of production." The vast majority of economists today would disagree with this statement, most quite vehemently.

12. TJ, § 11, at 62.

13. Samuel Fleischacker, *A Brief History of Distributive Justice* 116–119 (Cambridge, MA: Harvard Univ. Press, 2004).

14. Martha Craven Nussbaum and Amartya Kumar Sen, *The Quality of Life* (Oxford: Oxford Univ. Press, 1993); Martha C. Nussbaum, *Women and Human Development* (Cambridge: Cambridge Univ. Press, 2001).

15. These themes form the heart of Samuel Fleischacker, *A Third Concept of Liberty: Judgment and Freedom in Kant and Adam Smith* (Princeton, NJ: Princeton Univ. Press, 1999). See e.g., *id.*, at 181–183.

16. TJ, § 48, at 311.

17. There is some symmetry between Rawls's admission that special incentives may be appropriate in an egalitarian state, and the basic structure of IP law, which after all is based on the idea of incentives. From a Rawlsian perspective, the question is whether IP rights represent incentives designed solely to encourage the development of native endowments in a way that will benefit the least well off. In honesty, I do not think IP can meet the stringent justificatory standards of Rawls's second principle. The best that might be said is that there will at times be some benefit that flows from IP rights to the least well off, in the form of less expensive goods backed by innovative technology, widely accessible culture, and the like. As I argue below, a Rawlsian defense of IP rights turns not on complete satisfaction of his second principle, but rather on two different arguments: (1) IP is one type of property that fits under an expanded right to property, as many critics of Rawls have argued; and (2) IP is almost surely one type of entitlement that would be established early in the history of a fair Rawlsian state.

18. Fleischacker, *Distributive Justice*, supra, at 111–112.

19. Id. at 132–133. See also David Schmidtz, "How to Deserve," 30 *Pol. Theory* 774, 775 (2002) (collecting sources who agree with Rawls on this point).

20. See, e.g., Joel Feinberg, *Doing and Deserving* (Princeton, NJ: Princeton Univ. Press, 1970); George Sher, *Desert* (Princeton, NJ: Princeton Univ. Press, 1987).

21. Feinberg, *Doing and Deserving*, at 64–65.

22. Id. at 83.

23. Wojciech Sadurski, *Giving Desert Its Due: Social Justice and Legal Theory* 116 (Dordrecht, Holland: D. Reidel, 1985).

24. Julian Lamont, "The Concept of Desert in Distributive Justice," 44 *Phil. Q.* 45, 47 (1994). In particular, Lamont emphasizes (1) a careful identification of the reason why someone is said to deserve something—what he calls "the desert-basis"; and (2) a taxonomy between (a) those who believe that we must exercise a high degree of control over all aspects of a situation in order for our conduct to ground a desert claim in that situation; and (b) those who believe

that we need not exercise as much control over a situation for our conduct to ground a desert claim. Rawls obviously adopts a strong form of position (1), arguing in effect that we never exercise enough control over all circumstances (our family, upbringing, life opportunities, educational advantages or disadvantages, etc.). Heather Milne defends a version of desert that tends toward equal distribution of positive feelings—a sort of egalitarian desert theory. See Heather Milne, "Desert, Effort and Equality," 3 *J. Appl. Phil.* 235 (1986).

25. See, e.g., Lamont, "Concept of Desert in Distributive Justice, supra, at 52.

26. See, e.g., Heather Milne, "Desert, Effort and Equality," supra, at 240.

27. The "original position" is a hypothetical situation in which all the prospective members of a given society come together to agree on how to set up the society's basic institutions. Deliberations in the original position take place under a "veil of ignorance"—none of the participants know what jobs, skills, social rank, or other attributes they will have in society. The original position can be thought of as somewhat akin to the "state of nature" in the thought of Locke, Hobbes, etc.; it is a hypothetical moment in time before organized government or "civil society" is actually in place.

28. Waldron's indispensable book *The Right to Private Property* is an excellent guide to many of the theories of property acquisition I cover in this book. I have drawn from my former Berkeley colleague's work extensively, and anyone familiar with his book will quickly see its influence throughout mine. In this section, however, I come to correct Waldron (or at least, extend his thinking), and not to praise him.

29. Waldron's book is about two main topics: property acquisition and property distribution. He is concerned with the former topic primarily as it relates to the second. As befits the historical moment in which it was written (1980–1988), the book spends a fair amount of time traversing the Marxist landscape. While it for the most part renounces anything like a Marxist destination (part of why the book has aged well), it shows the signs of having negotiated the Marxist terrain of the times. This might be one reason why Waldron states unequivocally that people in the original position would not agree to a conventional property regime. (For the record, I find his later book, *God, Locke And Equality*, to be both much more balanced on distributional issues and much more convincing; see especially his very insightful thoughts on the Lockean "charity" proviso discussed earlier in Chapter 2.)

30. Jeremy Waldron, *The Right to Private Property* 274–278 (Oxford: Oxford Univ. Press, 1988).

31. Rawls, TJ, § 24, "The Veil of Ignorance," at 136–137: "The idea of the original position is to set up a fair procedure so that any principles agreed to will be just. . . . Somehow we must nullify the effects of specific contingencies which put men at odds and tempt them to exploit social and natural circumstances to their own advantage. . . . It is assumed [in the original position] . . . that the parties do not know certain kinds of particular facts. First of all, no one knows his place in society, his class position or social status; nor does he know his fortune in the distribution of natural assets and abilities, his intelligence and strength, and the like. . . . As far as possible, then, the only particular facts

which the parties know is that their society is subject to the circumstances of justice and whatever this implies."

32. As I mentioned earlier, it is possible to defend IP rights on the basis of Rawls's second principle instead. The inegalitarian distribution that comes with IP protection could be justified by the benefits flowing to the neediest. Even if one were not destined to have a job dependent on IP creation, these rights might well provide consumers with high-quality creative products (new inventions, entertainment products, and the like). Assuming that even the poorest could afford at least some of these products, IP protection could therefore contribute something quite positive to one's life whether or not it was reasonable to imagine a career as a creative professional. Hence one would rationally agree that society ought to grant IP rights.

33. Other types of property certainly have the capacity to contribute to independence and autonomy; think of the craftsperson and her tools, or the farmer and his land. I am not saying autonomy considerations do not apply to ownership for these types of resources. But given the importance of IP rights in shaping careers, earnings potential, and overall life prospects in modern economy, and given that I happen to know much more about conditions concerning resources covered by IP rights, I will limit my analysis to this special but important case.

34. These include film, publishing, the performing arts, scientific or technical research, or product design and development. I mean to include here not only the highly visible (and very limited) job categories of movie director, author, or award-winning product designer, but also all the ancillary creative professional jobs that go into supporting the creative aspects of these industries: light and sound professionals for film, editors for books, session musicians and studio recording engineers, product testing and development engineers, and the like. It is important to broaden the categories in this way, to accurately reflect the wide swath of employment cut by the IP-intensive industries, and therefore to not unduly limit the view of a person in the original position regarding the chances of actually being employed in a job like this. Actually, this move is a form of "covering my bases." There is an argument, based on various things Rawls says about other topics, that empirical predictions of one's life prospects—i.e., the probability that one would wind up doing or believing X as opposed to Y—have no place in the original position. An example comes from Rawls's discussion of principles of religious freedom: "[T]he parties [in the Original Position] must choose principles that secure the integrity of their religious and moral freedom. They do not know, of course, what their religious or moral convictions are, or what is the particular content of their moral and religious obligations as they interpret them. . . . Further, the partners do not know how their religious or moral view fares in their society, whether, for example, it is in the majority or the minority." Rawls, TJ, § 33, at 206. So the argument in the text, that, empirically speaking, people must carefully consider all the potential career paths that might lead them into the role of "creative professional," is perhaps unnecessary if one is committed to strict adherence to Rawls's version of the original position.

35. Rawls, TJ, § 13, at 78–79: "[T]hose starting out as members of the entrepreneurial class in property-owning democracy, say, have a better prospect than those who begin in the class of unskilled laborers. . . . What, then, can possibly justify this kind of inequality in life prospects? According to the difference principle, it is justifiable only if the difference in expectation is to the advantage of the representative man who is worse off, in this case the representative unskilled worker. . . . [T]he greater expectations allowed to entrepreneurs encourages them to do things which raise the long-term prospects of the laboring class. Their better prospects act as incentives so that the economic process is more efficient, innovation proceeds at a faster pace, and so on. Eventually the resulting material benefits spread throughout the system and to the least advantaged. . . . [S]omething of this kind must be argued if these inequalities are to be just by the difference principle."

36. Michael G. Titelbaum, "What Would a Rawlsian Ethos of Justice Look Like?" 36 *Phil. & Pub. Aff.* 289–322 (2008), at 289.

37. G. A. Cohen, *Rescuing Justice and Equality* 70, 374–375 (Cambridge, MA: Harvard Univ. Press, 2008) (citing the example of a doctor who must give up half of the compensation offered because to take the full amount would be to act contrary to the dictates of Rawlsian justice).

38. Titelbaum, "Rawlsian Ethos," supra, at 295.

39. Technically, as Titelbaum says, a full Rawlsian ethos would include correlates of the first principle and the first part of the second principle (fair and equal opportunity), as well as a correlate of the second part of the second principle, i.e., the difference principle. Titelbaum, "Rawlsian Ethos," supra, at 304–305 ("Freedom of occupation is also protected; perhaps a talented individual who could best benefit society by becoming a doctor chooses a career in the arts that she finds more fulfilling. [This] . . . would be consistent with a full ethos of justice.").

40. Id., at 290.

41. Id., at 314–315.

42. Titelbaum assumes the social worker would help more people at lower cost in the big city job.

43. Titelbaum, "Rawlsian Ethos," supra, at 321–322.

44. Of course, it is also quite possible, even likely, that a creator who makes a good living and who controls his or her own destiny will create things of higher quality than someone who works for less or who has less control. I have implicitly assumed away any quality differential in my discussion here, because—assuming that higher quality redounded to the benefit of all consumers—that would add weight to the argument that IP can be defended with reference to Rawls's second principle. Right now I am defending the idea that even if IP creates inequalities that do not benefit the worst off, it is still defensible as a necessary component of the occupational freedom and personal autonomy protected under Rawls's first principle, concerning basic human liberties.

45. Margaret Holmgren, "Justifying Desert Claims: Desert and Opportunity," 20 *J. Value Inquiry* 265 (1986).

46. See, e.g., Fleischacker, *Distributive Justice*, supra, at 116, 132. Cf. George Sher, *Desert* (Princeton, NJ: Princeton Univ. Press, 1987). Sher points out the illogic of Rawls's argument that because we do not deserve some of the grounds of our actions, we do not deserve any of the results of our actions (such as developing our natural talents): "If deserving the benefits of our actions did require that we deserve everything that makes our actions possible, then all such desert would immediately be canceled by the fact that no one has done anything to deserve to be born or to live in a life-sustaining environment." Sher, *Desert*, at 25. See also Alan Zaitchik, "On Deserving to Deserve," 6 *Phil. & Pub. Aff.* 373 (1977). Sher also notes the very widespread intuition that people who are diligent, and work hard, ought to be rewarded—that they are deserving. See George Sher, *Desert*, Chapter 4, "Desert and Diligence," at 53–66.

47. Holmgren, "Justifying Desert Claims," supra, at 274 (listing "inventing new products" as one of the reasons an individual may need and deserve greater resources than society would allocate under a strictly egalitarian arrangement).

48. Id.

49. Id.

50. Id. Holmgren also describes limits to her notion of desert, pointing out that the ability to develop one's talents fully should not come at the expense of the most basic needs of the destitute. There is an echo here of Kant's other-regarding concept of personal autonomy.

51. See, e.g., Royston M. Roberts, *Serendipity: Accidental Discoveries in Science* (New York: Wiley, 1989).

52. This is at the heart of Louis Pasteur's famous statement that "chance favors the prepared mind." See id., at x. Samuel Goldwyn put the same thought somewhat differently when he said, "the harder I work the luckier I get." See http://www.brainyquote.com/quotes/quotes/s/samuelgold122307.html. This strategy of moving the analysis to a higher conceptual level is also available to rebut an argument sometimes levied against Kantian and Hegelian conceptions of IP rights. We saw in Chapter 3 that Kant provides support for the claim that the purpose of property rights is to encourage the autonomous individual to imprint his personality onto an external object. Critics of the "personality theory" of IP rights point out that many IP-protected works are in fact quite prosaic, showing little of the residue of a human personality. See, e.g., Kim Treiger-Bar-Am, "Kant on Copyright: Rights of Transformative Authorship," 25 *Cardozo L. Rev.* 1059, 1066 (2008) (arguing that Kant is mistakenly associated with a personality theory of IP, and that such a theory is in any event not reflected in Anglo-American doctrine and legal requirements). But it is a mistake to associate a "personality theory" with the expression of authors' "innermost selves" (id., at 1066), or rather, to underestimate the range of expression that might embody one's innermost self. An individual personality is an assemblage of qualities. Among a person's qualities might be a highly efficient approach to problem solving, or a distinctively succinct manner of expression. The creative work of such a person might well bear the imprint of these qualities. The fact that it is these qualities that find expression in creative work does not mean those works are devoid of a personal imprint. Likewise, the decision to remove all traces of one's personal history from a creative work

is itself the expression of a highly personal aesthetic choice, and thus an in-
stantiation of one feature of one's personality. The same can be said about
someone who *chooses* to create works that are strictly and intentionally spontaneous and serendipitous (think Jackson Pollock or the stream-of-thought
novels of Jack Kerouac): such works are the product or expression of a highly
personal choice, and thus the expression of an individual personality.

53. Julian Lamont, "Problems for Effort-Based Distribution Systems," 12 *J. Appl.
Phil.* 215 (1995) (arguing that, due to problems with measuring effort, productivity measures will often be a superior way to test for desert). It should be
noted that, although productivity may at times be a plausible second-best
proxy for true desert, this may not always be so. As Sadurski notes, "output"
measures such as productivity can be the result of individual effort together
with various social inputs, "factors which are beyond our control and thus for
which we cannot claim any credit." Sadurski, Giving Desert Its Due, supra, at
134. Sadurski's suspicion of output measures suggests an interesting approach
to the institution of IP law, which has at times been criticized for requiring the
expenditure of social resources to make very complex determinations concerning individual contributions (was A an author; did B first invent something;
etc.) The IP system is a set of institutions that expresses society's judgment that
in some cases, with respect to certain creative products, it is important to dis-
entangle individual contributions from their social background. The "mea-
surement costs" imposed by IP law, from this point of view, are worthwhile
because society so highly values individual contributions in these fields. The
answer to Sadurski, in other words, is to spend societal resources to separate
out individual contributions from other background factors leading to a successful output. Note that from this perspective, employing productivity enhancement as a proxy for effort is not the same as pursuing a consequentialist
or utilitarian program; people are still to be rewarded not for maximizing
collective happiness, but on the basis that they are individually deserving because they have contributed something of value via the increases in productivity they are responsible for.

54. On this, see Sadurski, *Giving Desert Its Due,* at 121 ("Often it may happen
that the social costs of legal enforcement of justice based on desert are too
high and then the attempt should be abandoned without, however, changing
the criteria of what is desert." In the terminology I use in Chapter 5, this is an
example of the midlevel efficiency principle modifying or interacting with the
proportionality principle, which in the ideal tries to calibrate property rights
in accordance with the contribution/effort/desert they embody. Those steeped
in utilitarian philosophy will see an immediate analogy with rule-utilitarianism
(the idea that a practice is defensible if it generally, or as a rule, leads to an
increase in net utility) versus act-utilitarianism (the stricter requirement that to
be justifiable every specific act must increase net utility). See generally Lawrence
B. Solum, Legal Theory Lexicon: Utilitarianism, avail. at http://lsolum.typepad
.com/legal_theory_lexicon/2003/11/legal_theory_le_4.html. On this analogy, I
might be said to advocate a form of "rule desert" as opposed to "act desert."

55. For a fascinating account of the origin and diffusion of the word *serendipity*
by the well-known sociologists of science Robert K. Merton and Elinor Barber,

see Robert K. Merton & Elinor Barber, *The Travels and Adventures of Serendipity* (Princeton, NJ: Princeton Univ. Press, 2004).

56. See, e.g., many of the stories in Roberts, *Serendipity,* supra.

57. See *The Quote Verifier* 22 (London: Macmillan, 2006) (Pasteur included this sentence as part of a lecture in 1854).

58. Or "luck is the residue of design."

59. For a definitive account, see Gwynn Macfarlane, *Alexander Fleming: The Man and the Myth* (Oxford: Oxford Univ. Press, 1984).

60. This explains why Fleming shared the Nobel Prize for penicillin with Florey and Chain. See id.

61. Richard L. Gausewitz, *Patent Pending: Todays' Inventors and Their Inventions,* 54–66 (Old Greenwich, CT: Devin-Adair, 1983).

62. United States v. Adams, 383 U.S. 39 (1966) (upholding validity of Adams's battery patent in an action against the U.S. government for unauthorized use of batteries).

63. Justin Hughes has pointed out another distributional impact of IP rights: many of the people who rise furthest from their social class at birth benefit directly from IP rights and the industries where they predominate. I am speaking here of entertainment and the sports and endorsements industries. For well-understood historical reasons, the average income of African-Americans trails that of other major ethnic groups. But a quick glance at the list of wealthiest African-Americans shows that all of them work in entertainment, sports/endorsements, and publishing. Oprah Winfrey, who heads the list (and is one of the few African-American billionaires), spans all of these industries.

64. See Pew Research Center, Social and Demographic Trends, http://pewsocialtrends.org, link at Reports, link at 2006, "Things we can't live without: The list has grown in the past decade," avail. at http://pewsocialtrends.org/2006/12/14/luxury-or-necessity/, first link under heading "Income," link on "the pattern tends to play out in one direction only", table http identified as http://pewsocialtrends.org/files/legacy/214.gif (Survey Date: October 18–November 9, 2006). See also Alan Peacock, "Making Sense of Broadcasting Finance" (1986), Robbins Lecture, Univ. of Stirling, reprinted in *Cultural Economics: the Arts, the Heritage and the Media Industries* (Ruth Towse, ed.)(Aldershot: Edward Elgar Towse, 1997), vol. 1, at 435–448. (making the case for a subsidy for public service broadcasting on the equity grounds that TV should be universally available in remote parts of the country and also offer good quality information and entertainment to the less well off).

65. Karen E. Riggs, *Mature Audiences: Television in the Lives of Elders* 87 (Piscataway, NJ: Rutgers Univ. Press, 1998).

66. Paul Taylor & Wendy Wang, "The Fading Glory of the Television and Telephone," Pew Research Center Report (August 19, 2010), at 6, avail. at http://pewsocialtrends.org, link at Reports, link at 2010.

67. See, e.g., Bella Thomas, "What the World's Poor Watch on TV," *Prospect,* January 20, 2003, avail. at http://www.prospectmagazine.co.uk/2003/01/whattheworldspoorwatchontv/.

68. R. Moynihan, et al., "Coverage by the News Media of the Benefits and Risks of Medications," 342 *New Eng. J. Med.* 1645–1650 (1999); Centers for Dis-

ease Control and Prevention, "Folic Acid Campaign and Evaluation— Southwestern Virginia, 1997–1999," 48 *Morbidity and Mortality Weekly Rep.* 914–917 (1999); A. G. Ramirez, et al., "Prevention and Control in Diverse Hispanic Populations: A National Leading Initiative for Research and Action," 83 *Cancer* 1825–1829 (1998) (describing TV, newspaper, and radio campaign involving awareness of cervical cancer); E. M. Rogers, et al., "Effects of an Entertainment-Education Radio Soap Opera on Family Planning Behavior in Tanzania," 30 *Stud. in Family Plan.* 193–211 (1999).

69. See www.mpaa.org/movieattendancestudy.pdf; see also www.mpaa.org/research statistics.asp.

70. See http://en.wikipedia.org/wiki/Household_income_in_the_United_States (citing U.S. Census data).

71. Larry May, *Screening Out the Past: The Birth of Mass Culture and the Motion Picture Industry* (New York: Oxford Univ. Press, 1980).

72. See Jane Addams, *The Spirit of Youth and the City Streets* (New York: Macmillan, 1930), Chapter 4, "House of Dreams," at 75–79; see generally Jim Cullen, ed., *Popular Culture in American History* (Malden, MA: Blackwell, 2001). It is worth noting too that many of the film industry's early "moguls" (Harry Cohn, Sam Goldwyn, Louis Mayer, the Warner Brothers) were children of poor, often Jewish, immigrants. See A. Scott Berg, *Goldwyn: A Biography* (New York: Alfred A. Knopf, 1989).

73. Just from recent years, for example, see *Frozen River* (Cohen Media Group, 2008); *Ballast* (Alluvial Film Co., 2008); *Wendy and Lucy* (Field Guide Films, 2008); *Chop Shop* (Muskrat Filmed Properties, 2007).

74. Riggs, *Mature Audiences*, supra, at 130 (describing importance of telephone communication to the elderly: "Even among elders who live in poverty, telephone communication has become a way to collapse the space between oneself and loved ones. . . . Some of [these elders] live with cataracts or without air conditioning but still budget a few minutes a month to call Junior in Atlanta.").

75. See, e.g., Lester R. Brown, *Seeds of Change: The Green Revolution and Development in the 1970's* (New York: Praeger, 1970).

76. Raymond Arsenault, "The End of the Long Hot Summer: The Air Conditioner and Southern Culture," 50 *J. So. Hist.* 597–628 (1984) (positive effects of air-conditioning on mortality, economic growth, etc., in American south).

77. See, e.g., Frank Jordans, "World's Poor Drive Growth in Global Cell Phone Use," *San Francisco Chronicle*, March 9, 2009 (AP Wire story).

78. See, e.g., Frank R. Lichtenberg, "The Impact of New Drug Launches on Longevity: Evidence from Longitudinal, Disease-Level Data from 52 Countries, 1982–2001," 5 *Int'l J. Health Care Fin. & Econ.* 47–73 (2005) (showing connection between new drug launches and reduced mortality across a wide range of countries).

79. There is a large literature on the individual and collective aspects of property rights. See, e.g., Carol M. Rose, "Canons of Property Talk, or, Blackstone's Anxiety," 108 *Yale L.J.* 601, 603–606 (Sir William Blackstone, whose "absolutist" view of property is often cited, understood well that the legal reality of his time was in fact much more complex); Amnon Lehavi, "The Property

Puzzle," 96 *Geo. L.J.* 1987, 2000–2012 (2008) (intricate relationship between public and private interests in property law); Gregory S. Alexander, "The Social-Obligation Norm in American Property Law," 94 *Cornell L. Rev.* 745 (2009) (describing legal rules that reflect duties, as well as rights, of property owners).

80. Certain distributive policies are built into the initial grant of a right (e.g., a limitation on the term of protection, or exclusions from protectable subject matter, such as fact works in copyright or laws of nature in patent); others come into play when an IP-protected work is deployed (e.g., "fair use" in copyright, or limits on the availability of injunctions in patent cases). The final portion of the periphery represents the taxation of works covered by IP rights—general societal redistribution as it applies specifically in the IP context. In this way, each IP right recapitulates the blending of individual and social that goes into every work that IP covers.

81. I am speaking in generalities here; the median creative work, the typical one, is my concern. There will no doubt be outliers on both sides of the median.

82. For the most part, conventional thinking about IP law is an instance of a more general approach, under which efficiency or welfare is the paramount normative goal of law. This view can be expressed in a simple maxim, "don't use legal rules to achieve distributive goals." This idea is a staple of mainstream U.S. law and economics. It is best explained in certain coauthored works by Louis Kaplow and Steven Shavell. See Louis Kaplow & Steven Shavell, *Fairness Versus Welfare* (Cambridge, MA: Harvard Univ. Press, 2002). For an account of IP law grounded primarily in this school of thought, see William Landes & Richard Posner, *The Economic Structure of Intellectual Property Law* (Cambridge, MA: Harvard Univ. Press, 2003). (For example, Landes and Posner analogize IP to real property; they use the example of the English "enclosure" movement beginning in the sixteenth century, which is generally thought to have greatly increased overall economic productivity, though at the cost of serious distributive dislocation in the form of increased rural poverty. See Landes & Posner at 12). An exclusive focus on efficiency or welfare maximization obviously rules out any role for distributive justice or fairness. Many disagree with this approach, including me. In this book, I concentrate on normative accounts of IP law that go well beyond utilitarian/welfare maximization. Yet in Chapter 5, I describe efficiency as one of the bedrock "midlevel" principles of IP law as it is formulated and applied by legislatures and courts. For one statement of an approach like mine, see Jules Coleman, "The Grounds of Welfare," 112 *Yale L.J.* 1511, 1538–1539 (2003) (book review of Kaplow & Shavell, *Fairness Versus Welfare,* supra): "The deontologist need not, and likely does not, claim that the law ought not to be assessed by its impact on welfare. He claims only that in addition to being assessed by its impact on welfare, the law ought to be assessed as well by the extent to which it conforms to the demands of justice." Coleman aptly describes the differences between the deontological school and the welfare-only approach. And like me, Coleman in his work draws extensively from the tools of the "welfarist" (utilitarian) camp.

83. Indeed, George Sher's defense of desert, which depends on a complex understanding of individual agency and the persistence of identity over time, assumes that desert must always relate to past actions. See George Sher, *Desert,* Chapter 10, "Why the Past Matters," 175–193.

84. See, e.g., Sadurski, *Giving Desert Its Due,* supra, at 118 ("[D]esert considerations are always past-oriented.").

85. Schmidtz, "How to Deserve," supra, at 776 (emphasis in original; footnote omitted).

86. Schmidtz summarizes Rawls's position as follows: "[W]e can say no one deserves anything, and that is what we will say if we assume we deserve credit for working hard only if we in turn deserve credit for being 'destined' to work hard." This Schmidtz rejects. See id., at 777. There is obviously a good deal of overlap between Schmidtz's idea of earning our way into desert and Locke's idea of grounding property in a combination of that which we inherit by dumb luck (the things of the earth) and the application of something in our control, our labor. Likewise, Kant's notion of the willing application of control, which drives his account of possession and property, has a lot of similarity to Schmidtz's argument.

87. As he puts it, "We sometimes deserve X on the basis of what we do after receiving X rather than what we do before." Schmidtz, "How to Deserve," supra, at 778. The tone and spirit of this argument is strongly reminiscent of a virtue-based or "aretaic" view of ethics. This is a view that emphasizes virtues in the sense of the ancient Greeks (justice, charity, etc.); social institutions, from this perspective, ought to be set up to promote these virtues. Much of what I say about desert in this section would fit very comfortably in a virtue-based account of IP rights. See, e.g., Colin Farrelly & Lawrence Solum, "An Introduction to Aretaic Theories of Law," in *Virtue Jurisprudence* 1–23 (Colin Farrelly & Lawrence Solum, eds.) (New York: Palgrave Macmillan, 2008). Indeed, a broad-minded understanding of desert, and its place in a system of fundamental rights and entitlements, suggests that while the "aretaic" vocabulary is distinct, at the conceptual level it has enormous overlap with liberal-minded deontological ethical theory.

88. For a somewhat similar idea, see Zaitchik, "Deserving to Deserve," supra, at 378: "[T]here is something more basic than effort at one's task or job, namely the effort expended in preparing to make an effort at one's task or job." Note that effort expended at this "preparation stage" in Zaitchik's presentation will often require extended control over time, and it therefore fits closely with what I said in Chapter 3 about Kant's theories of possession and property.

89. Schmidtz calls this a "promissory model" of desert: we receive the reward first, and then earn it with later actions. See Schmidtz, "How to Deserve," supra, at 785. My understanding of IP law relates desert to autonomy, in a way that connects both these concepts to Rawls's first principle. IP gives creative people the chance to earn a living at what they do best, and then to fully develop (or come to deserve) their native talents.

90. To take one of literally millions of examples: there were many young Japanese artists employed to create manga and other mass-market commercial art in

postwar Japan, but only a few created vast and unique imaginary worlds, such as those represented in the Hayao Miyazaki films *Spirited Away* and *Howl's Moving Castle*. See Helen McCarthy, *Hayao Miyazaki: Master of Japanese Animation* 30 (Berkeley, CA: Stone Bridge Press, 1999) (describing Miyazaki's first job as a junior animator, filling in frames sketched by a senior animator).

91. Technically, in terms of Rawlsian doctrine, this statement can be interpreted two ways. It could mean that IP rights are a species of the "personal property" that Rawls admitted was a basic liberty under his first principle of justice. Alternatively, it could be read as an argument that Rawls was wrong to exclude all nonpersonal (or "productive") property from the list of basic liberties guaranteed by the first principle—that IP is an especially desert-worthy form of productive property that ought to be included and protected in the basic structure of a fair society. This might be described, because of the way it enhances individual autonomy, as personal-productive property, a sort of Rawlsian hybrid.

92. Sadurski makes this point as he criticizes extensions of Locke's labor theory of appropriation: "I do not see why one right (over the product of our work) is to follow from another (over our bodies). Not only our labor is invested in the product but also other resources to which we cannot claim similar rights: raw materials, know-how, technology, etc. A judgment about our right to a product requires, therefore, a prior judgment about our rights to all those resources and factors which were used in the production of the commodity concerned. This judgment would have to take into account very complex social relationships; for example, if my education were facilitated by someone's taxes, then this taxpayer has contributed . . . to the product of my work. . . . [T]here are many factors of production which are results of social co-operation and we cannot simply claim our 'rights' over them in the same way we can claim rights over our bodies." Wojciech Sadurski, *Giving Desert Its Due*, supra, at 135. While there is much to this argument, recall that in my view a proper understanding of Locke's theory includes careful attention to the idea of mixing labor with other inputs, and that in various aspects of Locke's theory a notion of proportional reward (property claim proportional to effort) can be found. In addition, I would claim that society has chosen (wisely, I think) to expend resources separating out individual from social factors in the production of certain creative works; the very complexity Sadurski identifies speaks, in the case of IP, to how highly society values these types of works. For more on the idea of proportional reward for individual effort, see Chapter 6, The Proportionality Principle.

93. Cf. Eldred v. Ashcroft, 537 U.S. 186 (2003) (largely rejecting the need for First Amendment limits on copyright law due to the "internal" limits provided by various copyright doctrines, such as the idea/expression dichotomy and the fair use defense).

94. It should be noted that the literature on IP and distributive fairness is mostly about the distributional effects of IP doctrines on people connected one way or another to the creative industries. The usual classes considered are creators/owners and consumers/users. Scholarship in this vein describes how IP doc-

trines affect the distribution of resources as between these two classes. Unlike the more general philosophical discussion of distributive justice, then, this literature does not address distribution at the broadest level, which would include people who neither make nor use things protected by IP rights. The relevant actors in the discussion are all participants in what might be called the IP-creative ecosystem. So when scholars talk about the distributive effects of IP law, they are really talking about the effect that IP doctrines have on the various participants in this ecosystem, as opposed to a discussion of fair distribution among all members of society. The group of users and consumers of IP-protected items is, however, vast, so there may not be that much difference in practice between fairness in the IP system and fairness at the highest possible level of generality. For an excellent contribution along these lines, see Molly Shaffer Van Houweling, "Distributive Values in Copyright," 83 *Tex. L. Rev.* 1535 (2005).

95. Details and citations for the examples in this and the following paragraph can be found in Chapter 6, the section entitled "What is Proportionality," beginning on p. 160.

96. See Robert Nozick, *Anarchy, State and Utopia* (New York: Basic Books, 1974).

97. One well-known critique comes from Barbara Fried, who attacks an example Nozick gives in *Anarchy, State and Utopia*. Barbara Fried, "Wilt Chamberlain Revisited: Nozick's 'Justice in Transfer' and the Problem of Market-Based Distribution," 24 *Phil. & Pub. Affairs* 226–245 (1995). Nozick's example concerns the basketball player Wilt Chamberlain. According to Nozick, people have the right to retain the proceeds from their natural talents as against redistributive claims from the state. Chamberlain can keep whatever part of the gate receipts he is paid for playing basketball, despite the fact that Chamberlain received his gifts of tallness and dexterity through no effort of his own. Fried says that Nozick's story is a sleight of hand, drawing the reader's attention to the uncontroversial idea that people such as the basketball fans who pay to see Chamberlain play may rightly transfer what they own, in this case the money to see the game. Nozick's discussion here, according to Fried, hides a classic controversy: whether one who receives something of value in a transaction is morally deserving of the full exchange price. The fans might have the right to transfer the money they possess, in other words, but that is not tantamount to saying that Chamberlain has the right to keep all the money so paid. The fans' fair title to their money does not somehow pass through to Chamberlain, insulating him from any redistributive claim from the state.

98. This is true for all property rights. See, e.g., Yoram Barzel, *A Theory of the State: Economic Rights, Legal Rights, and the Scope of the State* 13–58 (Cambridge: Cambridge Univ. Press, 2002) (analyzing state enforcement as essential to the stable functioning of a property system); Benito Arruñada, "Property Enforcement as Organized Consent," 19 *J.L. Econ. & Org.* 401 (2003) (justifying governmental monopoly in land recording and registration as facilitating private contracts and protecting third parties). This is even more true for IP rights, as I argue in the text.

99. In terms of Fried's critique of Nozick, I can state my point this way: it is fair to tax Wilt Chamberlain on some of the money he receives for playing basketball, because he benefits from the roads that allow fans to get to the game, police protection that makes the game a safe experience for fans, and other direct ways; and also because peace and order are necessary preconditions for people to have leisure and expendable income to spend on luxuries such as basketball games. I would add that I can hold this position while also maintaining that Chamberlain deserves to receive rewards from his efforts in developing his talents. Though, as a longtime Boston Celtics fan, I would have to add that Bill Russell deserved his rewards too—maybe even a bit more than Chamberlain!

100. See, e.g., Nordlinger v. Hahn, 505 U.S. 1 (1992) (upholding constitutionality of California Proposition 13, despite its creation of grossly disparate tax burdens for virtually identical properties, depending on whether properties are retained or sold); Stephen W. Mazza & Tracy A. Kaye, "Restricting the Legislative Power to Tax in the United States," 54 *Am. J. Comp. L.* 641 (2006) (surveying the very broad judicial deference to U.S. tax legislation). It has been argued that the sweeping deference to legislative taxing powers is matched by a great willingness on the part of courts to overturn legislation that intrudes on the formal incidents of ownership, such as in takings jurisprudence. See Amnon Lehavi, "The Taking/Taxing Taxonomy," 88 *Tex. L. Rev.* 1235 (2010). Lehavi's fascinating thesis is that U.S. property law strikes a curious balance under which formal ownership rights are protected zealously while state guarantees of continuing economic value are just as zealously avoided. See id., at 1235. Lehavi sees this logic at work in the IP field as well: "[N]otwithstanding any intrinsic autonomy-based benefits that a creator may enjoy when she is recognized as formal owner of her innovation, the actual economic value of such protected information is not in any way enshrined or guaranteed by the state, as opposed to the protection of the legal right in it." Id., at 1253.

101. See generally Richard A. Epstein, *Takings: Private Property and the Power of Eminent Domain* 283–305 (Cambridge, MA: Harvard Univ. Press, 1985) (arguing, in the context of a generally libertarian theory, that taxes and special assessments must be calibrated so that they confer benefits on those charged with them that are proportional to the cost or burden). Many tax scholars point out that the best way to preserve progressivity in tax rates (making wealthier people pay higher taxes) is via taxes on consumption rather than income. See, e.g., Edward J. McCaffery & James R. Hines Jr., "The Last Best Hope for Progressivity in Tax" (April 2009), University of Southern California Law and Economics Working Paper Series. Working Paper 92, avail. at http://law.bepress.com/usclwps/lewps/art92/ (arguing that, because income taxes create disincentives to earn more, they are a poor way to implement the principle of progressive taxation; and therefore consumption taxes, which tax purchases and not income, are a better alternative).

102. This brings to mind the famous statement by John Marshall, paraphrased from an oral argument by Daniel Webster: "That the power of taxing it [a federal

privilege] by the states may be exercised so as to destroy it, is too obvious to be denied." M'Culloch v. Maryland, 17 U.S. 316, 427 (1819) (Marshall, J.). The maxim that grows out of this—"the power to tax is the power to destroy"—might be used as a guiding principle in the IP context. When the tax rate climbs so high that it effectively eviscerates the core of the IP right, it works to destroy the strong individual entitlement that each creator should by rights enjoy. On takings issues with respect to federal IP law, see Adam Mossoff, "Patents as Constitutional Private Property: The Historical Protection of Patents under the Takings Clause," 87 *B.U. L. Rev.* 689 (2007). On the technical economics literature on optimal taxation, a helpful literature review is Alan J. Auerbach and James R. Hines, Jr., "Taxation and Economic Efficiency," in 3 *Handbook of Public Economics* 1347–1422 (Alan Auerbach and Martin Feldstein, eds., Amsterdam: North-Holland, 2002). Although economic models often emphasize the advantages of relatively low tax rates, historical and empirical evidence regarding the relationship between tax rates, economic growth, and overall social welfare, shows a much more complex story. Historical evidence shows no clear correlation between tax rates and economic growth. For example, three noted tax policy experts have written: "The United States has enjoyed rapid growth both when taxes were low and when taxes were high. The strongest recent extended period of growth in U.S. history spanned the two decades from the late 1940s to the late 1960s, when the top marginal personal income tax rates were 70 percent or higher. Economic growth accelerated after the top marginal tax rate was increased from 31 percent to 39.6 percent in 1993. Comparisons across countries confirm that rapid growth has been a feature of both high- and low-tax nations. These considerations suggest that well-designed revenue increases need not inflict significant damage and may even strengthen economic performance." Henry J. Aaron, William G. Gale, and Peter R. Orszag, "Meeting the Revenue Challenge," in *Restoring Fiscal Sanity: How to Balance the Budget* 111, 112 (Alice M. Rivlin & Isabel Sawhill eds., Washington, DC: Brookings Institution, 2004). As a guideline, it would seem that an overall average (as opposed to marginal) tax rate approaching 50 percent may be near the limit of what is fair for revenue for IP-protected works.

103. The idea for Harry Potter, in Rowling's words, "simply fell into my head." See www.jkrowling.en/biography.

5. Midlevel Principles of IP Law

1. See Jules Coleman, *The Practice of Principle* 54–55 (Oxford: Oxford Univ. Press, 2001).

2. Id. at 5–6.

3. Or, to put it another way, it is "a pragmatically oriented form of conceptual analysis." Stephen R. Perry, "Review: Method and Principle in Legal Theory," 111 *Yale L.J.* 1757, 1759 (2002) (book review of Coleman, *The Practice of Principle*).

4. Coleman, *The Practice of Principle*, supra, at 54.

5. It may seem confusing that I locate ethical commitments at the bottom of my schema, whereas Coleman puts his high-level principles at the top. I have always thought of Locke, Kant, and others as the foundation of the IP field, so that is where I put them in this book. There is surely an arbitrary quality to this sort of thing. Even so, it might be worth noting that I have spent most of my academic career attending to detailed doctrines and particular institutions in the world of IP, rather than high philosophical theory. So maybe it is significant that I place the details in the top, or privileged, position of my hierarchy, while assigning deep ethical principles to the bottom. Biography may not be the best source for theory, but it will inevitably find its way in.

6. See John Rawls, *Political Liberalism* (New York: Columbia Univ. Press, 1993).

7. See also Cass Sunstein, "Incompletely Theorized Agreements," 108 *Harv. L. Rev.* 1733 (1995) (idea very similar to overlapping consensus). For an interesting and concise introduction to the ideas of overlapping consensus and incompletely theorized agreements, see Larry Solum's Legal Theory Blog, "Legal Theory Lexicon: Overlapping Consensus and Incompletely Theorized Agreements," avail. at http://lsolum.typepad.com/legaltheory/2009/11/legal-theory-lexicon-overlapping-consensus-incompletely-theorized-agreements.html.

8. I prefer to add "nonremoval" to the usual phraseology of public domain, because it carries a reminder of Lockean ideas: some material is off limits to would-be appropriators, because it cannot be legitimately owned. There is far more discussion of "the public domain" than of "nonremoval," it is true, but I am not the only one in the IP field to speak in these terms. In cases involving inventions, for example, people often argue that wise policy should prevent removal of an obvious, and, therefore, soon-to-be-made invention, through award of a patent. The obvious variation on what is known is as yet only inchoately available; yet its removal represents a loss for the public. See, e.g., Richard H. Stern, "Structural Obviousness of Compounds And Compositions: The CAFC's En Banc *Dillon* Decision," 13 *Euro. Int. Prop. L. Rev.* 59, 61 (1991) ("The [patent office] argued that the effect of giving Dillon a patent on her compositions would be to remove from the public domain an obvious variant of known dewatering compositions. . . .").

9. Jane C. Ginsburg, "Sabotaging and Reconstructing History: A Comment on the Scope of Copyright Protection in Works of History after *Hoehling v. Universal Studios,*" 29 *J. Copyright Soc'y* 647 (1982).

10. Trade secrets and trademark can be protected indefinitely under the right conditions, so technically what I say here applies only to patents and copyrights. But even for trademarks and trade secrets, the legal requirements for continuing enforceability of the rights mean that in effect many of these will eventually become public too, at which point they also become essentially unremoveable from public availability. See generally Robert Merges, Peter Menell, & Mark Lemley, *Intellectual Property in the New Technological Age* (5th ed. 2010).

11. Independent creation is permissible in copyright, however; so if someone were to (improbably) create anew a work that just happens to coincide precisely with *Don Quixote*, that new work would be copyrightable, though of course the original could be copied because it is now in the public domain. See id. at 421. See also Jorge Luis Borges, "Pierre Menard, Author of the 'Quixote'," in *Labyrinths: Selected Short Stories and Other Writings by Jorge Luis Borges* (Donald A. Yates & James E. Irby, eds.) (New York: W. W. Norton, 2007) (fictional review of word-for-word recreation of *Don Quixote*, describing, as only Borges could, the subtle differences between original and new version). See also Feist Publ'ns, Inc. v. Rural Tel. Serv. Co., Inc., 499 U.S. 340, 345 (1991). ("Original, as the term is used in copyright, means only that the work was independently created by the author (as opposed to copied from other works), and that it possesses at least some minimal degree of creativity.")

12. These have been defined as "'incidents, characters or settings which are as a practical matter indispensable, or at least standard, in the treatment of a given topic." Atari, Inc. v. North American Phillips Consumer Electronics, 672 F.2d 607, 616 (7th Cir. 1982).

13. For a detailed history of the phrase "public domain," which was imported from French law into U.S. IP law, see Tyler T. Ochoa, "Origins and Meanings of the Public Domain," 28 *U. Dayton L. Rev.* 215 (2003). Ochoa says that "public property" was the phrase most commonly used to signify nonremoval in the nineteenth century; the Supreme Court first used "public domain" in 1911. See Baglin v. Cusenier Co., 221 U.S. 580, 598 (1911). Ochoa credits the great American jurist Learned Hand with popularizing "public domain" (and its earlier incarnation, public "demesne") in a series of opinions between 1915 and 1924. See Ochoa, "Public Domain," supra, at 243.

14. In re Hall, 781 F.2d 897 (Fed. Cir. 1986).

15. Titanium Metals Corp. v. Banner, 778 F.2d 775 (Fed. Cir. 1985) (invalidating a patent claim on the ground that one data point in one graph of a Russian metallurgy journal overlapped with the subject matter of the claim).

16. See, e.g., Robert P. Merges, "Economic Perspectives on Innovation: Commercial Success and Patent Standards," 76 *Cal. L. Rev.* 803–876 (1988); Robert P. Merges, "Uncertainty and the Standard of Patentability," 7 *(Berkeley) High Tech. L. J.* 1 (1993).

17. See, e.g., David McGowan, "Copyright Nonconsequentialism," 69 *Mo. L. Rev.* 1, 15–16 (2004) (arguing that although in general copyright scholars who appeal to utilitarian theories are in fact arguing from ethical/normative starting points, originality in copyright law is an example of a doctrine that can be explained along utilitarian/consequentialist lines).

18. The Canadian Supreme Court touched on this theme in a copyright opinion from 2004. See CCH Can. Ltd. v. Law Soc'y of Upper Can., [2004] S.C.R. 339, § 15 (citations omitted): "There are competing views on the meaning of 'original' in copyright law. Some courts have found that a work that originates from an author and is more than a mere copy of a work is sufficient to ground copyright. This approach is consistent with the 'sweat of the brow' or 'industriousness'

standard of originality which is premised on a natural rights or Lockean theory of 'just desserts [sic],' namely that an author deserves to have his or her efforts in producing a work rewarded. Other courts have required that a work must be creative to be 'original' and thus protected by copyright. This approach is also consistent with a natural rights theory of property law; however it is less absolute in that only those works that are the product of creativity will be rewarded with copyright protection." See generally, Lior Zemer, "The Making of a New Copyright Lockean," 29 *Harv. J. L. & Pub. Pol'y* 891 (2006) (arguing in general for a much more communitarian reading of Locke as applied to copyright, emphasizing the provisos, etc.).

19. See McGowan, "Nonconsequentialism," supra (arguing that, for this reason, copyright arguments conducted in the language of instrumental or utilitarian values are often in fact grounded in hidden or off-stage ethical commitments).

20. Another variant on this idea comes from a book by torts scholar Peter Gerhart, *Tort Law and Social Morality* (Cambridge: Cambridge Univ. Press, 2010). Gerhart argues that tort law can be explained by a single, integrated framework that incorporates both utilitarian and deontic elements. He explicitly rejects Coleman's concept of midlevel principles, partly because they derive from legal rules that themselves are grounded in ultimate normative commitments. Gerhart believes that you cannot induce principles upward from mere doctrine when that doctrine itself is rooted in deeper, if unarticulated, theory.

21. For excellent overviews of the large literature on this topic, which include taxonomic suggestions for identifying numerous distinct "public domains," see James Boyle, "The Second Enclosure Movement and the Construction of the Public Domain," 66 *Law & Contemp. Probs.* 33, 68 (Winter/Spring 2003); Pamela Samuelson, "Enriching Discourses on Public Domains," 55 *Duke L.J.* 783 (2006).

22. David Lange, "Reimagining the Public Domain," 66 *Law & Contemp. Probs.* 463 (Winter/Spring 2003).

23. Id., at 474 (arguing that the public domain should be "independently and affirmatively recognized in law, sometimes collective in nature and sometimes individual, but omnipresent, portable, and defining.").

24. See my article, "Locke for the Masses," 36 *Hofstra L. Rev.* 1179 (2008), where I explore the idea of rewarding group effort under Lockean principles by assigning some sort of IP right.

25. See, e.g., Lange, "Reimagining the Public Domain," supra, at 479–480, quoting from David Lange & Jennifer Lange Anderson, "Copyright, Fair Use and Transformative Critical Appropriation" (2001), later version available at http://www.law.duke.edu/pd/papers/langeand.pdf (last visited Dec. 21, 2010) ("Creative appropriation would be presumptively privileged in every instance, without primary concern either for exploitation adversely affecting the economic value of an antecedent work or for the reputation or sensibilities of its author or proprietor. . . ."). I disagree; for me, "the economic value" of a work and the "reputation or sensibilities" of authors are at the core of IP rights, as I argue based on Locke and Kant in Chapters 2 and 3. I address the specific issue

Lange is discussing—transformative uses of preexisting works, particularly in the digital or online world—in Chapter 8.

26. I address this in detail in Chapter 8.

27. There are actually two types of works represented here. One is works that are in fact covered by a valid and existing IP right, but for which the costs of enforcing that right are too high to be worthwhile. The other is works that could have been covered by an IP right but were not, because the creators of the works understood the enforcement situation and took it into account when deciding whether to even bother applying for a right. For our purposes here, the difference between these two subcategories is not important. In some contexts it can be.

28. Justin Hughes, "The Philosophy of Intellectual Property," 77 *Geo. L.J.* 287, 309–310 (1988) ("proportional contributions" concept in patent law as an example of the "value-added justification" for IP law).

29. See, e.g., Allen E. Buchanan, *Ethics, Efficiency and the Market* (Oxford: Oxford Univ. Press, 1985) at 11: "The best that can be said about the Paretian principles is that (1) both bear a remote resemblance to the common-sense notion of efficiency as taking the least-costly effective means to one's particular ends; and (2) the Pareto principles approximate the principle that social arrangements should be mutually advantageous in the sense that the attempt to achieve a Pareto Optimal state and the choice to achieve a Pareto Superior state over a Pareto Inferior state both acknowledge that advantages for some are to be gained if this can be done without disadvantaging others."

30. See, e.g., Buchanan, id.; Serena Olsaretti, *Liberty, Desert and the Market* 9 (Cambridge: Cambridge Univ. Press, 2004) (defending the basic fairness of a market economy, to the extent it rewards deserving and responsible choice, and subject to regulation when it deviates from this ideal).

31. See, e.g., Lewis A. Kornhauser, "Wealth Maximization," in *The New Palgrave Dictionary of Economics and the Law* 679–683 (Peter Newman, ed.) (New York: Stockton Press, vol. 3, 1998).

32. See Richard A. Posner, "Wealth Maximization and Tort Law: A Philosophical Inquiry," in *Philosophical Foundations of Tort Law* 99–111 (David G. Owen, ed.) (Oxford: Oxford University Press, 1995).

33. Deirdre McCloskey, *The Bourgeois Virtues: Ethics in an Age of Commerce* 480 (Chicago: Univ. of Chicago Press, 2006). McCloskey is a big believer in the "civilizing" benefits of economic and social systems based on market exchange, saying at one point: "Participation in capitalist markets and bourgeois virtues has civilized the world." Id., at 26. But her conception of capitalism situates market exchange in a larger system of "bourgeois virtues" which she traces to Adam Smith and beyond. For McCloskey, efficiency is an expression of the virtue of "prudence," which is one—but only one—of the requisite virtues necessary to promote economic growth and personal flourishing. Other virtues include justice, courage, temperance, and others with a more spiritual flavor (faith, hope, and love).

34. Amartya Sen, *Development as Freedom* 6, 112 (New York: Knopf, 2000).

35. See F. Scott Kieff and Troy A. Paredes, "Engineering a Deal: Toward a Private Ordering Solution to the Anticommons Problem," 48 *B.C. L. Rev.* 111. 140 (2007) (describing the "beacon effect" whereby a property right signals to others that the right holder must be located and dealt with if a given asset is to be used).

36. See, e.g., Thomas W. Merrill & Henry E. Smith, "Optimal Standardization in the Law of Property: The Numerus Clausus Principle," 110 *Yale L.J.* 1 (2000).

37. Henry E. Smith, "Intellectual Property as Property: Delineating Entitlements in Information," 116 *Yale L.J.* 1742 (2007).

38. Ashish Arora & Robert P. Merges, "Specialized Supply Firms, Property Rights, and Firm Boundaries," 13 *Indus. & Corp. Change* 451 (2004).

39. Robert P. Merges, "A Transactional View of Property Rights," 20 *Berkeley Tech. L.J.* 1477 (2005).

40. The efficiency principle can be expressed as an affirmative principle: only grant patents when they are likely to induce inventions that will not otherwise be made. See, e.g., Robert P. Merges, "Economic Perspectives on Innovation: Commercial Success and Patent Standards," 76 *Cal. L. Rev.* 803 (1988); Robert P. Merges, "Uncertainty and the Standard of Patentability," 7 (Berkeley) *High Tech. L.J.* 1 (1993).

41. Wendy Gordon, "Fair Use as Market Failure: A Structural and Economic Analysis of the Betamax Case and its Predecessors," 82 *Colum. L. Rev.* 1600 (1982).

42. Id.

43. In other scholarship, Gordon has engaged these issues in a deep and profound way. See, e.g., Wendy J. Gordon, "A Property Right in Self-Expression: Equality and Individualism in the Natural Law of Intellectual Property," 102 *Yale L.J.* 1533 (1993) (expounding Lockean theory of IP rights). For another influential example of Gordon's work at the level of midlevel principles, see Wendy J. Gordon, "On Owning Information: Intellectual Property and the Restitutionary Impulse," 78 *Va. L. Rev.* 149 (1992) (placing restitution, itself grounded in but not directly tied to ultimate normative principles, at the center of IP theory).

44. See Roberta Rosenthal Kwall, *The Soul of Creativity* 39-41 (Stanford, CA: Stanford Univ. Press, 2009) (analysis of Kantian and Hegelian influences in European moral rights law). See also Treiger-Bar-Am, "Kant on Copyright," supra (specifying that in Kantian theory, it is the presence of a unique individual as author, rather than evidence of a distinctive personality in the body of a given creative work, that merits protection).

45. Jane C. Ginsburg, "A Tale of Two Copyrights: Literary Property in Revolutionary France and America," 64 *Tul. L. Rev.* 991 (1990) reprinted in *Foundations of Intellectual Property* 285-291 (Robert P. Merges & Jane C. Ginsburg, eds.) (Mineola, NY: Foundation Press, 2004).

46. See, e.g., Adam Mossoff, "Rethinking the Development of Patents: An Intellectual History, 1550–1800," 52 *Hastings L.J.* 1255 (2001) (showing natural rights influence in development of patent law); Adam Mossoff, "Who Cares

What Thomas Jefferson Thought about Patents? Reevaluating the Patent 'Privilege' in Historical Context," 92 *Cornell L. Rev.* 953, 971–972 (2007) (refuting historians who argue that the early patent "privilege" was seen as purely a creature of state discretion and therefore distinct from true property, which by contrast has its roots in a natural right that precedes the state).

47. For background on moral rights, see Kwall, *Soul of Creativity*, supra; Martin A. Roeder, "The Doctrine of Moral Right: A Study in the Law of Artists, Authors and Creators," 53 *Harv. L. Rev.* 554 (1940); Henry Hansmann & Maria Santilli, "Authors' and Artists' Moral Rights: A Compartative Legal and Economic Analysis," 26 *J. Legal Stud.* 95, 105 (1997).

48. Jane C. Ginsburg, "The Right to Claim Authorship in U.S. Copyright and Trademark Laws," 41 *Hous. L. Rev.* 263 (2004).

49. See, e.g., Seshadri v. Kasraian, 130 F.3d 798, 803–804 (7th Cir. 1997) (Posner, J.) ("[T]here are glimmers of the moral-rights doctrine in contemporary American copyright law."); Ty, Inc. v. GMA Accessories, 132 F.3d 1167, 1173 (7th Cir. 1997) (Posner, J.) (stating that preliminary injunction "draws additional sustenance from the doctrine of 'moral rights' . . . a doctrine that is creeping into American copyright law").

50. On this point, see the illuminating essay by Neil Netanel, "Copyright Inalienability Restrictions and the Enhancement of Author Autonomy: A Normative Evaluation," 24 *Rutgers L.J.* 347 (1993). Netanel argues that "autonomy inalienabilities are generally desirable, not only to promote author interests, but also to foster cultural diversity." Id., at 354. This essay highlights the connection between autonomy, fostered here by the ability to rescind an old licensing agreement and make more money in a new one, and dignity; the reputational and personal interests protected by the termination right also lead to the chance for greater compensation, which often contributes to creator autonomy.

51. Gilliam v. Am. Broadcasting Co., Inc. 538 F.2d 14 (2d Cir. 1976). For background on *Gilliam*, see Justin Hughes, "American Moral Rights and Fixing the Dastar 'Gap,'" 2007 *Utah L. Rev.* 659.

52. Fantasy, Inc. v. Fogarty, 94 F.3d 553 (9th Cir. 1996).

53. Czarnik v. Illumina, Inc., 437 F. Supp. 2d 252, 256 (D. Del. 2006) (plaintiff has standing to correct inventorship because "he has suffered harm to his reputation and standing in the scientific community"). See also Chou v. Univ. of Chicago, 254 F.3d 1347, 1359 (Fed. Cir. 2001) ("being considered an inventor of important subject matter is a mark of success in one's field. . . . Pecuniary consequences may well flow from being designated as an inventor."). See generally, Paris Convention for the Protection of Industrial Property art. 4ter, Mar. 20, 1883, as revised at Stockholm July 14, 1967, 24 U.S.T. 2140, 828 U.N.T.S. 305 ("The inventor shall have the right to be mentioned as such in the patent.").

54. See, e.g., Robert P. Merges, "The Law and Economics of Employee Inventions," 13 *Harv. J.L. & Tech.* 1 (1999).

6. The Proportionality Principle

1. Jules Coleman, *The Practice of Principle* 54 (Oxford: Oxford Univ. Press, 2001): "Social practices turn abstract ideals into regulative principles; they turn virtue into duty. . . . In other words, the practices we have do not merely reveal the content of the principles to which we are committed; each practice partially constitutes the content." This is very similar to what Hans-Georg Gadamer says about legal interpretation. For Gadamer, meaning is not assigned to legal propositions in the abstract, before they are applied. For him, the application of the proposition to a specific fact pattern *constitutes* its meaning, it *is* its meaning. Hans-Georg Gadamer, *Truth and Method* 310, 325 (New York: Crossroad Publishing, 2d rev. ed., 1989).

2. See Rebecca Eisenberg & Robert P. Merges, "Opinion Letter as to the Patentability of Certain Inventions Associated with the Identification of Partial cDNA Sequences," 23 *Am. Intell. Prop. L. Ass'n Q.J.* 1 (1995).

3. See In re Fisher, 421 F.3d 1365 (Fed. Cir. 2005). The context for the case is explained in detail in Robert P. Merges & John F. Duffy, *Patent Law and Policy: Cases and Materials* 250–256 (Charlottesville, VA: LexisNexis Publishing, 4th ed., 2007).

4. Robert P. Merges, "The Trouble with Trolls: Innovation, Rent-Seeking and Patent Law Reform," 24 *Berkeley Tech. L.J.* 1583 (2010).

5. See, e.g., Robert P. Merges, "Uncertainty and the Standard of Patentability," 7 (Berkeley) *High Tech. L.J.* 1 (1993).

6. See, e.g., In re Fisher, 427 F.2d 833, 835 (C.C.P.A. 1970) (under the enablement requirement, patentee must disclose information "to a degree at least commensurate with the scope of the claims."). This requirement is discussed in Robert P. Merges & John F. Duffy, *Patent Law and Policy*, supra, 271–272.

7. See, e.g., Sega Enterprises, Ltd. v. Accolade, Inc., 977 F.2d 1510 (9th Cir. 1992); Sony Computer Entertainment, Inc. v. Connectix Corp., 203 F.3d 596 (9th Cir. 2000); Atari Games Corp. v. Nintendo of America, 975 F.2d 832, 843–844 (Fed. Cir. 1992).

8. For an application of the fair use defense to a case involving protection against anticircumvention under the Digital Millenium Copyright Act, see Chamberlain Group, Inc. v. Skylink Tech., Inc., 381 F.3d 1178 (Fed. Cir. 2004) (finding it fair use for defendant to have copied plaintiff's short garage door opener security codes, in case in which plaintiff sought effectively to use the short codes to protect its market in compatible garage door openers).

9. eBay, Inc. v. MercExchange, L.L.C., 126 S. Ct. 1837 (2006).

10. 547 U.S. 388, 396–397 (Kennedy, J., concurring) (joined by Justices Stevens, Souter, and Breyer).

11. MercExchange, L.L.C. v. eBay, Inc., 401 F.3d 1323, 1339 (Fed. Cir. 2005).

12. One implication here is that there is no rigid relationship between the physical area covered by Al's property claim and the amount of leverage a court might consider appropriate. Even a tiny parcel of land that everyone knows in advance occupies a crucially strategic location might well command a very high price; the small parcel size in such a case would not in other words preclude a

significant degree of economic leverage. I used a physical size/economic value metric in the bridge parable, but in reality the key relationship is between legitimate (intrinsic) and actual economic leverage.

13. The intuition here is quite in accord with a well-known article on doctrines relating to a mistake in the making of contracts. See Anthony Kronman, "Mistake, Information, Disclosure and the Law of Contracts," 7 *J. Leg. Stud.* 1 (1978). Kronman argued that where a contracting party could be expected to have invested significant resources to acquire valuable information, he should be able to use that information to contract to advantage. The other party to the contract, in other words, had no claim to be excused from performance even though that other party did not have access to the information in question. By contrast, where a person most likely acquired information fortuitously and without any effort, Kronman said it is not fair to enforce an advantageous contract made on the basis of that information. There is in this rationale more than a whiff of a combined emphasis on utilitarian incentives and moral desert—which is one reason I find it a close analogy to the proportionality principle in IP law. For an outstanding discussion and extension of Kronman's thesis, see Kim Lane Scheppele, *Legal Secrets: Equality and Efficiency in the Common Law* 32–36 (Chicago: Univ. Of Chicago Press, 1988).

14. *Oxford English Dictionary* (Oxford: Oxford Univ. Press, 1989, & Supp. 1997), entry for "Speculation."

15. Deirdre McCloskey, *The Rhetoric of Economics* (Madison: Univ. of Wisconsin Press, 2d ed., 1998).

16. See Richard A. Posner, "The Social Costs of Monopoly and Regulation," 83 *J. Pol. Econ.* 807, 808 1975 (discussing "monopoly rents," those backed by (usually temporary) market power or government-backed power to exclude). An instructive effort to distinguish between harmful or deleterious rents and rents generated by competition (and therefore in general of a less harmful nature) is made in Gordon Tullock, "Rent Seeking: The Problem of Definition," Chapter 5 in *The Economics of Special Privilege and Rent Seeking* 49–58 (Norwell, MA: Kluwer Academic Publishers, 1989).

17. The classic reference here is James M. Buchanan, Robert D. Tollison, & Gordon Tullock, *Toward a Theory of the Rent-Seeking Society* (College Station: Texas A&M University Press, 1980), at ix ("[Rent seeking] is meant to describe the resource-wasting activities of individuals seeking transfers of wealth through the aegis of the state."). It is probably not necessary to point out that the association between inefficiency, if not ethical questionability, and activities of the state bespeaks an affinity between the theory of rent seeking and conservative or libertarian politics. For a critique of the concept along these lines, see Steven G. Medema, "Another Look at the Problem of Rent Seeking," 25 *J. Econ. Issues* 1049, 1053 (1991) (criticizing the ahistorical assumption that there is a "natural" allocation of rights that governments "interfere with" and "artificially alter" due to rent-seeking lobbying).

18. William J. Baumol, "Entrepreneurship: Productive, Unproductive and Destructive," 98 *J. Pol. Econ.* 93, 93 (1990) ("The basic hypothesis is that, while the total supply of entrepreneurs varies among societies, the productive contribution of

the society's entrepreneurial activities varies much more because of their allocation between productive activities such as innovation and largely unproductive activities such as rent seeking or organized crime.").

19. See id., at 93 (arguing that it is up to social institutions to structure the rules of the game so as to channel entrepreneurs into productive activities). See also William J. Baumol, Robert E. Litan, & Carl J. Schramm, *Good Capitalism, Bad Capitalism, and the Economics of Growth and Prosperity* 7–8 (New Haven, CT: Yale Univ. Press, 2007) (contrasting entrepreneurial activity directed at productive innovation with "unproductive . . . activities [that] include criminal behavior (selling of illegal drugs, for example) as well as lawful 'rent-seeking' behavior (i.e., political lobbying or the filing of frivolous lawsuits designed to transfer wealth from one pocket to another")).

20. See, e.g., John Frederick Martin, *Profits in the Wilderness: Entrepreneurship and the Founding of New England Towns in the Seventeenth Century* 37–38 (Chapel Hill: Univ. of North Carolina Press, 1991) (describing distinction in the 1630s applied by the Massachusetts General Court [i.e., colonial legislature] between active land speculators who improved their landholdings, and passive absentee landowners who did little or nothing to make improvements; lands held by the latter were subject to repossession by the Court, as the goal was development and improvement). Overall, the prevailing social attitude was that land speculation was necessary to encourage European immigrant settlement of the vast American continent, though its more avaricious aspects were to be limited and condemned. See, e.g., James D. German, "The Social Utility of Wicked Self-Love: Calvinism, Capitalism and Public Policy in Colonial New England," 82 *J. Am. Hist.* 965, 983–984 (1995) (describing how New England preachers created a neo-Puritan theology demanding spiritual purity but admitting of a sphere of self-interest, in market exchange).

21. See, e.g., Alan Taylor, *William Cooper's Town: Power and Persuasion on the Frontier of the Early American Republic* 55 (New York: Vintage Books, 1995) (describing how partners in land development scheme hired Alexander Hamilton to secure their legal rights, which task he executed in a questionable negotiation with a titleholder experiencing some degree of economic duress).

22. Historian Stuart Banner describes a speculator who "instructed his associate to buy up as much Indian land west of the [British-enacted prohibited settlement] line as he could, and 'to keep this whole matter a profound Secret' because of its illegality. That speculator was George Washington." Stuart Banner, *How the Indians Lost Their Land: Law and Power on the Frontier* 100 (Cambridge, MA: Harvard Univ. Press, 2005).

23. Washington added value to the many acres of land he purchased (a total of 52,000 acres across six states) by surveying and mapping it, and taking the "political risk" that his titles would turn out to be worthless. See Andro Linklater, *Measuring America: How the United States Was Shaped by the Greatest Land Sale in History* 44–45 (New York: Plume Penguin Publishing, 2002).

24. Taylor, *William Cooper's Town*, supra, 101 (describing vigorous oversight, encouragement, and investment by developer William Cooper with respect to

the settlers he attracted to the township of Cooperstown, NY, in the late eighteenth century).

25. Linklater, *Measuring America*, supra, 70–71: "To prevent speculators from acquiring the best lands by bribing surveyors and land registry officials, the committee ruled out the Virginia method of metes-and-bounds surveys with its irregular shapes and complicated registration procedures. Instead, the country was to be surveyed before occupation and divided up into simple squares . . . so that no land would be left vacant."

26. J. Willard Hurst, *Law and Economic Growth: The Legal History of the Lumber Industry in Wisconsin, 1836–1915* (Madison: Univ. of Wisconsin Press, 1964), at 109. Hurst wrote further: "When the whole record is taken into account—actions as well as words—it appears that what this community most valued and insisted on, at bottom, was a rising curve of physical productivity. Insistently, the warnings and protests of the time come back to this; it is when large-scale speculative ownership threatens indefinitely to hold land out of active production that it is most often and surely pronounced contrary to public interest." Id., at 32–33. One can hear in this pronouncement a good deal of Locke's distaste for wasteful appropriation, and thus see parallels between nineteenth century economic regulation and Locke's spoilage proviso. The larger point, again is that over and over one can see the need for public institutions to apply superseding values to the ongoing process of economic acquisition and market exchange.

27. See John Umbeck, *A Theory of Property Rights: With Application to the California Gold Rush* (The Hague, Netherlands: Martinus Nijhoff Publishers, 1984).

28. Id., at 91–98.

29. See 30 U.S.C. § 23; "Comment, The General Mining Law and the Doctrine of Pedis Possessio: The Case for Congressional Action," 49 *U. Chi. L. Rev.* 1026, 1033–1034 (1982) (describing requirement of possession prior to filing federal mining claim).

30. Douglass North, Institutions, Institutional Change and Economic Performance 110 (New York: Cambridge Univ. Press, 1990) ("Because polities make and enforce economic rules, it is not surprising that property rights are seldom efficient.").

31. See Terry L. Anderson & Peter J. Hill, *The Not So Wild, Wild West* 13 (Stanford, CA: Stanford Univ. Press, 2004) ("The race to homestead land [under the Homestead Act] . . . induced people to move beyond the [economic] frontier and settle before the land commanded a positive rent. To wait meant to risk losing out to others who got there first. . . . Racing to beat others to catch fish, to pump oil or groundwater, and to occupy satellite orbits are other examples of how rents can be dissipated."). Anderson and Hill describe one private solution to some of these inefficiencies, a solution that mirrored the mining claim norms mentioned earlier. Groups of settlers established "claiming clubs" in the Midwest that required moderate expenditures of money and labor to secure title. On the general topic of efficient settlement on land frontiers, see Dean Lueck, "First Possession as the Basis of Property," in *Property*

Rights: Cooperation, Conflict and Law 200 (Terry L. Anderson & Fred S. McChesney, eds.) (Princeton, NJ: Princeton Univ. Press, 2003) (describing economic view of legal first possession rules, designed to minimize rent dissipation and overuse of resources).

32. While I see it as unavoidable that courts and other institutions must police against the worst manifestations of rent seeking, I want to be clear that I see this as a rare exception, the need for which will usually be quite apparent. The kind of institutional adjustment I am calling for here requires courts to only slightly adjust the entitlement structure to correct against a rent-seeking strategy that has gotten out of hand. This kind of regulation is small scale, need driven, modest in scope, and often almost hidden in the formal record. That is to say, courts that do this essential service will mention the rent-seeking issue only in passing, or only obliquely, or sometimes not at all. Thus this type of rebalancing action is a very far cry from extensive and pervasive governmental involvement in the details of private deal-making. Though it springs from the same sense of justice and fairness, it is much more humble than aggressive and pervasive regulation, such as restrictive usury laws or general policies for reviewing and overturning private deal making. See Brian M. McCall, "Unprofitable Lending: Modern Credit Regulation and the Lost Theory of Usury," 30 *Cardozo L. Rev.* 549 (2008) (tracing source of usury restrictions to the Bible, the classical era, and late antiquity, e.g., Aquinas); James Gordley, "Equality in Exchange," 69 *Cal. L. Rev.* 1587 (1981) (historical sources of the impulse to monitor exchange transactions for fairness). For a classic defense of usury, see Adam Smith, 1 *An Inquiry into the Nature and Causes of the Wealth of Nations*, Book 2, Chap. 4, par. 15 (Standard Edition) (London, 1776), at 44; reprinted (Oxford: Oxford Univ. Press, 1976), at 357 ("Where the legal rate of interest . . . is fixed but a very little above the lowest market rate, sober people are universally preferred, as borrowers, to prodigals and projectors. The person who lends money gets nearly as much interest from the former as he dares to take from the latter, and his money is much safer in the hands of the one set of people than in those of the other. A great part of the capital of the country is thus thrown into the hands in which it is most likely to be employed with advantage."). I am not defending usury laws; I merely point out once again the recurring recognition throughout history that government must regulate the basic conditions of economic exchange in order to preserve a sense of integrity and legitimacy.

33. For background, see Paul Goldstein, *Intellectual Property: The Tough New Realities that Could Make or Break Your Business* 56–58 (New York: Penguin Group, 2007) (describing Lemelson's tactics as "abuse" and "manipulation").

34. See Symbol Techs., Inc. v. Lemelson Med., Educ. & Research Found., 422 F.3d 1378, 1385 (Fed. Cir. 2005) (opining that purposely delaying the issuance of a patent for business reasons is an abuse of the patent system).

35. See 35 U.S.C. § 101 (2006).

36. David D. Haddock, "First Possession Versus Optimal Timing: Limiting the Dissipation of Economic Value," 64 *Wash U. L.Q.* 775 (1986).

37. See, e.g., Carl Shapiro and Hal R. Varian, *Information Rules: A Strategic Guide to the Network Economy* 187 (Boston, MA: Harvard Business School Press, 1999) (discussing "winner-take-all markets" in the context of "market tipping," i.e., the point at which a standard becomes "the winner" due to mutual adoption and the inception of strong network effects).

38. See W. Brian Arthur, "Competing Standards, Increasing Returns, and Lock-In by Historical Events," 99 *Econ. J.* 116 (1989) (discussing random events and "path dependency" in standards adoption).

39. Lotus Dev. v. Borland Int'l, 49 F.3d 807 (1st Cir. 1995).

40. 49 F.3d 807, 819, 821. Boudin added: "[I]t is unlikely that users who value the Lotus menu for its own sake—independent of any investment they have made themselves in learning Lotus' commands or creating macros dependent upon them—would choose the Borland program in order to secure access to the Lotus menu. . . . If Lotus is granted a monopoly on this pattern [of menu commands], users who have learned the command structure of Lotus 1-2-3 or devised their own macros are locked into Lotus. . . . So long as Lotus is the superior spreadsheet—either in quality or in price—there may be nothing wrong with this advantage. But if a better spreadsheet comes along, it is hard to see why customers who have learned the Lotus menu and devised macros for it should remain captives of Lotus because of an investment in learning made by the users and not by Lotus." 49 F.3d 807, 820, 821.

41. I briefly sketch this idea in Robert P. Merges, "Locke for the Masses," 36 *Hofstra L. Rev.* 1179 (2008).

42. Considerable conceptual groundwork on the general issue of groups and group rights already exists, and some of it may have valuable lessons to teach us about how group property rights ought to be structured and governed. See, e.g., Aviam Soifer, *Law and the Company We Keep* (Cambridge, MA: Harvard Univ. Press, 1995) (legal system needs to be much more sophisticated in its handling of group rights; needs to move away from exclusive focus on relations between individuals and the state); Marianne Constable, "Book Review," 26 *Contemp. Sociology* 362, 362 (1997) ("groups are important to individual identity and deserve legal recognition"); Eric R. Claeys, "The Private Society and the Liberal Public Good in John Locke's Thought," 25 *Soc. Phil. & Pol'y* 201 (2008) (describing Locke's views on voluntary private associations); Kevin A. Kordana & David H. Blankfein Tabachnick, "The Rawlsian View of Private Ordering," 25 *Soc. Phil. & Pol'y* 288 (2008) (discussing Rawls's two principles of justice and how they apply to private associations).

43. Frank Easterbrook, "The Supreme Court 1983 Term—Foreword: The Court and the Economic System," 98 *Harv. L. Rev.* 4 (1984).

44. Richard Epstein, *Takings: Private Property and the Power of Eminent Domain* (Cambridge, MA: Harvard Univ. Press, 1985). See also William A. Fischel, *Regulatory Takings: Law, Economics and Politics* (Cambridge, MA: Harvard Univ. Press, 1998) (includes an excellent overview of the extensive literature).

45. In the technical terms of economics, something akin to surplus value accrues to both producers and consumers. When a buyer pays less than he was willing

to pay, because larger market forces set the price below his personal value for the thing bought, he receives a kind of bonus: thus, consumer surplus, the aggregate value of these bonuses across all consumers. Producers receive surplus when they are paid more than the minimum price they would have accepted for something. (In both cases, values are for the marginal unit, the last one purchased or sold.) Market prices are set by the intersection of supply and demand factors, represented classically by curves on a graph. The point is this: Market prices are set by aggregate forces, but for any individual transaction the market price may provide a windfall in a sense (a marginal windfall might be a better term) for consumers or producers. This is labeled economic surplus. See, e.g., N. Gregory Mankiw, *Principles of Economics* 145 (Mason, OH: South-Western Publishing, 5th ed., 2007).

46. It has reared its head in the world of legal scholarship as well as many others. One manifestation comes in he "problem of judicial valuation," an old trope in the legal literature. A Columbia Business School professor in the 1920s and 1930s, James C. Bonbright, wrote a law review article on this issue in 1927, and later a book, that are both still cited. See James C. Bonbright, "The Problem of Judicial Valuation," 27 *Colum. L. Rev.* 522 (1927). For more recent sources, see, e.g., Keith Sharfman, "Judicial Valuation Behavior: Some Evidence from Bankruptcy," 32 *Fla. St. U. L. Rev.* 387, 388 n.2 (2005). It is a problem that reaches across a very large swath of the legal system. Consider: eminent domain in constitutional law, reorganization in bankruptcy, damages in contract law, "forced sale" of property interests in real property law; the list goes on and on. In all these settings legal actors—usually courts—are called upon to place a dollar value on an asset that is for some reason allegedly not appropriately transferred in a market transaction. Each area has its difficulties, and individual decisions of course are often not lacking for criticism. But judicial valuation is a ubiquitous practice in the legal system. Indeed, from one point of view, courts exist to substitute for the market when transfers of certain assets and interests are necessary but for some reason problematical.

47. Barbara Fried, "Wilt Chamberlain Revisited: Nozick's 'Justice in Transfer' and the Problem of Market-Based Distribution," 24 *Phil. & Pub. Affairs* 226–245 (1995).

7. Creative Professionals, Corporate Ownership, and Transaction Costs

1. See, e.g., Robert Andrew Macfie, *Copyright and Patents for Inventions* 79(Edinburgh: T. T. Clark Publishers, 1879) (in Socratic dialogue among pro- and anticopyright advocates, the procopyright position is quoted: "I hold that such men [authors] write for a livelihood and are entitled to expect from the State protection against those who would deprive them of their property and livelihood.").

2. It might well be asked: if I am so keen on the propertization of labor, why not extend the idea to types of work product not traditionally covered by IP rights? While some version of this idea might have merit, in this book I will

limit myself to the traditional subject matter of IP protection. These works and performances have for many years been judged to merit the award of a property right, while other types of work have, implicitly at least, been deemed so far not as worthy of the privilege of a property right.

3. This applies most strongly in the case of technical employees whose work may result in patented inventions. Because it is difficult to prove precisely when a person first arrived at an idea, an employee with a good idea may be able to leave a large company and then found a start-up company, later filing a patent on the idea. This "exit option" is possible despite rules about corporate ownership of employee inventions. One implication is that employers must treat inventive employees well, so those employees are less likely to avail themselves of the exit option. See Robert P. Merges, "The Law and Economics of Employee Inventions," 13 *Harv. J.L. & Tech.* 1 (1999).

4. Paul Goldstein, *Copyright's Highway: From Gutenberg to the Celestial Jukebox* (Stanford, CA: Stanford Univ. Press, rev. ed. 2003).

5. See, e.g., Paul J. Korshin, "Types of Eighteenth-Century Literary Patronage," 7 *Eighteenth-Century Stud.* 453 (1974).

6. Joseph Lowenstein, "The Script in the Marketplace," 12 *Representations* 101, 102 (1985).

7. Germaine de Rothschild, *Luigi Boccherini: His Life and Work,* 66–67 (Andreas Mayor, trans.) (Oxford: Oxford Univ. Press, 1965).

8. Thomas Carlyle, "Boswell's Life of Johnson (Book Review)," 5 *Fraser's Magazine* 396–398 (1832). For the text of Johnson's famous letter to Lord Chesterfield, perhaps the most eloquent critique of the indignities of the patronage relationship, see James Boswell, 1 *The Life of Samuel Johnson, LL.D.* (Alexander Napier, ed.) (London: George Bell & Sons, 1884), at 210–211.

9. Bach v. Longman et al., 2 Cowper 623 (1777).

10. F. M. Scherer, *Quarter Notes and Bank Notes: The Economics of Music Composition in Eighteenth and Nineteenth Centuries* (Princeton, NJ: Princeton Univ. Press, 2004).

11. See id. at 179–180. "During the late 1840s Verdi and Ricordi began to levy fees for each performance. Initially a fixed fee of 400 francs (£16, or three months' earnings for a building craftsman in southern England) was asked, with a 50 percent reduction in territories lacking a copyright law. This led theater impresarios in some of the smaller towns to ignore Verdi's copyright, obtaining their scores surreptitiously, and to lobby for the repeal of Sardinia's copyright law. In an exchange of letters during 1850, Ricordi explained to Verdi the principles of what economists now call second-degree price discrimination. 'It is more advantageous,' he wrote, 'to provide access to these scores for all theaters, adapting the price to their special means, because I obtain much more from many small theaters at the price of 300 or 250 Lire, than from ten or twelve at the price of a thousand.' Ricordi proposed to Verdi that each performance fee from a provincial theater be separately negotiated in accordance with ability to pay. Verdi would then receive 30 percent of the revenue from score rentals and 40 percent of score sale revenues for the first ten years of an opera's life. The arrangement was accepted, and later Verdi's share

was raised to 50 percent. To enforce it, Ricordi deployed a team of field agents to oversee the use of scores by provincial theaters and prevent theft. He also retained lawyers in the larger Italian cities to handle performance contract disputes. These transaction costs, Ricordi argued, justified his retaining a majority share of the provincial theater licensing revenues. Obtaining substantial revenues from score sales and performance fees, Verdi observed that he no longer needed to be a 'galley slave' and to compose at a frantic pace. Between 1840 and 1849 (he was thirty-six years old in 1849), Verdi composed fourteen operas. During the 1850s he composed seven, in the 1860s two, and one in each of the succeeding three decades."

12. Amusements, *N.Y. Times,* Sept. 25, 1885, at 5, quoted in Zvi S. Rosen, "The Twilight of the Opera Pirates: The Prehistory of the Exclusive Right of Public Performance for Musical Compositions," 24 *Cardozo Arts & Ent. L.J.* 1157, 1178 (2007).

13. See Zorina Khan, *The Democratization of Invention: Patents and Copyright in American Economic Development, 1790–1920* (New York: Cambridge Univ. Press, 2005).

14. The early, exuberant period of state-supported artistic experimentation in the post-revolutionary Soviet Union is perhaps the best example. See Austin Harrington, *Art and Social Theory: Sociological Arguments in Aesthetics* 78–79 (Malden, MA: Polity Press, 2004). Perhaps predictably, the flowering of state-backed art was brief, and was followed by a brutal crackdown on all forms of personal, subjective creativity; after Lenin's death, art was required by the Soviet state to promote state purposes such as solidarity and commitment to the ongoing revolution, and this policy was promoted not only through funding mandates but also repressive tactics such as deportation. Id. See generally David R. Shearer, "Stalinism," in 3 *The Cambridge History of Russia: The Twentieth Century* 192, 208 (Ronald Grigor Suny, ed., Cambridge: Cambridge Univ. Press, 2006): "The Stalinist regime enforced aesthetic norms by extending monopoly control over the organization of all cultural production." This movement to purely socialist art was captured perfectly in Boris Pasternak's novel, and later the film by David Lean, *Doctor Zhivago,* when the revolutionary general Strelnikov declares to the poet and doctor Yuri Zhivago, "The personal life is dead in Russia . . . . History has killed it." It is obvious from this, and from the plot of the story as a whole, that exclusive state support for the arts ends in the very opposite of autonomy.

15. See, e.g., Judith Huggins Balfe, ed., *Paying the Piper: Causes and Consequences of Art Patronage* 251 (Champagne: Univ. of Illinois Press, 1993) (citing "the recognized difficulties of direct state patronage" in discussion of indirect state support of the arts).

16. For an overview of difficult issues historians face in sorting out just how much autonomy was retained by artists and artisans under patronage arrangements, see Jill Caskey, "Whodunit? Patronage, the Canon, and the Problematics of Agency in Romanesque Gothic Art," in *A Companion to Medieval Art: Romanesque and Gothic in Northern Europe* 193–200 (Conrad Rudolph, ed.) (Malden, MA: Blackwell, 2006).

17. See http://www.bls.gov/oco/cg/cgso31.htm#emply.
18. U.S. Dept. of Commerce, Bureau of Labor Statistics, avail. at http://www.bls.gov/oco/cg/content/charts/cht_cgs_031_1.gif.
19. Occupational Outlook Handbook, 2010–2011 Edition: Artists and Related Workers, http://www.bls.gov/oco/ocos092.htm (visited Dec. 30, 2010).
20. Id., at Table 3, "Employment of wage and salary workers in arts, entertainment and recreation by occupation, 2008 and projected change, 2008–2018".
21. Source: U.S. Bureau of labor Statistics, Occupational Employment Statistics May 2009, NAICS 511000 - Publishing Industries (except Internet), http://www.bls.gov/oes/current/naics3_511000.htm. For similar data, see Robert G. Picard, The Economics of the Daily Newspaper Industry, in Alison Alexander Picard et al., *Media Economics: Theory and Practice* 109, 110, 116 (Mahwah, N.J.: Lawrence Erlbaum Assocs., Publishers, 3rd ed. 2004) (Newspapers employed 445,000 people as of 2001, with 7–10 percent of budget in editorial, but that number appears to be dropping fast).
22. Adapted from U.S. Dept. of Commerce, Bureau of Labor Statistics, Occupational Outlook Handbook 2010–2011 edition (current data), Projections Data, http://www.bls.gov/oco/ocos095.htm.
23. See, e.g., Marco Iansati & Roy Levien, *The Keystone Advantage: What the New Dynamics of Business Ecosystems Mean for Strategy, Innovation, and Sustainability* 82–83 (Boston: Harvard Business School Press, 2004) (describing how "keystone companies" unify a far-flung network of large and small companies in a business ecosystem, using Microsoft as an example in the software industry).
24. See Richard N. Langlois, "The Vanishing Hand: The Changing Dynamics of Industrial Capitalism," 12 *Indus. & Corp. Change* 351 (2003); Naomi R. Lamoreaux, Daniel M. G. Raff & Peter Temin, "Beyond Markets and Hierarchies: Toward a New Synthesis of American Business History," 108 *Am. Hist. Rev.* 404 (2003).
25. The classic accounts are by the business historian Alfred D. Chandler; see his *The Visible Hand: The Managerial Revolution in American Business* (Cambridge, MA: Harvard Univ. Press, 1980), and *Scale and Scope: The Dynamics of Industrial Capitalism* (Cambridge, MA: Harvard Univ. Press, 1994). For a perspective on Chandler's work, placing it in the context of more recent developments, see Richard N. Langlois, "Chandler in a Larger Frame: Markets, Transaction Costs, and Organizational Form in History," 5 *Enterprise & Soc'y* 355 (2004). For a historical perspective, arguing that much of our history consists of moving, albeit slowly at times, toward realization of the ideal of Lockean individualism, see Peter Karsten, "Review: Labor's Sorrow? Workers, Bosses, and the Courts in Antebellum America," 21 *Rev. Am. Hist.* 447–453 (No. 3, September, 1993).
26. See Naomi Lamoreaux & Kenneth Sokoloff, "The Decline of the Independent Inventor: A Schumpterian Story?" Nat'l Bureau Econ. Res. Working Paper 11654, September, 2005, at 9, avail. at http://www.nber.org/papers/w11654.
27. Bronwyn H. Hall, Adam B. Jaffe, & Manuel Trajtenberg, "The NBER Patent Citations Data File: Lessons, Insights and Methodological Tools," Nat'l Bureau

Econ. Res. Working Paper 8498, October 2001, at 12, avail. at http://www
.nber.org/papers/w8498. For perspective on some of the intervening years, see
Lowell Juilliard Carr, "The Patenting Performance of 1,000 Inventors During
Ten Years," 37 *Am. J. Soc.* 569 (1932) (in the sample, many inventors were
independents or from small companies); Barkev S. Sanders, Joseph Rossman,
& L. James Harris, "Patent Acquisition by Corporations," 3 *Pat. Trademark &
Copy. J. Res. & Ed.* 217, 217 (1959) (In the years 1936–1955, 59 percent of
issued patents were assigned to corporations, 41 percent to individuals). Between 1963 and 1995, 24.2 percent of issued patents owned by U.S. entities
went to individuals. There seem to be even fewer non-U.S. individual inventors; in 2008, of the 74,465 patents issued to foreign entities, only 3,615 were
issued to foreign individuals. See USPTO, Patent Counts by Class by Year—
Independent Inventors, 12/31/08, avail. at http://www.uspto.gov/web/offices/
ac/ido/oeip/taf/cbcby_in.pdf. For general background, see John R. Allison &
Mark A. Lemley, "The Growing Complexity of the United States Patent System," 82 *B.U. L. Rev.* 77 (2002).

28. See, e.g., David C. Mowery & Nathan Rosenberg, *Technology and the Pursuit
of Economic Growth* 71 (Cambridge: Cambridge Univ. Press, 1989) ("In-
house research was better able to combine the heterogeneous inputs necessary
for commercially successful innovation, to use and increase the stock of firm-
specific knowledge gleaned from marketing and production personnel, and to
exploit the close link between manufacturing and acquisition of certain forms
of technical knowledge."); Christopher Freeman, *The Economics of Industrial
Innovation* 103 (London: Routledge Publishing, 1st ed.,1974) ("[C]orporate
R&D has come to dominate the major revolutionary leaps in technology. . . .").

29. Richard N. Langlois, "Modularity in Technology and Organization," 49 *J.
Econ. Beh. & Org.* 19–37 (2002); Richard N. Langlois, "The Vanishing Hand:
The Changing Dynamics of Industrial Capitalism," 12 *Indus. & Corp. Change*
351–385 (2003).

30. Henry Chesbrough, *Open Innovation: The New Imperative for Creating and
Profiting from Technology* (Boston: Harvard Business School Press, 2003).

31. See Stuart J. H. Graham et al., "High Technology Entrepreneurs and the Patent
System: Results of the 2008 Berkeley Patent Survey," 24 *Berkeley Tech. L.J.*
1255 (2009). Indeed, this recent survey showed that the holding of patents by
technology-based start-ups is even more widespread than previously believed.

32. See Jonathan M. Barnett, "Private Protection of Patentable Goods," 25 *Cardozo L. Rev.* 1251, 1252 (2004) (established firms, or incumbents, have many
ways to recoup R&D costs, such as linking innovative products to other products they sell, whereas new entrants must rely disproportionately on legal
protection). I and several others have made a similar argument: that legal IP
rights make it possible for the makers of specialized, technology-intensive
components to constitute themselves as an independent company as opposed
to a division or specialized group situated in a larger company. See Robert P.
Merges, "A Transactional View of Property Rights," 20 *Berkeley Tech. L.J.* 1477
(2005); Ashish Arora & Robert P. Merges, "Specialized Supply Firms, Property
Rights, and Firm Boundaries," 13 *Indus. & Corp. Change* 451–475 (2004).

Some related ideas are presented in Dan L. Burk, "Intellectual Property and the Theory of the Firm," 71 *U. Chi. L. Rev.* 3 (2004) and Paul J. Heald, "A Transaction Costs Theory of Patent Law," 66 *Ohio St. L.J.* 473 (2005).

33. See Merges & Arora, "Specialized Supply Firms," supra, for a formal version of this argument.

34. See Graham et al., "High Technology Entrepreneurs," supra, at 34–35. Contrary to anecdotal evidence, this survey found that start-up companies file for patents primarily to prevent other entities from copying their products and services.

35. For evidence that entrepreneurs value autonomy very highly, see Tobias J. Moskowitz & Annette Vissing-Jorgensen, "The Returns to Entrepreneurial Investment: A Private Equity Premium Puzzle?" 92 *Am. Econ. Rev.* 745–778 (2002) (entrepreneurs often motivated by desire for increased autonomy, and therefore they have different risk preferences than the average person).

36. Henry Sauermann & Wesley M. Cohen, "What Makes Them Tick? Employee Motives and Industrial Innovation," Nat'l Bureau Econ. Res. Working Paper 14443, September, 2008, at 4, avail. at http://www.nber.org/papers/w14443 .pdf ("[F]irms' R&D personnel exercise substantial autonomy—arguably more than other types of employees. . . ."). Cf. Phillipe Aghion, Mathias Dewatripont, & Jeremy C. Stein, "Academic Freedom, Private-Sector Focus, and the Process of Innovation," 39 *Rand J. Econ.* 617 (2008) (presenting a model showing the advantages of academic research, which permits maximum creative control by researchers, against industrial research, which allows management to direct the activities of its R&D personnel, though not completely).

37. Zoltán J. Ács & David B. Audretsch, *Innovation and Small Firms* 40 (Boston: MIT Press, 1990) ("Smaller enterprises make their impressive contributions to innovation because of several advantages they possess compared to larger-size corporations. One important strength is that they are less bureaucratic. . . .").

38. See, e.g., Langlois, "Modularity in Technology," supra. There is at least some empirical support for the idea that small firms are becoming more important. See CHI Research, Inc., "Small Firms and Technology: Acquisitions, Inventor Movement, and Technology Transfer," Report to the Small Business Administration, January 2004, at ii, avail. at http://www.sba.gov/advo/research/ rs233tot.pdf: "The technological influence of small firms is increasing. The percentage of highly innovative US firms (those with more than 15 US patents in the last five years) that are defined as small firms increased from 33% in the 2000 [study of 1,070 companies with 15 or more patents] to 40% in the 2002 database [of 1,270 such companies]." See also id., at iii: "The share of highly productive inventors [i.e., those with at least ten patents] at large firms fell from 72% to 69%, and the share at small firms rose from 12% to 16%, between the mid 1990s and early in the next decade."

39. For example, few think that the law needs to supply incentives to create trademarks for their own sake. It is fairly easy to think up potential product names; compared to inventing something or writing a novel or song, the costs are quite low. The incentive associated with a trademark has more to do with investing in the promotion of a brand or mark or design, so consumers come to

associate the trademark with a particular product sold by a particular company. See generally Robert P. Merges et al., *Intellectual Property in the New Technological Age* 735 (New York: Aspen Publishers, 5th ed. 2010). For a different, and quite illuminating, perspective see Mark P. McKenna, "The Normative Foundations of Trademark Law," 82 *Notre Dame. L. Rev.* 1839 (2007).

40. Cf. McKenna, "The Normative Foundations of Trademark Law," supra, at 1843 ("Modern law . . . sees a trademark as a repository for value and meaning, which may be deployed across a wide range of products and services. In other words, twenty-first century trademark law amounts to little more than industrial policy intended to increase brand value." [footnote omitted]).

41. See, e.g., Harvey Luskin Molotch, "Inside Stuff: How Professionals Do It," in *Where Stuff Comes From* 23, 26 (New York: Routledge, 2003) (noting "low pay and power of designers" especially as compared to engineering and marketing professionals).

42. Molotch, *Where Stuff Comes From*, supra, at 23–24.

43. Jack W. Plunkett, *Plunkett's Advertising and Branding Industry Almanac 2008* (Houston, TX: Plunkett Research, Inc., 2008), at 29.

44. What I mean is that if all the toymaker wanted to do was use the thing covered by the IP right (as opposed to the legal right itself), he might have no need to deal with the IP owner. Mickey Mouse is such a familiar image that there is no need to get a master drawing from the Disney Company; one could just draw it from memory and apply it to a toy such as a ball or a board game. Of course, doing so might well invite a lawsuit from Disney. But that is just my point: the reason for the toymaker to get a license from Disney is to acquire the *legal right* to use the Mickey Mouse image. The information content, i.e., how to draw Mickey, is already well known. A license to use the Mickey Mouse image is therefore an example of a "pure" IP license: the only thing acquired is the legal right and no separate information content comes with the license. This is the purest example of the additional transactional burden that IP rights creates. Apart from IP, there is no reason whatsoever for the Disney license. The justification for IP rights, then, must explain how this additional transaction benefits the creative team at Disney, while effective IP policy must seek to minimize the costs of such transactions.

45. See Oliver Williamson, *The Mechanisms of Governance* (Oxford: Oxford Univ. Press, 1996); Oliver Williamson, *The Economic Institutions of Capitalism* (New York: Free Press, 1985).

46. See Sanford J. Grossman & Oliver D. Hart, "The Costs and Benefits of Ownership: A Theory of Vertical and Lateral Integration," 94 *J. Pol. Econ.* 691 (1986); Oliver Hart & John Moore, "Property Rights and the Nature of the Firm," 98 *J. Pol. Econ.* 1119 (1990). A good overview of NPR theory is Oliver Hart, *Firms, Contracts and Financial Structure* (Oxford: Oxford Univ. Press, 1995). For an in-depth application of this body of theory—often called the "new property rights" approach—to intellectual property rights, see Robert P. Merges, Intellectual Property Rights, Input Markets, and the Value of Intangible Assets (1999), http://www.law.berkeley.edu/7937.htm (filed under "older articles").

47. U.S. International Trade Commission, "The Migration of U.S. Film and Television Production" 15 (2001) avail. at http://www.ita.doc.gov/media/filmreport .html.

48. In Chapter 8, I explore in more depth the need to maintain incentives for professional creators of digital content.

49. See Thomas Hellmann, "When Do Employees Become Entrepreneurs?" Working Paper, University of British Columbia (August 2006), avail. at http:// strategy.sauder.ubc.ca/hellmann/pdfs/MSRevision_August_2006-All.pdf (citing sources indicating that 70 percent of all entrepreneurs come from established firms where they receive training and inspiration for new ideas).

50. See John Hannigan, *Fantasy City: Pleasure and Profit in the Postmodern Metropolis* 120 (London: Routledge, 1998).

51. See "Now Even Disney Goes Digital to Put Drawing Out of the Picture," *Timesonline*, July 21, 2006, avail. at http://entertainment.timesonline.co.uk/ tol/arts_and_entertainment/article690659.ece; http://eddiepittman.com (website of freelance animator Eddie Pittman, former Walt Disney employee). For a detailed study on the dynamics of spinoffs in another industry, see Steven Klepper & Sally Sleeper, "Entry by Spinoffs," 51 *Mgt. Sci.* 1291 (2005) (detailed study of numerous spinoffs in precision laser industry).

52. M. William Krasilovsky, *This Business of Music* 31–32 (New York: Billboard Books, 2003) ("Independent producers with particularly desirable artists under contract may be able to establish a *label deal* with a major record label. A label deal may provide that records will be released under the trade name and label of the producer. Producers claim that a label deal helps them attract artists to their fold.").

53. It should be noted here that on one view of things, greater diversity of creative content actually *increases* the rewards to big media companies. The idea is that, in a crowded market where production and distribution costs are low (i.e., today's era of digital production and Internet distribution), the returns for "premium content" made and sold by big media actually increase. See Paul Seabright & Helen Weeds, "Competition and Market Power in Broadcasting: Where Are the Rents?" at 12, avail. at http://privatewww.essex.ac.uk/~hf-weeds/SeabrightWeeds_paper.pdf.; published in *The Economic Regulation of Broadcasting Markets* (Paul Seabright & Jürgen von Hagen, eds.) (Cambridge: Cambridge Univ. Press, 2007).

54. Providing a living is of course an important, practical aspect of the more idealized goal of autonomy described and defended in Chapters 2 through 4.

55. As I explain in Chapter 4, by privileging here I mean helping or assisting. Property rights continue to be useful and profitable, and can therefore assist those who make and sell high-quality content, and who have the wherewithal to enforce their rights. I do not mean to imply that low-value content does not or ought not qualify for property rights; it often does. Nor am I arguing that IP policy ought to go out of its way to create disproportionate harm to the creators of low-quality content. My proposals for easier ways to dedicate IP-protected content to the public, to promote sharing—which I lump under the rubric of a "right to include," described later in this chapter—push in just the

opposite direction, toward an even-handed treatment of amateur content and sharing-based models of production. My point is simply that, when we look at the "law in action," the fact is that robust IP rights help or assist individual proprietors of high-quality content more than others, and that this is as it should be given societal goals (as expressed through IP policy) of creative autonomy and equality. This is all I mean by "privileging."

56. See, for example, my essays "A New Dynamism in the Public Domain," 71 *U. Chi. L. Rev.* 183 (2004) (need for a simple way for creators to dedicate works to the public domain); and "Locke for the Masses," 36 *Hofstra L. Rev.* 1179 (2008) (need for property theory to account for aggregated labor of crowd-sourced products).

57. I do not mean to imply that only canonical works ought to be protected by IP rights. In Chapter 8, which delves more deeply into the "remix" phenomenon and ideology, I explain that many original creators and profit-oriented companies have incentives to waive their IP rights and give away content for free to remixers. Canonical works are not the only works that should be protected by IP rights, but they are often the most likely to be worth the cost and bother of protecting. Put another way, the practical effect of high enforcement costs in the world of IP is to create strong incentives for IP owners to waive their rights. IP protects autonomy, but only when a creator chooses to enforce his rights (often because it is worth the cost).

58. I am apparently not alone in this respect. See, e.g., Jaron Lanier, *You Are Not a Gadget: A Manifesto* 83 (New York: Alfred A Knopf, 2010) ("[I]f some free video of a silly stunt will draw as many eyeballs as the product of a professional filmmaker on a given day, then why pay the filmmaker?"); Andrew Keen, *The Cult of the Amateur: How Blogs, MySpace, YouTube, and the Rest of Today's User-generated Media Are Destroying Our Economy, Our Culture, and Our Values* (New York: Doubleday, 2008).

59. For background, see Pamela Samuelson, "Google Book Search and the Future of Books in Cyberspace," (February, 2010), avail. at http://people.ischool.berkeley.edu/~pam/GBSandBooksInCyberspace.pdf; Pamela Samuelson, "Academic Author Objections to the Google Book Search Settlement," avail. at http://people.ischool.berkeley.edu/~pam/JTHTL.pdf.

60. See, e.g., Business Review Letter, U.S. Dept. of Justice, Joel I. Klein, Acting Assistant Attorney General, June 26, 1997, avail. at http://www.justice.gov/atr/public/busreview/215742.pdf (giving Department of Justice approval to consortium of nine patent holders in formation of licensing organization for licensing essential patents over data compression technology); Antitrust Guidelines for the Licensing of Intellectual Property, April 6, 1995, at § 2.3, "Procompetitive Benefits of Licensing," avail. at http://www.justice.gov/atr/public/guidelines/0558.htm#t23. For a historical overview, see Richard J. Gilbert. "Antitrust for Patent Pools: A Century of Policy Evolution" 2004 *Stan. Tech. L. Rev.* 3 (2004).

61. For historical background and theoretical discussion of patent pools, ASCAP, and related organizations, see Robert P. Merges, "Contracting into Liability Rules: Intellectual Property Transactions and Collective Rights Organizations," 84 *Cal. L. Rev.* 1293 (1997); Robert P. Merges, "Institutions for Intellectual

Property Exchange: The Case of Patent Pools," in *Intellectual Products: Novel Claims to Protection and Their Boundaries* (Rochelle Dreyfuss, ed.) (Oxford: Oxford Univ. Press, 2001).

62. United States v. American Society of Composers, Authors and Publishers, 208 F. Supp. 896 (S.D. N.Y. 1962), aff'd, 331 F.2d 117 (2d Cir. 1963) (reviewing and revising original 1941 ASCAP consent decree); Philips Corp. v. International Trade Commission, 424 F.3d 1179 (Fed. Cir. 2005) (challenging Compact Disc patent pool under various antitrust theories).

63. For an overview of the economics of content bundling, which explains some features of record label–digital music platform deals, see Yannis Bakos & Erik Brynjolfsson, "Bundling Information Goods: Pricing, Profits, and Efficiency," 45 *Mgmt. Sci.* 1613 (1999).

64. See, e.g., "Norway: Apple's FairPlay DRM is illegal," MacNN, January 24, 2007, avail. at http://www.macnn.com/articles/07/01/24/norway.rules.against .drm/: "Norway today ruled that Apple's digital rights management technology on its iPod and iTunes store is illegal, following a report earlier this week that both France and Germany have also decided to go after Apple's closed iPod/iTunes ecosystem. . . . [T]he Consumer Ombudsman in Norway has ruled that the closed system is illegal because the songs, encoded with Apple's FairPlay DRM cannot be played on any music device other than an iPod, breaking Norway's laws. 'It doesn't get any clearer than this. Fairplay is an illegal lock-in technology whose main purpose is to lock the consumers to the total package provided by Apple by blocking interoperability' Torgeir Waterhouse, senior adviser at the Consumer Council, told the publication."

65. Douglas Lichtman, "Property Rights in Emerging Platform Technologies," 29 *J. Leg. Stud.* 615 (2000) (arguing that double marginalization and self-interested pricing decisions lead to less-than-optimal production of platform-compatible content, and therefore that policy ought to encourage integrated production of content and platforms).

66. Urs Gasser & John Palfrey, "Breaking Down Barriers: When and How ICT Interoperability Drives Innovation," Berkman Center for Law and Society, Publication Series (November 2007), at 6, avail. at http://cyber.law.harvard. edu/interop. For a detailed discussion of Apple's strategy of exclusively bundling its DRM technology (FairPlay) to music content, and the antitrust actions brought by public officials and private parties in an effort to thwart it, see Nicola F. Sharpe & Olufunmilayo B. Arewa, "Is Apple Playing Fair? Navigating the iPod FairPlay DRM Controversy," Northwestern Univ. School of Law, Public Law and Legal Theory Series, No. 07–18, 5 *Nw. J. Tech. & IP* 331 (2007).

67. Walt Mossberg, "The Way We Read: Amazon.com's Jeffrey Bezos on Why Books Are Like Horses," *Wall St. Journal,* June 9, 2009, at R3, R10.

68. See Robert Hahn & Peter Passell, "Microsoft: Predator or Prey?" Economist's Voice (Berkeley Electronic Press), April 2008, at 1–2, avail. at http://www.be-press.com/cgi/viewcontent.cgi?article=1335&context=ev: ("The real story here is the ever-briefer period in which companies with clear leads in technology and marketing seem able to sustain their advantages. As a consequence, antitrust policy built around traditional tests of market power are at best a way to

keep lawyers well remunerated and, more likely, a significant barrier to productive change. While Microsoft's ongoing disputes with [European] regulators are many and varied, they generally follow from the company's past successes achieved at the expense of faltering rivals. . . . [W]hatever market power Microsoft possessed was already ebbing by the time the company became mired in battles with regulators over which software applications could be bundled with operating systems, and what sorts of proprietary information must be shared with rivals.").

69. Another example comes once again from the publishing industry, where entry by multiple manufacturers of electronic book readers has given publishers greater leverage over the pricing of their content. The leverage extends to pricing negotiations with other platform owners, including Google, which sells online access to digital versions of books. See Mokoto Rich, "Publishers Win a Bout in eBook Price Fight," *New York Times,* February 8, 2010, at B1 (entry of eBook sellers has allowed publishers to ask for higher royalties and more pro-author terms of use in negotiations with Google).

70. In their analysis of innovation in iPods and notebook computers, Jason Dedrick, Kenneth L. Kraemer, and Greg Linden show that the gross margins for Apple's high-end iPod products are generally higher than those earned by notebook PC makers. Furthermore, they argue that these enhanced gross margins enjoyed by Apple are in part due to the innovation represented in the iPod, a product that "is not just a hardware innovation but also an integrated system comprising the iPod product family and closely integrated with its iTunes software and iTunes Store." Jason Dedrick, Kenneth L. Kraemer, & Greg Linden, "Who Profits from Innovation in Global Value Chains? A Study of the iPod and Notebook PCs," 19 *Indus. & Corp. Change* 81 (2009).

71. For some ideas along this line, see Robert P. Merges, "Who Owns the Charles River Bridge? Intellectual Property Rights and the Software Industry," working paper, April, 1999, avail. at http://papers.ssrn.com/sol3/papers.cfm?abstract_id=208089; Peter S. Menell, "Tailoring Legal Protection for Computer Software," 39 *Stan. L. Rev.* 1329 (1987) (proposing the novel idea of copyright "genericide" for software that becomes a widely used standard).

8. Property in the Digital Era

1. Some material in this chapter is drawn from Robert P. Merges, "The Concept of Property in the Digital Era," *Hous. L. Rev.* 1239 (2008). This is taken from a famous line by the screenwriter Gene Fowler: "Writing is easy. All you do is stare at a blank sheet of paper until drops of blood form on your forehead." See http://en.wikipedia.org/wiki/Gene_Fowler. There is a long tradition of similar quotes, all attesting to the difficulty of creating anything worthwhile. See, e.g., Ben Jonson, "To the Memory of My Beloved, The Author William Shakespeare," Introduction to the 1623 Folio edition of Shakespeare's works, lines 58–59, quoted in Jonathan F. S. Post, *English Lyric Poetry: The Early Seventeenth Century* 45 (London: Routledge, 2002) ("he/ Who casts to write a living line must sweat.").

2. Lawrence Lessig, *Remix: Making Art and Commerce Thrive in the Hybrid Economy* xviii (New York: Penguin, 2008). See also Don Tapscott & Anthony D. Williams, *Wikinomics: How Mass Collaboration Changes Everything* 52–53 (New York: Portfolio, 2006) (For young Internet users, the "ability to remix media, hack products, or otherwise tamper with consumer culture is their birthright, and they won't let outmoded intellectual property laws stand in their way.").

3. For a thorough exploration, see *Does Technology Drive History? The Dilemma of Technological Determinism* (Merritt Roe Smith & Leo Marx eds., Cambridge MA: The MIT Press, 1994). For more on the historiography of this idea see John M. Staudenmeier, S.J *Technology's Storytellers: Reweaving the Human Fabric* (Cambridge, MA: The MIT Press, 1985).

4. See Carroll Pursell, *The Machine in America* 230 (1995). Pursell describes one reaction to the Great Depression, the call for new political structures that would better accommodate the massive economic changes brought on by the mechanization and industrialization of the first thirty years of the twentieth century. See id., at 268–269.

5. There is a long association between technological boosterism and technological determinism. See Staudenmeier, *Technology's Storytellers*, supra, at xv ("[T]he myth of progress. . . . came to be the ideological justification for Western colonialism. . . . It was the destiny of the West to be the cutting edge of human progress."). On Americans' peculiar inclination to treat new technologies as a sort of secular religious experience, see David Nye, *American Technological Sublime* (Cambridge, MA: The MIT Press, 1994). The breathless assurances that "the Internet will change everything," common in the 1990s when the Internet was new, are a good recent example of this sort of boosterish enthusiasm. Sober observers have long noted the tendency of contemporaries to overstate the importance of the new technologies of the day. See, e.g., George Orwell, "As I Please," *Tribune*, May 12, 1944, reprinted in 3 *Collected Essays, Journalism and Letters of George Orwell: As I Please* (Boston: Godine, 2000): "Reading recently a batch of rather shallowly optimistic 'progressive' books, I was struck by the automatic way people go on repeating certain phrases which were fashionable before 1914. Two great favorites are 'the abolition of distance' and the 'disappearance of frontiers' [i.e., borders]. I do not know how often I have met with statements that 'the aeroplane and the radio have abolished distance' and 'all parts of the world are now interdependent.' "

6. See, e.g., Wiebe Bijker, *Of Bicycles, Bakelite, and Bulbs: Toward a Theory of Sociotechnical Change*, 281 (Cambridge, MA: The MIT Press, 1995): "Determinism inhibits the development of democratic controls on technology because it suggests that all interventions are futile. . . . [I]f we do not foster constructivist views of sociotechnical development, stressing the possibilities and the constraints of change and choice in technology, a large part of the public is bound to turn their backs on the possibility of participatory decisionmaking, with the result that technology will really slip out of control."

7. Some scholarly writings on digital IP fully recognize the socially determined nature of technologies, and argue that entrenched interests such as large media

companies are currently attempting to steer the Internet and other digital technologies in a direction favorable to their interests. See, e.g., Larry Lessig, *Code Version 2.0* (New York: Basic Books, 2006); Tarleton Gillespie, *Wired Shut: Copyright and the Shape of Digital Culture* (Cambridge, MA: The MIT Press, 2007). The narrative in these works is not centered around an inevitable path of technical development, but instead around the idea of the co-optation of an inherently liberating technological force by self-interested economic actors. There is a political economy dimension to these writings, in other words, inconsistent with a strict version of technological determinism. There is much one could say about this issue, but here I will limit myself to one observation: the growth of content "aggregators" such as Google and YouTube is rapidly creating a natural counterforce against these older media interests, which obviously changes the political economy of IP policy. My main point in raising the idea of digital determinism is to argue that many IP scholars believe that digital technology has an *inherent logic* that society ought to conform to, by way of IP policy. It is this "softer" determinism I take aim at in this chapter. I think we ought to adapt digital technology to our ends and goals, rather than striving always to adapt ourselves to it. And I further think that our ends and goals ought to include promoting individual autonomy and supporting creative professionals—both of which are furthered by the institution of property rights.

8. See, e.g., Yochai Benkler, *The Wealth of Networks: How Social Production Transforms Markets and Freedom* (New Haven, CT: Yale Univ. Press, 2006); Tapscott & Williams, *Wikinomics*, supra. In *Wikinomics*, the authors exuberantly claim that the benefits of this new mass collaboration mean it "will eventually displace the traditional corporate structure as the economy's primary engine of wealth creation." *Wikinomics*, at 1–2. They also claim that the opportunity to bring Internet consumers "into the enterprise as cocreators of value possibly presents the most exciting, long-term engine of change and innovation that the business world has ever seen." *Wikinomics*, at 53.

9. Jeremy Waldron, *The Right to Private Property* 38–40 (Oxford: Oxford Univ. Press, 1988).

10. Gordon Hull, "Digital Copyright and the Possibility of Pure Law," 14 *Qui Parle* 21, 25 (2003) ("[A]bsent the baseline of visual intelligibility, there is no criterion for knowing which object legitimately embodies its eidos and which does not. The effects of this absence stand behind many of the battles surrounding digital reproduction."), avail. at http://ssrn.com/abstract=1019702.

11. See, e.g., N. D. Batra, *Digital Freedom: How Much Can You Handle?* 4 (Lanham, MD: Rowman & Littlefield, 2007) (speaking of the impact of the Internet and related technologies, and their "digital fluidity," on traditional cultures). I should note here that some believe individual authorship was a problematic concept long before digital technology—that in fact *all* works are essentially assembled from social or collective sources. See, e.g., Lior Zemer, *The Idea of Authorship in Copyright* 2 (Hampshire, England: Ashgate Publishing, 2007) (arguing that "the public" should be recognized as a formal joint author in all copyrighted works).

12. See, e.g., Gillespie, *Wired Shut*, supra; David Trend, ed., *Reading Digital Culture* (Malden, MA: Blackwell, 2001). See also Rosemary J. Coombe, *The Cul-*

tural Life of Intellectual Properties: Authorship, Appropriation and The Law 82–83 (Durham, NC: Duke Univ. Press, 1998) (writing of the "dialogic culture" we now inhabit). As Lessig explains it, digital technology that enables perfect copies and allows widespread and anonymous distribution, combined with an already existing norm that if we legally own copyrighted content we can do anything we want with it (for instance, loan a book we own to a friend), now make massive sharing of copyrighted material across the Internet seem like a reasonable and legal act. Lessig, supra, 173.

13. As the authors of *Wikinomics* tell us, we have truly entered a "new era of collaboration and participation." *Wikinomics*, supra, 18.

14. See Simon Winchester, *The Meaning of Everything: The Story of the Oxford English Dictionary* (New York: Oxford Univ. Press, 2003).

15. I am bracketing here (1) cases where the original creation serves a truly unique cultural role, entitling others to make use of it, which I think will be very rare; (2) cases where the remixer is making fun of the original work; and (3) cases where the original creation is essential for the remixer to make a political or social statement. In other words, put aside First Amendment issues. It should be clear that I do not define legitimate First Amendment issues nearly as broadly as some recent commentators, who would have the First Amendment swallow large chunks of IP law, at least in the digital domain.

16. See, e.g., James Boyle, *Shamans, Software, and Spleens: Law and the Construction of the Information Society* (Cambridge, MA: Harvard Univ. Press, 1996).

17. See, e.g., http://remixtheory.net/.

18. Doris Estelle Long, "Dissonant Harmonization: Limitations on 'Cash 'n Carry' Creativity," 70 *Alb. L. Rev.* 1163, 1168 n.20 (2007).

19. Important note: remixing is fun, and people like to do it a lot. So there are good reasons for people to share their own original creations with each other, and there is also an excellent business in providing *free* inputs for people who want to remix things. As I argue later, this is one of the great advantages of property rights: you can easily waive them if you want to, and many in the remix community will want to. See generally Robert P. Merges, "Locke Remixed ;-)," 40 *U.C. Davis L. Rev.* 1259 (2007). This means that property rights will apply only to people who want them. *Wikinomics* authors Tapscott and Williams argue that remixes actually promote the underlying music such that original artists and their music labels should benefit from the additional exposure of this development. *Wikinomics*, supra, 139–140. But it is different to say these labels should consider allowing remix of their property out of self-interest than to say such labels should be legally obligated to do so. Again, waiver may be advisable here, but an individual artist should retain the right to refuse the use of her song in a remix for aesthetic or other reasons despite any potential profit to be made.

20. The original distinction was described by economist Bruno Frey as "institutional motivation" versus "personal motivation." See Bruno Frey, *Arts and Economics* (Berlin: Springer, 2000). The Internet may be changing industry structure for artists, ameliorating the age-old problem that (oligopolistic) industry structure traditionally has diluted the individual incentive effects of IP for

the artist. On this, see Ruth Towse, "Partly for the Money: Rewards and Incentives to Artists," 54 *Kyklos* 473 (2001); Joelle Farchy & Heritiana Ranaivoson, "DRM and Competition: The Consequences on Cultural Diversity for the Case of the Online Music Market," Society for Economic Research on Copyright Issues, 2005 Annual Conference, Montreal, Canada, avail. at http://www.serci.org/documents.html (visited Dec. 31, 2010); Ronald Bettig, *Copyrighting Culture* (Boulder, CO: Westview Press, 1996); Richard Caves, *Creative Industries* (Cambridge, MA: Harvard Univ. Press, 2000). David Throsby has provided some evidence that artists do work partly for the money and that their labor supply responds positively to financial rewards, though intrinsic motivation and preference for arts work is strong. David Throsby, *Economics and Culture* (Cambridge: Cambridge Univ. Press, 2001). Ruth Towse, "Copyright and Artists: A View from Cultural Economics," 20 *J. Econ. Surv.* 567, 578 (2006) (well-known "winner take all" aspects of art labor market).

21. Henry H. Perritt Jr., "Flanking the DRM Maginot Line Against New Music Markets," 16 *Mich. St. J. Int'l L.* 113, 145–146 (2007) (describing intrinsic motivation of two creative people known to the author).

22. See, e.g., F. M. Scherer, *Quarter Notes and Bank Notes: The Economics of Music Composition in the Eighteenth and Nineteenth Centuries* (Princeton, NJ: Princeton Univ. Press, 2003).

23. See James Heilbrun & Charles M. Gray, *The Economics of Art and Culture: An American Perspective* 300 (Cambridge: Cambridge Univ. Press, 1993) ("Second jobs [for artists] are a double-edged sword: they enable artists to attain a higher standard of living, but they inhibit investment in human capital by reducing practice, class, and rehearsal time.").

24. See, e.g., Eric von Hippel, *Democratizing Innovation* (Cambridge, MA: The MIT Press, 2005).

25. This is question asked by Yochai Benkler, who says society should be very cognizant of the costs incurred when it regulates technology and passes laws— both part of the "institutional ecology" in his terminology—that hinder the free operation of digital networks, sharing norms, and the like. See Benkler, *The Wealth of Networks*, supra, at 428–429.

26. This does not, by the way, mean that one must support *all* expansions of IP rights, and oppose all public-domain-enhancing policies. I am arguing only for a commitment to maintaining the economic conditions needed to nurture and support a viable class of creative professionals. Not all expansions of IP rights have that effect. The economist Ruth Towse has provided a good starting point for the kind of analysis we need. See Ruth Towse, "Copyright and Economic Incentives: An Application to Performers' Rights in the Music Industry," 52 *Kyklos* 369 (1999). Towse produces data about the additional income provided to musicians by the advent of the performance right in Britain. She argues that the median income is not worth the transaction costs necessitated by the new right. This is the right approach to the problem; the only question remaining on this particular topic is whether, over time, systems will evolve that might lower the transaction costs enough to make this right worthwhile.

27. Consider for example Steven Heller, *The Education of a Design Entrepreneur* (New York: Allworth Press, 2002). Heller describes his experiences teaching

students web page design. Heller relates that he tries to teach students that, if they want to become good designers, they must learn how to make original content, and not just assemble preexisting components. Id., at xiv. He tells of one student who wanted to use preexisting content to assemble a website but ran into permissions problems with owners of some of the content. In response, the student changed course: "[H]e . . . decided to expand the parameters to include original material that he will author—a virtuous goal. . . ." Id., at xiii. This is just an anecdote, but the point is straightforward: there are many people like this designer.

28. See, e.g., Lawrence Lessig, *Remix: Making Art and Commerce Thrive in the Hybrid Economy* (New York: Penguin Press, 2008).

29. Larry Lessig suggests at times that remixing is analogous to fair use and wonders why, if it's considered legal and normal to quote an author's words in an essay or other piece of writing, it is not legal or normal to "quote"—or remix—a section of a film or song or video. Lessig, *Remix*, supra, at 53–54. Lessig also argues that the meaning of the remix comes from the "cultural references" that form the basis of the remix, that is, that a remix leverages the meaning created by the reference in order to build something new. Lessig, *Remix*, supra, at 74–75.

30. See, e.g., Bill Thompson's essay "The Public Domain and the Creative Author" in *Intellectual Property: The Many Faces of the Public Domain* 138 (Charlotte Waelde & Hector MacQueen, eds.) (Northampton, MA: Edward Elgar, 2007): "The interest in these new forms of creativity [remixes, mashups, and the like] and the enthusiasm with which they are circulated would seem to indicate that the current conception of what constitutes fair use may be too limited, stifling creativity where it should not be, and this in turn should lead us to reflect on the need to enhance the public domain."

31. 17 U.S.C. § 107.

32. Wendy Gordon, "Fair Use as Market Failure: A Structural and Economic Analysis of the *Betamax* Case and Its Predecessors," 82 *Colum. L. Rev.* 1600 (1982).

33. See Rebecca S. Eisenberg, "Bargaining over the Transfer of Proprietary Research Tools: Is This Market Failing or Emerging?" in *Expanding the Boundaries of Intellectual Property: Innovation Policy for the Knowledge Society* 223 (Rochelle Dreyfuss et al., eds.) (Oxford: Oxford Univ. Press, 2001).

34. Am. Geophysical Union v. Texaco, Inc., 60 F.3d 913 (2nd Cir. 1994).

35. See, e.g., MGM Studios, Inc. v. Grokster, Inc., 45 U.S. 913 (2005).

36. See, e.g., Bridgeport Music, Inc., et al. v. Dimension Films, et al., 410 F.3d 792 (6th Cir. 2005).

37. See Pierre N. Leval, "Toward a Fair Use Standard," 103 *Harv. L. Rev.* 1105–1136 (1990).

38. One way to loosen property rights' stranglehold on this effort to freely share and alter content, in the view of some of these enthusiasts, is to allow "transformative uses" of copyrighted material [e.g., remixes] without the owners' permission, together with a scheme of compulsory licensing for commercial (but not noncommercial) transformations. See, e.g., Michael A. Einhorn, *Media, Technology and Copyright: Integrating Law and Economics* 13 (Northampton,

MA: Edward Elgar, 2004) (arguing, from a law and economics perspective, that remixing is transformative and permitting the original creator to control it would be inefficient).

39. See, e.g., id. Einhorn argues that remixes (at least among amateurs) should be considered fair use: "... [T]ransformative works with new meanings tend to reach largely new audiences, and do not predictably displace sales of primary goods or interfere with later undertakings of derivative licenses. Accordingly, it is unlikely that any creator's incentive to produce primary work depends on whether a small class of transformative uses can be published or not. ..." Moreover, he argues, imposing traditional licensing requirements upon remixes and fan fiction could create prohibitive transaction costs and could deter many noncommercial users from creating interesting works. Id. at 29, 36–37.

40. I have described a similar situation in patent law. One who files a patent application, and then amends it while it is pending to embrace an idea first pioneered by a competitor, ought not be given title to the material covered by the broadening amendment—a situation I describe as "misappropriation by amendment." See Robert P. Merges, "Software and Patent Scope: A Report from the Middle Innings," 85 *Tex. L. Rev.* 1627, 1653 (2007).

41. Thus remix "contests" are common, including some that have been conducted by museums and other arts-related institutions. So for example the Brooklyn Museum asked remixers to download the tracks from its Soundcloud page and remix them for a "Who Shot Rock & Roll: Remix!" contest. See http://www.brooklynmuseum.org/exhibitions/rock_and_roll/remix.php.

42. See Locke, *Two Treatises of Government, Second Treatise*, § 33–34: "He that had as good left for his improvement, as was already taken up, needed not complain, ought not to meddle with what was already improved by another's labor." See also Jeremy Waldron, *God, Locke and Equality: Christian Foundations in Locke's Political Thought* 172 (Cambridge: Cambridge Univ. Press, 2002) ("[P]rejudice to others' interests is the main heading under which objections to acquisition can reasonably be lodged."). This principle is also found in the traditional law of restitution, which since Roman times has prohibited labor subsequently added from justifying a legitimate claim to an asset that is already owned by another. See, e.g., James Tully, *A Discourse on Property: John Locke and His Adversaries* 118 (Cambridge: Cambridge Univ. Press, 1980) (quoting excerpt from Justinian's Digest attributed to the Roman jurist Paulus).

43. See John Locke, *Second Treatise*, supra, § 28 (discussing an employer's ownership of "the Turfs my Servant has cut").

44. These artists participated in making a CD sponsored by *Wired* magazine, which was distributed by the magazine and made available online by the Creative Commons organization. See http://ccmixter.org/view/media/samples.

45. See "Open Source Record Label," Wikipedia, avail. at http://en.wikipedia.org/wiki/Open_source_record_label.

46. In discussing the virtues of remixes, the authors of *Wikinomics* argue that there is good reason for record companies to "fall[] over backwards" to encourage remixing rather than fight it because it is illegal under current copyright law. *Wikinomics*, supra, at 139.

47. See www.creativecommons.org/ ("Find licensed works you can share, remix, or reuse . . ."); http://ccmixter.org/ ("Remixers: If you're into sampling, remixing and mash-ups grab the sample packs and a cappellas for download and you can upload your version back into ccMixter, for others to enjoy and re-sample. All legal").

48. The notion of "tolerated use" was hatched by IP scholar Tim Wu of Columbia University. See Tim Wu, "Does YouTube Really Have Legal Problems?" *Slate,* October 26, 2006, avail. at http://www.slate.com/id/2152264/; see also Tim Wu, "Tolerated Use," Columbia Law and Econ. Working Paper No. 333 (May 2008), avail. at http://papers.ssrn.com/sol3/papers.cfm?abstract_id=1132247. On expanded implied licensing online, see Orit Fischman Afori, "Implied License: An Emerging New Standard in Copyright Law," 25 *Santa Clara Computer & High Tech. L.J.* 275 (2009).

49. See, e.g., Pamela Samuelson, "The Copyright Grab," *Wired* 4.01 (January, 1996); Jessica Litman, *Digital Copyright* (Amherst, MA: Prometheus Books, 2001) (describing DMCA, including expanded criminal provisions).

50. Metro-Goldwyn-Mayer Studios, Inc., et al. v. Grokster, Ltd., et al., 545 U.S. 913 (2005). The substantial noninfringing use standard comes from Sony Corp. v. Universal City Studios, 464 U.S. 417 (1984).

51. See Peter S. Menell & David Nimmer, "Unwinding Sony," 94 *Cal. L. Rev.* 941 (2007) (advocating an alternative reasonable design standard from tort law); Peter S. Menell & David Nimmer, "Legal Realism in Action: Indirect Copyright Liability's Continuing Tort Framework and Sony's De Facto Demise," 55 *UCLA L. Rev.* 1 (2007).

52. See Peter Menell, "Chilled Innovation v. Balanced Evolution: Reflecting on Indirect Copyright Liability in the Digital Age," avail. at http://www.mediain-stitute.org/new_site/IPI/072409_ChilledInnovations.php (documenting robust developments in new digital distribution technologies post-*Grokster.*).

53. Thomas Merrill & Henry Smith, "Optimal Standardization in the Law of Property: The Numerus Clausus Principle," 110 *Yale Law J.* 1 (2000).

54. See Lawrence Lessig, *The Future of Ideas* 201 (New York: Vintage, 2002) ("Compensation without control." [footnote omitted]); William W. Fisher, *Promises to Keep: Technology, Law and the Future of Entertainment* (Stanford, CA: Stanford Law and Politics, 2004), at Chapter 6 ("An Alternative Compensation System").

55. Had compulsory licenses been in use in recent times, says Lessig, ". . . there would have been an explosion in innovation around these [digital remixing] technologies. . . . Anyone who had an idea could have deployed it, consistent with the terms of the compulsory license." Lessig, *Remix*, supra, at 111.

56. See, e.g., Robert P. Merges, "Contracting into Liability Rules: Intellectual Property Rights and Collective Rights Organizations," 84 *Cal. L. Rev.* 1293 (1996); Robert P. Merges, "The Continuing Vitality of Performance Rights Organizations" (Working Paper 2008).

57. Lawrence Lessig, *Free Culture* 8 (New York: Penguin, 2005).

58. Jeremy Waldron, "From Authors to Copiers: Individual Rights and Social Values in Intellectual Property," 68 *Chi.-Kent L. Rev.* 841 (1993).

59. Merges, "Locke Remixed," supra.

60. For this perspective, see Lessig, *Code 2.0*, supra, at 183 (distinguishing real property from IP; claiming that society needs an incentive to produce and protect real property, but only needs an incentive to produce IP—no need to protect or control it).

61. On the importance of this in U.S. IP law, see the outstanding book by Roberta Rosenthal Kwall, *The Soul of Creativity: Forging a Moral Rights Law for the United States* (Stanford, CA: Stanford Law Books, 2010).

62. This section borrows from Robert P. Merges, "Locke for the Masses," 36 *Hofstra L. Rev.* 1179 (2008).

63. Robert P. Merges & Jeffrey Kuhn, "An Estoppel Doctrine for Patented Standards," 97 *Cal. L. Rev.* 1–50 (2009).

64. For background on this phenomenon, see Steven A. Hetcher, "Using Social Norms to Regulate Fan Fiction and Remix Culture," 157 *Penn. L. Rev.* 1869 (2009).

65. This concern is highlighted in Debora Halbert, "Mass Culture and the Culture of the Masses: A Manifesto for User-Generated Rights," 11 *Vand. J. Ent. & Tech. L.* 921, 947 (2009).

9. Patents and Drugs for the Developing World

1. See World Health Organization, "Global Health Risks" (2009), at 3, avail. at http://www.who.int/healthinfo/global_burden_disease/GlobalHealthRisks_report_part1.pdf.

2. On mortality from malaria, see Mark S. Klepner, Thomas N. Unnash, & Linden Hu, "Taking a Bite Out of Vector-Transmitted Infectious Diseases," 356 *New Eng. J. Med.* 2567, 2567 (2009) ("[M]alaria . . . kills 1 million to 2 million people annually, most of them children under 5 years of age.").

3. World Health Organization, "Global Burden of Disease: 2004 Update" (2008), at 28 (TB rates: 1.4 million in Africa, 2.8 million in Southeast Asia, and .4 million in the Americas; HIV: 1.9 million in Africa, .2 million in the Americas; diarrheal disease incidents: 912 million in Africa, 1.2765 billion in Southeast Asia, and 543 million in the Americas).

4. "Pharmaceuticals: Quagmire to Goldmine?" *The Economist*, May 17, 2008, at 102 ("Tachi Yamada of the Gates Foundation, who was at GSK when the firm faced the South African backlash over HIV drugs, 'pharma companies can't possibly survive without recognising their responsibilities to the poor.'").

5. John Locke, *Two Treatises of Government, First Treatise*, Chap. IV, § 42, (Cambridge: Cambridge University Press, 3rd ed., 1988) (Peter Laslett, ed.) (hereafter "Laslett") at 170.

6. Samuel Fleischacker, *A Short History of Distributive Justice* 49 (Cambridge, MA: Harvard Univ. Press, 2004).

7. See, e.g., Michel Mollat, *The Poor in the Middle Ages: An Essay in Social History* 44 (Arthur Goldhammer, trans.) (New Haven, CT: Yale Univ. Press, 1986); Peter Lamont Brown, *The Rise of Western Christiandom* 69 (Oxford: Wiley-Blackwell, 2nd ed., 2003). To be sure, the poor were also sometimes

seen as Christlike figures whose poverty emulated the virtues of simplicity and "non-attachment to worldly things" that were also valued highly by the medieval church. See, e.g., Mollat, *The Poor in the Middle Ages,* supra.

8. B. Sharon Byrd & Joachim Hruschka, "The Natural Law Duty to Recognize Private Law Ownership: Kant's Theory of Property in His Doctrine of Right," 56 *U. Tor. L.J.* 217, 219–221 (2006).

9. See id. at 221.

10. For background on the necessity defense, see Fleischacker, *A Short History of Distributive Justice,* supra, at 28–32 (describing the view of Thomas Aquinas); James Gordley, *Foundations of Private Law* (Oxford: Oxford Univ. Press, 2006), at Chapter 7, "Loss of Resources Without the Owner's Consent: Necessity and Adverse Possession," 130–154 (describing progression from Aristotle through Aquinas to medieval canon law scholars).

11. I. Kant, *The Metaphysics of Morals,* 236 (trans. and ed. Mary J. Gregor) (Cambridge: Cambridge University Press, 1996). See also Arthur Ripstein, "In Extremis," 2 *Ohio St. J. Crim. L.* 415 (2006). Ripstein gives a nice summary of how Kant's ideas about criminal liability for harm to property flow from his basic conception of property as a (private) right that promotes individual autonomy: "The structure of the criminal law follows the structure of private wrongs, since the latter law defines the basic categories of wrongs against persons and property that are the main subject of the criminal law. Kant's account of private wrongdoing is not harm-based, but rights based: a private wrong is an interference with the freedom of another person. There are two basic types of interference: injury and trespass. An injury involves depriving a person of some power to which he had a right—by damaging or literally depriving him of it. Injuries to person, property and reputation deprive their victims of powers that they had—their ability to use their own bodies, their goods, or their good name. Injuries restrict freedom, depriving persons of means that they had with which to set and pursue their own purposes. A trespass involves using another person or his goods in pursuit of an end that the latter person does not choose to pursue. Trespasses against person, property and reputation use what properly belongs to one person for another's purposes: one uses another's powers, and in so doing subjects the powers of the first to the other's choice." Ripstein, supra, at 416.

12. See, e.g., Ripstein, "In Extremis," supra; Khalid Ghanayim, "Excused Necessity in Western Legal Philosophy," 19 *Can. J.L. & Juris.* 31 (2006). Although Ghanayim's discussion of Kant is centered on the famous kill-someone-else-to-save-your-own-life hypothetical, it clearly encompasses the sort of necessity that would apply in the case of taking a patented pharmaceutical to save immediate lives. See Ghanayim, at 56: "Although Kant treats only of the case of a life for a life, his theory, or the spirit of his theory, allows us to argue that necessity as a defence that negates criminal punishment is appropriate when the threatened harm to the actor in the case of injuring legally protected interests does not outweigh the harm that awaits him if he refrains from harming those interests, as would be the case, for example, in a situation of life versus other protected values, like physical integrity, health, liberty, or property."

13. Bill & Melinda Gates Foundation, "Neglected Diseases Overview," avail. at http://www.gatesfoundation.org/topics/Pages/neglected-diseases.aspx.

14. See, e.g., Frank H. Easterbrook, "Foreword: The Court and the Economic System," 98 *Harv. L. Rev.* 4 (1984).

15. Although some current patients might be affected, because pharmaceutical firms would presumably scale back distribution, advertising, etc., if their operations were curtailed as a result of widespread patent overrides, I am assuming that pharmaceuticals already in existence would for the most part reach patients who could use them.

16. Richard C. Levin et al., "Appropriating the Returns from Industrial Research and Development," 18 *Brookings Papers on Econ. Activity* (Special Issue) 783 (1987); Wesley M. Cohen, Richard R. Nelson, & John P. Walsh, "Protecting Their Intellectual Assets: Appropriability Conditions and Why U.S. Manufacturing Firms Patent (or Not)," Working Paper 7552, National Bureau of Economic Research, Cambridge, MA, (February, 2000, revised 2004); Stuart J. H. Graham, Robert P. Merges, Pam Samuelson, & Ted Sichelman, "High Technology Entrepreneurs and the Patent System: Results of the 2008 Berkeley Patent Survey," 24 *Berkeley Tech. L. J.* 1256 (2010) (survey of 1,332 small and start-up companies formed since 1998; finding that patents are much more important in biotechnology industry than in computer hardware and software).

17. Joseph A. DiMasi, Ronald W. Hansen, & Henry G. Grabowski, "The Price of Innovation: New Estimates of Drug Development Costs," 22 *J. Health Econ.* 151–185, 151 (2003). See also Michael Dickson & Jean Paul Gagnon, "Key Factors in the Rising Cost of New Drug Discovery and Development," 3 *Nature Reviews* 417–429 (2004). The DiMasi et al. estimate has been criticized because (1) none of the pharmaceuticals in the sample received government support, which makes them somewhat unusual in a field where many drugs are based on publicly funded research; and (2) the "discount factor" used to reduce future payments to net present value figures is said to be too high. See http://www.citizen.org/pressroom/release.cfm?ID=954. Despite this criticism, many drugs are developed completely by private pharmaceutical companies, and the risk-adjusted discount factor is a standard technique in investment analysis and finance. The controversial issue is the *level* of the relevant discount factor. On one hand, drug R&D is surely risky; many examples can be found of development projects costing hundreds of millions of dollars that had to be abandoned when late-stage clinical testing revealed insoluble problems. On the other hand, stock analysts consistently note that, partly due to entry barriers including massive required investments and extensive government regulation, financial returns in the pharmaceutical sector have been steadily high for many years, which suggests that the large companies involved are good at mediating project-specific risk by diversifying their portfolio of drug development projects. Research reviewed by Dickson & Gagnon confirms that pharmaceutical R&D is indeed very risky and that the overall economic return on all but the very top drugs is only average for standard investments. Dickson & Gagnon, at 420.

18. Dickson & Gagnon, "Key Factors," supra, at 418.

19. See Pharmaceutical Research and Manufacturing Association (PhRMA), Pharmaceutical Industry Profile 2009, at 2, avail. at http://www.phrma.org/files/attachments/PhRMA%202009%20Profile%20FINAL.pdf. Total spending by the National Institutes of Health, the major funder of health-related scientific research, has held steady at about $30 billion for the past several years. See http://www.nih.gov/about/budget.htm (NIH invests $30.5 billion in health-related research annually).

20. David Schwartzman, *Innovation in the Pharmaceutical Industry* 63 (Baltimore, MD: Johns Hopkins, 1976) (describing advantages of large, vertically integrated pharmaceutical firms).

21. See, e.g., Alfred D. Chandler, *Scale and Scope* 456, Chap. 12 (Cambridge, MA: Harvard Univ. Press, 1994) (describing emergence of German chemical and pharmaceutical giants and their American competitors in the late nineteenth and early twentieth centuries).

22. Rebecca Henderson, Luigo Orsenigo, & Gary P. Pisano, "The Pharmaceutical Industry and the Revolution in Molecular Biology: Interactions Among Scientific, Institutional, and Organizational Change," in *Sources of Industrial Leadership: Studies in Seven Industries* 267–311 (David C. Mowery and Richard R. Nelson, eds.) (Cambridge: Cambridge Univ. Press, 1999).

23. See id. at 294.

24. Patents are also of course crucial to *large* pharmaceutical companies, and indeed to pharmaceutical manufacturers of all sizes. See Barry Werth, *The Billion Dollar Molecule* (New York: Touchstone Simon & Schuster, 1994) (recounting the story of Vertex, Inc., a start-up pharmaceutical company based on principles of advanced chemistry known as "rational drug design").

25. See generally Kevin Outterson, "Pharmaceutical Arbitrage: Balancing Access and Innovation in International Prescription Drug Markets," 5 *Yale J. Health Pol'y, L. & Ethics* 193, 262–264 (2005) (reviewing reported case of drug "diversion" from West Africa to Europe; though the facts of this case were overblown, e.g., very few diverted drugs originated with charitable gifting programs in Africa, the author recognizes that arbitrage is a real threat to global pharmaceutical companies).

26. "Pharmaceuticals: Quagmire to Goldmine?" supra, at 102: Evidence of research focused on developing countries: "Novartis has opened a research centre in Shanghai and has another outpost in Singapore focused on tropical diseases. Merck has struck several deals with firms in emerging markets to do early-stage research. The drugs giants argue that this new approach allows them to tap a global network of innovation, and also provides insights into local markets." These programs have been beneficial for pharmaceutical companies in terms of public relations and humanitarian reputation. See, e.g., Julian Chauveau, Constance Marie Meiners, Stephane Luchini, & Jean Paul Moatti, "Evolution of Prices amd Quantities of ARV Drugs in African Countries: From Emerging to Strategic Markets," in *The Political Economy of HIV/AIDS in Developing Countries* 94 (Benjamin Coriat, ed.) (Northampton, MA: Edward Elgar, 2008) (selective nonenforcement of patents: "the policy of

brand companies in not enforcing pharmaceutical patent protection in Africa," a form of "strategic philanthropy," is pursued so that firms may "burnish their image").

27. Doha Development Agenda, "Decision Removes Final Patent Obstacle to Cheap Drug Imports," (August 30, 2003), avail. at http://www.wto.org/english/news_e/pres03_e/pr350_e.htm (applauding administrative decision "allowing poorer countries to make full use of the flexibilities in the WTO's intellectual property rules in order to deal with the diseases that ravage their people.").

28. $2.5 billion was invested in neglected diseases in 2008, led by NIH and the Gates Foundation; private pharmaceutical firms were the third-leading source of funding. Center for the Study of Drug Development, Tufts University, "Neglected Diseases in the Developing World: Progress, Current Challenges, and Promising Approaches," Summary Proceedings (October 16, 2009), at 1, avail. at http://csdd.tufts.edu/files/uploads/ndfinproceed.pdf.

10. Conclusion

1. The *Oxford English Dictionary* defines one sense of the word "exclude"—that pertaining to a "monopoly or grant"—as "[e]xcluding all other persons from the rights conferred. Hence of a right, privilege, possession, quality, etc.: In which others have no share. . . ." *Oxford English Dictionary* (electronic version) (Oxford: Oxford Univ. Press, 1989), at "Exclusive."

2. Jeremy Waldron, *The Right to Private Property* 258 (New York: Oxford Univ. Press, 1988).

Index